Margot Hamilton Hill
Peter A Bucknell

The Evolution of Fashion:
Pattern and Cut from 1066 to 1930

B T Batsford Ltd, London

Drama Book Publishers, New York

Drawings © Margot Hamilton Hill
Text and patterns © Peter A Bucknell
1967, 1987

First published 1967
First published in the United States of America 1968
Fifth impression 1976
Sixth impression 1978
Seventh impression 1981
Eighth impression 1983
Ninth impression 1984
First published in paperback 1987
Eleventh impression 1989
Twelfth impression 1992
Thirteenth impression 1994
Library of Congress Catalog Card No. 68–10504

Printed and bound in Great Britain by
Butler & Tanner Ltd, Frome and London
for the publishers, B T BATSFORD Ltd
4 Fitzhardinge Street, London W1H 0AH

Published in the United States of America
by Drama Book Publishers
260 Fifth Avenue
New York, NY 10001

ISBN 0-7134-5818-6 (UK)   646.4009 HIL
ISBN 0-89676-099-5 (USA)

Contents

Introduction

This book is a history of the development of English costume and cutting covering nearly ten centuries: from the Norman Conquest to the Second World War. It is divided into 56 sections. Each section illustrates a man and woman wearing the typical attire of the upper middle classes. A feeling for the period style is reflected in the background, plus an aim to capture their ideal of beauty, deportment and poise.

It is not an academic history of costume in the strictest sense. It does not attempt to show all the minor developments and idiosyncrasies of dress. It is a guide, rather, to an understanding of costume evolution with its subtly changing shapes and forms reflected by the spirit and mood of each given period. Special costumes – such as seasonal or evening wear, ceremonial dress, bizarre or eccentric fashions – are omitted, unless they relate specifically to this basic evolution.

We chose to trace the evolution of fashion from the point where the earliest shaped garment – the T-shaped tunic – evolved by cutting the cloth into the shape to fit the body, rather than by draping, as had been done previously in the classical world of Greece and Rome. From this simple beginning, the basic shape was constantly improvised and adapted to suit the wearer's needs and the dictates of society. Society also dictated the manner of wearing dress, the style of movement and deportment, to point and draw attention to those areas of the body chosen for emphasis. To achieve a new image and acquire more individualistic garments, the proportions of the body were changed by lengthening, seaming, padding, stiffening, corsetry and so on.

Clothes arrive through necessity and function, the demands of climate, the fabrics available. But 'fashion' in dress is highly complex. It does not necessarily aspire towards beauty, since the ideal of beauty changes. Fashionable dress is more a visual symbol of an idea the wearer wishes to excite in the spectator. For example, an abundance of jewellery and costly materials will suggest a grandeur and social superiority to which the majority cannot lay claim. In high fashion purely aesthetic considerations, such as weight and balance of detail, tension of angles and curves, the distribution of tones, textures and colours, etc., are always in evidence. Fashion is the translation of the wearer's personality into the language of clothes. But people do not always adhere to the immediate fashions of their time. They often cling to styles of their youth from personal taste or familiarity. The average man or woman wore costume that was invariably a composite of several years of fashion.

Fashions change when the impetus that inspired them has been accepted and modified by the majority, more particularly so since the 18th century. Before the 16th century fashion often took fifty years or more to change, gradually gaining momentum, as the dates of the illustrations show; it is in fact only in the past two hundred years or so that 'fashion' in the modern sense can be used with any degree of accuracy. From the Industrial Revolution onwards gentlemen of fashion were adopting new and more varied styles of dress. Factors of etiquette such as suitability to the occasion, the season, the hour of day, for town or country wear, whether for formal, semi-formal or informal wear, were now considered important. As a result it becomes increasingly difficult within the scope of this book to trace a precise evolution of male dress as distinct from female dress. There were, however, four basic styles of coat which ran parallel and were characteristic throughout the period: the Cutaway Tailcoat, the Frockcoat, the Morning Coat and the Lounge Suit. Other styles were designed for outdoor or sporting pursuits. We can show the 19th and 20th century men in only a selection from these clothes.

Until the 19th century it is highly conjectural to form any absolute laws governing cutting or to establish any principles on the grain of the fabric in relation to the shape of the body. Cut was invariably determined by the width of the cloth or the enormous cost of the fabrics, all hand woven and embroidered. As a result the patterns were often interlocked, turned upside down, or had small off-cuts joined together so that no scrap of material was wasted. Fabric often determined the method of cut and shaping. During all periods, fashion has been greatly influenced by the fabric which was available at the time. Materials today usually require the addition of a light lining, and in some cases an interlining as well, as they have not sufficient weight to be suitable substitutes for the real thing.

There is usually a marked difference in elegance and style between existing costumes (often of poor workmanship) in relation to the idealized concept of dress as recorded by the artist. This idealization has to a certain extent influenced this book. Our interpretation is made up from a study of paintings, prints, sculpture and manuscript drawings rather than from measured-up museum costumes. (Although the colours revealed in mediaeval heraldry and illuminated manuscripts are bright and clear, the brilliance and simplicity of these colours were undoubtedly exaggerated for artistic effect. It was unlikely that the animal and vegetable dyes used could match the intensity of those developed in the 19th century. The general effect of the dyes would be softer and more mellow.) No great liberties, to our knowledge, have been taken. The result, we hope, is a comprehensive picture of fashion to serve as a basis for the understanding of cut, construction, colour, fabric and the manner of wearing dress.

The sequence of illustrations, patterns and notes in relation to colour, fabrics, movement and deportment have been developed, however, from known sources of historical costumes and cutting. All available facts and existing costumes and visual records have likewise been consulted. Therefore we hope the book will prove valuable to the theatre designer, the cutter, the illustrator, the student of costume history and dress design, and the actor, and encourage further reading research.

Peter A Bucknell
Margot Hamilton Hill
1967

Introduction to the Patterns

The scale of the patterns is $\frac{1}{8}$ inch to 1 inch. In some cases where space does not permit, a few patterns are cut $\frac{1}{16}$ inch to 1 inch. Where this departure occurs, the scale is marked on the patterns. (Because of this small scale, the taking of accurate measurements from the patterns should be avoided. Specific measurements from the person for whom the costume is to be made and the drafting of basic blocks adapted to the character of these patterns is considered advisable).

The patterns are:

a arranged with the men's patterns shown on the left-hand side of the book and the women's on the right-hand side, unless otherwise stated.

b positioned in relation to the edges of the book wherever possible to establish grain of fabric.

c cut without allowance for seams.

d cut in most cases without giving front or placket overlaps, overlaps to buttoned fastenings, under flaps to vents, etc.

e basic measurements:

Men: Chest: 38–40 inches

Waist: 30–32 inches

Height: 5 feet 10 inches–6 feet.

Women: Bust: 35–36 inches

Waist: 25–26 inches

Height: 5 feet 5 inches–5 feet 7 inches.

All the foundation garments and patterns have been developed from the available historical information. They have been drafted to fit an average figure and to give maximum freedom of movement (at times certainly very limited), for the wearer. Foundation garments, padding, restrictive devices such as corsets, and panniers, bustle, extensions, etc., are a very essential part of costume and establish silhouette and posture. All top garment patterns should be cut from measurements taken from the figure wearing the necessary foundation garments. The patterns should be considered only as a basis for adaptation. They give fundamental principles and guidance from which adaptation can commence in the interpretation of costume drawings, plates, designs, etc. They will require re-proportioning in relation to the wearer.

The patterns, until the middle of the 17th century, are in most cases conjectural, there being very few existing garments and little or no information on cutting—the main source being paintings, drawings, carving of the time, often stylised and very formal, from which to draw conclusions. Sometimes, in exceptional cases, where complexities in the making or the arrangement of a garment, or head dress, can be simplified for the wearer or the costume maker, this has been done, and wherever possible, these devices or convenient short cuts have been mentioned. (Construction notes are only given when it is considered absolutely necessary.)

From the middle of the 17th century on, patterns follow closely the fundamental principles of cutting from the sources available—cutting books, patterns, existing garments, etc. Men's patterns after 1700 are almost entirely taken from the existing patterns and books on tailoring of the time—these will require, in some instances, alterations to fit the average contemporary male figure.

Tailoring is a very specialised art and craft, and no attempt has been made to give instructions in construction. Tailoring is work for specialists, and it is not advisable for costume makers to consider constructing male costume after about 1800 without expert advice from a tailor. Cutting, pressing, stretching, shrinking, moulding, interlining, sewing and certainly not forgetting fitting, are all too complex in nature without the help of a specialist. Tailoring was essentially created as an art to make the best of the human figure, or to reveal a good one, to give elegance and beauty of line and to permit movement without disturbance to the actual look, style and fit of the costume.

Elegance of movement within a good suit of clothes is essential. All tailoring commences from a careful observation of the person for whom one is to cut a suit of clothes, and to correct stoop, paunch, rounded shoulders, square shoulders, etc., by skilful padding, cunning cutting, re-proportioning, etc.

A good figure is determined by its society. Therefore, the ideal is constantly changing. Scientific rules are the commencement for the making of a good suit of clothes but in the end it depends upon a personal and sensitive appraisal of style in relation to a particular man and his environment.

Peter A Bucknell

Bibliography

Arnold, J.: Patterns of Fashion. Englishwomen's dresses and their construction. 1660–1860. Wace & Co. 1964.

Blum, A.: The Last Valois 1515–90. Costume of the Western World. Harrap. 1951.

Blum, A.: Early Bourbon, 1590–1643. Harrap 1951.

Bracket, O. & Smith, H. Clifford: English Furniture Illustrated. Ernest Benn Ltd.

Boehn, M.: Modes and Manners. 8 Volumes. Harrap. 1932–5.

Boucher, F.: Histoire du Costume. Flammarion 1965.

Brinson & Wildeblood. The Polite World. A guide to English manners and deportment from the 13th to the 19th Century. O.U.P. 1965.

Carman, W. X.: British Military uniforms from contemporary pictures. Henry VII to present day. Leonard Hill 1957.

Connoiseur Period Guides:
1500–1603 Tudor. 1956.
1603–1714 Stuart. 1957.
1714–1760 Early Georgian. 1957.
1760–1810 Late Georgian. 1956.
1810–1830 Regency. 1958.
1830–1860 Early Victorian. 1957.

Corson, R.: Fashions in Hair. The first 5,000 years. Peter Owen 1965.

Cunnington, C. W.: A Dictionary of English Costume. 900–1900. Black. 1960.

Cunnington, C. W: The Art of English Costume. Collins. 1949.

Cunnington, C. W: English Women's Clothing in the 19th Century. Faber. 1956.

Cunnington, C. W.: English Women's Clothing in the Present Century. Faber & Faber. 1952.

Cunnington, C. W. & P.: Handbook of English Mediaeval Costume. Faber. 1952.

Cunnington, C. W. & P.: Handbook of English Costume in the 16th Century. Faber. 1952.

Cunnington, C. W. & P.: Handbook of English Costume in the 17th Century. Faber. 1955.

Cunnington, C. W. & P.: Handbook of English Costume in the 18th Century. Faber & Faber. 1959.

Cunnington, C. W. & P.: The History of Underclothes. Michael Joseph. 1951.

Cunnington, P.: Costume in pictures. Dutton Vista. 1964.

Davenport, M.: The Book of Costume. Crown Publishers. New York, 1948.

Edwards, M.: Modes and Manners of the 19th Century as represented by the pictures and engravings of the time. Dent. 1909.

Evans, J.: Dress in mediaeval France. O.U.P. 1952.

Flemming, Ernst.: Encyclopaedia of Textiles. Zwemmer.

Garland, Madge: The Changing Face of Beauty. Weidenfeld & Nicolson.

Gernsheim, A.: Fashion and Reality. Faber. 1963.

Gorsline, D.: A History of Fashion; a visual survey of costume from ancient times to the present day. Batsford. 1953.

Gregor, J.: Das Bühnenkostüm in Historischer. Amalthea-Verlag, c.1925.

Hottenroth, Friedrich: Le Costume chez les peuples anciens et modernes. Armand Guerinet, Paris.

Houston, M.: Ancient Greek, Roman and Byzantine costume. Black. 1947.

Houston, M.: Mediaeval costume in England and France, 13th, 14th and 15th centuries. A. & C. Black. 1939.

Hussey, C.: English Country Houses Open to the Public. Country Life Ltd.

Jourdain, M.: English Interior Decoration. 1500–1830. Batsford.

Kelly, F. M.: Shakespearian Costume for Stage and Screen. Black. 1938.

Kelly, F. & Schwabe, R.: Historic costume. A chronicle of fashion in Western Europe 1490–1790. Batsford. 2nd Edn. 1929.

Kohler & Sichart: A History of Costume. Harrap. 1929.

Kretschmer & Rohrbach: The Costumes of All Nations from earliest times to the 19th century. Dresses and habits of all classes. Henry Sotheran & Co. 1832.

Laver, J.: British Military Uniforms. Penguin. 1948.

Laver, J.: Costume. Cassell. 1963.

Laver, J.: Style in Costume. O.U.P. 1949.

Laver, J.: Costume through the Ages. Thames & Hudson. 1963.

Laver, J.: Early Tudor, 1485–1558. Harrap. 1951.

Laver, J.: Le Costume des Tudor à Louis XIII. Horizons de France. Paris, 1950.

Laver, J.: Costume Illustration: 17th and 18th Centuries. H.M.S.O. 1951.

Martin, P.: Military costume. Herbert Jenkins. 1963.

Morse, H.: Elizabethan pageantry. 1560–1620. Studio. 1934.

Norris, H.: Costume and Fashion. Evolution of European dress. Dent. 1924.
Vol. 2 1066–1485.
Vol. 3 The Tudors. (2 vols.).
Vol. 6 The 19th Century.

Piton, C.: Le Costume Civil en France du XIII au XIx siècle. Paris 1913(?).

Planche, J. R.: A Cyclopaedia of costume or dictionary of Dress. Chatto & Windus 1876–9.

Praz, Mario: An Illustrated History of Interior Decoration. Thames & Hudson.

Reynolds, G.: Elizabethan & Jacobean costume 1558–1625. Harrap. 1951.

Ronsdorf, M.: The Wheel of Fashion. 1689–1929. Thames & Hudson. 1963.

Smith, C. H.: The Fashionable Lady in the 19th century. H.M.S.O. 1960.

Thienen, F.: The Great Age of Holland, 1600–60. Harrap. 1951.

Tilke, M.: Costume patterns and designs. Zwemmer. 1956.

Victoria & Albert Museum: A guide to the collection of costumes. Board of Education. 1924.

Victoria & Albert Museum: 19th Century Costume. Ministry of Education. 1947.

Victoria & Albert Museum: European Printed Textiles.

Waugh, N.: The Cut of Men's clothes 1600–1900. Faber & Faber. 1964.

Waugh, N.: Corsets and Crinolines. Batsford. 1954.

Acknowledgements

The authors would like to express their thanks to all those people who have encouraged and assisted in the development of this book.

Margot Hamilton Hill wishes to thank especially Margaret Simeon, Mrs Cecil A. Wilcox, the Victoria and Albert Museum, the London Library, the Bethnal Green Museum, the Bath Museum of Costume and the National Portrait Gallery.

Peter A Bucknell would like to express his thanks particularly to Margaret Simeon, A.R.C.A., Michael Pope, Alex Ginnett, Stella Marsden, A.R.C.A., Victor Hackett, Richard Negri, Robert Stanbury, Geoffrey Sussams, Elizabeth Rapsey, and Joan Taylor who so carefully typed the manuscript; and to the numerous students who have by trial and error worked in experiments in the making up of costumes, in particular past and present students of the Wimbledon School of Art, past students of the Royal College of Art, past students of the Carnegie Institute of Technology (Drama Department), students of the Webber Douglas Academy of Dramatic Art; and to the numerous actors who have, in the end, worn the costumes.

The illustrations that follow are by Margot Hamilton Hill;
the text and patterns by Peter A Bucknell.

1066 William I

Fabrics: Thick and heavy woollen cloths. Linen. Silks (woven and embroidered) used only on *very* formal occasions.

Colours: Large range of warm colours; small range of greens and blues. Shirt, chemise, and women's head linen white. Only vegetable dyes are used, with a gradual increase in the range of colours, until the middle of the 19th century when vegetable dyes are supplemented with aniline dyes.

Decoration: Simple bands of embroidery and weaving (formal and geometric in design) edge openings, hems, borders, etc. Motifs, of similar design, are appliquéd to the skirts (fronts or hips) and other parts of the top tunic (C.F. neck opening) or mantle.

Movement, men: Tough, athletic people. The stance is natural with the legs set well astride and the arms held away from the body.

Movement, women: Natural, easy and graceful costume to wear. Adjustment is needed in the positioning of the arms, the straightening of the back, and the method of walk, to take the weight of the large circular mantle and veil.

Men

General characteristics: Simple wardrobe consisting of braies (trousers), leather shoes, shirt, under tunic, and over tunic (Dalmatic). Under and top tunics are usually knee length. Cape or mantle rarely longer than mid calf. The costume is essentially practical.

Shirt — rarely if ever seen.

Under tunic — T-shaped with long sleeves.

Top tunic (Dalmatic) — T-shaped with the sides strongly flared from waist to hem. The skirt side seams are closed or left open. The arrangement of the hem is controlled by the girdle or belt — with most of the fullness arranged at the sides. Sleeves are short or three-quarter length.

Cloak or mantle — semi-circular or rectangular and fastened by a brooch, ring, or tied on the right shoulder.

Braies — similar in cut to pyjama trousers, held at the waist with cords and controlled in the legs by various methods of gartering — crossed, braided, bound, etc. What seem to be thickly knitted knee-length hosen are frequently worn under the gartering.

Shoes — of leather or thick cloth constructed to follow the natural shape of the foot and ankle.

Head dress — very rarely seen. Usually a simple fillet binds the hair.

Hair — allowed to grow to a moderate length all round and curled under towards the head, giving a soft, round, cap-like shape. Though moustaches and small beards are seen, the face is usually clean shaven. (Throughout history until well into the 17th century it will be noted from contemporary portraits that the upper lip and chin show a three or four days' growth of hair. Shaving was painful and it is unlikely that men shaved regularly.)

Accessories — accessories of fighting: swords, daggers, shields, spears, etc.

Women

General characteristics: Similar in cut to men's costume. Essentially practical.

Chemise — very rarely seen.

Under tunic — cut full, ground length, and with long narrow sleeves.

Top tunic — knee or calf-length and controlled at the waist by the girdle, with most of the fullness arranged around the hips.

Cloak or mantle — semi-circular, rectangular, or a full circle with a hole cut in the circle to take the head. Portraits show this mantle worn over and in the manner of the circular veil. The semi-circular or rectangular mantle is generally fastened over the chest by means of a brooch.

Leg covering — apparently coarsely knitted or cloth stockings.

Shoes — similar to the men's.

Head dress — the hair, entirely hidden under the voluminous veil, is most likely parted in the middle, braided, and twisted into a coil at the nape of the neck. The veil, arranged in a variety of ways and fastened with pins, is semi-circular, rectangular, or fully circular with a hole cut in the circle to take the face. (It is very probable that a fillet is first placed on the head to which the veil can be secured.)

Accessories — knotted girdles. Purses, brooches. All accessories are functional and not primarily used for decoration.

Notes on patterns: Men

Over tunic (Dalmatic) — for extra side flare extend the patterns at the side seams from waist to hem.

Under tunic — the sleeve is placed to an embroidered wristband and allowed to wrinkle up the length of the arm. (For theatre costume it is advisable to tie-catch these sleeves to a false under sleeve.)

Shirt — use under tunic pattern.

Notes on patterns: Women

Chemise — use under tunic pattern.

Under tunic — for extra skirt fullness extend the patterns at the side seams from waist to hem (for theatre costume tie-catch the long sleeve to an inner sleeve).

Circular veil — the arrangement of the veil illustrated requires the head opening to be cut nearer to the centre of the circle. It is secured to a fillet with the front part, which lies across the chest, drawn up high under the chin and around under the veil to the back, where it is pinned to the plait of hair. (It is advisable, for theatre costume, to sew the veil arrangement in place, fastening at the back with hooks and eyes. The mass of flutings over the forehead, represented in a stylized manner by painters of the time, can be achieved by inserting and whipping godets into the top curve of the head opening.)

PORTANT:ARMAS: ADNAVES: ETHIC
TRAHVNT: CARRVM
CVMVINO:ETARM IS:

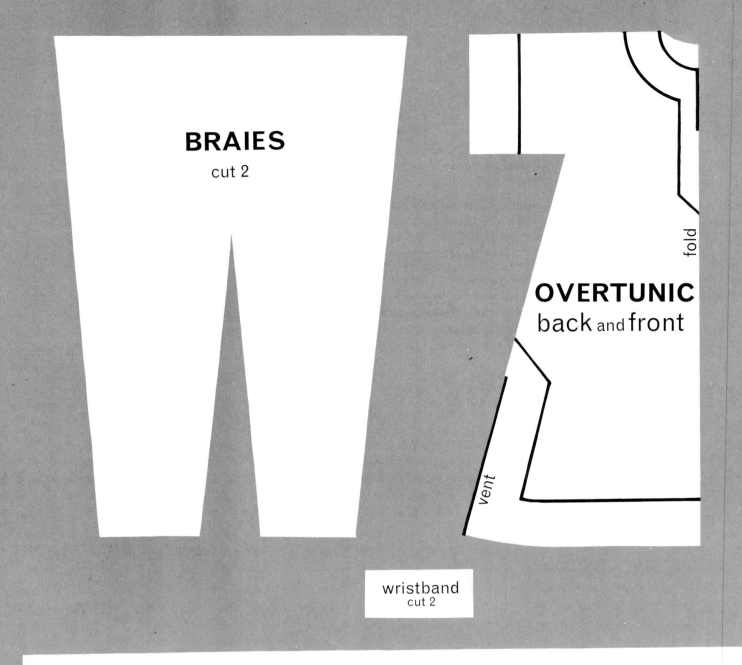

BRAIES
cut 2

OVERTUNIC
back and front

fold

vent

wristband
cut 2

GIRDLE

CLOAK
rectangular or semicircular
(1/16 scale)

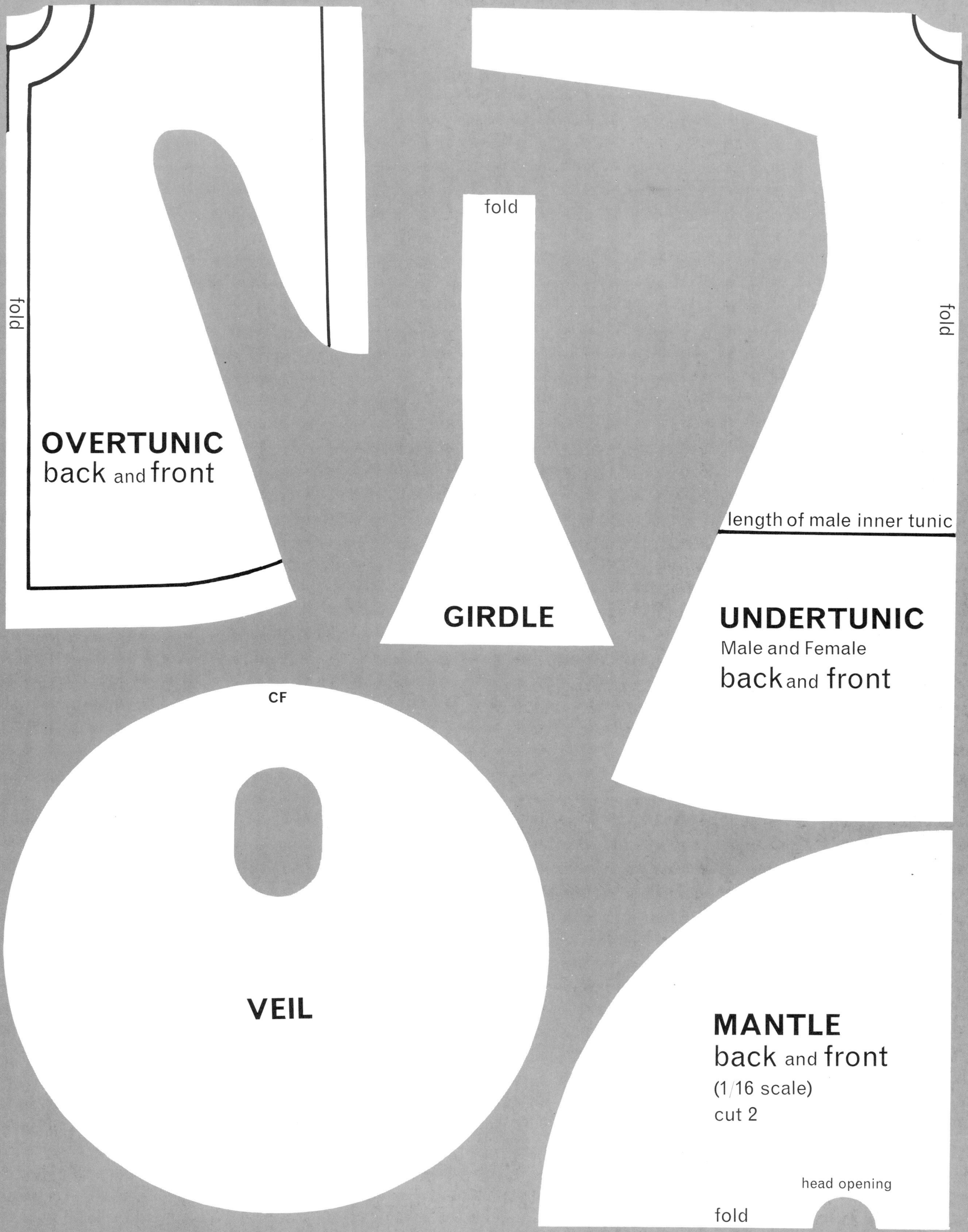

OVERTUNIC
back and front

fold

fold

fold

length of male inner tunic

GIRDLE

UNDERTUNIC
Male and Female
back and front

CF

VEIL

MANTLE
back and front
(1/16 scale)
cut 2

head opening

fold

1100 Henry I

Fabrics: Similar to the previous fashion — of various weights, both fine and coarse in texture.

Colours: Fresh and brighter in hue.

Decoration: Embroidered or woven stripes and formal motifs decorate the robe and mantle.

Padding and restriction, women: Indications of a desire to reveal and control the shape of the body suggests that a simple form of body binder is worn under the robe.

Movement, men: The quantity of fabric in the robe and mantle, and the wide variety of methods of girdling and draping, determines flamboyant movement and gesture. To free the mantle from the long robe and to relieve the shoulders from its weight, it is convenient to place the palms of the hands on the hips. The fullness and length of the skirts necessitates a slow walk.

Movement, women: Natural, with a straight back. Elbows are held inwards to complement and free the long sleeves.

Men

General characteristics: Garments are full, ground length, and richly decorated with bands of embroidery. The skirts are frequently draped, pouched, and arranged in pleats at the waist, to form hem-lines of varying length.

Shirt — similar to the previous fashion.

Under tunic — ground length with long ruckled sleeves to wrist.

Robe — T-shaped with ground-length flared skirts — pulled up high on one side and controlled by the belt. Sleeves are cut very long to extend over the hand.

Mantle — semi-circular, ground length, fastened on right shoulder and edged with a patterned band.

Hosen — possibly poorly fitting long stockings held up by cords attached to an inner belt.

Shoes — shaped like a slipper with a stuffed and padded long pointed toe ("fishtail" or "scorpion's tail").

Head dress — simple hoods.

Hair — long, with one or more partings, and elaborately arranged in tight curls and plaits. Beards are dressed in three or more points. Long, wispy moustaches.

Accessories — belts, purses, daggers.

Women

General characteristics: More individualistic than the preceding fashion, with indications of an attempt to arrange and cut clothes to reveal the figure.

Chemise and under robe — rarely seen. The tight sleeves of the under robe appear beneath the long, wide sleeves of the top robe.

Robe — the robe is probably back-laced to reveal and fit the body. Examples are seen where the side seams of the body part, from underarm to hips, are cut in such a manner that when tied or knotted they tighten the robe to accentuate the contour of the figure. The robe is secured at the waist by a cloth girdle. Skirts show strong development of flare at the side seams, and the sleeve is now cut tightly to develop into a long, wide sleeve at the wrist.

Mantle — semi-circular, ground length, with a hole scooped out to take the neck. Held in place by a brooch or thongs tied across chest.

Stockings — likely to be poorly fitting.

Shoes — similar to men's.

Head dress — the hair, more elaborately dressed, is centrally parted and formed into one or more sheathed plaits (length of the plaits indicate addition of false hair). Veils, as described in the previous fashion, are arranged to reveal the form of the head, neck and shoulders. The fillet is now placed over the veil.

Accessories — similar to the previous fashion.

Notes on patterns: Men

Robe — for extra fullness extend flares at the side seams.

Under tunic — cut as robe using sleeve from the previous pattern.

Belt — knotted thongs are threaded through holes to secure the belt.

Notes on patterns: Women

Chemise and under robe — cut as in previous pattern.

Robe — side flare emphasis is increased by developing the side seams or inserting godets. (For the theatre, control the stretched folds across the body by tie-catching to a lining, use an inserted sleeve, and make up in a soft stretchy material, e.g., jersey.)

Veil — the back shoulder-parts of the veil are brought forward over the shoulders and arranged into folds to fall down over the chest.

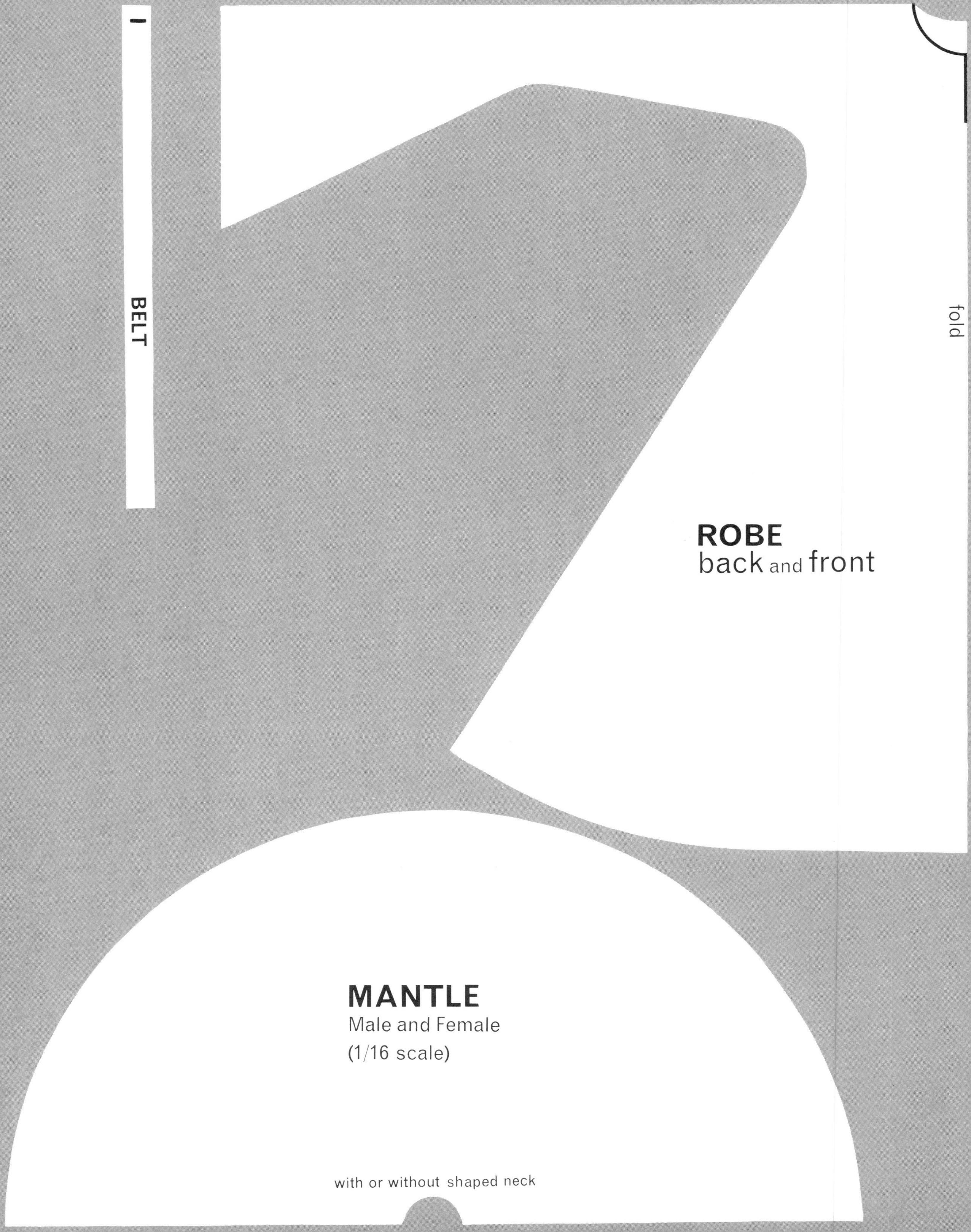

BELT

fold

ROBE
back and front

MANTLE
Male and Female
(1/16 scale)

with or without shaped neck

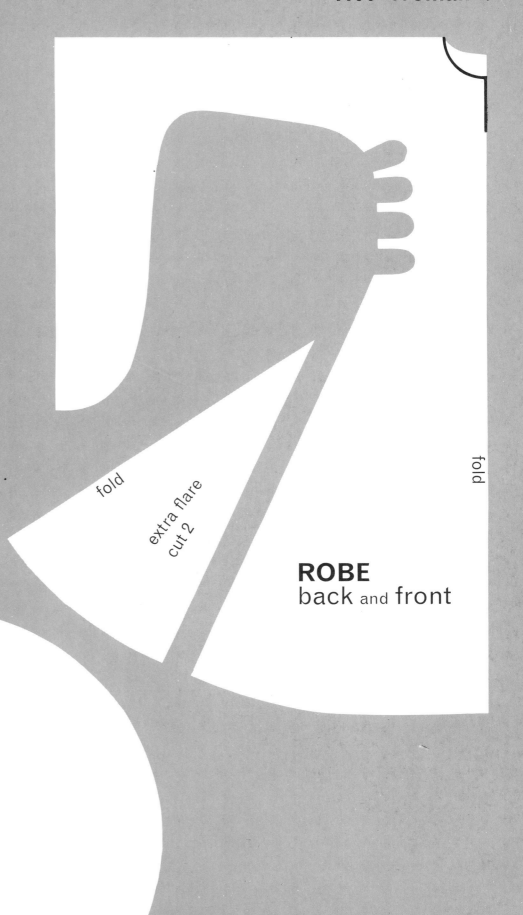

fold

GIRDLE

fold

extra flare
cut 2

fold

ROBE
back and front

VEIL

1150 Stephen

Fabrics: New and very costly fabrics (introduced by soldiers returning from the First Crusade), such as silks, gauzes, damasks, woven gold, etc., are occasionally worn at Court. Clinging drapery and arrangements of pleating indicate a large range of soft, very fine woollen fabrics.

Colours: Lighter in hue.

Decoration: The most distinctive decorative feature is the variety of methods used in the draping and pleating of garments. Continued use of woven and embroidered bands.

Padding and restriction, women: A simple form of body corsetry worn over the bliaut.

Movement, men: Care and elegance exercised in the handling of the mantle and the long skirts of the under robe.

Movement, women: An extremely graceful costume to wear — a gliding movement with arms held well away from the body to display to advantage the very long, — sometimes trailing the ground — rippling sleeves. (For convenience the sleeves are frequently arranged in knots to keep them off the ground.)

Men

General characteristics: Less eccentric than the preceding fashion. Increasing originality in the cutting of the tunic to achieve a variety of skirt arrangements. Body parts fit close to the figure, the waistline is lower and the sleeves narrower in cut from the shoulder to elbow, from whence they widen. All garments indicate extravagant use of material.

Shirt — probably knee length.

Under tunic — the skirts, strongly flared on the side seams, are decorated with bands of embroidery.

Bliaut — (probably back-laced) a sophisticated development of the tunic with body part and skirts separated by a waist seam. The skirts, longer at the back than in the front, are pleated to the low-positioned waistline. Sleeves are cut in one with the body. The belt is usually placed twice around the figure (below chest and hips).

Mantle — similar to the previous fashion.

Hosen — similar to the previous fashion.

Shoes — form-fitting, covering the ankle, with a modest, pointed toe.

Head dress — hoods and simple Phrygian caps.

Hair — similar to the previous fashion, but less formal and more natural and flowing.

Women

General characteristics: A very sophisticated fashion lasting for only a few years. The vast quantity of pleated material used in the costume, and the body corsetry, are the most characteristic features of this period.

Chemise and under tunic — similar to the cut of 1066 but very much fuller in width and made of fine materials.

Bliaut — entire costume cut with sufficient fullness to produce fine, radial, knife pleatings. Upper parts of the body and upper parts of the sleeves (sleeves separate and set into armholes) fit the form by means of smocking. Neck opening fastened with a brooch.

Corselet or body belt — (worn over the bliaut) a form-revealing, sleeveless, hip-length, quilted waistcoat with back-lacing, or a wide body belt tightly laced at the back or on the sides.

Mantle — almost a three-quarter circle cut long enough to trail the ground. Secured across the chest by thongs laced through eyelet holes.

Girdle or belt — decorated with embroidery, passed twice around the figure and fastened in front with knotted, decorated thongs.

Shoes — similar to men's.

Hosen — likely to be poorly fitting.

Head dress — the hair is centrally parted and arranged in two very long braided plaits. A circular veil, of various lengths, is worn over the hair and kept in place by a decorated fillet.

Accessories — similar to the previous fashion.

Notes on patterns: Men

Shirt — adapt under tunic pattern terminating at knee.

Bliaut — attach the skirts to the body parts, forming pleats on the sides — back and front. The skirt side seams are left open. (A, marked on the skirt pattern, indicates termination of the waistline and commencement of the side seam.) Tighten body part of bliaut by means of back-lacing or, for theatre purposes, by darting and forming a side or back placket.

Under tunic — the heavy pleating is controlled by the belt. As an alternative, terminate the body parts at hip level and attach to a skirt similar in shape to that of the bliaut — cut ground length with an even hemline, and with the side seams closed.

Notes on patterns: Women

Chemise and under tunic — develop by flaring and spreading pattern of 1066 from neckline to hem, gathering excess fullness at the neck into a narrow band.

Bliaut — cut from the patterns in fine, pre-pleated (radial) material. The pleatings run from shoulder to hem and through the length of the sleeve. Patterns should be opened up and developed to the length of sleeve and fullness of skirt required. Smock top part of the bodice and upper part of the sleeves — if necessary insert an underarm gusset. Apply an embroidered band to the neckline and neck opening.

Corselet — advisable to cut the material on the cross and to attach to a made-up corselet foundation (see pattern). Lace at the back.

Girdle — advisable to cut and shape the girdle to the figure and to tie-catch it to the costume.

Veil — the fine fluting can be exaggerated, theatrically, by cutting the circle in pre-pleated (radial) material of the finest and softest fabric available. (It should not be transparent.)

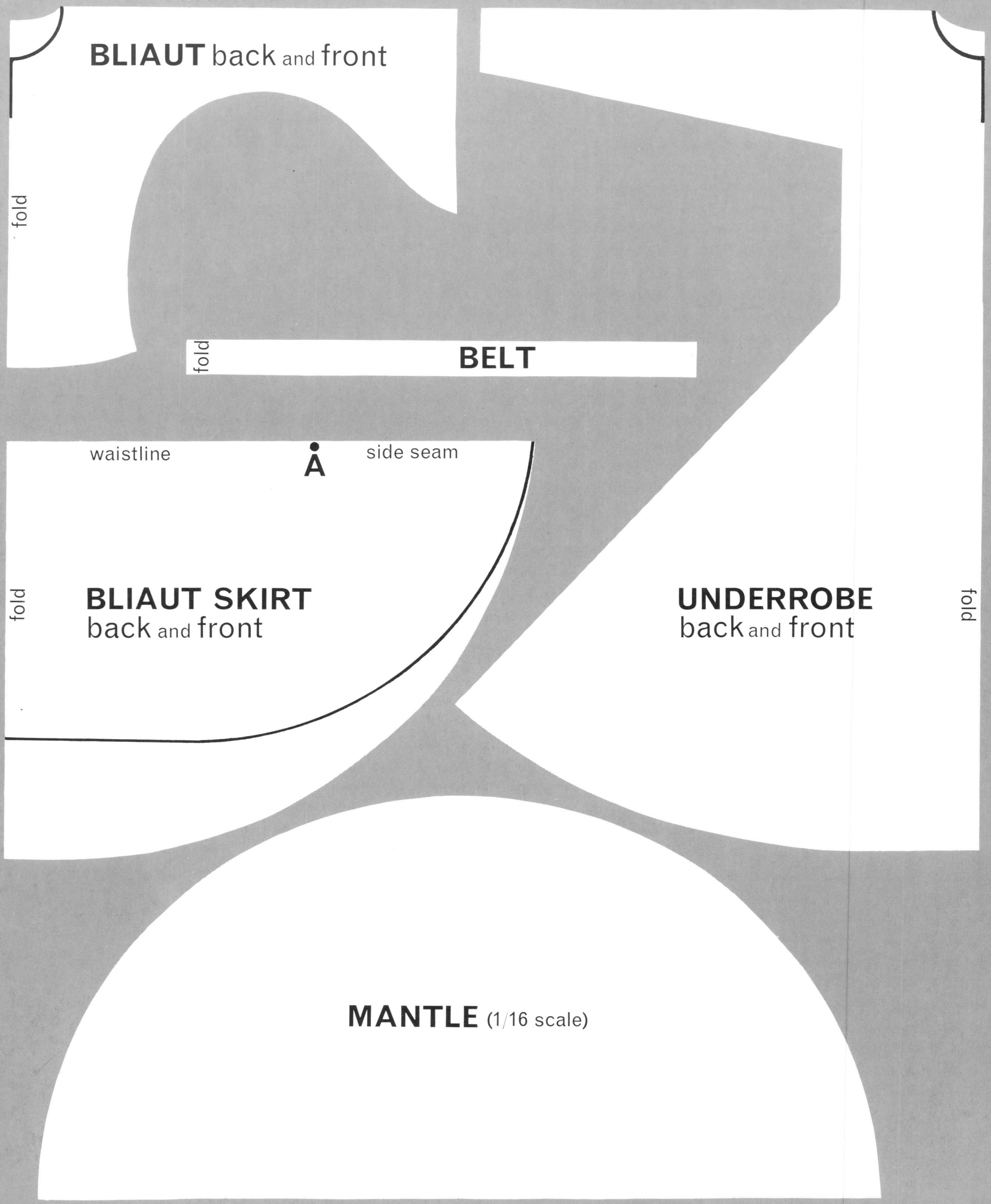

BLIAUT back and front

fold

fold **BELT**

waistline Å side seam

fold **BLIAUT SKIRT** back and front

UNDERROBE back and front fold

MANTLE (1/16 scale)

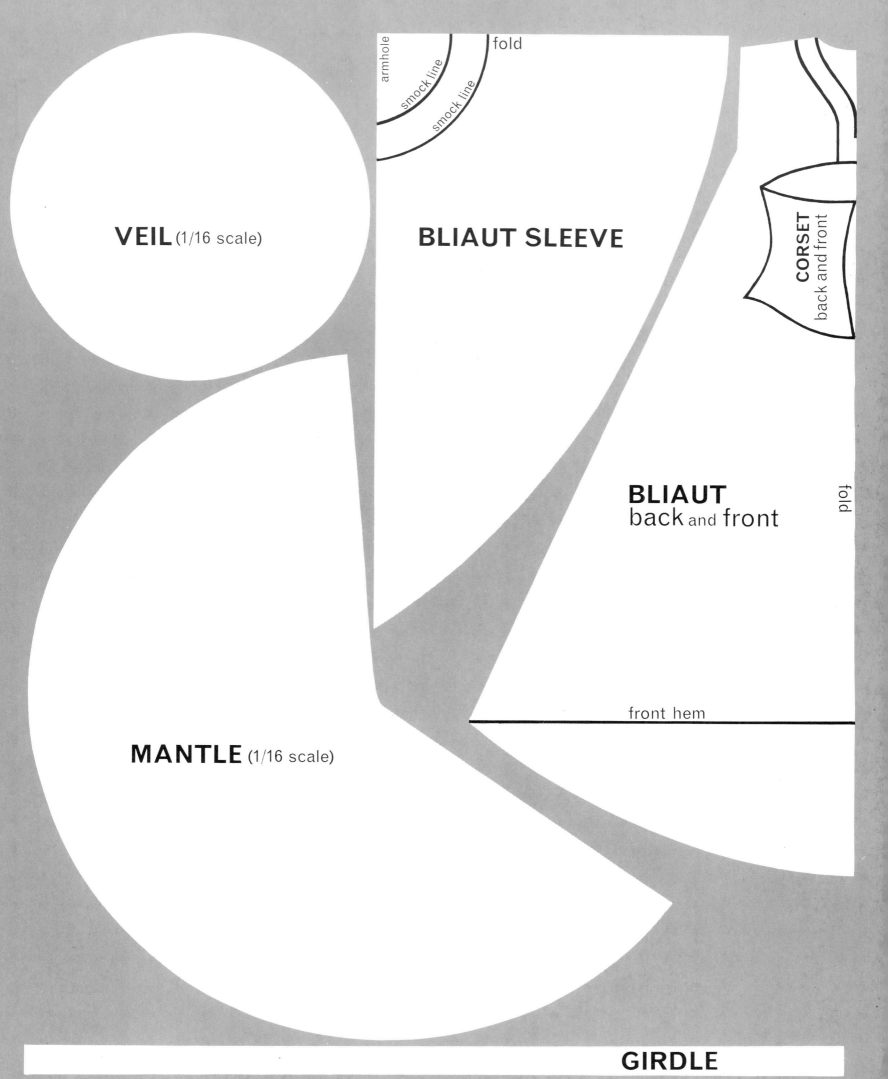

VEIL (1/16 scale)

BLIAUT SLEEVE

armhole
smock line
smock line
fold

CORSET
back and front

BLIAUT
back and front

fold

front hem

MANTLE (1/16 scale)

GIRDLE

1190 Richard I

Fabrics: Similar to the previous fashion. The mantle is frequently lined with fur — small, shorthaired pelts cut into formal shapes and sewn together.

Colours: Clear and bright.

Decoration: Generally confined to the neck and wrist edges of the tunic or robe, the edge of the mantle, and the belt.

Movement, men: Natural.

Movement, women: The simple robe permits natural and easy movement. When taking corners or turning about, a curved line of walk is necessary.

Men

General characteristics: Essentially a simple wardrobe. Men's and women's clothes are similar in cut save for length of skirts and mantle.

Shirt — similar to the previous fashion.

Under tunic — similar to the previous fashion (possibly discarded).

Tunic — the line of the sleeve is now cut at an angle and no longer developed at 90° from the body parts. It forms a very deep armhole, springing from the waistline, and tapers to fit the wrist. Fullness of the body parts and the skirts is controlled at the natural waist by a belt from which a purse, dagger, etc., are usually suspended. The neck opening, cut low, suggests that a placket is unnecessary. The centre front and the centre back of the skirts are open from crotch to hem.

Mantle — usually the same length as the tunic and somewhat fuller than the half circle. Kept in place over the chest by a strap.

Hosen — somewhat loose in fit with V-shaped insertions positioned at the front and back from crotch point to waist. The hosen are held up by a drawstring.

Shoes — similar to the previous fashion, neat and close in fit with a front or side fastening. Tubes of material or soft leather are sometimes sewn to the ankle part to form simple high boots.

Head dress — a hood cut with a shoulder cape.

Hair — waved with a short fringe. Hair is cut to terminate at the nape of the neck in a continuous, horizontal curl from ear to ear. Beards and moustaches are rarely worn by younger men.

Accessories — belts, elaborate purses, daggers, gloves (simple in cut with a short gauntlet and no insertions between the fingers).

Women

General characteristics: Simple and graceful fashion with an absence of applied decoration — depending for its effect on line and flow of material.

Chemise — rarely seen.

Under robe — seen only when the top robe skirts are held up in the process of walking.

Robe or kirtle — similar in cut to the men's tunic. Ground length with side and back skirts developing into a short train. The robe is usually longer than the wearer with the excess material controlled and pouched at the waistline by the belt.

Mantle — (the inside edge is shaped to take the curve of the neck) fastened across the chest with a strap.

Hosen — similar to the previous fashion.

Shoes — similar to men's.

Head dress — plaits now coiled, frequently encased in a net or caul, give added width to sides of the face and in particular to the back of the head. The barbette (a strip of cloth placed under the chin, taken up over the ears and fastened on top of the head by pinning) is worn with a deep fillet placed over it. Both fillet, when not decorated, and the barbette are always white.

Accessories — belts, brooches (to fasten robe neckline) and purses.

Notes on patterns: Men

Tunic — (wider pattern) if necessary form a placket at the C.F. or C.B. neck, and at the wrist if a really tight sleeve is required. To control the excess of material at the waistline add a casing and drawstring — concealed by the belt.

Notes on patterns: Women

Robe or kirtle — (narrower pattern) to control the length and width of the garment at the waistline add a casing and drawstring — concealed by the belt.

Head dress — cut fillet and barbette from measurements taken after the hair has been arranged. The fillet should be pulled well down on the sides of the head to form a concave curve over the forehead.

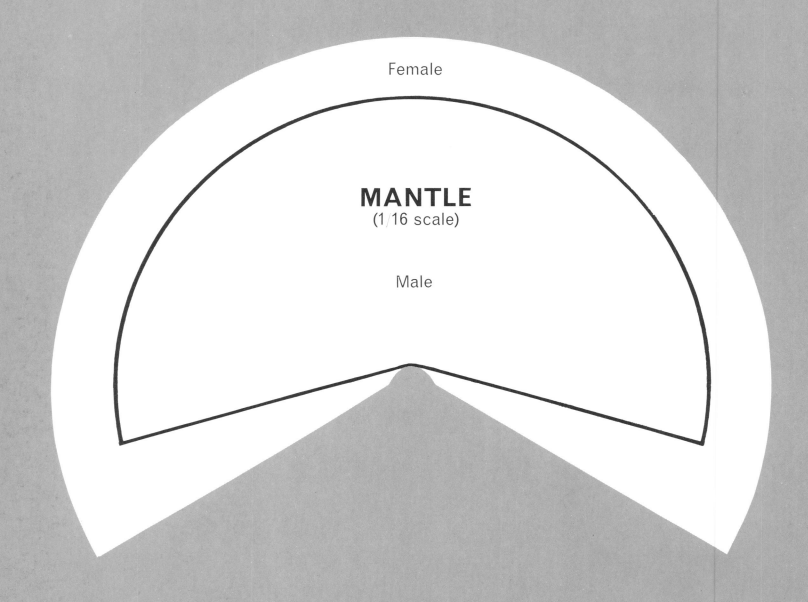

Female

MANTLE
(1/16 scale)

Male

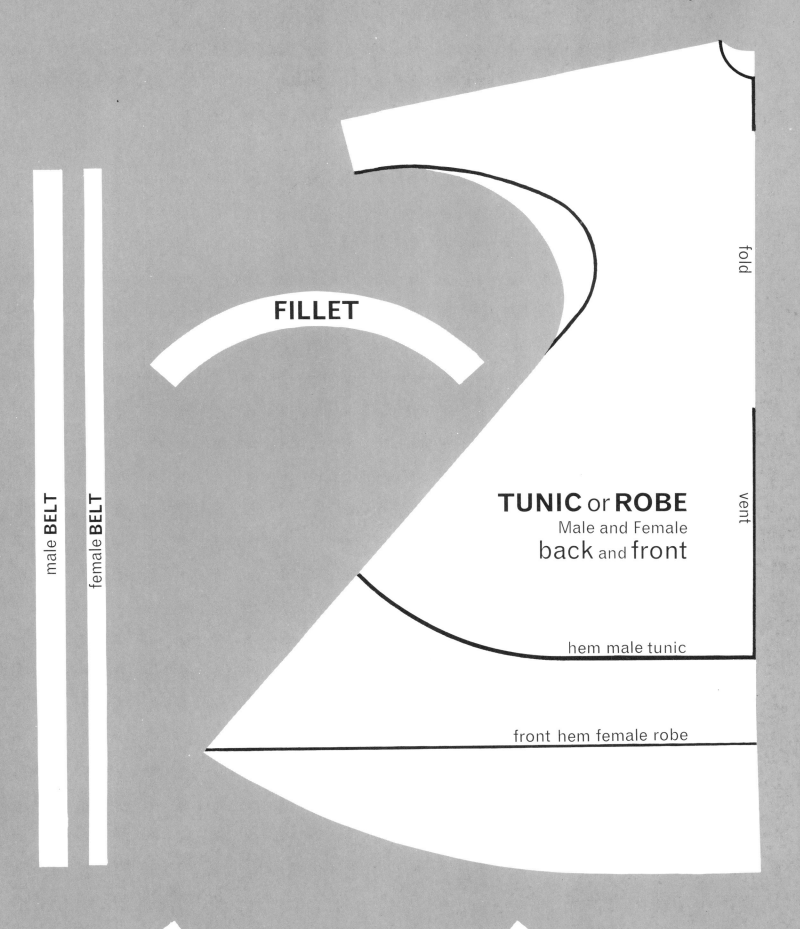

FILLET

male **BELT**

female **BELT**

fold

vent

TUNIC or ROBE
Male and Female
back and front

hem male tunic

front hem female robe

BARBETTE

1210 John

Fabrics: Wider range of materials including silks, of various weights, and woven and printed textiles. (Middle classes imitate patterns of woven fabrics by printing.)

Colours: Rich and heraldic.

Decoration: Strong influence of Byzantine ornament — roundels, diamonds, hexagons, etc., either in all-over simple repeats or confined to wide bands. Skirts (men) are cut and slit up from the hemline at regular intervals all round to form scallops, castellations, zig-zags, pendulant streamers, etc. (dagging). By the middle of the 15th century this form of decoration becomes very extravagant and elaborate — appearing anywhere on areas of the costume capable of being serrated, foliated, or snipped.

Movement, men: Easy and natural.

Movement, women: Easy and natural.

Men

General characteristics: More formal and robust in style. All body garments are cut with considerably less fullness. Fit becomes progressively more important. A return to the habit of banding and edging parts of the costume with woven or embroidered strips of material.

Shirt — rarely seen (possibly tucked into the waistline of the hosen).

Under tunic — possibly dispensed with.

Tunic — mid calf in length and cut with fairly tight sleeves. It is possible that the dagging of skirts was introduced to permit greater freedom of movement for the lower limbs. Vents are still cut in the skirt at C.F. and C.B. The garment is controlled at the natural waist by a belt. Another belt holding the sword is placed lower, about the hips.

Mantle — usually lined throughout. Semi-circular, gathered and fastened by a large brooch over the chest.

Hosen — closer in fit and often cross-gartered. Simple, soft leather high boots are sometimes worn over the hosen and under the cross gartering.

Shoes — elegantly pointed, cut low at the sides and front, and fastened with an ankle strap.

Head dress — a variety of simple, low-crowned hats with the brim frequently made of fur. Hoods.

Hair — dressed in soft, neat waves. Cut with a fringe, and terminating in length at the base of the neck. Heavy moustaches — with or without the beard.

Accessories — richly ornamented gloves with a short gauntlet, purses, daggers, sword and sword belt.

Women

General characteristics: Formal and matronly in style compared to the essentially youthful costume of the previous fashion.

Chemise — seen above the low neck of the robe when the wimple is not worn.

Under robe — cut in similar fashion to the robe.

Robe (kirtle) — cut with a low curved neckline, tight sleeves, and narrower body parts — the skirts lengthening into a small train at the C.B. A long sash, belt, or girdle is worn about the waist.

Mantle — usually lined throughout. Cut larger than the half circle, often to trail the ground, and kept in place over the chest by a strap fastened to buttons sewn to the mantle edges.

Hosen — similar to the previous fashion.

Shoes — similar to men's.

Head dress — hair rarely seen but probably neatly braided and placed in a caul fastened to a narrow fillet. The neck is covered by the wimple (a rectangular piece of white fabric). It is placed loosely under the chin, brought up over the ears and pinned on top of the head or at the sides of the fillet, with the lower edge usually tucked into the neckline of the robe. A veil, of varying lengths, is placed over the head and attached to the fillet.

Accessories — brooches, purses.

Notes on patterns: Men

Tunic — (line throughout). For a neater-fitting sleeve add an underarm gusset.

Mantle — (line throughout). Use the man's pattern of 1190.

Hosen — use thick woollen tights, two or three sizes too large.

Hat — for a more subtle form, block the crown from heavy felt, adding a covered button to the central point.

Sword belt — attach the scabbard to the two rings and place the buckle at A.

Notes on patterns: Women

Chemise — cut full and gather excess material at the neck to a narrow band.

Robe (kirtle) — for a neater-fitting sleeve add an underarm gusset. The bands around the neck and wrists are appliquéd to the robe.

Mantle — line throughout.

Wimple and veil — make up in very soft fine material (wool or cotton).

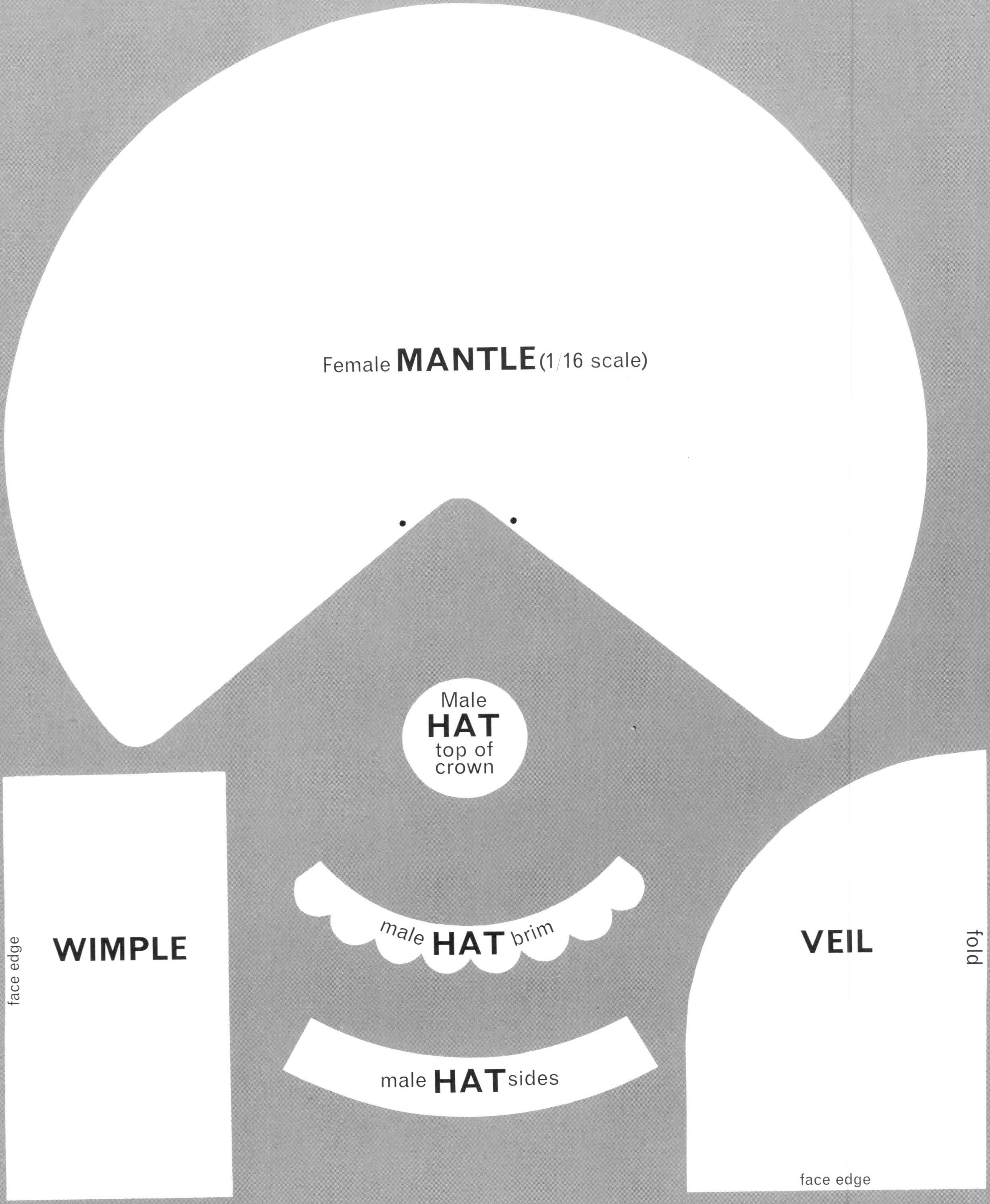

Female **MANTLE** (1/16 scale)

Male **HAT** top of crown

WIMPLE

face edge

male **HAT** brim

male **HAT** sides

VEIL

fold

face edge

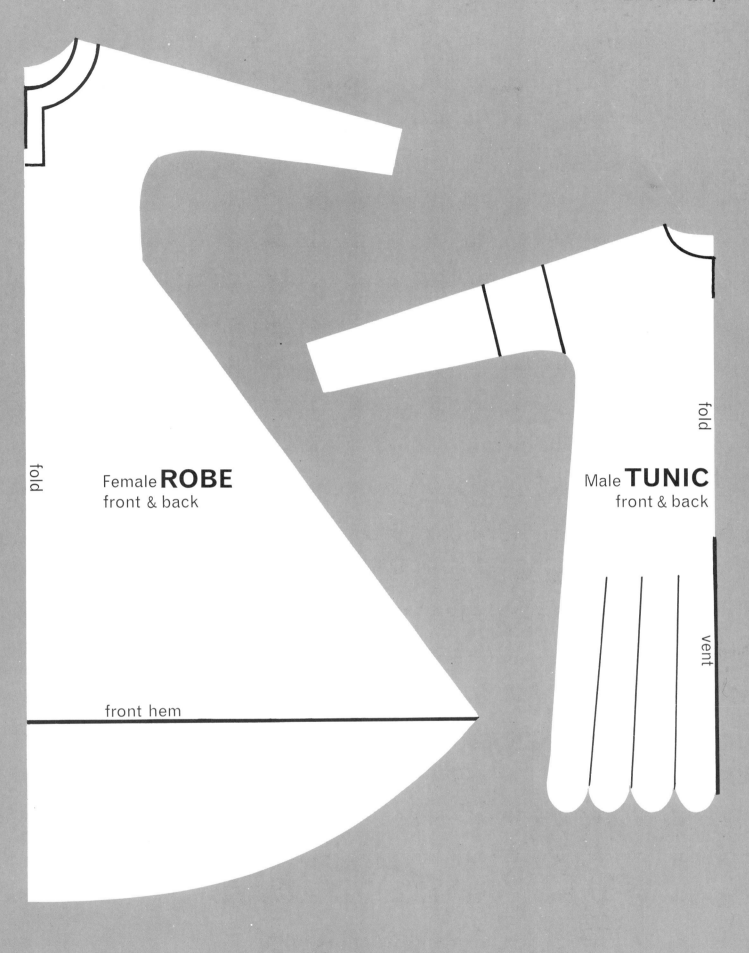

Female ROBE
front & back

fold

front hem

Male TUNIC
front & back

fold

vent

BELT female

A

Sword **BELT** male

Waist **BELT** male

1260 Henry III

Fabrics: Large range of materials including a small quantity of brocades and silks. Garments are lined throughout in fur made up from the small pelts of short-haired animals or in material of contrasting colour or tone.

Colours: Heraldic.

Decoration: Simple parti-colour (costume divided vertically back and front), quartering (costume divided vertically, and horizontally at the waist, back and front), and appliquéd or embroidered heraldic charges decorate the cyclas (originally worn to identify the wearer on the battlefield) and the sideless gown. Decoration becomes very elaborate and rich, especially in women's dress, when the coat of arms of the woman and her husband are embroidered and appliquèd over the entire ground of the mantle and the sideless gown. (This fashion, with minor adaptations, continues to be worn for formal and ceremonial dress until the commencement of the 16th century.)

Movement, men: Natural, but with elbows held away from the body.

Movement, women: The back is arched and the pelvis leads the walk due to the considerable weight and length of the mantle and the train of the sideless gown. Elbows are held well away from the body. The front skirts of the sideless gown are usually gathered up and placed in the crook of the arm.

Men

General characteristics: Low-waisted and narrow silhouette. The sleeves and skirts are possibly cut independently of the body parts. Buttoned openings at C.F. or C.B. and down the length of the arm (elbow to wrist) indicate improved cutting to achieve better fit.

Shirt — rarely seen.

Under tunic — seen from wrist to elbow.

Tunic — knee length, lined throughout and buttoned down the C.F. The sleeves are tight and terminate just below the elbow where they develop into long, flowing ends.

Cyclas (or sleeveless tunic) — low-necked tabard form with the sides left open to the hips, where they are either buttoned or seamed through to the hem. Vents are cut in the skirts at C.F. and C.B. A belt is worn low on the hips.

Hosen — improvement in cut and fit due to the length of leg exposed by the short tunic.

Shoes — elegantly pointed. Cut away at the sides and front leaving a high back and narrow ankle strap.

Head dress — little white bonnets or coifs. The point at the back of the hood develops in length (liripipe).

Hair — similar in style to the previous fashion; shorter in length with the ends curled outwards in a continuous roll. Beards and moustaches worn by older men.

Accessories — belt, dagger, purse, and sword.

Women

General characteristics: Dress is more complex. Cutting reveals one garment below the other (short-sleeved robe and sideless gown).

Chemise — rarely seen.

Under robe — similar in cut to the robe with tight-fitting, buttoned sleeves.

Robe (kirtle) — low necked and cut closer to the form. The skirts are flared and develop into a train at the back. Sleeves are similar in cut to the men's.

Sideless gown — worn over the robe, low necked, without sleeves and cut away at the sides to hip level. The skirts, strongly flared on the side seams, are usually longer than ground length and cut with a train at the back. Many early examples of the sideless gown show side lacing.

Mantle — similar to the fashion of 1190.

Stockings — similar to the previous fashion.

Shoes — similar to men's.

Head dress — the hair is centrally parted and placed in cauls. The wimple is stretched tightly under the chin and fastened on top of the head, with the lower edge tucked into the neckline of the sideless gown. The form of the throat is accentuated by drawing the material tightly around the neck and pinning it together at the back. The pinning and excess material is hidden by the veil, which is pleated across its width and placed over the pillbox-type hat (a development of the fillet of 1190).

Accessories — similar to the previous fashion.

Notes on patterns: Men

Under tunic — cut body parts similar to the body parts of the tunic. Add a C.F. buttoned opening and buttoned openings to the lower parts of the sleeves.

Tunic — line throughout adding a C.F. buttoned opening.

Cyclas — line throughout.

Hood — line throughout.

Coif — sew edges B to B and gather from A to A to fit the head, adding strings at the corners (or a draw ribbon) to tie under the chin.

Notes on patterns: Women

Chemise — cut full with a gathered neckline.

Under robe — use body parts and skirts of the robe pattern. Add a C.B. placket, and buttoned openings to the lower parts of the sleeves (elbow to wrist).

Robe — line throughout, adding placket at C.F. or C.B.

Sideless gown — line throughout and cut at least 9 inches longer than the height of the wearer, extending the train to the required length. Loops should be sewn at intervals to the side openings, back and front, if the gown is to be laced.

Mantle — use women's pattern of 1190.

Head dress — (for theatre purposes these head dresses are best made up and not left for the wearer to arrange. It is, however, very essential that the drapery should look natural — head dresses were originally arranged daily by hands well accustomed to the folding and often elaborate arrangements of simple-shaped pieces of material).

Wimple: (cut on the cross) pre-arrange on the wearer to get a close fit around the neck and sides of the head — cut away excess material, form a placket at the C.B. and fasten with hooks and eyes.

Hat: control top rim pleating by tie-catching. Pull the hat well down at the sides to form a concave curve over the forehead.

Veil: reduce to 6 inches the distance A to B by pleating. Place over the hat and secure with pins.

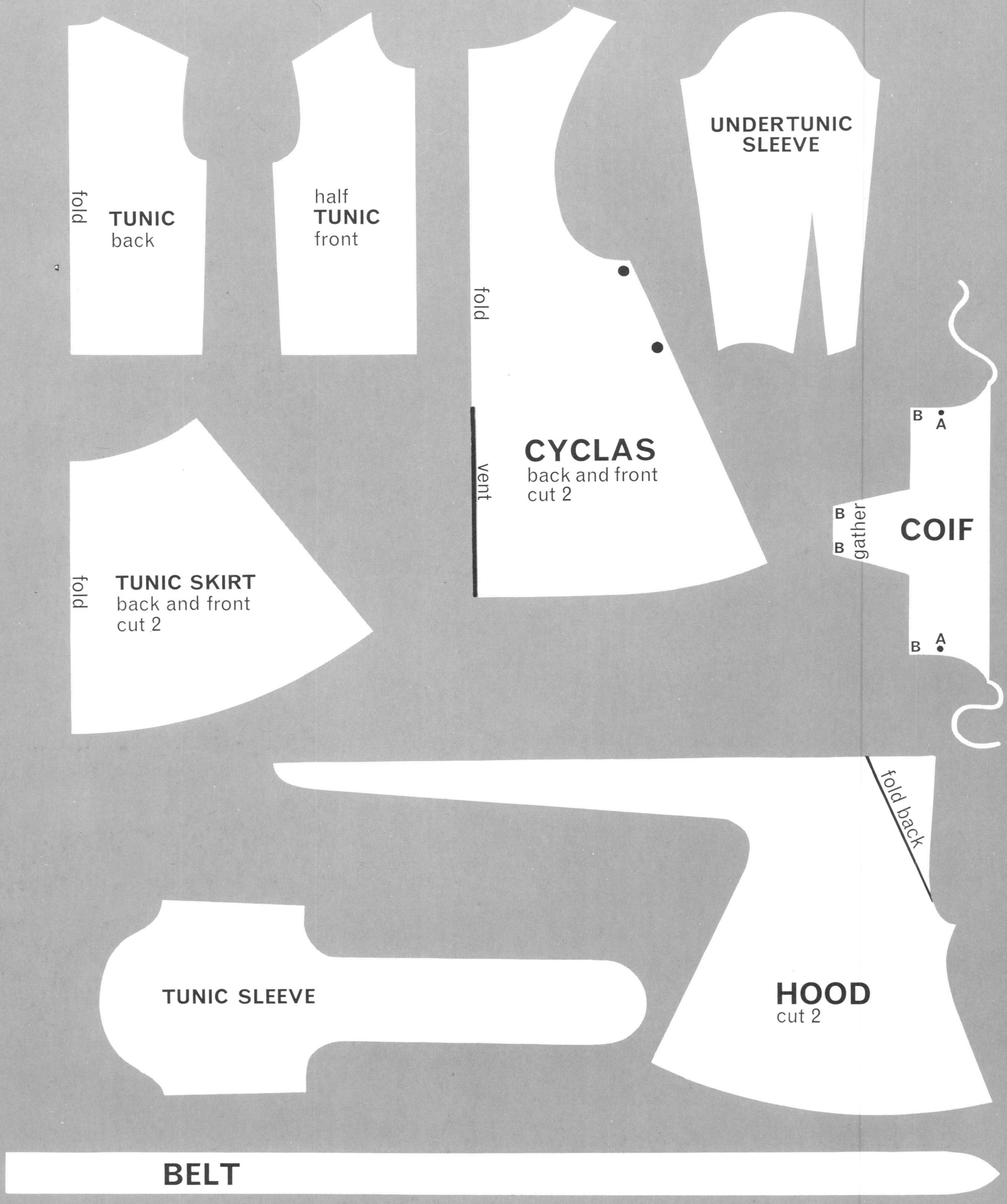

TUNIC back

fold

half **TUNIC** front

UNDER TUNIC SLEEVE

fold

vent

CYCLAS back and front cut 2

B A

B gather

B

COIF

B A

TUNIC SKIRT back and front cut 2

fold

fold back

TUNIC SLEEVE

HOOD cut 2

BELT

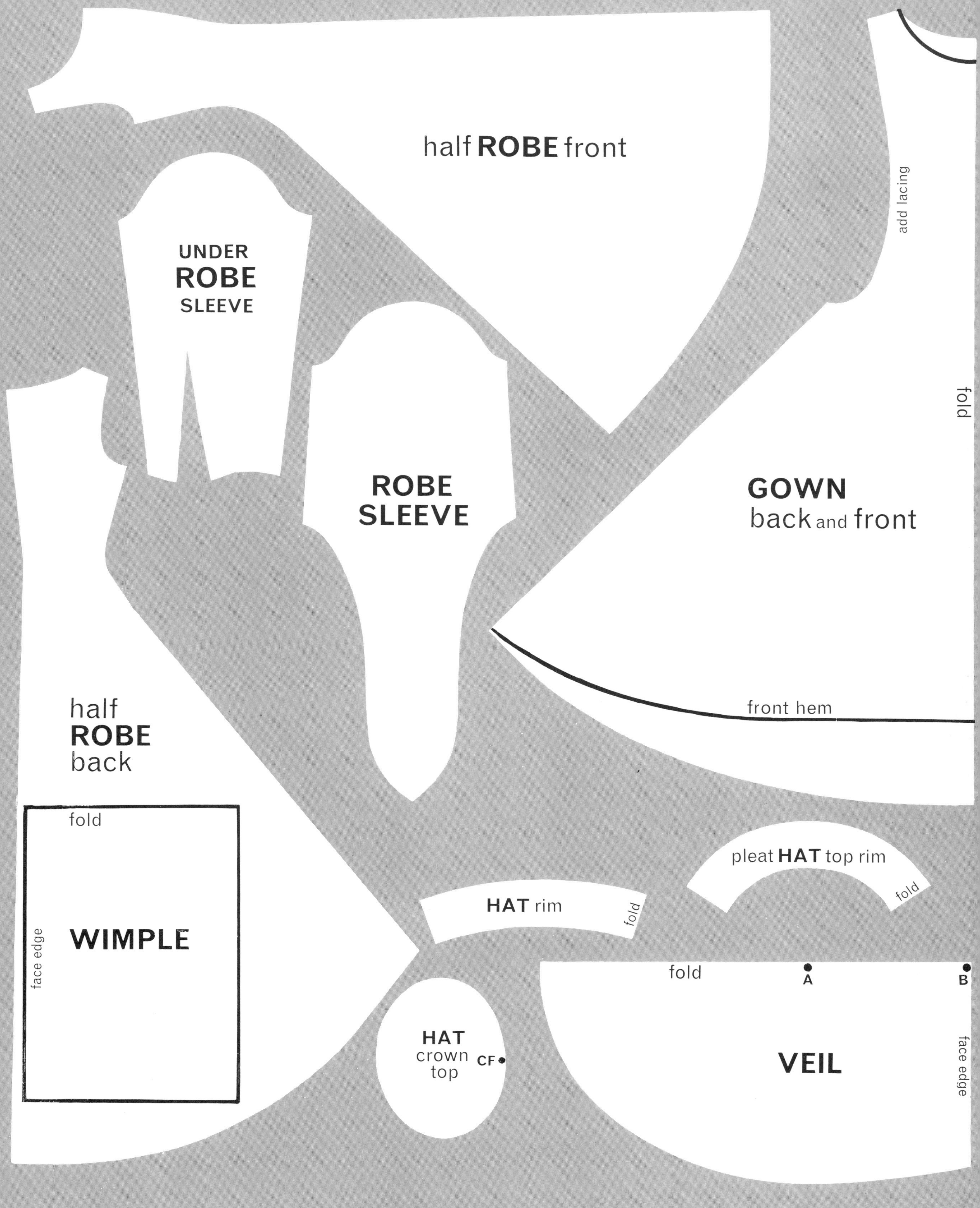

half **ROBE** front

UNDER
ROBE
SLEEVE

add lacing

fold

**ROBE
SLEEVE**

GOWN
back and front

front hem

half
ROBE
back

fold

pleat **HAT** top rim

fold

HAT rim

fold

fold

face edge

WIMPLE

fold · A · B

HAT
crown
top

CF ·

VEIL

face edge

1300 Edward I

Fabrics: Similar to the previous fashion.

Colours: Heraldic.

Decoration: Small pelts sewn together to form linings and edgings.

Movement, men: Similar to the previous fashion.

Movement, women: The weight and great size of the pelican (top garment) dictates slow movement and dignified and upright posture. The head is held high with the chin tucked in.

Men

General characteristics: Similar to the previous fashion.

Shirt — rarely seen.

Under tunic — similar to the previous fashion.

Cyclas — similar to the previous fashion.

Gard-corps — a flared, below knee-length, top garment with hood attached. It falls straight from the shoulders and is lined throughout. The very full pleated sleeves are cut with a second and alternative opening for the hand. Vents are placed at the C.F. and C.B. of the skirts. The gard-corps frequently replaces the cloak.

Hosen — similar to the previous fashion.

Shoes — similar to the previous fashion.

Head dress — similar to the previous fashion.

Hair — similar to the previous fashion. ·

Accessories — similar to the previous fashion.

Women

General characteristics: The cyclas or sideless gown, the robe, the full mantle or pelican, and the veil and wimple, completely cover the figure to reveal only the face and hands.

Chemise and under robe — similar to the previous fashion.

Robe — similar to the previous fashion.

Sideless gown — similar to the previous fashion.

Pelicon — (usually lined throughout with fur), a fully circular top garment with holes cut to take the head and arms. Two large radial pleats develop from the shoulders to the ground. A travelling hood buttoned down the C.F. is attached to the neckline.

Mantle — similar to the previous fashion.

Stockings — similar to the previous fashion.

Shoes — similar to men's.

Head dress — similar to the previous fashion. The straight edge of the semi-circular veil frames the face and neck. A decorated fillet is worn as an alternative to the pillbox-shaped hat.

Accessories — rarely seen. Purses, knife, etc. are fastened to a girdle worn under the sideless gown.

Notes on patterns: Men

Adapt patterns of 1260.

Gard-corps — body parts: (line throughout). Form a C.F. placket at the neckline.
Hood: (line throughout). Form hood by sewing AB to BA and attach neckline to the neckline of the body parts. Add buttons and buttonholes for fastening down the centre front.
Sleeves: (line throughout). Pleat width of sleeves until they are equal in measurement to the armhole opening. (Pleating should be stitched down to a distance of 6 inches.) In fitting the sleeve to the armhole add an underarm gusset.

Coif — either extend sides of coif into narrow straps for tying under chin or insert drawstring into the neck edge of the existing pattern.

Notes on patterns: Women

Adapt patterns of 1260 fashion.

Pelicon — (line throughout). Form a placket at the C.F. neckline. In making up, form a large radial pleat on either shoulder to B.B. (stiching down a short distance to hold the fold).
Hood: (line throughout). Form hood by sewing A to A and attach neckline to the neckline of the pelicon. And buttons and buttonholes for fastening down the centre front.

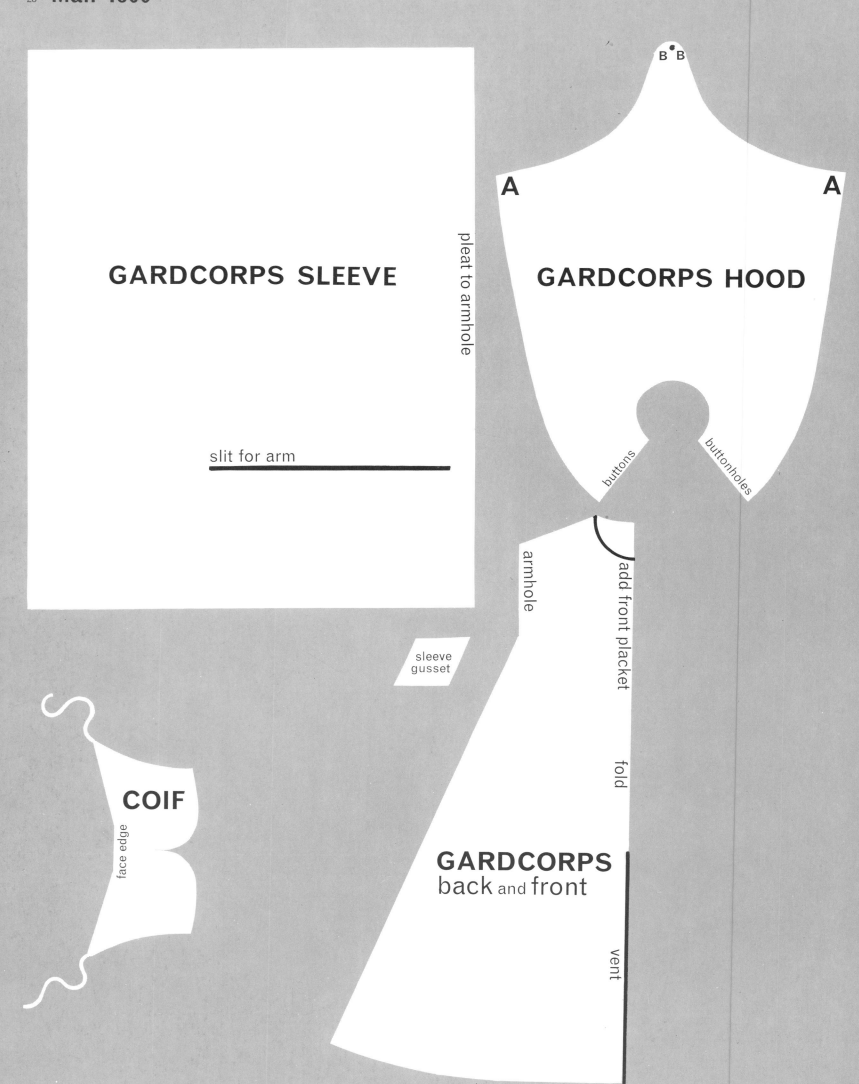

GARDCORPS SLEEVE

pleat to armhole

slit for arm

GARDCORPS HOOD

A

A

B B

buttons

buttonholes

add front placket

armhole

sleeve gusset

COIF

face edge

fold

GARDCORPS
back and front

vent

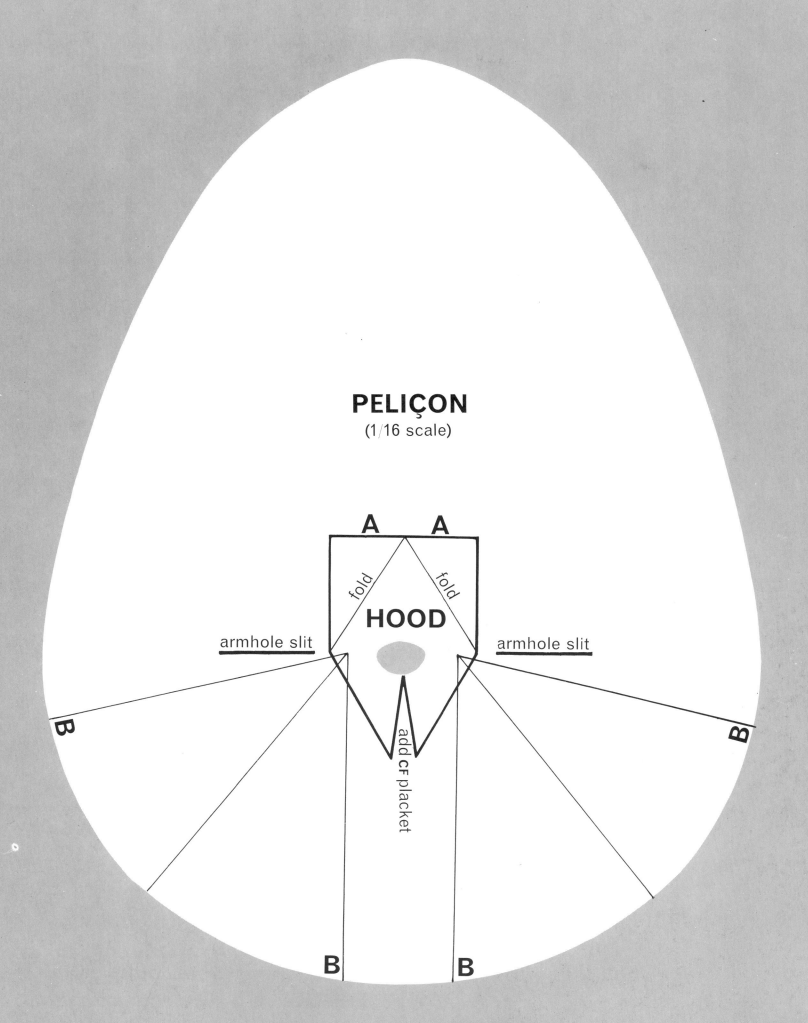

PELIÇON
(1/16 scale)

A   A

fold   fold

HOOD

armhole slit   armhole slit

B   B

add CF placket

B   B

1340 Edward III

Fabrics: as used in 1300.

Colours: Heraldic.

Decoration: All-over patterns of a heraldic nature or delicate scroll repeats based on foliated plant forms. Parti-colour or quartering of costume (including the hosen). Formal dagging of the skirts of the cotehardie and the shoulder cape of the hood. Buttons as a method of fastening.

Padding and restriction, men: Cotehardie cut double with the chest parts padded to give the wearer a pigeon-chested appearance.

Padding and restriction, women: Clothes are cut and fastened (buttoning and lacing) to fit the body tightly.

Movement, men: With the figure totally revealed by the tight cutting of all garments, and the short length of the cotehardie, emphasis is placed on elegant posture, both in the stance and the holding of the arms up and well away from the body.

Movement, women: A walk with the pelvis gently thrust forward, straight backed, with arms bent and the elbows carried away from the body to display the tippets or pendant sleeves. To prevent the great weight of the mantle slipping backwards, the fastening cords are usually held, by one hand, pulled well down on the chest.

Men

General characteristics: A youthful, simple, but somewhat effeminate style. Garments are cut to reveal the figure — chest, waist, hips, thighs, etc.

Shirt — rarely seen.

Under tunic — dispensed with.

Cotehardie — cut double, tightly fitting to emphasise a small waist, the shaped body parts cut in four sections. The front is buttoned through to the hem, the neckline low and boat-shaped. Tight, inserted sleeves button through from elbow point to cover most of the hand. Arm bands, with long white pendulant streamers (tippets), fasten about the upper arm.

Mantle — three-quarters, or full circular with an opening and placket formed to take the head. Varying in length from buttocks to ankle.

Hosen — improvement in cut, construction and fit (material probably cut on the cross).

Shoes — similar to the previous fashion. Toes are longer and pointed.

Head dress — hoods with very long liripipes and shoulder capes — possibly darted at the neck to improve the fitting. Narrow fillets.

Hair — centrally parted, loosely waved, terminating at the nape of the neck. Young men sport light moustaches and small pointed beards.

Accessories — wide, richly decorated metal hip belts, daggers, purses.

Women

General characteristics: Very simple, neat, youthful, and lyric in style. The under robe and cotehardie skirts are very strongly flared, the body parts laced to fit tightly and reveal the figure.

Chemise — never seen.

Under robe — areas visible (buttoned sleeve and hem of skirts when cotehardie skirts are lifted) made up in richly woven or embroidered cloth, the remaining parts of the robe in some simpler and less expensive material. The four sections of the body parts are strongly flared from the hips, particularly on the side seams. Laced or buttoned opening at C.B. or C.F.

Cotehardie — (lined throughout) similar in cut to the under robe. The skirts are more heavily flared and usually longer than the wearer. The front opening is laced or buttoned, the neckline low and boat-shaped. Sleeves terminate at the elbow where they develop long pendulant streamers. The two slits, forming openings in the front skirts, might either give access to the belt and accessories, or be used to aid the lifting of skirts when walking.

Mantle — three-quarter circle, with large scoop cut to take the shape of the neck, and fastened across the chest by cords.

Hosen — only seen when the skirts are held high. Bright colours.

Shoes — similar to the men's.

Head dress — similar to the previous fashion. Married and older women wear the veil, and barbe or wimple. Young women wear their hair very long and loose, falling about the shoulders, or braided and neatly pinned and looped up, echoing the silhouette of the men's hair style.

Accessories — purses, rosary, etc.

Notes on patterns: Men

Cotehardie — cut double. Pad between surfaces of fabric to form the pigeon chest. Add a buttoned placket to the C.F., and from the elbow points down on the sleeves.

Hosen — use thick woollen tights a size larger than the wearer.

Mantle — (line throughout) cut as in previous patterns.

Hood — (line throughout) for better fit, dart at intervals around neckline and form a buttoned C.F. opening.

Belt — construct of metal ornaments, either sewn to a foundation, hinged, or threaded together on two or more cords.

Notes on patterns: Women

Under robe — use cotehardie pattern. Cut skirts with less flare and without train. Add buttoned plackets, from the elbow points down, to the sleeves.

Cotehardie — (line throughout) cut skirts at least 9 inches longer than the wearer. Work eyelet holes down the C.F. edges if lacing is used as a method of fastening.

Mantle — (line throughout) cut as in previous patterns.

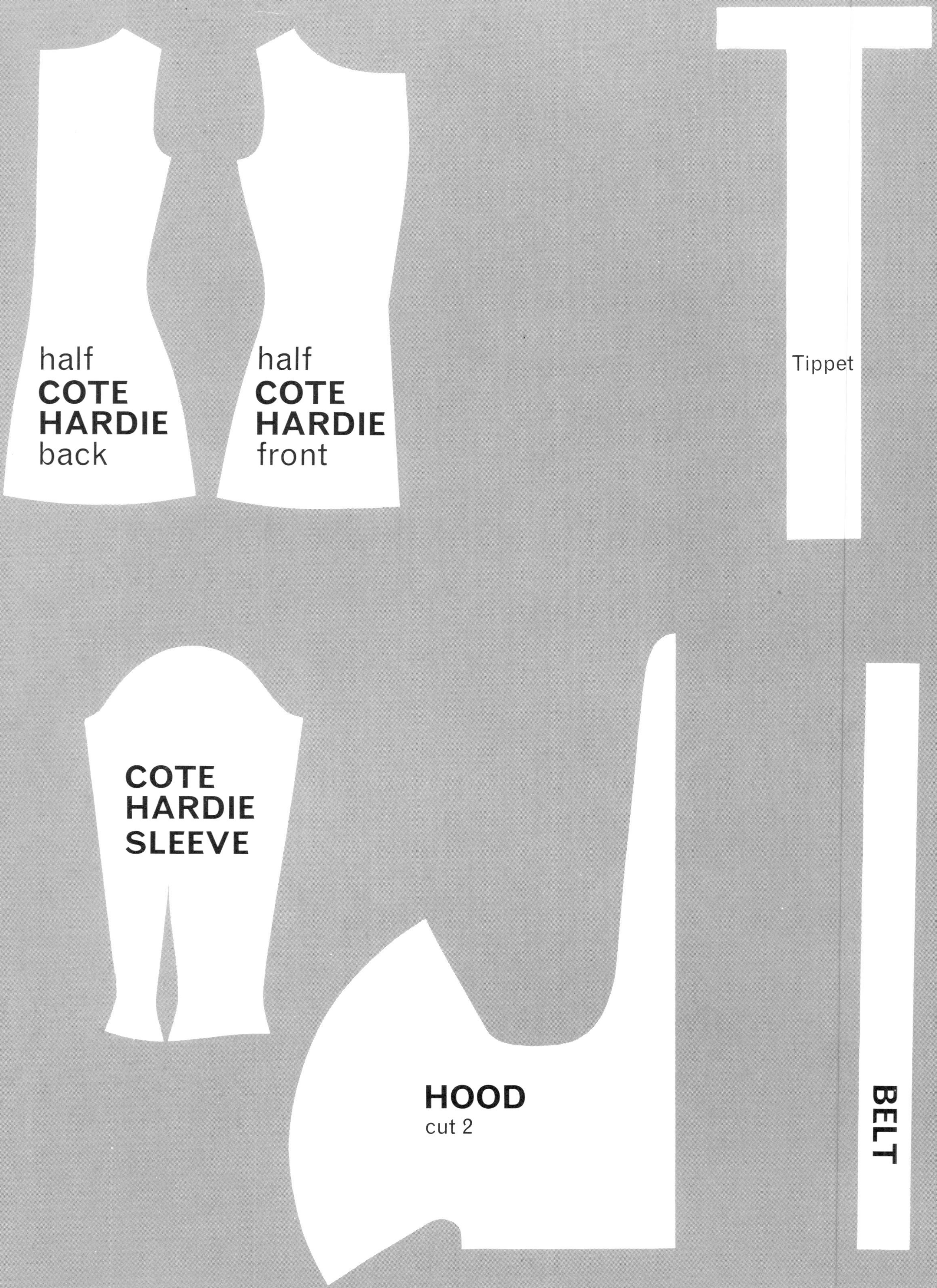

half
COTE HARDIE
back

half
COTE HARDIE
front

Tippet

COTE HARDIE SLEEVE

HOOD
cut 2

BELT

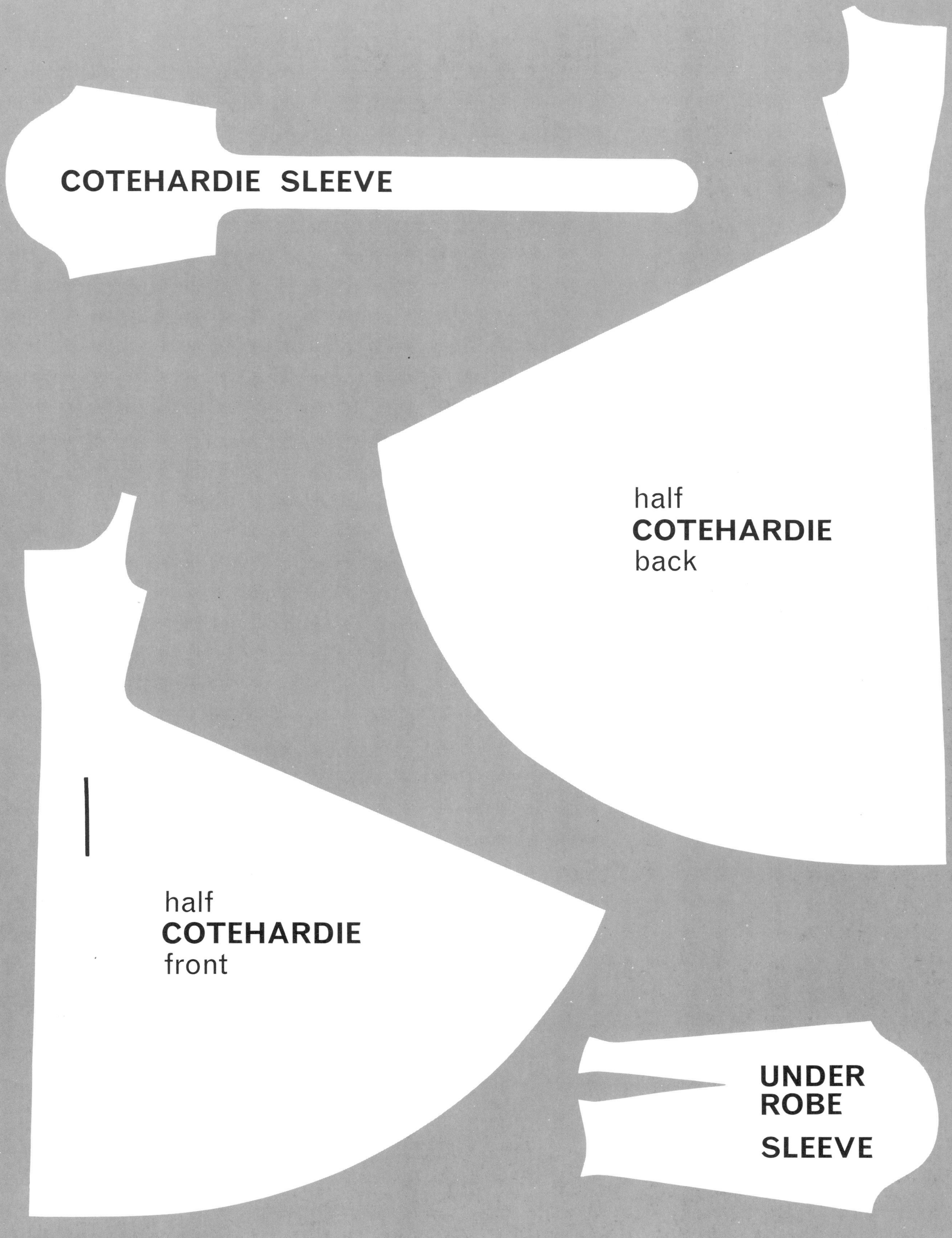

COTEHARDIE SLEEVE

half
COTEHARDIE
back

half
COTEHARDIE
front

**UNDER
ROBE**

SLEEVE

1380 Richard II

Fabrics: Frequently embroidered.

Colours: Large range of light and bright colours.

Decoration: Formal heraldic decoration and all-over scroll patterns or half-drop repeats based on delicate rhythmical plant forms.

Movement, men: Less lyrical and "poetic" than the previous fashion. The standing collar of the cotehardie forces the head to be held high. The arms are carried away from the body to display the voluminous sleeves.

Movement, women: The weight of the costume determines formal dignified movement and posture with the back held rigid to support the mantle. Skirts, always cut longer than the wearer, are lifted in the process of walking. Care should be exercised in turning (a curved line of walk), as the very full and long skirts can easily twist about and trap the legs.

Men

General characteristics: The top garment, with high-standing collar, is looser in cut and high-waisted. Sleeves and hats are of all shapes and sizes.

Shirt — not seen.

Cotehardie — line throughout, often with fur (seen at wrists and neckline), hip length or shorter, fastened down the C.F., the excess fullness formally pleated at the C.F. and C.B. and held in place by a wide leather belt. The sleeves, fitting the upper arm, are full and wide at the wrist where they are left open or gathered into a wristband (bagpipe or bag sleeves). The standing collar is stiffened.

Hosen — similar to the previous fashion.

Shoes — toes longer and pointed.

Hats — wide variety with stiff or floppy, small or large, bag-shaped crowns and small turned-up brims. Feathered mounts decorate the front of the hat.

Hair — dressed to frame the face by being rolled smoothly around a small pad of material from the nape of the neck up and around the sides of the head, to terminate (diminishing in size) at the centre of a high forehead.

Accessories — belts, sword belts, daggers, purses, short gauntlet gloves. Chains of gold or silver worn about the neck. Collarettes of jewelled ornaments hinged together or threaded on ribbons.

Women

General characteristics: Formal and less youthful wardrobe consisting of a close-fitting robe, the sideless gown, and a three-quarter circular mantle.

Chemise — rarely seen.

Robe — similar to the previous fashion. A belt made from a series of hinged, decorated, metal sections is worn low on the hips.

Sideless gown — (lined throughout) the arm openings are cut away in front in deep, scooped-out curves to form a narrow central panel which is usually enriched with a decorated and jewelled plastron. The back is cut straight from the shoulders to form a wide flare and long train. Deep fur bands edge the openings.

Mantle — similar to the previous fashion.

Stockings — similar to the previous fashion.

Shoes — similar to men's.

Head dress — the hair, centrally parted, is plaited, coiled, and placed in metal cylindrical constructions (templers) which are positioned well forward to cover the ears. The templers are secured to a fillet. The back part of the head is usually covered by the veil.

Accessories — similar to the previous fashion.

Notes on patterns: Men

Hosen — for theatre purposes use coarse woollen tights a size too large.

Cotehardie — line throughout, and form a C.F. fly fastening. It is advisable to pre-arrange and secure the pleating at the waistline.
(The wrist band is sewn to BB marked on the sleeve pattern.)

Hat — (cut double) pleat or dart crown to fit the brim.

Notes on patterns: Women

Chemise and robe — cut as in previous pattern. Sleeves of the robe require plackets which should button to well above elbow point.

Mantle — line throughout and cut as in previous patterns.

Sideless gown — line throughout, cutting skirts to form a long train at the back and at least 12 inches longer than the wearer in front. Stiffen plastron front.

Head dress — the templers, fastened to a fillet, should be made of metal and sufficiently rigid to lie flat against the sides of the head. Further control can be achieved by fixing a rigid metal band, shaped to fit the nape of the neck, to the lower part of the templers. Should a wimple be worn, tapes can also be attached to the fronts of the templers and tied under the chin.

Veils — rectangular, semi-circular or circular. If the wimple is worn it should be tucked into the robe neckline.

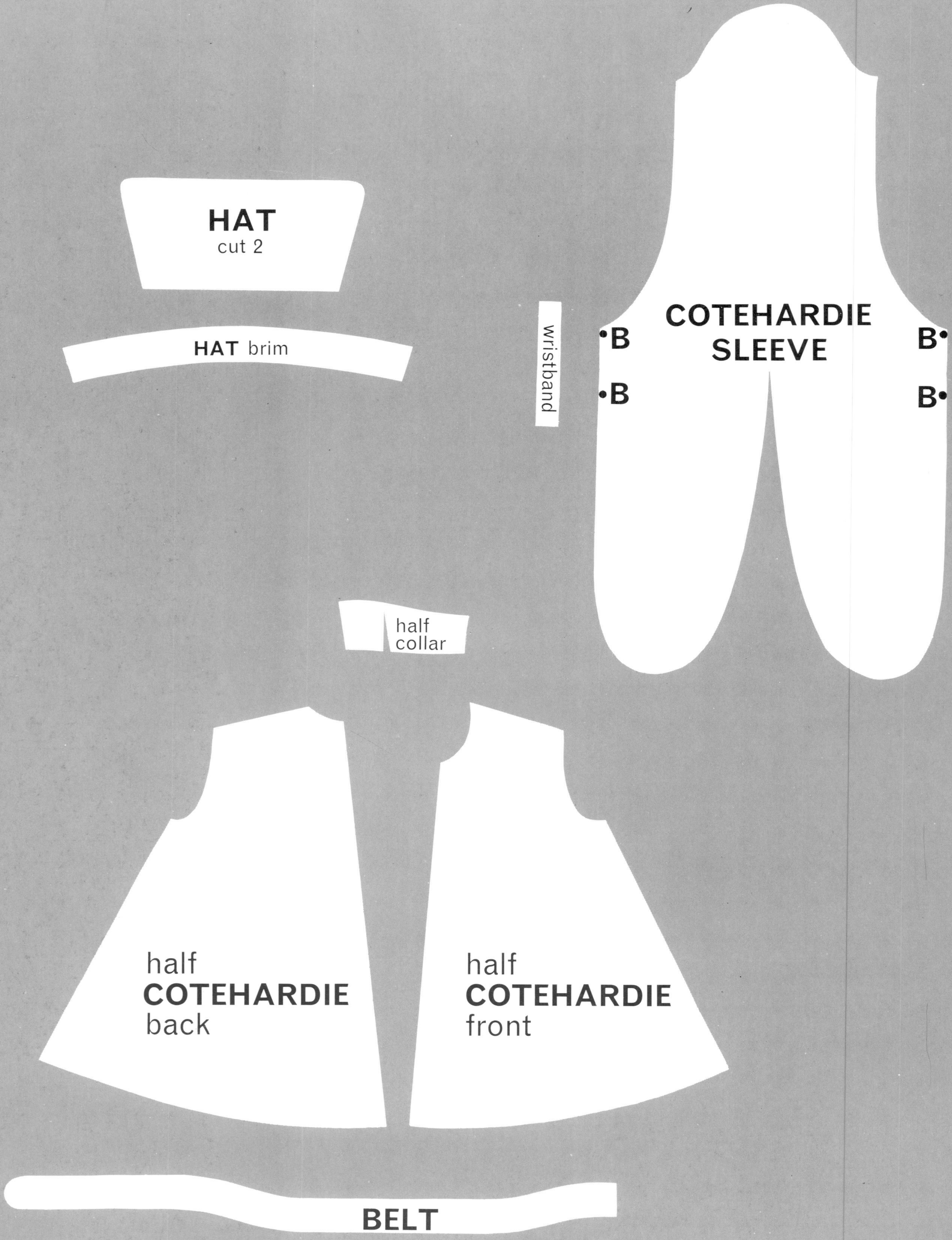

HAT
cut 2

HAT brim

wristband

COTEHARDIE SLEEVE

•B

•B

B•

B•

half collar

half **COTEHARDIE** back

half **COTEHARDIE** front

BELT

Plastron

fold

GOWN
back and front

front hem

1420 Henry V

Fabrics: Sturdy and rich cloths. Fur trimmings and linings. (Decorative value of sewing short-haired pelts together less evident.)

Colours: Bright and fresh. Black rarely used. White seen in the body linen and women's head-dresses.

Decoration: Fabrics woven and embroidered in large or small repeating patterns with beasts, birds and flowers incorporated in the designs. Elaborate dagging varies in size from very large formal castellations and complex foliated serrations to very small zig-zag cuts.

Movement, men: Foppish and eccentric. The volume of fabric in the houppelande dictates a flamboyance of movement, particularly in the play of the arms — which are always carried up and well away from the body — and the walk, either a glide, or flicking movement from the knee through to the pointed toe. The high positioning of the belt forces the chest forward. The stiff-standing collar stretches and straightens the neck.

Movement, women: Similar to the men's. The fullness of the houppelande and the tight high waist gives a rounded and pregnant look to the figure. The long-front skirts are carried in the crook of the arm.

Men

General characteristics: A very extravagant, though dignified, fashion. The gown (houppelande) is full, long, and high waisted. Sleeves are open and very deep — often cut to trail the ground and merge into the train of the back skirts.

Shirt — rarely seen.

Under tunic or doublet — body parts fit the figure. The sleeves are tight, covering the hand to the knuckles.

Houppelande — (C.F. fastening) high-collared, lined throughout and flared from shoulders to hem. The C.F. skirts are frequently left open from crotch point to ground. Fullness is set into deep folds and controlled by a belt. The enormously large and wide sleeves narrow to fit the armhole.

Hosen — similar to the previous fashion.

Shoes — well-fitting, pointed bootees, laced or buckled at the sides or front.

Head dress — derived from the hood, with the face opening placed on the top of the head and the liripipe, up to 9 feet in length, wound around the head to form a turban. The remaining length of liripipe is brought forward across the chest and flung over the shoulder to hang down the back. The shoulder part (now the cockscomb) is arranged in pleats and forms a fan of material to emerge from the centre of the turban. The example shown is made in pre-pleated material, running the length of the hood, with the edges of the cockscomb and liripipe serrated (diminutive form of dagging).

Hair — fashionable to shave the nape of the neck up to or above ear level. The hair is brushed to radiate from the centre of the crown and to curl under to form a basin shape. Faces are usually clean-shaven, although small pointed beards and moustaches are seen.

Accessories — belts, collars, purses. A second belt, richly ornamented and decorated with tassels or hung with little bells, is worn over the shoulder and across the body (baldrick).

Women

General characteristics: Silhouette almost identical to that of the man. High-waisted with neckline rising into a buttoned or unbuttoned stiffened collar.

Chemise — rarely seen.

Under robe — cut similar to the houppelande with a tight-fitting sleeve covering the hand to the knuckles.

Houppelande — similar in cut to men's.

Stockings — coloured.

Shoes — similar to men's.

Head dress — the front of the head is shaven to create a high forehead. The hair is centrally parted, braided and tightly arranged in two buns over the ears. The hair is kept firmly in place by two white linen bands — one tightly fitting around the head and concealing the hairline, the other covering the nape of the neck, passing in front of the ears and fastened at the temples to the first band. The braided hair over the ears is placed into templers (cones, boxes, quarter spheres, pyramids, etc., rigid in construction and shaped to fit close to the sides of the head). The top, sides, and back of the head are covered by a circular veil. (The example shown is set in minute radial pleatings with the raw edge pinked.)

Accessories — collarettes in metal, enamelled and set with semi-precious stones. Richly embroidered and decorated belts.

Notes on patterns: Men

Under tunic or doublet — (line throughout). Cut to fit the figure adding a C.F. fastening. For theatre purposes this garment can usually be omitted and inner false sleeves (commencing from the elbow) substituted.

Houppelande — (line throughout) form placket at C.F. For extra fullness develop the patterns by opening up to extend the flares. Cut skirts longer than ground length to develop into a train at the back. The width and flare of the sleeve is increased by extending the pattern out from line A at X. To lengthen the sleeve, open up and extend the pattern at its widest.

Head dress — for theatre purposes pre-arrange and secure.

Notes on patterns: Women

Under robe — use houppelande pattern. (For theatre costume substitute with false sleeves, adding a placket at the wrists.)

Houppelande — (line throughout) cut the skirts longer than the wearer. Construct in a similar manner to the men's houppelande. Form a short buttoned opening at the C.F.

Head dress — white bands, securing hair, should be cut on the cross (2 inches deep). Control templers as in previous fashion. (For theatre costume a narrow tape placed under chin, and covered with grease paint, would assist in holding the templers close to the sides of the face.) The circular veil, of light and fine material, is unhemmed and fastened with pins to the head dress.

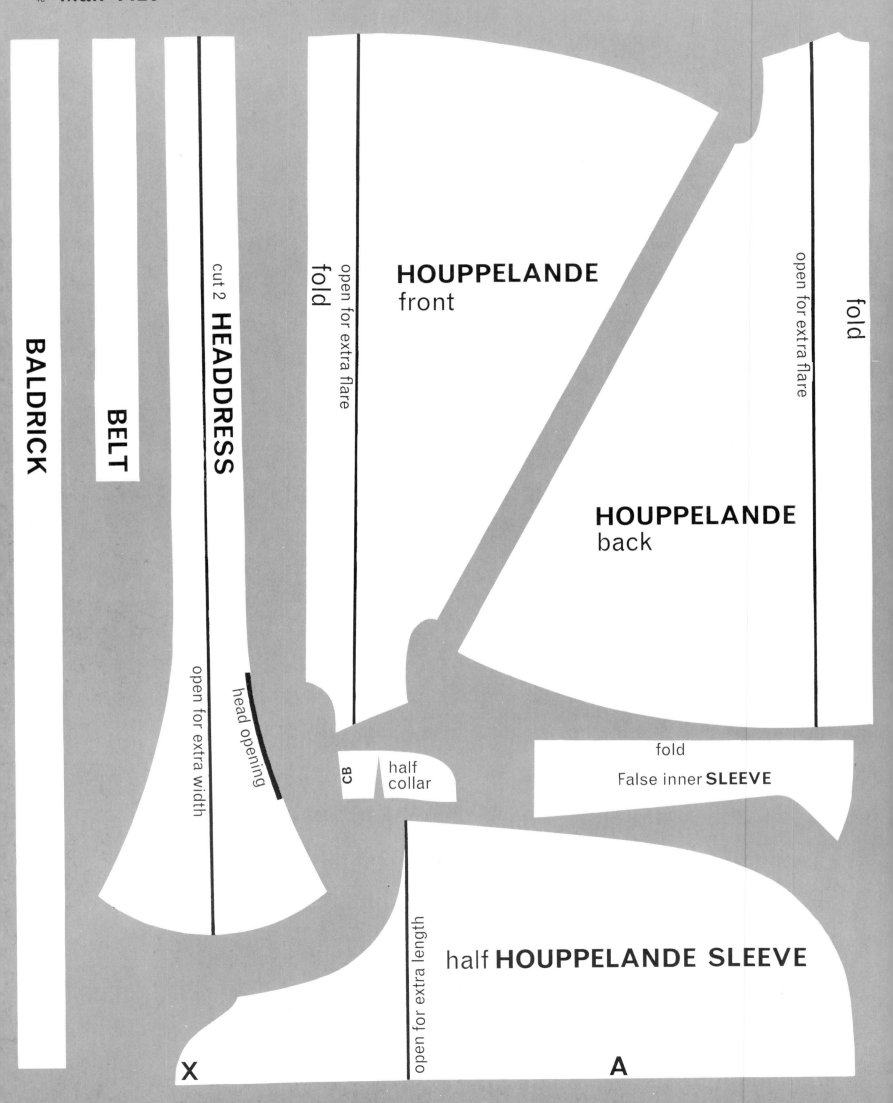

BALDRICK

BELT

cut 2 **HEADDRESS**

open for extra width

head opening

fold

open for extra flare

HOUPPELANDE
front

open for extra flare

fold

HOUPPELANDE
back

CB half collar

fold
False inner **SLEEVE**

open for extra length

half **HOUPPELANDE SLEEVE**

X

A

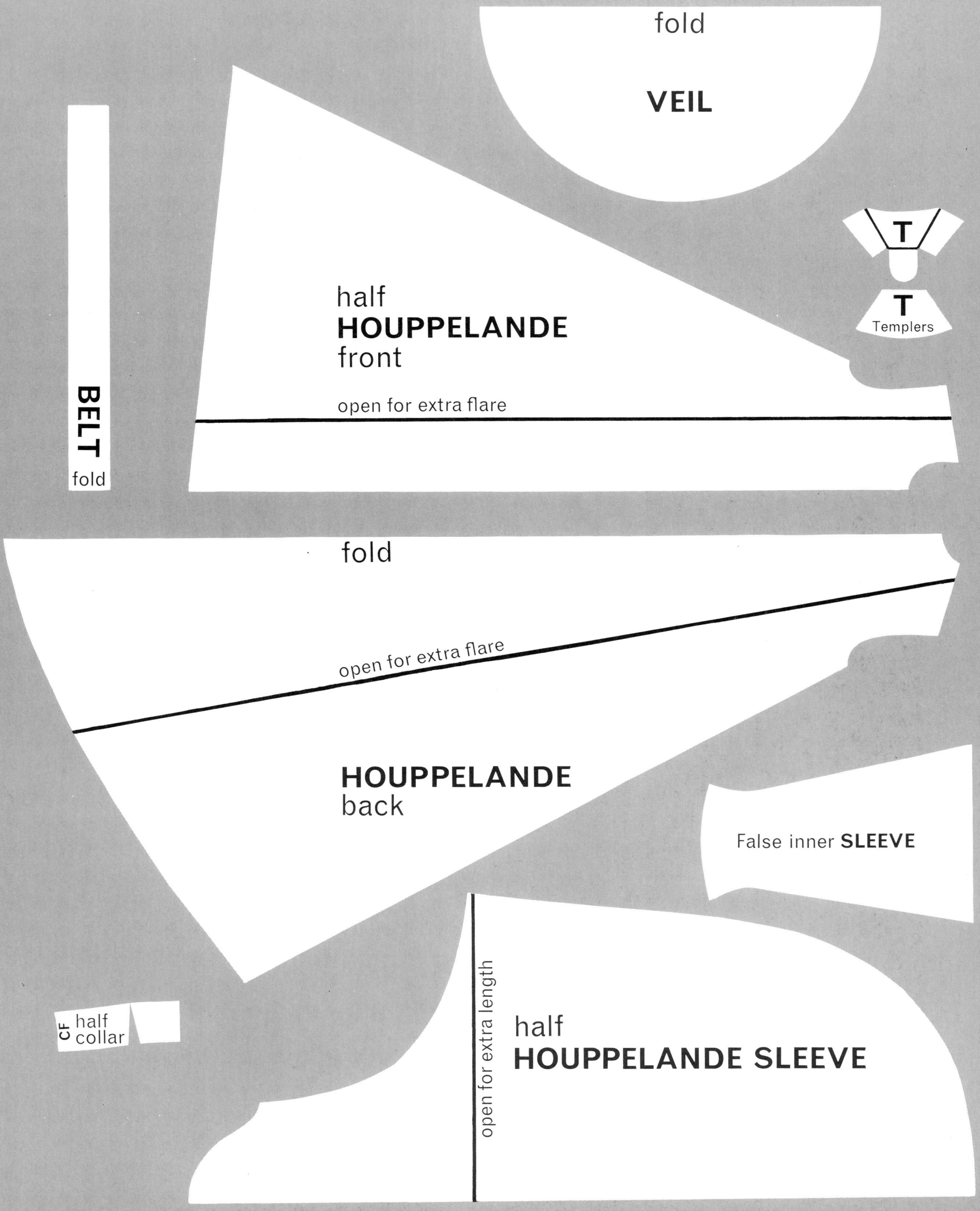

fold

VEIL

T

T

Templers

BELT

fold

half
HOUPPELANDE
front

open for extra flare

fold

open for extra flare

HOUPPELANDE
back

False inner **SLEEVE**

CF half
collar

open for extra length

half
HOUPPELANDE SLEEVE

1440 Henry VI

Fabrics: Heavy and substantial.

Colours: Similar to the previous fashion.

Decoration: Garments are patterned (woven or embroidered) with large flowing drop, half-drop, or ogee repeats based on highly stylized plant and animal forms.

Padding and restriction, men: The rigid pleating at the top of the sleeves and the pleated body parts of the houppelande are interlined and/or padded.

Padding and restriction, women: The tight belt forces the breasts up and the stomach out.

Movement, men: The broad shoulder line, large sleeves and the shorter, stiffer skirts dictate a formal and somewhat rigid and mannered carriage. The desire to display the legs is evident in the general trend towards short skirts. The movement of the head is often severely restricted by the very large hat or head dress.

Movement, women: Lyrical and graceful movement similar to the previous fashion.

Men

General characteristics: Squarish in silhouette with broad shoulders, low-placed waistline, knee-length skirts and large open sleeves. Legs are slender and clad in dark hosen. Headgear, some of the largest recorded in male fashions, is very bizarre and eccentric.

Shirt — never seen.

Under tunic or doublet — form-fitting, tight-sleeved, with high-standing collar set well away from the neck.

Short houppelande — the formally arranged pleating of the body parts is controlled by a belt placed low on the hips. The low boat-shaped neckline reveals the high-standing collar of the tunic worn beneath. The sleeves are similar to the previous fashion or cape-shaped and open up the fronts. The entire garment is lined throughout. Padded bands, or padded rolls of material decorate the hemline, neckline, and edges of the sleeves.

Hosen — laced to the waistline of the doublet or inner tunic.

Shoes — similar to the previous fashion.

Head dress — the formalised turban arrangement of the hood is composed of a padded roll (burlet), a false cockscomb, and long liripipe. Other hats range from elaborately draped and padded forms and enormous turbans, to small pillboxes, coifs, and tall blocked brimless hats — pepperpot in shape.

Hair — wide variety of hair styles — shaven heads, formally cut caplike heads of hair, fully-curled shoulder-length pageboy styles with fringes, etc. Absence of beards and moustaches.

Accessories — belts, daggers, purses, walking canes.

Women

General characteristics: A sophisticated development of the previous fashion emphasising an awareness of the body — plucking of the hair to achieve a high forehead, plucking of eyebrows, ivory or alabaster complexion, small cup-shaped breasts and rounded stomach, long neck and sloping shoulders, etc.

Chemise — rarely seen.

Under robe — similar in cut to the houppelande with tight-fitting buttoned sleeves extending in length to the first finger joint. The collar lies over the collar of the houppelande.

Houppelande — similar to the previous fashion. The collar lies flat, the neckline cut to reveal more of the throat and chest.

Stockings — brightly coloured.

Shoes — similar to men's.

Head dress — hair is brushed back from the forehead, tightly coiled and plaited, and kept in place by a deep fillet worn well on the back of the head. The sides and back of the head are encased in a richly-decorated templer (fastened to the fillet) to form a sweeping line up and away from the nape of the neck. On the top of the templer is placed a padded roll shaped to curve down to the centre of the high forehead. (A false cockscomb and liripipe frequently accompanies this head dress.)

Accessories — richly decorated metal collarettes shaped to follow the curve of the throat. Belts, finger rings.

Notes on patterns: Men

Under tunic or doublet — cut double, stiffen collar, and form C.F. placket. The sleeve is cut with or without a wrist placket.

Short houppelande — line throughout, interline with a thin wadding, bullet-pleat head of sleeve to fit armhole, and control pleating of the body parts by sewing each pleat down, a little, below the natural waistline. (Place extra padding in the pleats.)

Head dress — cut burlet on the cross and softly pad. The crown of the hat is cut double and gathered to the inner egde of the burlet. Formally pleat and stiffen cockscomb.

Notes on patterns: Women

Under robe — cut similar to the houppelande with tight sleeves buttoned through from elbow point to waist. (For theatre purposes this garment can be omitted and false sleeves substituted — the collar sewn to the inside edge of the houppelande neckline.)

Houppelande — line throughout. Cut considerably longer than the wearer, adding a C.F. fastening (laced) to terminate at the natural waist. Control pleating by pre-setting and stitching down each pleat to the depth of the belt. If necessary extend and develop the flare and length of the sleeve.

Head dress — pull hair tightly back from the forehead and sides and bind it with the deep fillet which should be placed well to the back of the head (obliterate hairline with grease paint). The templer foundation should be padded and stiffened before decorating. It is essential to cut and shape the foundation of the templer to fit the nape of the neck and sides of the head. Secure the fronts of the templer to the fillet. Attach the padded roll to the top edge of the back of the templer and to the C.F. of the fillet. The unstiffened false cockscomb and liripipe are positioned, inside the padded roll, at the C.B.

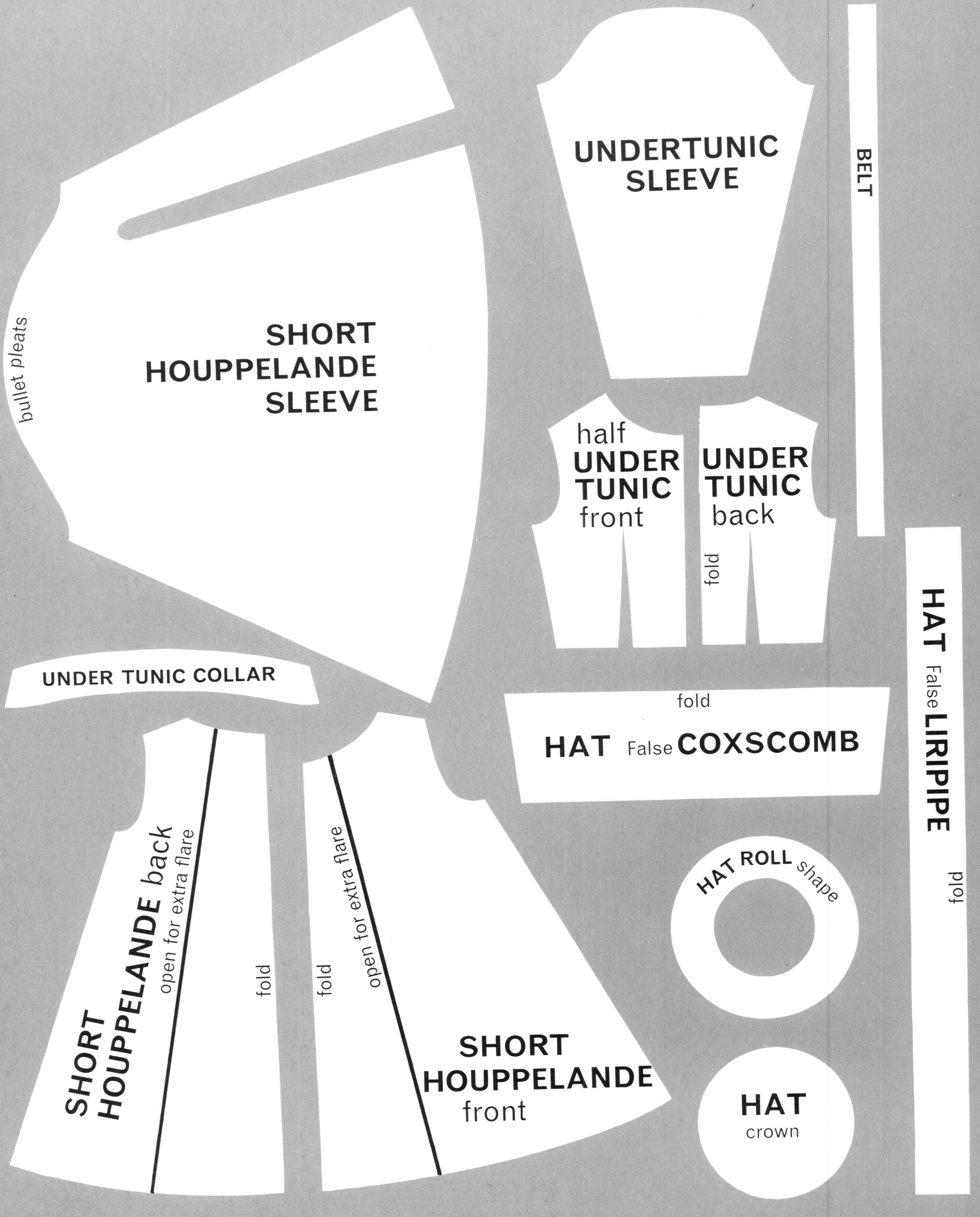

SHORT HOUPPELANDE SLEEVE

bullet pleats

UNDERTUNIC SLEEVE

BELT

half **UNDER TUNIC** front

UNDER TUNIC back

fold

UNDER TUNIC COLLAR

fold

HAT False **COXSCOMB**

HAT False **LIRIPIPE**

fold

SHORT HOUPPELANDE back

open for extra flare

fold

fold

open for extra flare

SHORT HOUPPELANDE front

HAT ROLL shape

HAT crown

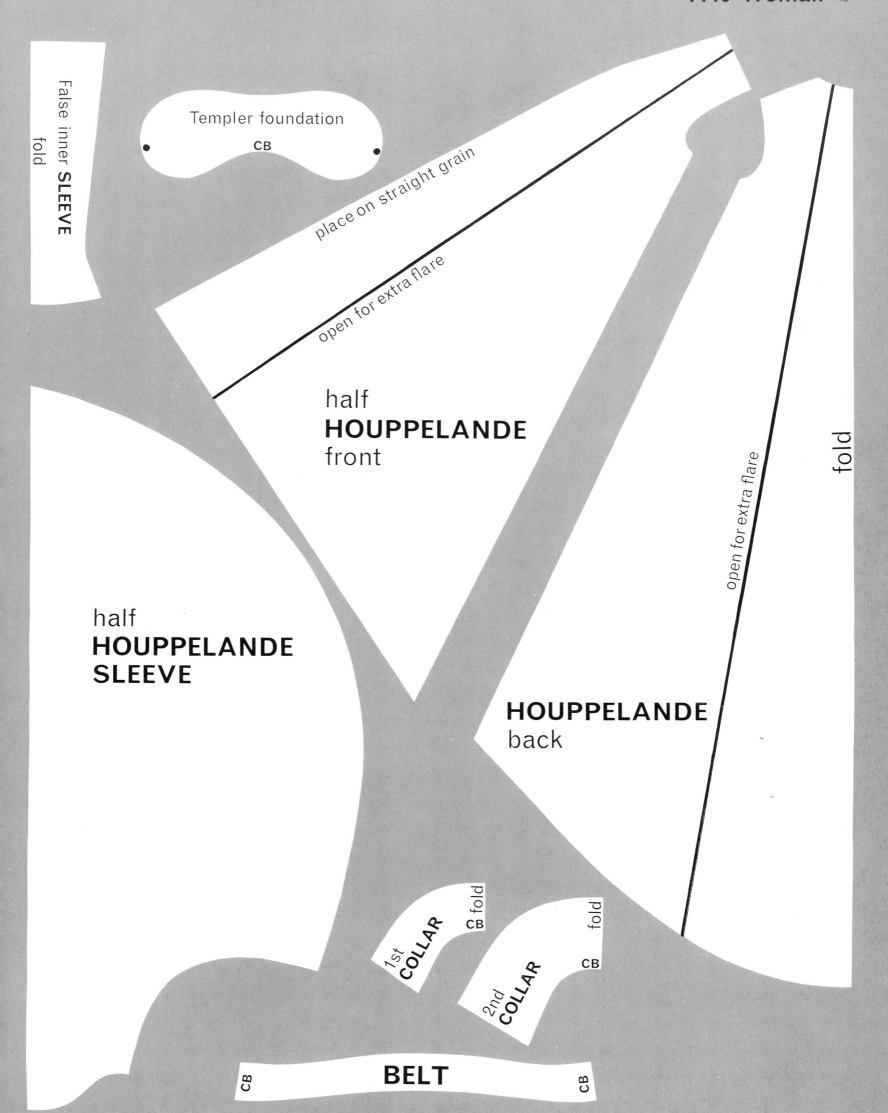

False inner **SLEEVE** fold

Templer foundation
CB

place on straight grain

open for extra flare

half
HOUPPELANDE
front

fold

open for extra flare

half
**HOUPPELANDE
SLEEVE**

HOUPPELANDE
back

COLLAR 1st
CB fold

2nd **COLLAR**
fold
CB

CB **BELT** CB

1470 Edward IV

Fabrics: Men — similar to the previous fashion. Women — soft rich materials including velvet (real or imitation).

Colours: Wide variety, from deep and rich colours to light muted pastel shades. Black very fashionable.

Decoration: Similar to the previous fashion.

Padding and restriction, men: The costume, lined throughout, stiffly encases the figure. The rigid and formal arrangement of pleatings indicates a further increase in the use of padding and stiff interlinings.

Padding and restriction, women: A high, broad curved belt restricts the waist, accentuating the breasts and the stomach.

Movement, men: Stiff, upright, and angular in carriage. The costume restricts the movement of the limbs. Walk and gesture are mechanical and without grace.

Movement, women: Similar to the previous fashion. Posture emphasises the stomach, breasts, shoulders, sweeping length of neck and set of the head.

Men

General characteristics: Bizarre proportions — sleeves, body parts and hat all tubular in shape. Square shouldered and long waisted.

Shirt — rarely seen.

Under tunic or doublet — cut with or without skirts. Tight-sleeved.

Robe — lined, padded and stiffened throughout. (Controlled at the hips by a narrow belt.) The body parts (fly fastened through C.F.) are cut without a waist seam with the front, and sometimes back fullness, arranged in pleats or sewn down to form padded tubes. The sleeves are pleated into the armholes — vertical slits form a second and alternative opening for the arm. Padded bands or fur decorate the hem, sleeve slits, wrist openings, and the edge of the standing collar.

Hosen — similar to the previous fashion.

Shoes — similar to the previous fashion with accentuated long, padded points to the toes. Over-shoes or clogs, with high cork or wooden soles and straps fastening over the instep and toes, are worn for out-of-doors.

Head dress — the burlet, with liripipe thrown over the shoulder, is frequently carried as an accessory. A second hat, black and pepperpot in shape is worn on the head (a white coif often worn beneath).

Hair — carefully arranged in a similar manner to the previous fashion.

Accessories — narrow belts, purses, collarettes, chains, daggers, gloves, finger rings (placed on first or second joint). Men frequently carry their hats on the tops of their walking canes — held high like batons.

Women

General characteristics: The shoulders and breasts are revealed by a low and wide neckline forming a deep V at the back and front. The waistline is very high and restricted by a wide stiffened belt. The style emphasises sloping shoulders, rounded stomach, and small cup-shaped breasts. The hair is plucked from the forehead, tightly pulled back, and encased in the templer.

Chemise — possibly discarded.

Under robe — probably discarded in favour of a high-waisted, ground-length, pleated petticoat.

Gown — lined throughout and trimmed with fur. The skirts, separate and attached to the waistline of the body parts, are cut circular to develop into a train at the back. The deep V-front of the neckline is partially filled with a triangular plastron (stomacher). Sleeves, tighter in fit and covering the hand, are sometimes turned back to form cuffs.

Stockings — similar to the previous fashion.

Shoes — similar to the men's.

Head dress — the templer (hiding the hair) is placed well to the back of the head to fit closely at the temples and nape of the neck. It is secured to a deep fillet binding the hair. A coronet, curving down to meet the forehead, is frequently worn secured to the top edge of the templer. A small black loop, lying flat on the forehead, is attached to the front of the coronet (origin and purpose dubious).

Accessories — a broad enamelled and jewelled collarette with pendant, emphasises the curve of the throat and the separation of the breasts.

Notes on patterns: Men

Inner tunic or doublet — cut double adding a C.F. placket.

Robe — (add C.F. fly fastening) line and interline all pieces, placing extra stiffening in the collar. Sew down flares 1, 2 and 3 to the equivalent marks shown on the foundation pattern, arrange in pleats, or pad each section to produce a deep broad rib. The padded band at the hem should be sewn to the skirts before the pleats or ribs are sewn down to the foundation.

Burlet — make up as in previous pattern.

Hat — interline with stiffening or make up in heavy fur felt.

Notes on patterns: Women

Petticoat — line throughout. Skirts are flared and set in deep pleats to a waistband.

Gown — line throughout. The shape of the body-part pattern should be adapted to the specific slope and width of the shoulders. The stomacher, stiffened, is secured to the inside edges of the neckline and controlled by the belt (lined, stiffened and boned).

Head dress — similar in construction to the previous fashion, (rigid and preferably made in metal). The coronet replaces the padded roll. Shape and construct the coronet to follow the shape and angle of the templer. The sides of the coronet should be straight and not flared.

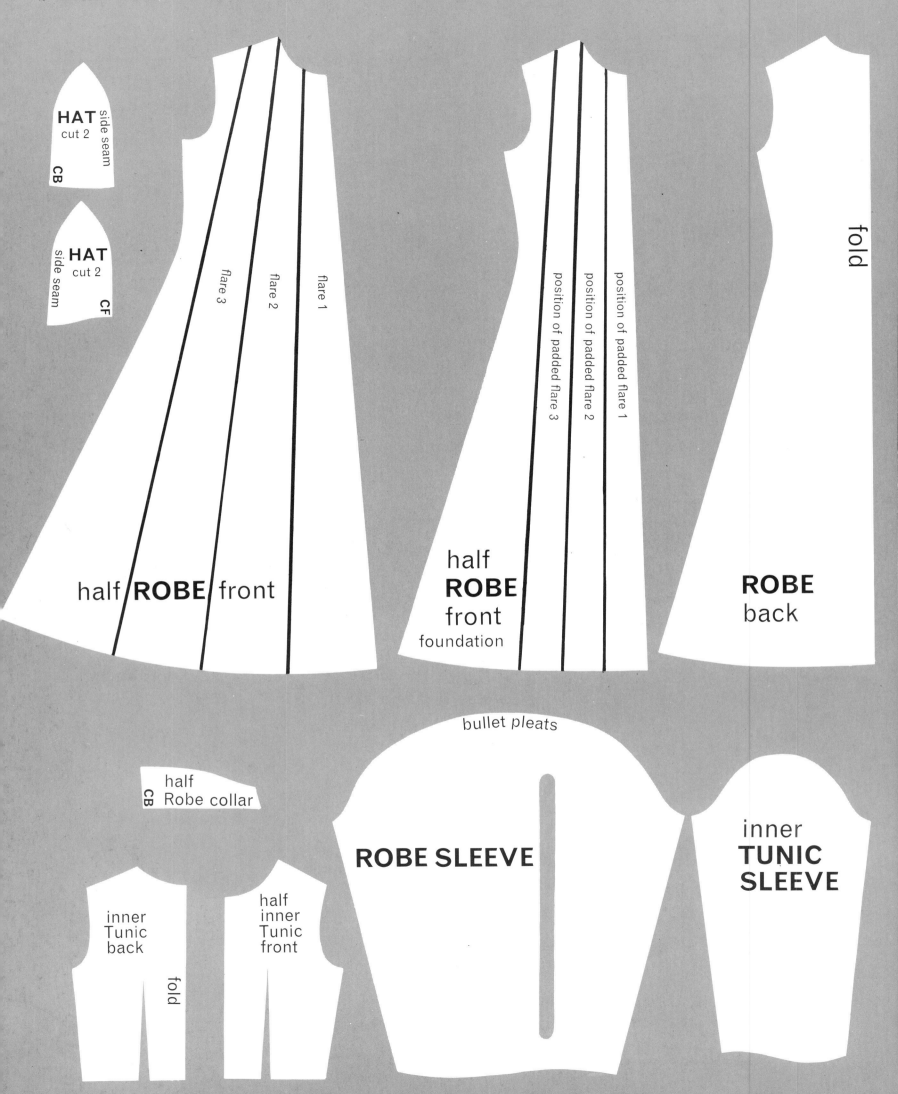

HAT
cut 2
side seam
CB

HAT
cut 2
side seam
CF

flare 3
flare 2
flare 1

half **ROBE** front

position of padded flare 3
position of padded flare 2
position of padded flare 1

half
ROBE
front
foundation

fold

ROBE
back

half
Robe collar
CB

bullet *pleats*

ROBE SLEEVE

inner
**TUNIC
SLEEVE**

inner
Tunic
back

half
inner
Tunic
front

fold

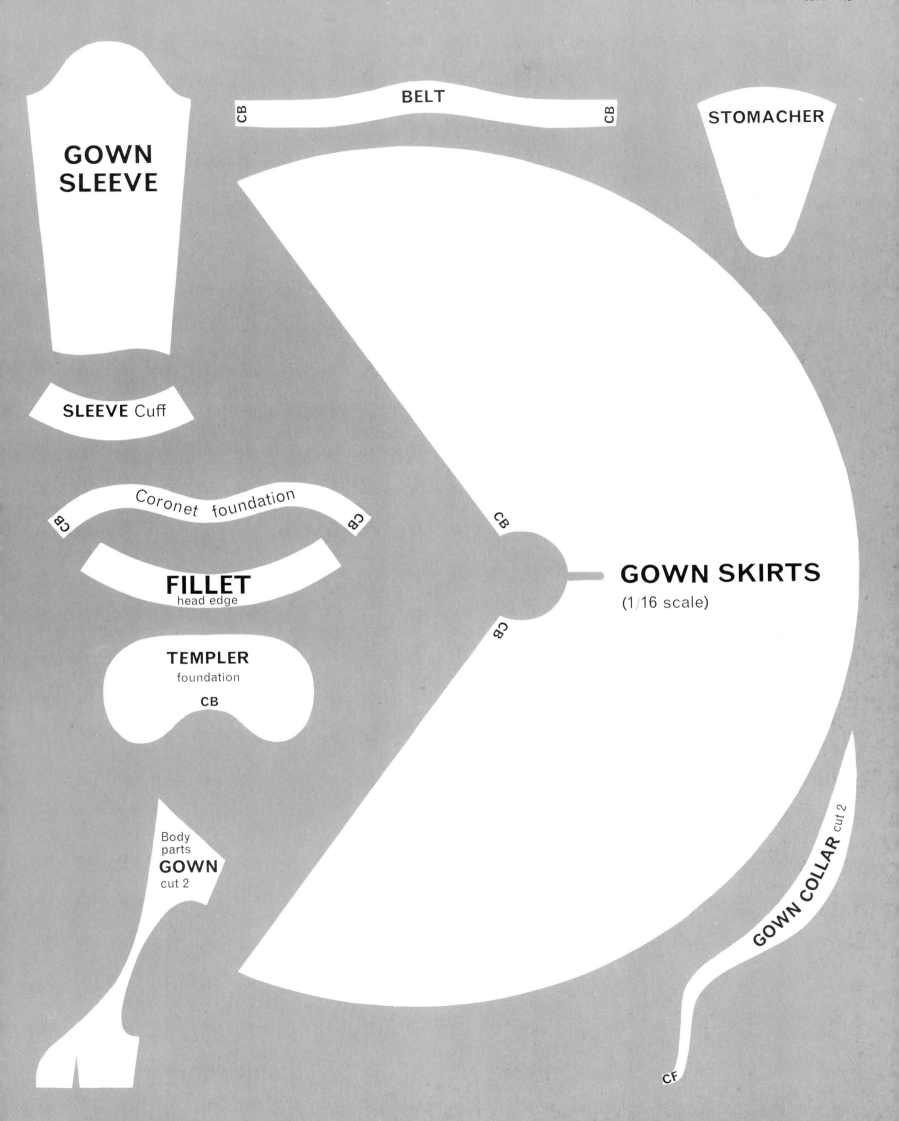

GOWN SLEEVE

BELT

CB

CB

STOMACHER

SLEEVE Cuff

Coronet foundation

CB

CB

FILLET
head edge

CB

GOWN SKIRTS

(1/16 scale)

CB

TEMPLER
foundation

CB

Body
parts
GOWN
cut 2

GOWN COLLAR cut 2

CF

1485 Richard III

Fabrics: Velvets, damasks, silks (chiefly imported) cloths and furs.

Colours: Darker, richer, colours dominate, relieved by the white chemise or shirt.

Decoration: strong decorative feature, particularly in men's costume, develops with the habit of lacing garments or garment parts together with ribbons or cords (points) terminating in metallic ornamental tags (aglets), e.g. securing hosen to doublet waistline, lacing doublet front or securing the two-piece tubular sleeve at the wrist, elbow and armhole. The underlying fabric of the underlinen is puffed out and revealed between the ties.

Padding and restriction, women: The figure is possibly controlled by body binding or an unboned corselet (laced at the back or on the side seams).

Movement, men: The removal of rigid padding and the new form of dress allows considerable freedom for natural and easy movement.

Movement, women: An age of vanity, posturing and posing, with emphasis placed on the sensuous shape of the torso and the cup-shaped breasts. The backward thrust of the fez-shaped hat and butterfly veil is countered by the forward thrust of the pelvis. The very long front skirts are usually lifted up and carried.

Men

General characteristics: Square silhouette. Wardrobe consists of hosen, shirt, doublet or vest, and short flared over robe.

Shirt — low necked with body parts and sleeves cut full.

Doublet — (Vest — sleeveless version) body fitting with short skirts. The front is cut in a deep V to the C.F. waistline. The sleeves are laced together and pointed to the armhole.

Robe — knee-length, open down the fronts and lined throughout. Long pendant sleeves terminate a little below the length of the skirts. (Sleeves have the characteristic second opening.)

Hosen — (frequently striped) laced to the waistline of the doublet. A triangle of cloth (codpiece) is laced to the crotch point and waistline of the fronts.

Shoes — the toes are less pointed to form a rounded bulbous shape. Calf length, form-fitting, richly decorated boots with side lacing, also worn.

Hats — soft beret-like crowns with turned up brims (the brim often slashed and held together with brooches or lacing).

Hair — usually shoulder-length, with or without a short fringe. Beards and moustaches rarely seen.

Accessories — finger rings, jewelled collars, chains, belts, daggers and purses.

Women

General characteristics: Very simple and elegant line. The gown, clinging to the body to below hips and then flaring into a very long, full skirt, is cut in seven pieces.

Chemise — rarely seen.

Under robe — discarded or similar in shape to the gown.

Corselet — controls the figure from breasts to thighs.

Gown — back-laced, strongly flared (fully circular) with tightish sleeves, the cuffs extending to well over the fingers. The fur-collared neckline, low and boat shaped, reveals the plastron or top of the corselet. A richly decorated belt, worn low about the waist, emphasises the stomach.

Stockings — similar to the previous fashion.

Shoes — similar to men's.

Head dress — a small fez-shaped hat, worn on the back of the head, reveals the ears and side hair (reduced by plucking). The transparent stiffened veil, extending well out beyond the back of the head, is supported by wire antennae. (The antennae form a small loop which lies flat on the top of the forehead — possibly a means of securing the head dress to the hair.)

Accessories — collars enamelled and set with coloured stones. Richly decorated belts, finger rings.

Notes on patterns: Men

Shirt — pleat or smock to a narrow neckband. Extend the patterns of the body parts and the sleeves to the desired fullness.

Doublet or vest — cut double and interline. Fasten the sleeves to the body parts by means of eyelet holes and lacing. (The sleeves are also laced at elbow and wrist. Similar lacing, placed at regular intervals, secures the sleeve around the upper and lower parts of the arm.)

Robe — interline and line throughout (extend flare at C.B. for extra fullness). Gather or pleat head of sleeve to armhole.

Hosen — should be laced to eyelet holes worked at regular intervals around the doublet waistline. A triangle of material (codpiece) is laced to the C.F.

Hat — line and stiffen both crown and brim, gathering or pleating the crown to the brim.

Notes on patterns: Women

Foundation garment — an unboned, tightly-laced strapless corselet (the top is revealed above the gown neckline). Always take measurements for the drafting of the gown pattern from the corseleted figure.

Gown — (cut entire garment on the cross, extending length of skirts 2 feet longer than the wearer), back-lace to fit the figure. The collar should be lightly padded and cut to roll gently out and away from the neckline.

Belt — adapt foundation to curve over and around the hips and stomach of the wearer.

Head dress — comb hair away from the forehead, tightly pinning it at the back. (If wearer has a low hairline, tightly bind the forehead with a strip of fine and soft material and cover with make-up.) The fez-shaped hat, cut to fit tightly the back of the head, is secured with pins to the hair. Attach wire structure to support the veil, to the C.F. of the hat, controlling the angle with upright wires fastened to the back of the head dress. Arrange the veil lightly over the antennae — securing the central fold of the material to the depth of the top part of the fez.

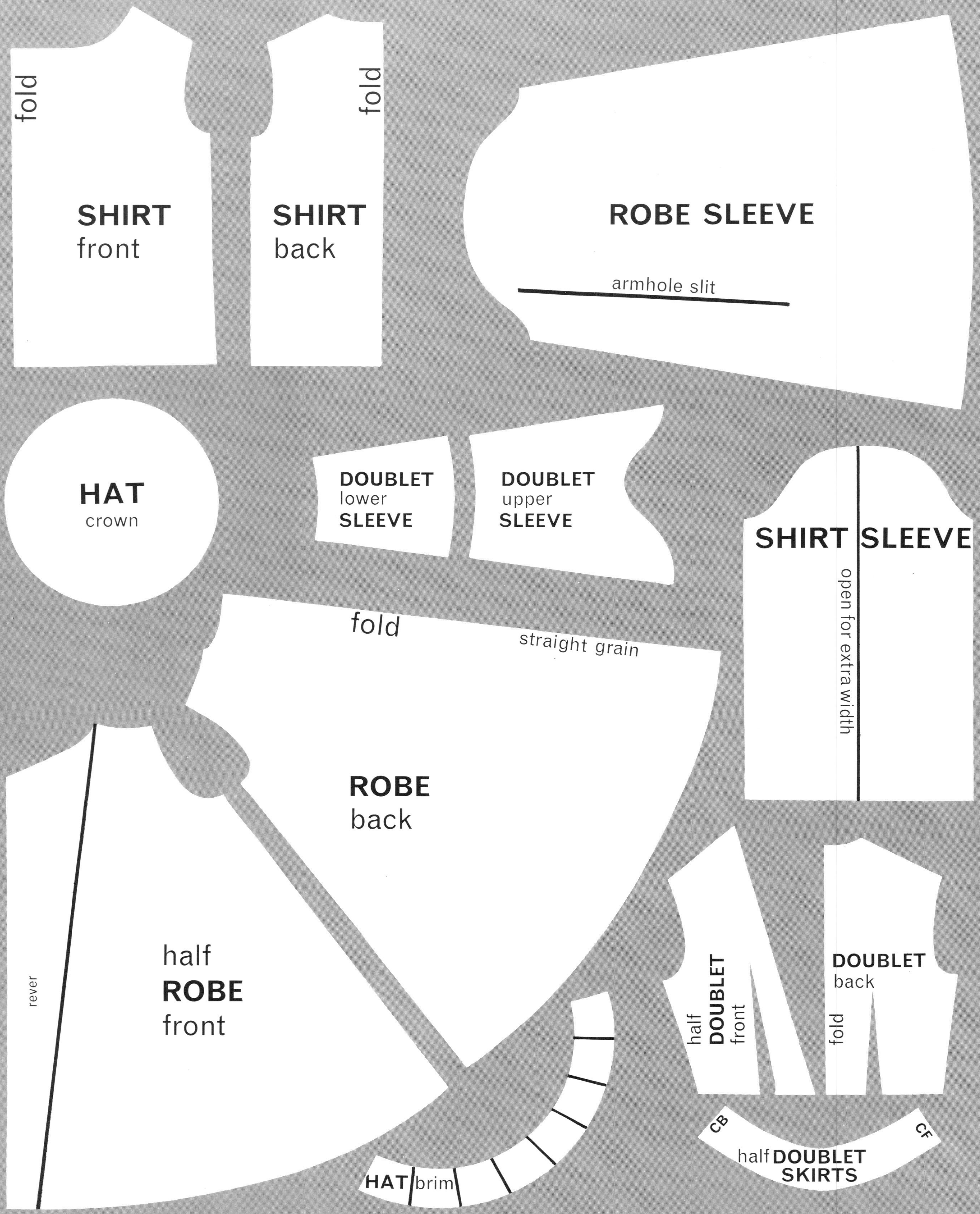

fold

SHIRT front

fold

SHIRT back

ROBE SLEEVE

armhole slit

HAT crown

DOUBLET lower **SLEEVE**

DOUBLET upper **SLEEVE**

SHIRT SLEEVE

open for extra width

fold

straight grain

ROBE back

rever

half **ROBE** front

DOUBLET half front

DOUBLET back

fold

CB

CF

HAT brim

half **DOUBLET SKIRTS**

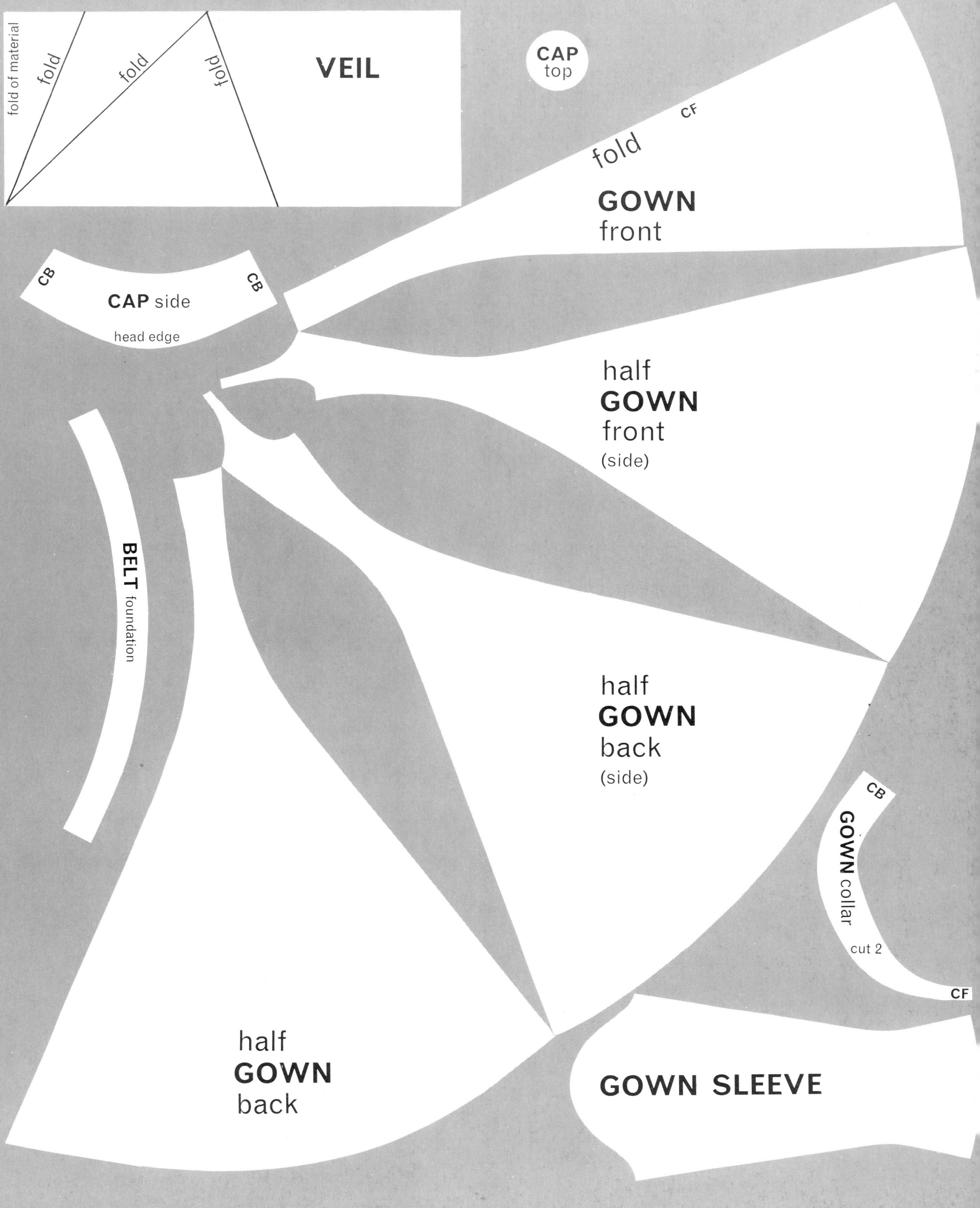

VEIL

fold of material

fold

fold

fold

CAP top

CAP side

CB

CB

head edge

fold

CF

GOWN front

half **GOWN** front (side)

BELT foundation

half **GOWN** back (side)

half **GOWN** back

CB

GOWN collar

cut 2

CF

GOWN SLEEVE

1500 Henry VII

Fabrics: Stout brocades, velvets, silks, satin, taffetas (real and imitation).

Colours: Black and a variety of warm colours — yellows, honeys, golds, reds and browns. The shirt and chemise add accents of white at the neck and wrists (a habit which will persist in men's dress to the present day).

Decoration: Large formal all-over patterns, based on conventional flower and plant forms, with background and design close in tone. (Plain fabrics equally popular.) Garments are bordered at neckline and hems with deep bands of contrasting colour or tone.

Padding and restriction, women: Body binding or an unboned corselet.

Movement, men: Natural and unaffected.

Movement women: Modest and dignified — similar to the mode of the preceding 60 years, but with an absence of exaggeration and affectation.

Men

General characteristics: Similar to the previous fashion — the doublet skirts knee length, the outer robe, ground-length.

Shirt — similar to the previous fashion.

Doublet — square-necked, laced up the C.F.s, with loose-fitting sleeves, the skirts set in deep pleats.

Robe — cut full and made of rich substantial material lined throughout — often with fur.

Hosen — similar to the previous fashion.

Shoes — broader across the toes (duckbilled), with latchets or ribbons tying across the instep.

Hats — similar to the previous fashion (usually black and made in thick cloth, felt, beaver or velvet). The brim is turned up and sometimes cut away in front. The crown is taller and blocked or shaped.

Hair — shoulder-length and centrally parted, with or without a fringe.

Accessories — belts, pouches, daggers, finger rings, chains, collars decorated with enamel work and set with semi-precious stones. The black ribbon worn around the neck and disappearing below the shirt probably holds a cross, talisman or reliquary.

Women

General characteristics: A simple and flowing gown with bell-shaped sleeves. The head dress, elaborate in construction (gable or kennel).

Chemise — seen covering the chest above the neckline of the gown.

Under robe — back-laced, cut similar to the gown but with less fullness in the skirts. Sleeves are laced to the armholes.

Gown — (lined throughout). The neckline is square and edged with a contrasting material. The body parts are narrow shouldered and tight fitting, flattening the breasts. The skirts are flared and develop into a train. The sleeve fits very tightly into a narrow armhole to develop into a large, flared bell-form at the wrist.

Stockings — similar to the previous fashion.

Shoes — similar to men's.

Head dress — the gable or kennel head dress is composed of:
1. a white undercap tied under the chin. It reveals the front part of the hair, which is centrally parted and allowed to fall loosely down the back.
2. a stiffened coif, the front part and lappets covered in black material. The front edge is decorated and made rigid by a band of metalwork set with coloured stones. (The coif is pinned to the undercap).
3. a semi-circular black hood decorated on both sides of its front edge with a band of embroidery — folded back. The lappets, formed by vents cut at the side of the embroidery, fall over the chest; the rest of the hood falls down the back, hiding the hair (the hood is pinned to the coif).

Accessories — finger rings and richly ornamented belts and girdles.

Notes on patterns: Men

Shirt — gather body fullness to a narrow neck band (extend patterns if extra fullness is required). The sleeve is cut similar to the sleeve of the doublet.

Doublet — line and interline throughout, pleating skirts (C.F. opening) to the waistline. Fasten doublet down C.F. by lacing.

Robe — (develop length of robe sleeve from the previous pattern). Line and interline throughout.

Hat — fit brim from the C.B. to leave a space at the C.F., where it is secured with ribbons.

Notes on patterns: Women

Chemise — cut ground length (cut top body parts double). Extend and flare at A to the required length.

Corselet — adapt top body parts of the gown, cutting to restrict the waistline and breasts.

Petticoat and false sleeves — a flared petticoat (light material) should be cut with a fitted waistline so that the line of the waistline is *not* revealed through the material of the gown. Add a deep band (some 30 inches in depth) of rich and heavy material to the hem. The sleeves terminate at the elbow point or are sewn or laced into the armholes of the chemise or under robe (adapt gown pattern if under robe is required).

Gown — (line throughout) back-laced and cut to fit the corseted figure. (Extend the underarm panel pattern at A to the required length of the skirts.)

Head dress — add a drawstring to the under cap for tying under the chin. Stiffen the sides of the coif, adding a rigid ornamental band to the face edge. Cover lappets with black material and pin the coif securely to the under cap. Lightly pad the embroidered edge of the black hood, and secure with pins to the coif.

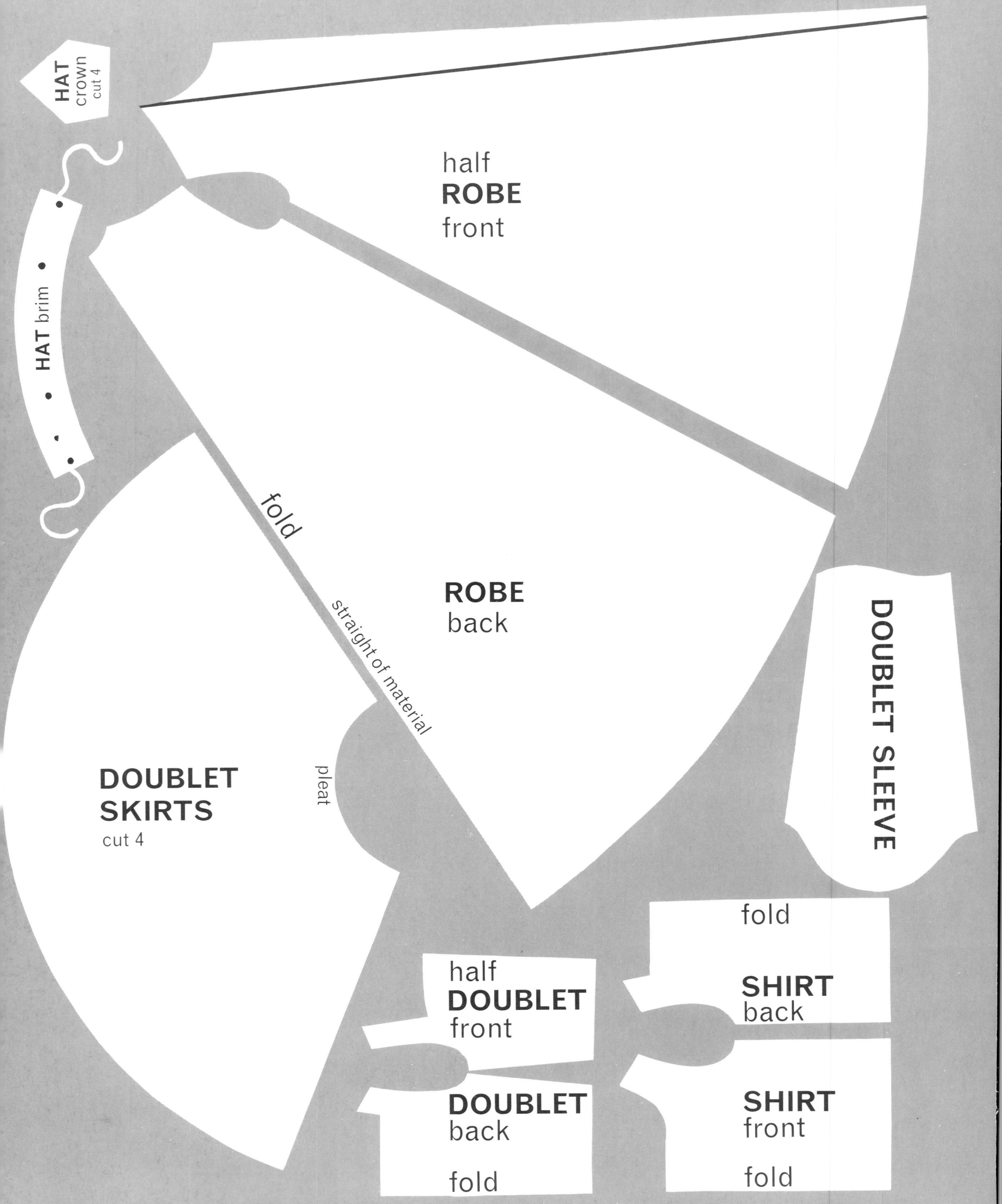

HAT crown cut 4

HAT brim

half
ROBE
front

fold

straight of material

ROBE
back

DOUBLET SLEEVE

**DOUBLET
SKIRTS**

cut 4

pleat

fold

half
DOUBLET
front

SHIRT
back

DOUBLET
back

fold

SHIRT
front

fold

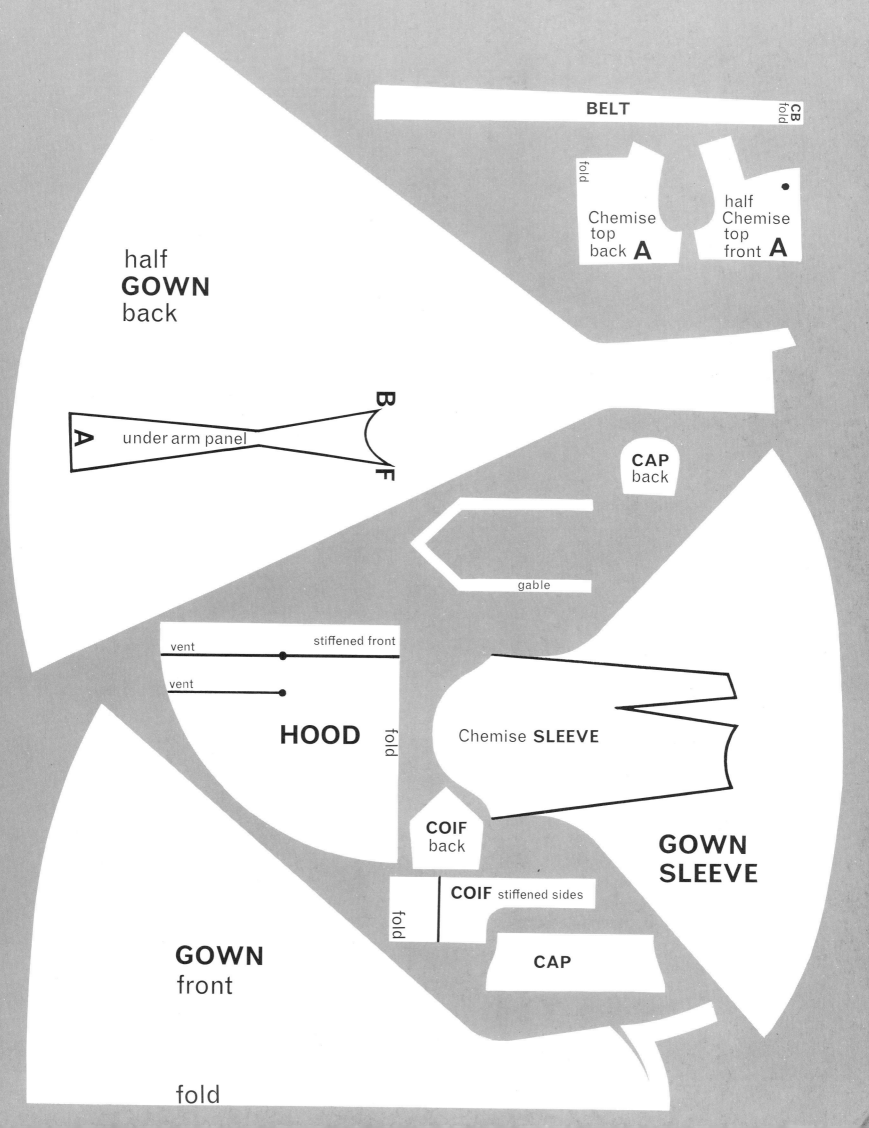

BELT **CB** fold

fold

Chemise top back **A**

half Chemise top front **A**

half **GOWN** back

B

A under arm panel

F

CAP back

gable

vent stiffened front

vent

HOOD fold

Chemise **SLEEVE**

GOWN SLEEVE

COIF back

COIF stiffened sides

fold

CAP

GOWN front

fold

1530 Henry VIII

Fabrics: Similar to the previous fashion. Expensive fabrics are always used with economy and show only in the areas of the costume visible.

Colours: Similar to the previous fashion.

Decoration: Similar to the previous fashion. Black embroidery decorates the shirt. Bands and braids of formal geometric design are used not only as a decoration but also to strengthen the seams and give good finish. Fabric is embroidered and enriched with slashing (noticeable in the doublet where the body parts and sleeves are slashed through to reveal the shirt beneath). The slashes are held together at regular intervals by jewelled ornaments, laced or tied to the fabric. This fashion becomes increasingly more varied throughout the 16th and early part of the 17th century.

Padding and restriction, men: All garments are lined and interlined—the large melon-shaped sleeve of the top robe, heavily bombasted.

Padding and restriction, women: The corselet, restricting the breasts and waist, is similar to the previous fashion. The head of the sleeve tightly fits the armhole (giving restriction of movement), the inside lower part of the sleeve frequently padded or lined with fur. The false inner sleeve is stuffed and filled out by the full chemise sleeve.

Movement, men: Upright, broad-chested, swaggering. The legs are splayed with feet turned out. Arms are forced out well away from the body due to the heavy bombasting of the sleeves. It is common for the hands to be placed on the hips—holding back the edges of the outer robe well away from the front of the body.

Movement, women: More formal than the previous fashion. Walking is made simpler by the shorter length of the front skirts. The elbows are carried well away from the body, the hands held lightly together over the stomach.

Men

General characteristics: Solid, square proportion. Heavy bombasting and use of rich and substantial materials. Basically similar in shape and cut to the previous two fashions.

Shirt — tied with ribbons down the C.F., full, sleeved, smocked or gathered to a neck band. The neck edge and wrists terminate in pleated frills.

Doublet — heavily lined throughout, fastened down the C.F., and cut to terminate at the waist. The sleeves are laced into the armholes.

Vest — worn over the doublet. Sleeveless, with pleated knee-length skirts. The body parts are cut away in front to reveal the doublet.

Robe — lined throughout, knee length, with a heavily pleated back. The revers develop into a sailor collar. The sleeves are composed of short large padded melon-shaped tops with hanging dummy sleeves attached to the back parts at the elbow point.

Hosen — (laced to the waistline of the doublet) the bombasted codpiece, laced to the fronts of the hosen, protrudes through the C.F. opening of the vest skirts. Upper parts of the hosen are sometimes slashed—the underlinen pulled and puffed out through the openings.

Shoes — similar to the previous fashion, broader across toes (frequently slashed).

Hats — flat, with a gathered or fitted crown and an upturned brim—decorated with a brooch and an ostrich feather.

Hair — shorter version of the last fashion, with or without the fringe, or cut very short to an even length all over. Beards, carefully trimmed and of various shapes, follow the jaw line up to and joining the side-boards. The moustache, accompanying the beard, is also carefully trimmed in a variety of ways.

Accessories — jewelled metal collars and chains. Finger rings worn *over* short gauntlet gloves (slashed and pounced). Belts, sashes, purses, pomanders, and daggers.

Women

General characteristics: More formal and stiffer than preceding fashion. The large bell sleeve is folded back and pinned tightly around the upper arm. The head dress is smaller and neater.

Chemise — loosely fitting, and cut to follow the shape of the neckline of the gown. Full bishop sleeves.

Petticoat — stiffened to form a cone-shaped foundation to the skirts.

Gown — similar in cut to the previous fashion. Laced down the C.B. The folded-back sleeve reveals a false inner sleeve which is held together at regular intervals along its lower edge by jewelled ties.

Stockings — similar to the previous fashion.

Shoes — similar to men's.

Head dress — the gable head dress terminates on a line with the mouth. The hair is no longer revealed, but secured and hidden by a padded embroidered band, forming a turban, to which the coif is fastened. The ends of the embroidered band of the hood (now with a single central vent) are looped up and pinned on top of the head. One side of the hood is twisted and secured to the top back part of the head dress, the other side remains loose to fall over the shoulder. An alternative head dress is the French hood (cf. portrait of Anne Boleyn, by Holbein). It is worn well on the back of the head and tied with ribbons under the chin. A flared, stiffened, crescent-shaped form (billement), handsomely bordered with an edging of metalwork set with jewels, is worn on top of the hood and set well back from the stiffened front edge.

Accessories — fine necklaces, pomanders, chains, pendants enamelled and set with coloured stones and pearls. Finger rings. Jewelled ornaments threaded on laces to secure the slashings.

Notes on patterns: Men

All garments, other than underlinen and hosen, should be lined and if necessary interlined.

Shirt — (C.F. tied opening) cut full and gather to a plain or smocked collar band terminating in a pleated frill. A wrist frill also terminates the sleeve.

Doublet — for theatre purposes sew sleeves (padded) into armholes.

Vest — adapt skirts from previous pattern.

Robe — pleat back robe to front shoulders—pleatings continue along B.A. (top front patterns form the back neckline). Sew edges C.B. together to form centre back seam of sailor collar. The melon-shaped sleeve, gathered or pleated into the armhole, is mounted onto a heavily padded foundation and the elbow band. The dummy sleeve is sewn up and attached to the lower edge of the elbow band, from the seam out to B., with the points A.A. falling away in front.

Hat — gather the crown to fit the brim (stiffened). Insert stiffened band (A) to support the sides of the crown.

Codpiece—(for theatre purposes sew to the front of the tights). Cut 2 sides (A) and 2 fronts (B). Join 2 fronts together and attach to the side pieces. Bone each seam and heavily bombast.

Notes on patterns: Women

Chemise — (pattern for the neckline is shown above the neckline of the gown pattern). The body parts fit the figure to develop into flared skirts. Form a C.B. placket. The sleeve (use pattern of 1550) is gathered to a wristband and pleated frill. Form a placket at the wrist.

Petticoat — similar to the previous fashion. Add stiffening to the lower parts.

Gown — similar to the previous fashion. The tight-fitting upper part of the sleeve is sewn to the lower part (lightly padded) which is folded back and tightly pinned around the upper arm at B.B. (remaining width of the sleeve falls away down the back of the arm).

False sleeves — (stiffen) tuck to fit the wrist measurement (lengthwise). Attach A.A. to armband (hook and eye fastening). Fasten the lower edge, at intervals, with ties and jewelled ornaments. (Pull out the chemise sleeve through the openings formed.)

Head dress — secure the stiffened coif by pinning to the turban, and tying under the chin.

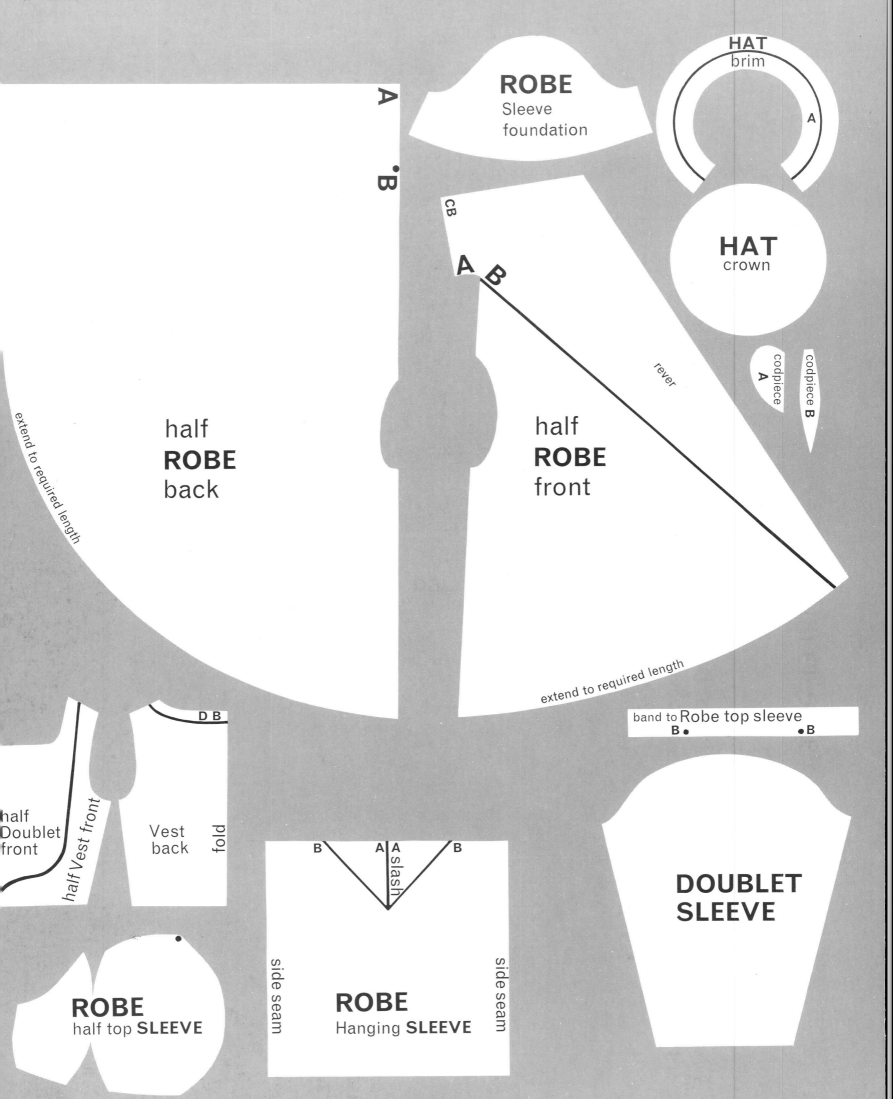

ROBE Sleeve foundation

HAT brim

A

HAT crown

A B

CB

rever

codpiece A

codpiece B

A B

half **ROBE** back

extend to required length

half **ROBE** front

extend to required length

D B

band to Robe top sleeve
B • • B

half Doublet front

half Vest front

Vest back

fold

B A A B
slash

side seam

ROBE Hanging **SLEEVE**

side seam

DOUBLET SLEEVE

ROBE half top **SLEEVE**

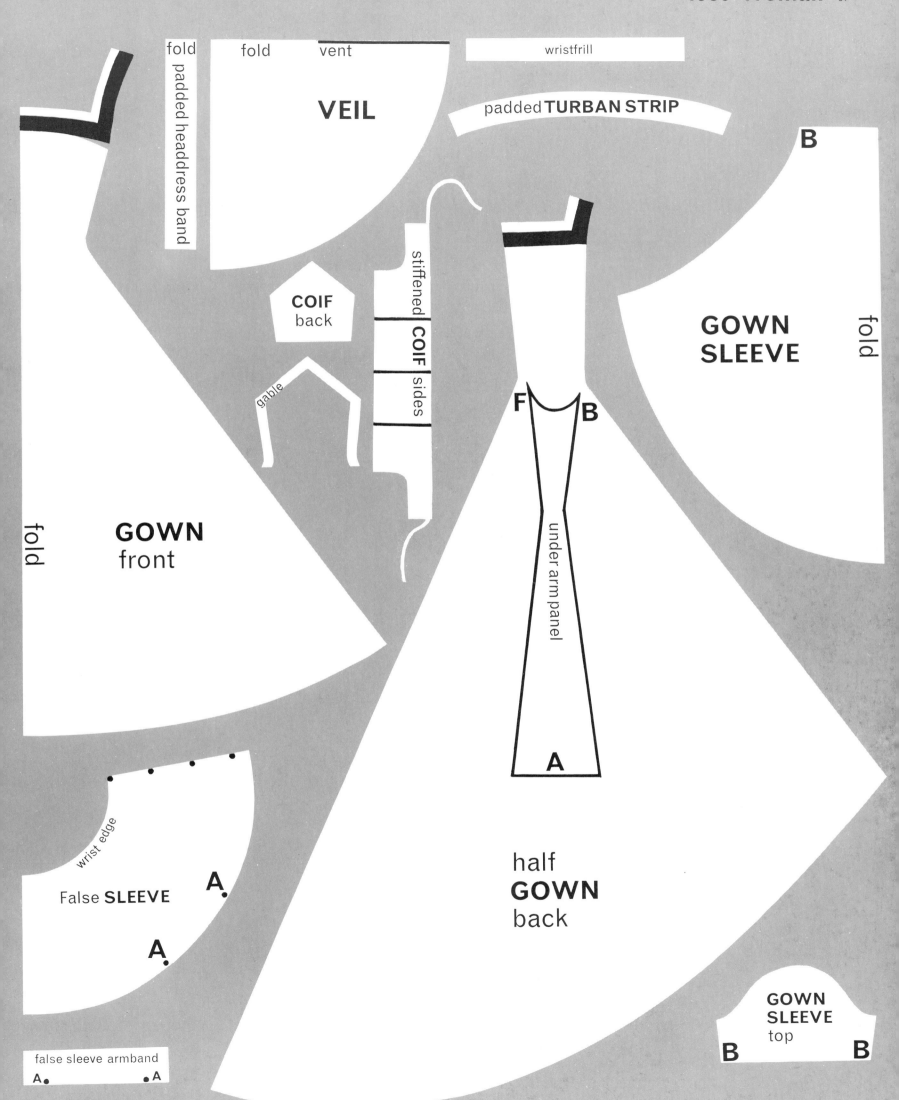

fold

fold

vent

VEIL

wristfrill

fold padded headdress band

padded **TURBAN STRIP**

B

GOWN SLEEVE

fold

COIF back

stiffened **COIF** sides

gable

F **B**

fold

GOWN front

under arm panel

A

wrist edge

False **SLEEVE**

A

A

half **GOWN** back

false sleeve armband

A **A**

GOWN SLEEVE top

B **B**

1550 Edward VI

Fabrics: Similar to the previous fashion.

Colours: More sombre than the previous fashion, with domination of black.

Decoration: Rich and formal floral patterns, woven and embroidered. Braiding or banding of most seams and edges, particularly on men's costume, will continue until the end of the 17th century. Slashing and puffing enriches the surface of most fabrics from simple large vertical slashes, and cuts forming all-over patterns, to very small cuts, pricks or pounces — too small to allow the underlinen to protrude, but giving an elasticity to the cloth and a tight wrinkle-free fit. Jewellery, real and imitation, becomes increasingly popular.

Padding and restriction, men: Most parts of the garments are lined and interlined. Padding consciously alters the natural shape of the figure.

Padding and restriction, women: Iron corsets flatten the chest and restrict the waistline to give a totally rigid inverted triangular silhouette to the body. The triangular bell form of the skirt is supported by a petticoat stiffened with boning, parchment or iron hoops.

Movement, men: Natural with the head held high and the arms carried away from the body.

Movement, women: Formal, upright, rigid and stiff, with the elbows angled and carried away from the body, the hands held together over the stomach.

Men

General characteristics: Suit of clothes, consisting of shirt, doublet or jerkin, the short robe or cloak, and upper and nether hosen. Hat, gloves, and sword worn to complete the wardrobe.

Shirt — (less voluminous) frequently embroidered, fastening down the C.F. with collar band and wrists terminating in pleated frills or ruffs.

Jerkins — (similar to the vest with short sleeves), buttoned through the C.F.s, with a standing collar and hip-length flared skirts. False, full-length sleeves are laced into the armholes.

Robe — similar to the previous fashion.

Cloak — worn in preference to the robe, usually circular and hip length.

Upper and nether hosen — upper hosen, laced or hooked to waistline of doublet, terminate at mid-thigh. They are heavily bombasted and a codpiece is laced to an opening formed at the C.F. Broad strips of stiffened material (panes), attached only at the waist edge and around the leg openings, reveal the underlying fabric. Nether hosen (stockings) are sewn into the leg openings of the upper hosen. (Knitted stockings appear at the end of the century.)

Shoes — natural in shape resembling a heelless slipper. Decorative slashing and pricking gives elasticity to the fit of the shoe.

Hats — flat black caps or berets with stiffened brims — decorated with jewelled ornaments and small ostrich feathers.

Hair — cut short. Beards and moustaches similar to the previous fashion.

Accessories — belt, sword and dagger belt, purses, finger rings, short gauntlet gloves, brooches.

Women

General characteristics: Similar to the previous fashion, stiffer and angular in form.

Corsets — hinged, laced, and beautifully ornamented.

Chemise — very full and of fine material. The fullness is gathered to a high neckband edged with a narrow pleated ruff. The sleeves are similar to the previous fashion.

Petticoat — this foundation determines the rigid shape and bell form of the skirt. The front panel, of rich material, is flat and probably terminates at the side seams.

Gown — (body parts and skirts cut separately), the gown laced up the C.B., has a square neckline and V-shaped waist. The flared skirts, developing into a train at the back, are closed or cut away in the front to form an inverted V-shaped opening revealing the petticoat beneath. The bell-shaped sleeve, fastened back to form a deep cuff, exposes the false inner sleeve — stiffer, larger and more elaborately decorated than the preceding fashion.

Partlet — a yoke with a V-neck and standing collar. It is worn over the gown and tied under the armpits with tapes. A brooch secures it to the C.F. of the bodice.

Stockings — similar to the previous fashion.

Shoes — similar to men's.

Head dress — the hair is centrally parted, gently waved, and puffed out over pads at the sides to give a flat broad top to the head. The French hood, secured with ribbons tied under the chin, and stiffened along its front edge, forms a tube at the back to encase the hair. The billement, worn at an acute angle to slope forward onto the cheek bones from the back part of the head, is stiffened and decorated on its outer edge by a band of fine metalwork set with jewels.

Accessories — brooches, pendants. A pomander, prayer book or crucifix is fastened to the long end of the belt or girdle.

Notes on patterns: Men

Line and interline all garments save shirt and nether hosen.

Shirt — stiffen collar band. Ribbon ties form the fastening down the C.F.s. The wrist and neck frills or pleatings are made from a strip of material 3 inches in width and folded down its length (the folded edge forms the outer circumference).

Jerkin — stiffen collar band and skirts. The belt is cut to follow the line of the V-shaped waist.

False sleeve — tie-catch and arrange at intervals the excess length to the lining. Sew to the jerkin armhole.

Upper and nether hosen — (add C.F. placket) make up lining and foundation separately (pattern of foundation terminates at W.W. and A. Front and back are marked F and B). Gather waist edge and leg openings of the lining, to the waist edge and leg openings of the foundation (lightly tie-catch at intervals the excess material to padding sewn to the foundation surface). Attach codpiece (bombasted and boned) to the C.F. with the centre panel gathered to a point at the base. Attach stiffened panes (12 in number), to the waist edge and leg openings. Ease the waist edge to the waistband, and the leg openings to the stiffened thigh bands. (For theatre purposes substitute tights for nether hosen.)

Hat — similar in construction to the previous fashion.

Notes on patterns: Women

Chemise — develop and extend at A to required length. Add ribbons to form the fastening at the C.F. Stiffen the collar band, (plain or smocked), and attach two pleated frills to the top edge. The sleeve is gathered at the wrist to a wristband and pleated frill. (Add wrist placket.)

Gown — (laced placket down C.B.) Interline throughout — save head of the sleeve. As a substitute for the corsets, closely bone the bodice to the level of the neckline, adding extra interlining around the armhole (formed by sewing A to A). The skirts are eased to the waistline of the bodice and, if necessary, arranged in pleats at the back. The sleeves are similar in construction to the previous fashion.

Petticoat — set on a waistband. For theatre purposes, a series of stiff buckram flounces graduating from waist to hem and further stiffened with bones, can be used instead of hoops to achieve the necessary formal bell-shaped silhouette. Cover the front with a panel of material sewn flat and without fullness.

False sleeves — stiffen and line. AB joins AB to form the armband (hooked and eyed). The large formal slashes and CC, DD, EE, and FF are fastened with laces and jewelled ornaments. Pull the chemise sleeve out through the openings.

Yoke — line. Stiffen the collar. Attach ribbons for tying at X, X, X, X.

Head dress — construct the hood by sewing AB to AB and BC to BC (forming the back tube). Stiffen and wire the face edge to fit and follow the contour of the hair style. Stiffen, wire, and shape the crescent to angle backwards. The crescent should fit the head and secure the hood. (Ribbons, sewn to the front sides, tie under the chin.)

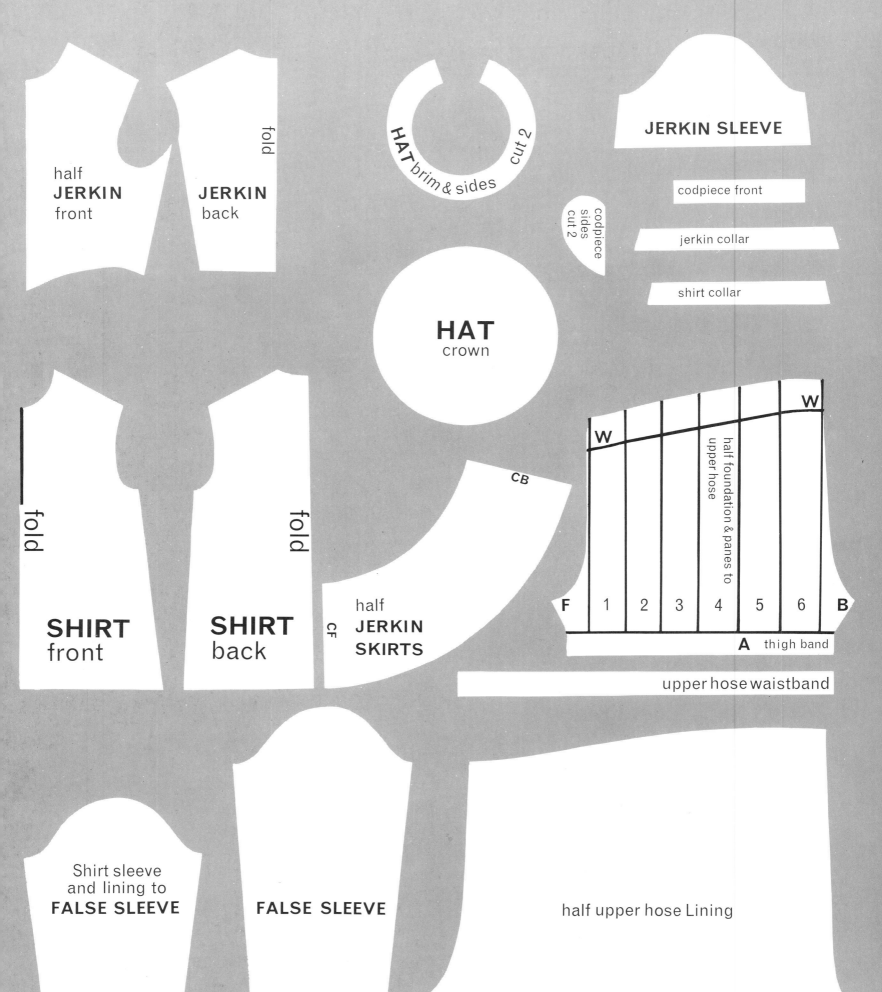

half
JERKIN
front

JERKIN
back

fold

HAT brim & sides cut 2

codpiece
sides
cut 2

JERKIN SLEEVE

codpiece front

jerkin collar

shirt collar

HAT
crown

fold

SHIRT
front

fold

SHIRT
back

CB

CF

half
**JERKIN
SKIRTS**

W

W

half foundation & panes to
upper hose

F   1   2   3   4   5   6   B

A   thigh band

upper hose waistband

Shirt sleeve
and lining to
FALSE SLEEVE

FALSE SLEEVE

half upper hose Lining

F

B

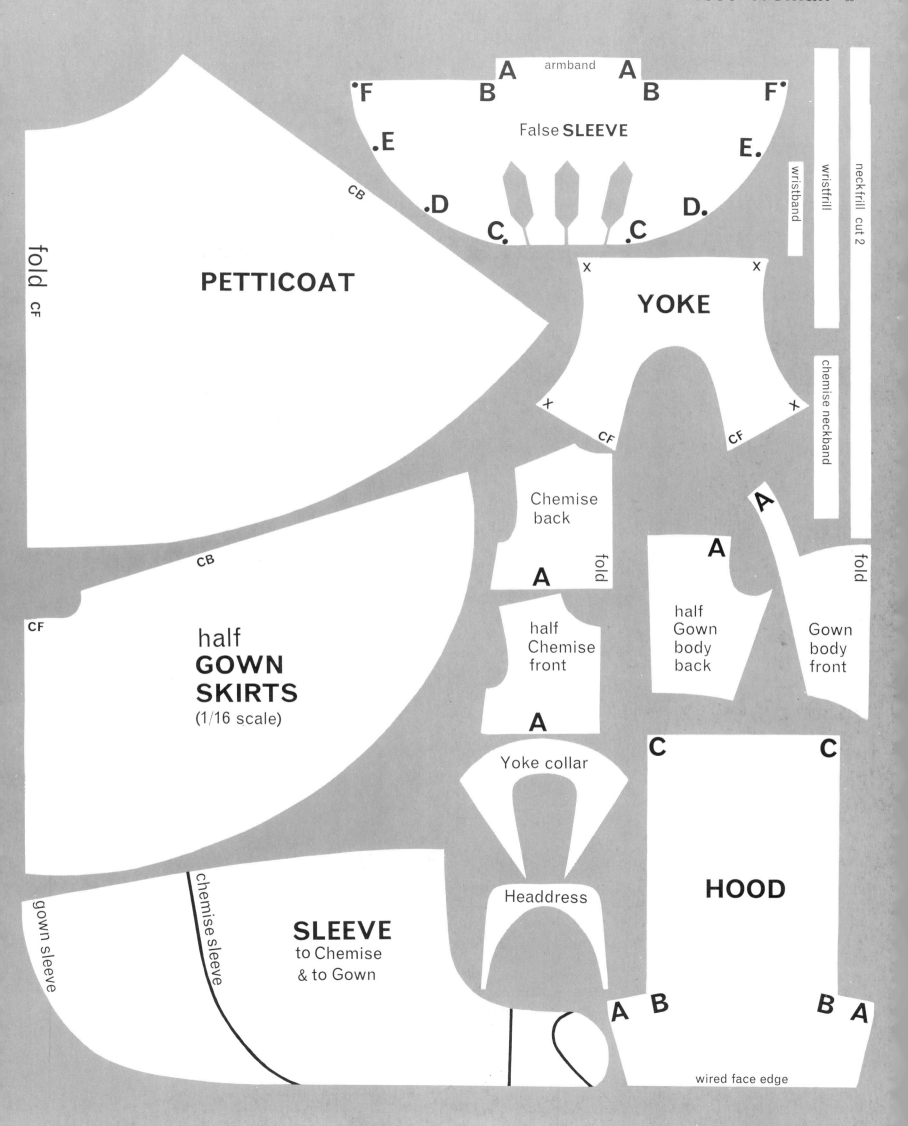

armband

F **B** **A** **A** **B** **F**

.E E.

False **SLEEVE**

CB

.D D.

C. **C**

fold cf

PETTICOAT

x x

YOKE

x

x CF CF

wristband

wristfrill

neckfrill cut 2

chemise neckband

Chemise back

A

fold

A

half Chemise front

CB

half Gown body back

Gown body front

fold

A

CF

A

half **GOWN SKIRTS** (1/16 scale)

A

Yoke collar

C **C**

HOOD

gown sleeve

chemise sleeve

SLEEVE to Chemise & to Gown

Headdress

A **B** **B** **A**

wired face edge

1560 Elizabeth I

Fabrics: Strong tough velvets, satins, silks, damasks, etc. Doublets of leather.

Colours: Profusion of black. Rich dark colours. White always seen at wrists and neck and in the puffings and pullings out of the underlinen through the slashes and panes.

Decoration: Patterned or plain braids of various widths stripe fabrics, cover seams, and decorate the edges of most garments.

Padding and restriction, men: The V-shaped extended belly form of the doublet, the high neckband and the pumpkin-shaped upper hosen (trunk hose, round hose, slops, etc.) are boned and stiffened to retain their shape. The waist is restricted by simple corsetry (C.F. edges of the lining of the doublet laced or hooked and eyed together independently from the top surface). Most fabrics are interlined or lightly padded. The cavities formed by the extended belly of the doublet and the trunk hose are filled out with bombast — wool, horsehair, horses' tails, bran, sawdust and even rags. This desire to deform the natural shape of the figure and to eliminate folds and creases in the fabric will continue to be fashionable (at times very bizarre and exaggerated) during the next 70 years.

Padding and restriction, women: Heavy corsets, with a V-shaped waist, flatten the chest and reduce the size of the waistline. Hip pads, and a bell-shaped stiffened under skirt. Padding increases the height of the sleeves.

Movement, men: Formal. Arms curve away from the body with one hand placed on the hip — the elbows helping to support and display the cloak.

Movement, women: Posture is less rigid than the previous fashion. The arms curve away from the body and come to rest on either side of the padded hip roll. The collar band and neck frill forces the head high.

Men

General characteristics: A sober and dignified suit of clothes with doublet, cloak and trunk hose often of matching fabric and decoration.

Under garments — the shirt, open down C.F.s (tied with ribbons or cords), terminates at the wrists and neck in pleated frills. Under drawers, (tied with drawstring at waistline) with a C.F. opening, are cut short and close to the leg.

Jerkin — usually slashed through its length to reveal the padded inner lining. Short skirts are attached to the waistline, and epaulettes or wings hide the join of sleeve to armhole.

Trunk or upper hose — similar to the previous fashion.

Cloak — fully circular (with or without dummy sleeves) with revers and standing collar.

Nether hosen — similar to the previous fashion.

Shoes — similar to the previous fashion.

Hats — black hats with narrow brims and pleated crowns.

Hair — short and neat in cut. All men wear the beard and moustache. Older men favour a larger and fuller beard.

Accessories — a pendant or talisman, attached to a cord or fine chain worn about the neck. Sword belt (straps supporting the sword are frequently slotted through a section of the panes of the trunk hose). Gloves.

Women

General characteristics: Less rigid and angular, somewhat masculine, reflecting men's fashions. The deep, pinned-back bell sleeve disappears.

Under garments — the corset is made of metal or cloth — heavily boned, with wooden busks placed down the C.F.s. The full ground-length chemise is rarely seen. The partlet, which covers the exposed areas of neck, shoulders and breasts, is finished off with a pleated frill at the neck. A hip pad, bum roll or bolster, together with several stiffened flared petticoats (sometimes set with hoops), hold out the skirts of the gown.

Gown — body parts (boned) resemble the shape of the corset. Sleeves, padded and puffed, with small ruffs fastened about the wrists, are usually laced into the armholes. The skirts, (closed in front, and set in a deep inverted box-pleat simulating the line of the inverted V-shaped opening of the skirts of the previous fashion) are separate, attached to a waistband, and heavily pleated.

Shoes — similar to men's.

Head dress — the French hood, or hats similar in shape to those worn by the men.

Hair — brushed back and rolled over a small pad surrounding the forehead and temples, with the back hair arranged in a bun.

Accessories — finger rings, metal and jewelled belts, chains, pendants, etc.

Notes on patterns: Men

In future all parts of the costume (other than under garments) should be lined, and in many cases interlined, unless otherwise stated.

Shirt — sleeve and neck frills are box or knife pleated.

Jerkin — separately make up foundation, lining body parts, and jerkin top. Attach lining body parts to foundation, gathering the waist edge to the waist edge of the foundation. Add a side and neck placket. Padding should be placed between the surfaces at the C.F., diminishing towards the side seams and the neck opening. Place strips of whalebone down the length of the slashes of the jerkin fronts. Attach skirts and collar band (with extra stiffening) to the jerkin top, which is fastened at the neck and C.F. waistline. Secure back waist and neck edge of jerkin top to the back waist and neck edge of body parts. Pad sleeves.

Trunk hose — (add C.F. opening) make up as in previous fashion. A formal melon shape is achieved by attaching heavy padding between the two surfaces.

Hat — wire brim and the support to the crown.

Belt — add attachments to XX marked on the sword straps and belt. Attachments are also placed at OO to support the sword and scabbard.

Notes on patterns: Women

In future all parts of the costume (other than under garments) should be lined, and in many cases interlined, unless otherwise stated.

Corsets — adapt bodice pattern adding tabs around the waistline. Bone closely throughout save around the armhole which should be strongly interlined. (Boning should *not* stop at the waistline but continue through into the tabs.) The corset is back-laced.

Hip roll — pad or make of cork and attach to the corset tabs.

Petticoat — cut full, gather at the waistline by means of a drawstring and stiffen either with flounces of buckram reinforced with whalebone, or with graduated hoops of whalebone or steel set into the skirts.

Partlet — attach a drawstring to the lower edge and tie at the C.F. Add a pleated frill to the collar (hook and eye). If the collar band is to be smocked, extend and widen the pattern.

Gown — (bodice and skirts separate, the bodice fastening at the C.F.) lightly bone bodice. Construct sleeve by attaching the lower lining to the foundation at BB, the double puff at the head of the sleeve being formed at AA and BB. 6 panes cover these puffs, and panes sewn to form a series of chevrons cover the lower arm BB to CC. (Pad head of sleeve.) The skirts, set to a waistband, are pleated at sides and back — bullet pleating to take up excess material. A deep pleat is formed at AB to AB on either side of the C.F. Form placket at the side or C.B.

Wrist ruff — (1 inch deep) is set in the figure 8 and controlled by catching the arrangement of pleats together at regular intervals around the outer edge. Made from band 3 inches wide, folded down its length (about 80 inches long — 4 to 5 pleats to the inch) sewn to 1 inch wide wristband (add tapes for tying).

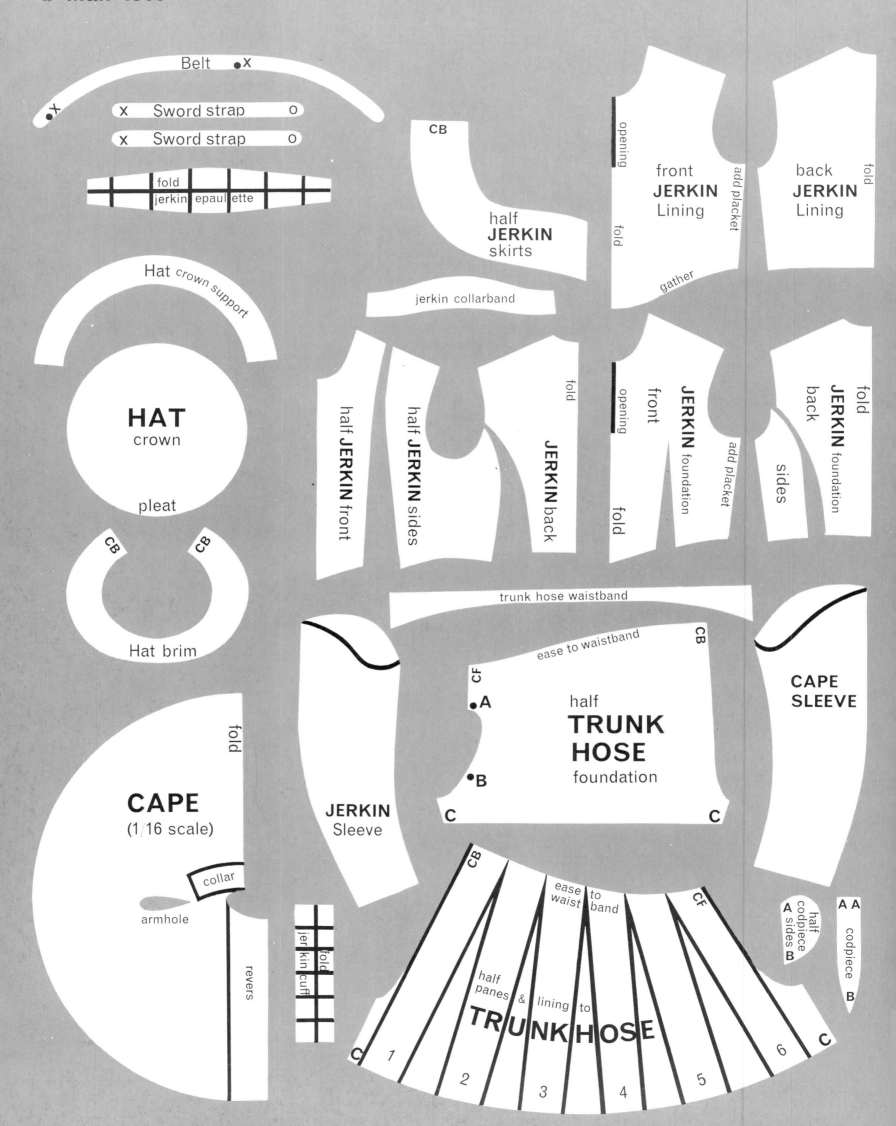

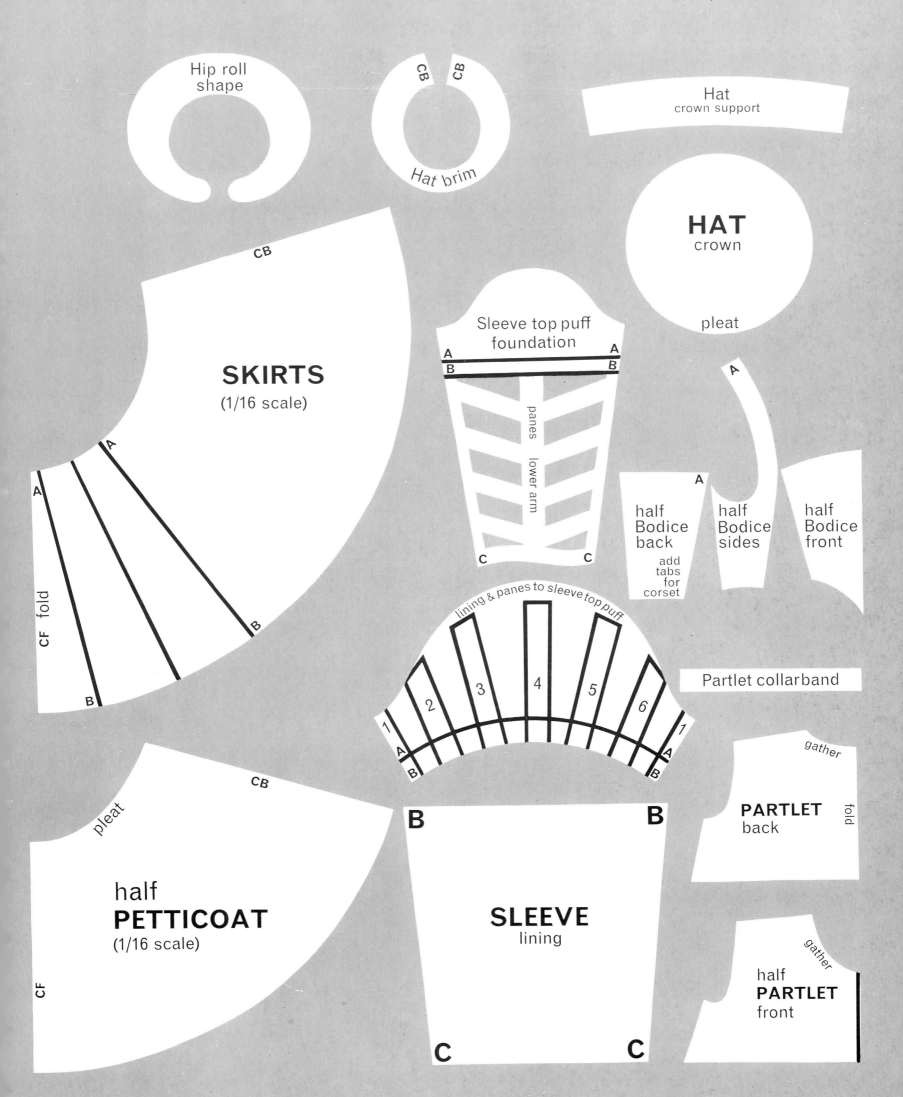

Hip roll shape

CB CB

Hat brim

Hat
crown support

HAT
crown

pleat

SKIRTS
(1/16 scale)

CB

A

A

CF fold

B

B

Sleeve top puff
foundation

A A
B B

panes

lower arm

C C

A

half
Bodice
back

add
tabs
for
corset

half
Bodice
sides

A

half
Bodice
front

Partlet collarband

lining & panes to sleeve top puff

1 2 3 4 5 6 1
A A
B B

B B

pleat

CB

half
PETTICOAT
(1/16 scale)

CF

SLEEVE
lining

C C

gather

PARTLET
back

fold

gather

half
PARTLET
front

1575 Elizabeth 1

Fabrics: Similar to the previous fashion. Softer, finer materials employed in the making of sleeves and linings.

Colours: Brighter and lighter. Black continues to be popular and will remain so throughout the history of fashion.

Decoration: Embroidered braids, decorative pinking, piercing and pricking. Black or coloured embroidery, in all-over scroll patterns incorporating realistic motifs of plant, flower, and animal forms.

Padding and restriction, men: Similar to the previous fashion. Sleeves and peascod belly more heavily padded.

Padding and restriction, women: Similar to the previous fashion. Sleeves larger and more heavily padded.

Movement, men: Similar to the previous fashion.

Movement, women: Similar to the previous fashion.

Men

General characteristics: Less uniform with a greater originality and variety in cut and decoration.

Under garments — similar to the previous fashion.

Doublet — the belly part begins to extend over the pointed waistline. A stiffened, flared basque replaces the skirt. Ruffs are tied around the high neckband and wrists.

Trunk hose — similar to the previous fashion, shorter in form and less bulky. They are joined to tubes extending to the knee (canions).

Cloak — shorter in length.

Stockings — worn over the canions and kept in place by ties of soft fabric cross-gartered above and below the knee.

Shoes — similar to the previous fashion. Made of leather and usually of the same colour as the stockings. Over shoes (pantofles), composed of a wedge-shaped sole and toe piece, are frequently worn.

Hats — the crown is fuller and taller and set further back on the head.

Hair — similar to the previous fashion.

Accessories — similar to the previous fashion.

Women

General characteristics: More feminine and individual in choice of detail and decoration.

Under garments — similar to the previous fashion. The partlet of very fine, almost transparent, material terminates at the neck in a deep ruff forming a series of figure 8 pleats. The top petticoat is richly embroidered and decorated.

Gown — a diminutive stiffened skirt or basque terminates the body parts and covers the join of the skirts proper to the waistline. Skirts, bullet-pleated to a waistband or laced to the body parts, are open in front and reveal the top petticoat. The lacing of the sleeve (fuller, interlined and padded, gathered or pleated at both wrist and head) to the armhole is hidden by a very large epaulette rising at a sharp angle away from the shoulder point.

Stockings — similar to the previous fashion.

Shoes — similar to men's.

Head dress and hair — similar to the previous fashion.

Accessories — profusion of necklaces looped around the throat, pendants enamelled and set with pearl drops and semi-precious stones, waistbelts of metal and jewelled ornaments. Finger rings, and fans — feathers formally arranged and mounted onto an ornamental stick.

Ruffs — always a separate item of apparel and referred to as "suites of ruffs" or "sets of ruffs". Basically composed of a long strip of material (band) gathered and fastened by a drawstring threaded along the inner edge (Band-strings). With the introduction of starching and the supportasse (a framework of wire, whipped all over with coloured silk, fastened to the neckband to support the starched ruff or collar), ruffs become very large, formal, and complex in contrast to the earlier simple methods of knife or box pleating. The tubular folds are formed by moulding the wet starched material around heated setting sticks. These ruffs, mounted onto wrist or neckbands, are fastened (open or closed) at throat and wrists by the bandstrings.

Notes on patterns: Men

Doublet — (add C.F. button fastening). Cut fronts of the lining (adding whalebone) to restrict the size of the natural waist. Hooks and eyes fasten these fronts. The stiffened fronts of the doublet are eased or gathered at the waistline edge to the waistline edge of the front linings with the majority of the easing or gathering placed at the C.F.s. In addition to the whaleboning and stiffening of the fronts it may be necessary to insert, between the lining and top surface, a bolster cut to the form of the peascod belly, before buttoning the doublet across. The sleeve, gathered into the armhole, should be interlined with soft padding.

Cape — use sleeve pattern from the previous fashion.

Trunk hose and canions — (add C.F. opening). Make up in a similar manner to the previous fashion. The leg extensions (canions) are covered by a top surface AA/BB which should be controlled by tie-catching.

Ruffs — (1½ inches deep) made from band 4 inches wide, folded down its length (about 240 inches long — 4 to 5 pleats to the inch). Sewn to 1½ inches wide neckband.

Wrist ruff — (1½ inches deep) made from band 4 inches wide, folded down its length (about 140 inches long — 4 to 5 pleats to the inch). Sewn to 1½ inches wide wristband.

Notes on patterns: Women

Corset — (laced at C.B.) Adapt bodice pattern by adding tabs. Heavily bone throughout.

Petticoats — similar to the previous fashion. The front of the top petticoat, exposed by the open skirts of the gown, is covered by a large triangle of material cut to lie flat over the surface, without gathering or pleating at the waist edge.

Partlet — cut from previous pattern omitting gathering at the throat. For theatre purposes as an alternative to tying, the ruff can be closed with press studs or very small hooks and eyes.

Gown — the bodice should be rigidly boned, and laced or hooked and eyed at C.B. Add a layer of padding between the two surfaces of the sleeve. The skirts are mounted to a waistband, with pleating commencing from A marked on the fronts. Epaulettes and basque require extra stiffening.

French hood — wire and stiffen the hair crescent. The hood, attached to the head edge of the crescent, forms a tube at the back. The head dress should be secured to the sides of the head or tied with tapes under the chin.

Ruff — (2 inches deep) made from band 4½ inches wide, folded down its length (about 300 inches long — 4 to 5 pleats to the inch) sewn to 2 inch wide neck band.

Wrist ruffs — (2 inches deep) made from band 4 inches wide folded down its length (about 140 inches long — 4 pleats to the inch) sewn to 2 inch wide wristband.

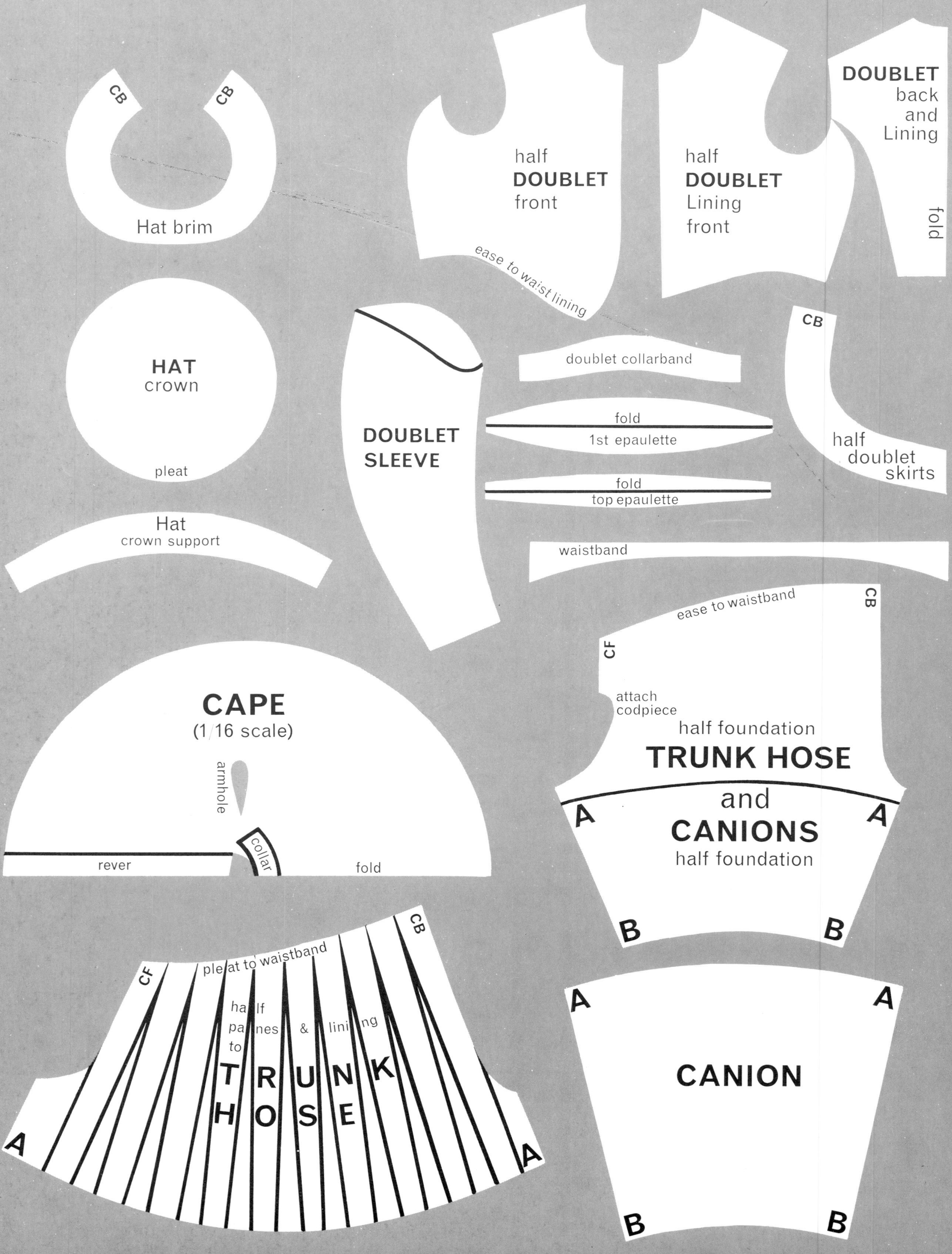

CB   CB

Hat brim

HAT
crown

pleat

Hat
crown support

half
DOUBLET
front

ease to waist lining

half
DOUBLET
Lining
front

DOUBLET
back
and
Lining

fold

CB

DOUBLET SLEEVE

doublet collarband

fold
1st epaulette

fold
top epaulette

half
doublet
skirts

waistband

CAPE
(1/16 scale)

armhole

rever   collar   fold

ease to waistband   CB

CF

attach
codpiece

half foundation
TRUNK HOSE
and
CANIONS
half foundation

A   A

B   B

CF   pleat to waistband   CB

half
pannes & lining
to
**T R U N K
H O S E**

A   A

B

A   A

CANION

B   B

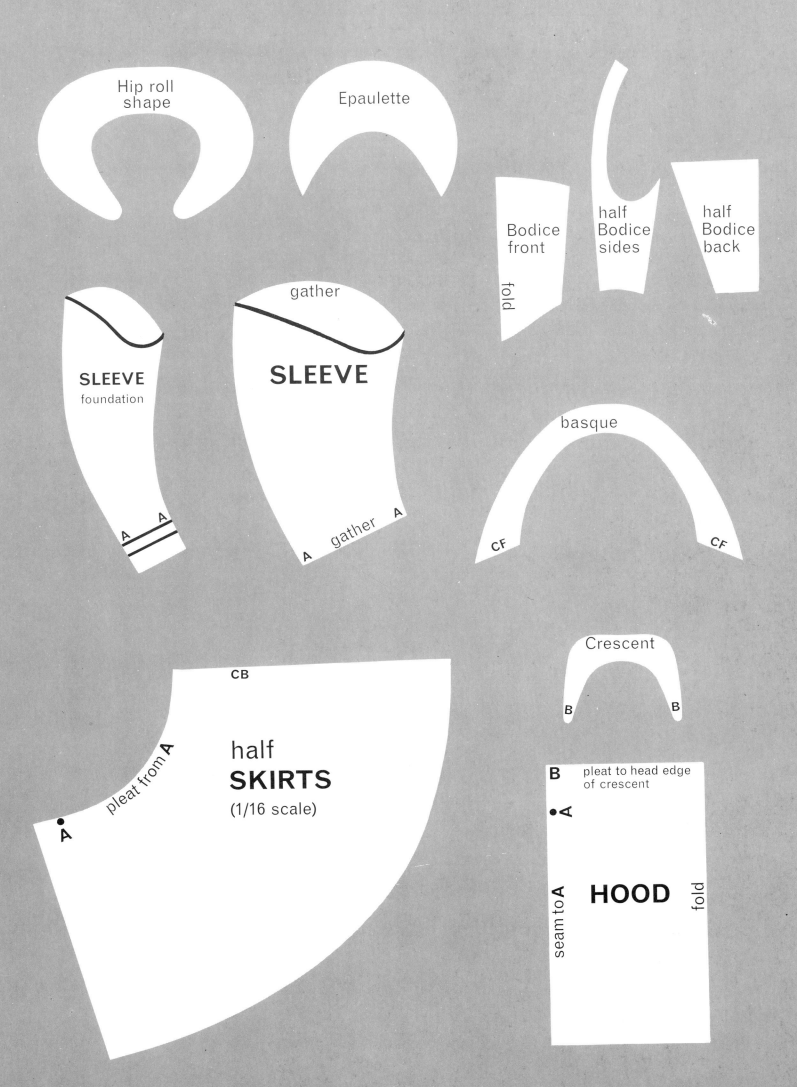

Hip roll shape

Epaulette

Bodice front
fold

half Bodice sides

half Bodice back

SLEEVE foundation

gather

SLEEVE

A A

A gather A

basque

CF

CF

half **SKIRTS** (1/16 scale)

CB

pleat from A

A

Crescent

B B

B
pleat to head edge of crescent

A

seam to A

HOOD

fold

1585 Elizabeth I

Fabrics: Similar to the previous fashion.

Colours: Soft colours — beige, carnation pink, greens, honeys, golds and greys. Little or no blue (relegated to servants and lower classes).

Decoration: Similar to previous fashion with profusion of embroidery, often raised and incorporating metallic braids, in formal interlocking patterns, with naturalistic plant and animal forms frequently worked into areas of the same design.

Magnificent lace, drawn-thread work, cut work, reticella, punto-in-aria or bobbin, further enriches the costume — the early simple bands of geometric patterns worked into the linen are now edged with large scallops, triangles, circles and squares. These rich patterns are formed by cutting the linen away leaving only a framework of threads to support the needlework filling of geometric forms.

Padding and restriction, men: Padding, boning and stiffening used in all garments. Doublet front develops a very large hanging stuffed paunch, whaleboned to make it stand away from the body.

Padding and restriction, women: The corset and bodice, both with a very low V pointed waistline, are heavily boned and busked (pieces of wood shaped to fit and make rigid the front parts of the bodice). The farthingale, a large oval wheel-shaped hoop (constructed of iron, wood or whalebone), supported by a bolster or hip pad (secured to the corsets), replaces the bell-shaped petticoat to extend the skirts well out and away from the hips. Sleeves are heavily bombasted. Padded rolls hide the join of sleeve to armhole.

Movement, men: Formal. Natural movement is made impossible by the excess of padding.

Movement, women: Rigidly controlled and limited by the size of skirt, sleeves, long corsets and bodice, the shoulder rolls, and supportasse.

Men

General characteristics: Large peascod belly. The trunk hose are reduced in size to a short bombasted and paned skirt (pansid slops).

Under garments — similar to the previous fashion.

Doublet — the large peascod belly, hanging well over the belt, is forced out by whalebone busks and stiffened with layers of parchment glued together (as much as 4 or 5 pounds of bombast placed in the cavity). Diminutive skirts are attached to the waistline, and the C.F. opening is fastened with rich and elaborate buttons. Falling bands and cuffs frequently replace the suite of ruffs. Surface of the doublet decorated with pricking and piercings.

Upper hosen — pansid slops worn over Venetians (tight fitting knee breeches). The codpiece disappears.

Stockings — silk knitted stockings, extending over the lower parts of the Venetians, are protected by a second pair of stockings (shorter in length) made of fabric or fine leather pounced and

pricked in elaborate geometric designs. Both pairs of stockings are gartered below the knee.

Shoes — the front of the shoe, neater and closely fitting the shape of the foot, is cut to form a long and stiffened narrow tongue. Footwear, delicately pricked, is usually of the same colour as the stockings.

Coat — as an alternative to the cape — a short, flared hip-length coat worn (with revers and a sailor collar).

Hats — the crown, much taller and often stiffened, resembles an extended bowler. Trimmings of twists of fabric, jewelled brooches, and feathers.

Hair — similar to the previous fashion.

Accessories — similar to the previous fashion.

Women

General characteristics: Large extended ankle-length skirts, narrow body, very low pointed waist, and very broad shoulders.

Under garments — the corset (laced down C.B.) projects out from the waist into a basque skirt and a series of tabs to which the bum roll or bolster of leather is attached. The petticoats, placed over the rigid oval of the farthingale, are stiffened to extend the skirts further out at the ankles. The chemise, worn under the corsets, is never seen.

Gown — body parts are elaborately fastened down the C.F. A supported circular lace collar, fastened to the high neckband, totally frames the head. The two sets of sleeves, one large and padded and terminating in lace cuffs and diminutive ruffs, the other ground length and open, are laced into the armholes. The shoulder rolls are richly decorated. The skirts are pleated, and cut in a deep curved opening at the front to reveal the richly embroidered petticoat beneath.

Stockings — knitted (silk stockings).

Shoes — similar to men's.

Hair — (wigs of bright colours worn) crimped, frizzed or curled, dressed high and out on either side of the head and plucked away in front to give a high forehead. The back hair is braided and covered by a cap of lace or linen — the front edge wired out and starched to form a double crescent.

Accessories — profusion of formally tied bows, earrings, brooches, necklaces and beads — as many as eight or nine strings falling to the waist. Richly decorated gauntlet gloves, stick fans.

Notes on patterns: Men

Shirt — cuffs and collar are attached to neck and wristbands or, for theatre purposes, sewn directly to the doublet.

Doublet — constructed in a similar manner to the previous fashion. The fronts are more heavily boned and stiffened (possibly with light papier mâché), and the waistline of the top surface is gathered or darted at the C.F.s to form a large pouch. Add a boned C.F. placket to both lining and top surface. Interline and pad sleeves.

Coat — interline throughout with light padding. The sleeve is composed of a padded foundation, a lining gathered at the head and wrist, and a top fabric — fastened (Ionic) at regular intervals down its outside seam.

Venetians — (use the foundation pattern of the trunk hose and canions of the previous fashion omitting the codpiece). Interline with a light layer of padding, adding a C.F. opening.

Pansid slops — (add a C.F. buttoned opening). Gently pad the foundation, increasing the quantity of padding at skirt edge. The panes are folded around the foundation and pleated or eased to the waist edge. The waist edge is eased to the lower edge of the waistband.

Notes on patterns: Women

Corsets — add tabs and bone throughout.

Hip bolster — a large hip bolster (padded or made of cork) should be fastened to the tabs of the corset to support the farthingale.

Farthingale — (add placket at C.F.) insert heavy whalebone or an iron hoop to hold out the top circumference of the farthingale. Reinforce with strips of whalebone radiating from the waist edge to the circumference, like the spokes of a wheel. Place waist edge to a waistband or insert strong drawstring. The top of the drum should be lightly padded, the skirts stiffened.

Petticoat — (use farthingale pattern) the embroidered front panel should be cut to lie flat.

Gown — heavily bone the seams of the bodice. Insert wooden busks down the front edges (edge to edge hook and eye fastening). The sleeves should be heavily interlined with padding to remove as much wrinkling as possible. The padded shoulder roll, set at an angle well out from the shoulder, is caught at intervals to the armhole. The skirts, bullet-pleated to a waistband, are fastened at the C.F. It may be necessary to cut away the fronts of the skirt and secure them to the petticoat in order to preserve the character of the deep curved opening.

Supportasse and standing collar — the supportasse should be made from heavy wire and set at an angle to the neckband of the bodice. The standing collar should be starched and wired to lie flat. For theatre purposes the standing collar and supportasse could be made as one, attached to a neckband, and hooked and eyed down the C.B.

Cap — wire edge and curve to form a double crescent in front.

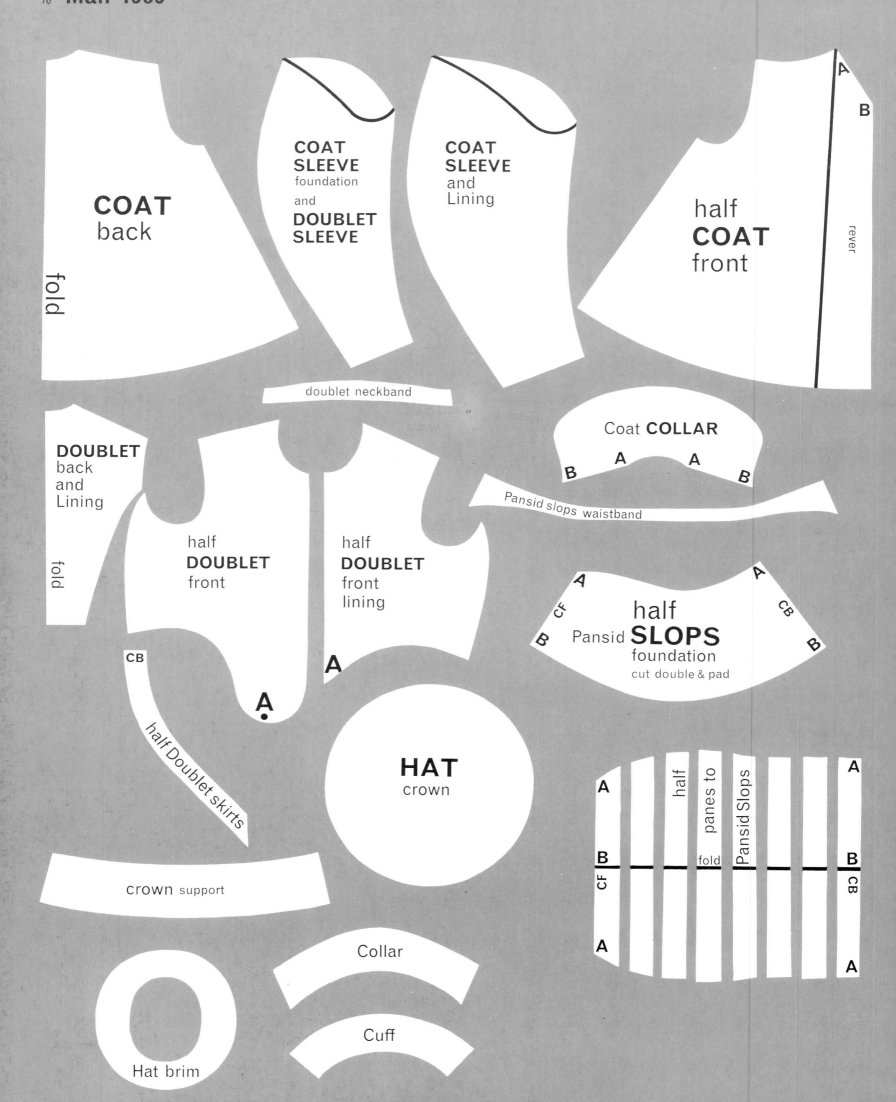

COAT back

fold

COAT SLEEVE foundation and **DOUBLET SLEEVE**

COAT SLEEVE and Lining

half **COAT** front

A

B

rever

doublet neckband

DOUBLET back and Lining

fold

half **DOUBLET** front

half **DOUBLET** front lining

Coat **COLLAR**

B A A B

Pansid slops waistband

A

CF

B

A

CB

B

half Pansid **SLOPS** foundation cut double & pad

CB

half Doublet skirts

A

A.

HAT crown

crown support

A

half panes to fold Pansid Slops

A

B

CF

A

B

CB

A

Collar

Cuff

Hat brim

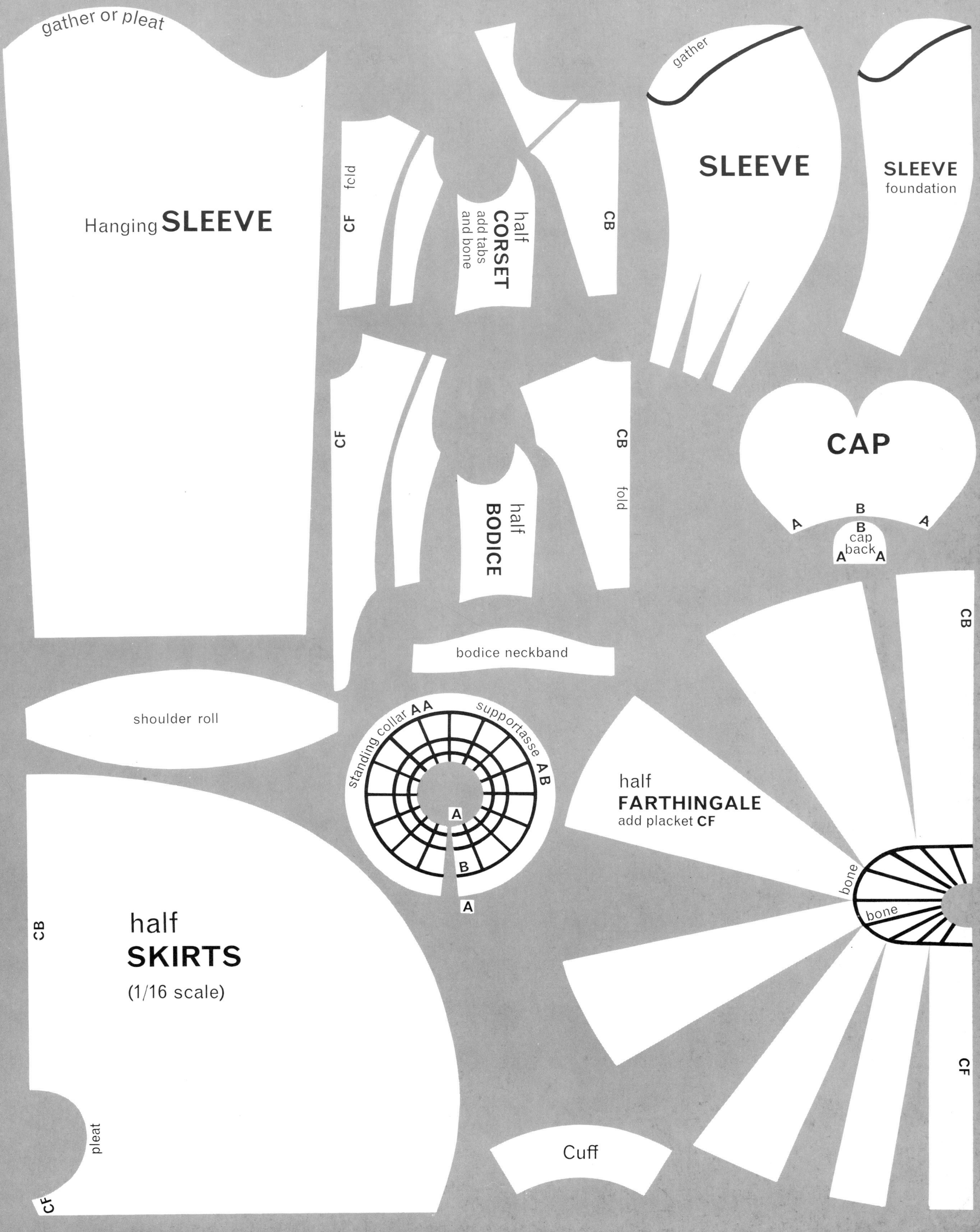

gather or pleat

Hanging **SLEEVE**

CF fcld

CF

half **CORSET**
add tabs
and bone

CB

half **BODICE**

CB fold

SLEEVE

SLEEVE
foundation

gather

CAP

A   B   A
B
cap
A back A

CB

bodice neckband

shoulder roll

standing collar **A A**   supportasse **A B**

A

B

A

half
FARTHINGALE
add placket **CF**

bone

bone

CB

half
SKIRTS

(1/16 scale)

CF

pleat

Cuff

CF

1595 Elizabeth I

Fabrics: Similar to the previous fashion. Noticeable increase in soft "novelty" fabrics — tissues, gauzes (sprinkled with sequins), light-weight silks, etc.

Colours: Much lighter and brighter range of colours including pinks, greys, oyster, silvers and white.

Decoration: Embroidery, appliqué, braiding, slashing and cutting, together with jewelled ornaments, combined to form a very rich surface texture.

Padding and restriction, men: Similar to the previous fashion.

Padding and restriction, women: Similar to the previous fashion. The farthingale now resembles a circular drum.

Movement, men: Lyric and romantic. Legs are given prominence, being totally revealed in tight-fitting hosen.

Movement, women: Similar to the previous fashion. Arms, due to the excess of bombasting, size of sleeve and great shoulder roll, are severely restricted in movement and held well away from the body. The lower part of the arm always rests on the wheel of the farthingale.

Men

General characteristics: Essentially a youthful costume. A large, heavily bombasted doublet worn with diminutive trunk hose (pansid slops). From the waist down the body is covered in tight-fitting hosen. Very large standing ruffs or collars.

Under garments — similar to the previous fashion.

Doublet — similar to the previous fashion.

Pansid slops — very small.

Nether hosen — knitted or made up in material cut on the bias.

Cloak — near circular with revers and collar. Short in length — sometimes barely covering the buttocks.

Shoes — elegant in shape, with a pointed toe and low broad heel. The top part of the shoe, cut away at the sides (developing into straps for fastening), forms a narrow tongue over the instep.

Hat — less stiff and worn at an acute angle on the back of the head.

Hair — combed away from the forehead, is fuller, curled and frizzed. (A small light beard and moustache worn by the man of fashion.)

Accessories — similar to the previous fashion. A locket hanging from a long chain or cord is worn about the neck.

Women

General characteristics: Entire costume is more feminine — light and lyrical in shape, dominated by large ruffs and collars, large sleeves and the drum-shaped farthingale.

Under garments — basically similar to the previous fashion. The farthingale, supported by the hip pad, bum roll, or bolster, is set at an angle to dip down in the front to well below stomacher point.

Gown — composed of body parts, stomacher, sleeves and skirts. The body parts, cut with a low square neckline and following the shape of the corset, terminate at the waist edge in a series of tabs (picadils). The stomacher, heavily boned, and covering the C.F. fastening of the body parts, is secured with pins, brooches or ties. The square neckline is framed by a large open ruff, frequently wired, of one or more layers, and edged with lace. (Fine gauze or tissue tucked into the sides of the neckline hides the join of ruff to bodice.) The open hanging sleeves, wired and stiffened to spring away from the armholes, fall to the ground like massive wings. The ankle-length skirts, set in pleats, are frequently arranged and secured around the outer edge of the wheel of the farthingale to form a top not unlike the closed ruff (Frounce).

Veil — a very large transparent veil wired about the shoulders to form butterfly wings. The method of cut is dubious. It is possible that a corner of the veil was placed over the forehead and gathered into a small cap, with the remaining part of the veil wired out to produce the two wing forms (tied under the armpits) and a cape to fall down the back to the ground. It is equally possible that this was not a veil but a very full cape of transparent material with the top parts stretched over a cane foundation to form the large collar — worn under the great ruff, and tied or pinned to the front parts of the bodice.

Stockings — similar to the previous fashion.

Shoes — similar to the previous fashion.

Hair and head dress — hair is brushed well away from the forehead, over a crescent-shaped padded roll, and frizzed or curled at the temples and sides. The back hair is coiled into a bun at the nape of the neck or on the top of the head. Delicate and richly made ornaments decorate the hair. Hats rarely seen.

Accessories — finger rings, baldricks of chains and beads, hip length and short necklaces, pendants, earrings, bracelets of several ropes of beads, stick fans. Real flowers and little jewelled insects decorate the ruff.

Notes on patterns: Men

Doublet — construct as in previous fashion. The top surface of the doublet should be made up in broad bands of fabric, plaited together and then cut to the required pattern.

Pansid slops — construct as in previous fashion.

Cloak — similar in cut to the pattern of 1560 (omit sleeves).

Ruff — (C.B. fastening), wear with supportasse. 32 sets of pleats (diagram shows arrangement) are required to form the ruff which should be starched and set to a $\frac{1}{2}$ inch wide neckband. The outer edge of the ruff can be wired to help control the pleat formation.

Notes on patterns: Women

Corsets — similar to the previous pattern. Cut with a low neckline.

Farthingale wheel — (support with a hip bolster), attach to a waistband cut to follow the line of the waist of the bodice (plunging down in front to a deep point). Form a C.B. placket. Insert very heavy whalebone, cane, or a steel or iron hoop to the outer circumference of the wheel and pad the top surface.

Petticoat — cut to follow the shape of the farthingale and gather to the waist by a drawstring.

Gown — (C.F. edge to edge fastening) bone the bodice. The tabs, joining the waistline, should be so positioned that they lie flat on the top surface of the farthingale wheel. The stomacher, stiffened, is securely fastened to the fronts of the bodice with ribbon ties or large hooks and eyes. Pad the sleeves, adding an inner structure of whalebone or cane to make them stand up and well away from the armholes. The hanging sleeves are wired and stiffened. A shoulder roll covers the join of sleeve to armhole. The waist edge of the skirts are attached to the waist edge of the farthingale wheel, or to a separate waistband (C.F. opening) which follows the line of the pointed front of the bodice. The frounce can be permanently arranged and sewn to a lining, or gathered up by inserting a drawstring.

Open ruff — (one or more tiers) wire outer edge to control the arrangement of pleats. Attach supporter to the collar band of the bodice.

Veil — gather the transparent collar to the foundation of heavy wire or cane. The back part of the veil, 9 feet wide and 5 feet deep, is gathered to the neck edge B.B. The points B.B. are fastened securely to the fronts of the bodice, under the open ruff.

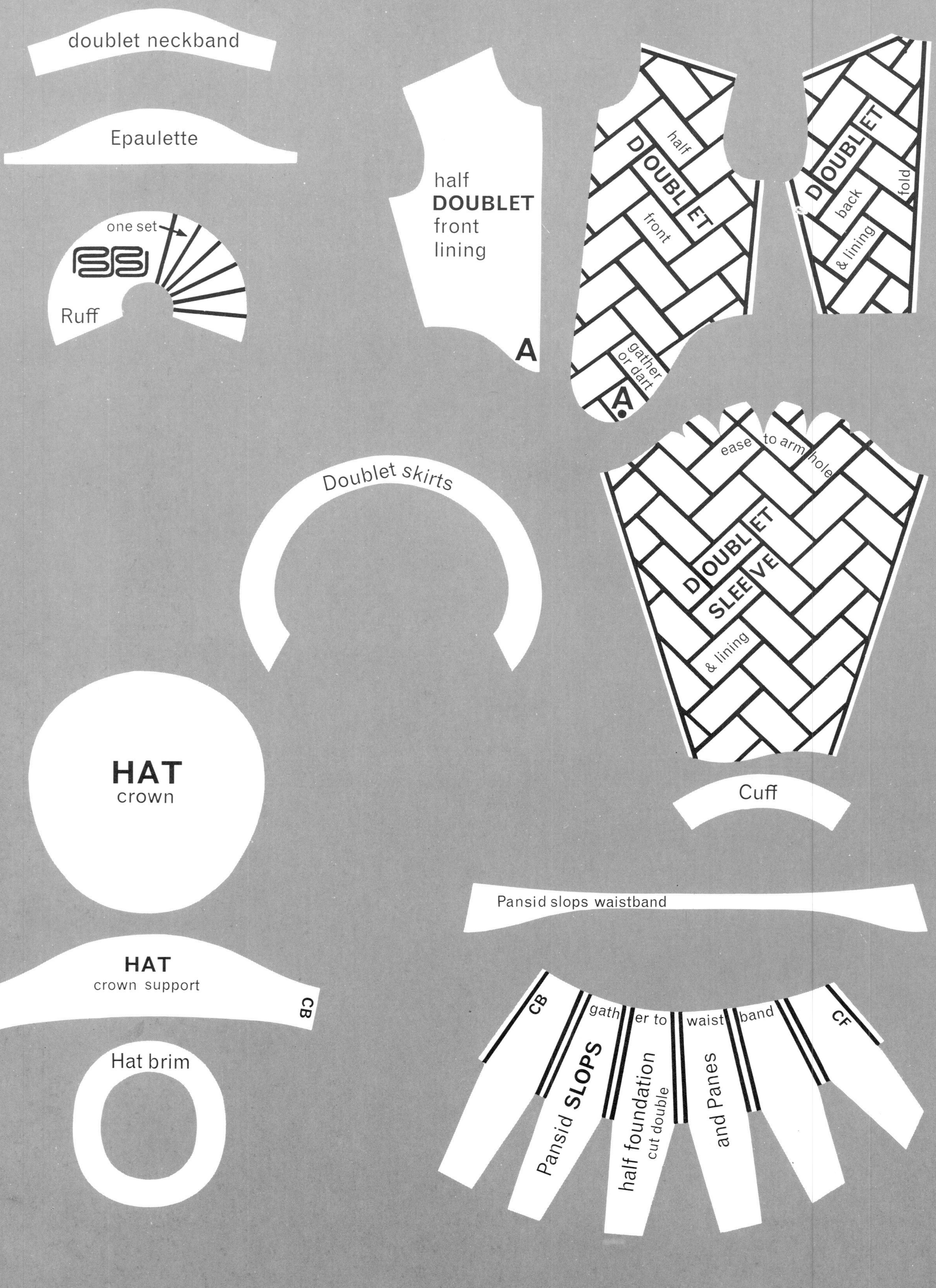

doublet neckband

Epaulette

one set

Ruff

half
DOUBLET
front
lining

A

half
DOUBLET
front

gather
or dart

A.

DOUBLET
back
& lining
fold

Doublet *skirts*

ease to armhole

DOUBLET
SLEEVE
& lining

HAT
crown

Cuff

Pansid slops waistband

HAT
crown support

CB

CB

Hat brim

CB

gather to waist band

CF

Pansid **SLOPS**

half foundation
cut double

and Panes

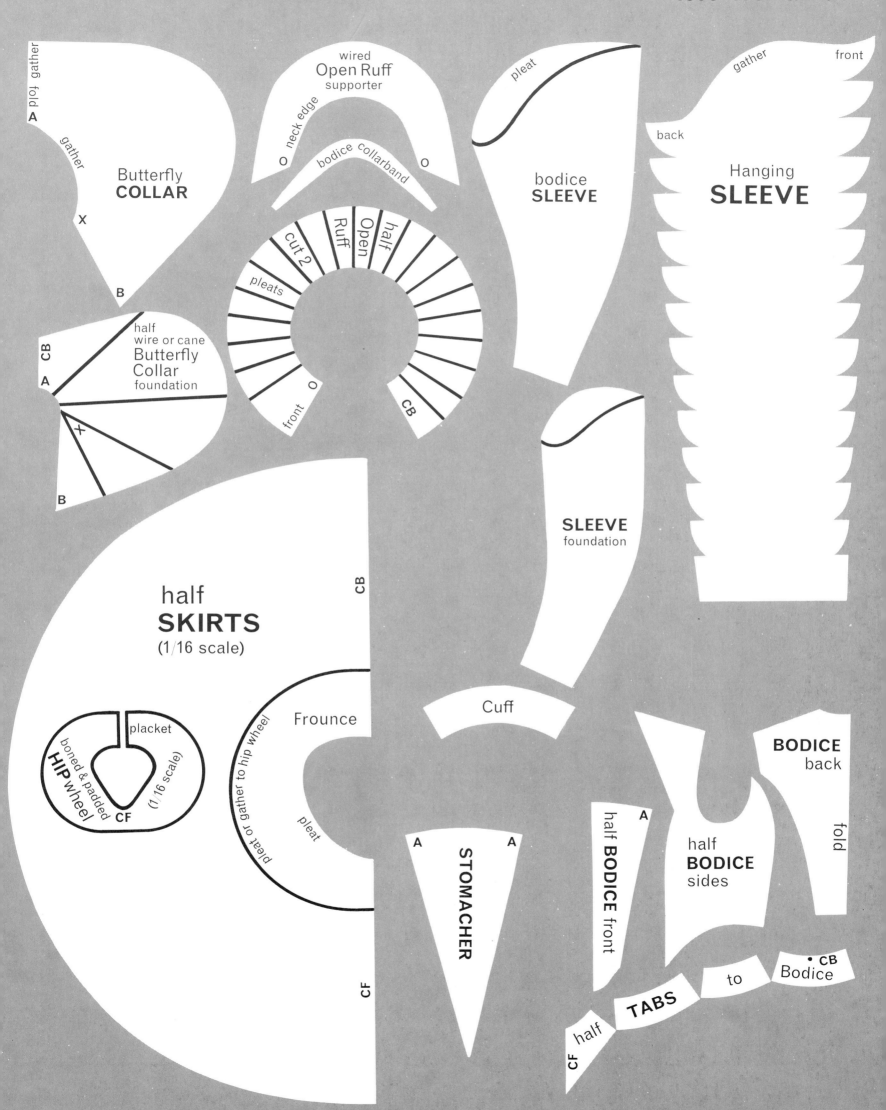

Butterfly **COLLAR**

A fold gather

gather

X

B

CB

A

half
wire or cane
Butterfly
Collar
foundation

X

B

wired
Open Ruff
supporter

O neck edge

O bodice collarband O

half Open Ruff Cut 2

pleats

front O

CB

pleat

bodice **SLEEVE**

gather front

back

Hanging **SLEEVE**

SLEEVE foundation

half **SKIRTS**
(1/16 scale)

CB

placket

boned & padded **HIP** wheel (1/16 scale)

CF

Frounce

pleat or gather to hip wheel

pleat

Cuff

A A

STOMACHER

CF

half **BODICE** front

A

half **BODICE** sides

BODICE back

fold

CF half

TABS

to

• CB Bodice

1605 James I

Fabrics: Stiffer and heavier.

Colours: Wide range of reds, buffs, browns and yellows.

Decoration: Embroidery, braiding, slashing, pricking, etc. covers the costume in geometric patterns, zig-zags and stripes.

Padding and restriction, men: The large peascod belly disappears. The body parts are stiffly interlined and boned.

Padding and restriction, women: Similar to the previous fashion. Length of the corset is shorter, the placing of the wheel farthingale higher.

Movement, men: Less elegant and poised than the previous fashion. The movement of the arm is restricted by a narrow, tightly-fitting sleeve.

Movement, women: Stiff and awkward, lacking lyricism and grace. The high position of the drum-shaped farthingale forces the arms up and out into a sharp angle — the elbows resting on the back parts of the wheel.

Men

General characteristics: Clumsy and awkward, lacking balance and sense of proportion. The doublet is short-waisted, the neckline frequently cut low, the sleeves are very tight, and the small slops, giving width and bulk to the hips, narrow to open tubes at the knee.

Under garments — similar to the previous fashion.

Doublet — all seams and edges are heavily braided. A falling band (collar) is attached to the low open neckline. The waistline terminates in tabs. The armhole curves inwards towards the chest. The join of the sleeve is covered by an epaulette which rises up and away from the shoulder line to fit closely around the upper arm.

Small slops — heavily pleated to a waistband and tied or hooked and eyed to the waistline of the doublet.

Cloak — longer in length.

Stockings — supported by large swagged bands of material knotted below the knee.

Shoes — similar to the previous fashion. The fastening of the latchets over the instep is concealed by a large elaborate rosette — often of gold or silver lace.

Hats — stiff tall crowns, trimmed with wide hatbands and clusters of formally arranged feathers — the brim often pinned up in front.

Hair — longer and brushed away from the forehead with one side grown to fall in ringlets or soft waves onto the chest. Beards are frequently very small.

Accessories — gauntlet gloves, shoe rosettes, a single earring. A baldrick, of fine material terminating in a large bow on the hip, holds the sword.

Women

General characteristics: Stiff, angular, ill-proportioned adaptation of the previous fashion. The farthingale no longer dips gracefully to the stomacher point but is set square to a higher waistline. Garments frequently give the appearance of being taut and a size too small for the wearer.

Under garments — similar to the previous fashion. The corset terminates at natural waist in a short sharp point.

Gown — the body parts, (elaborately fastened dowr. C.F.) follow the shape of the corset. The low-curved, deep neckline frequently exposes the breasts — partly covered, though not always, by a piece of semi-transparent material. A standing collar of lace, wired and stiffened, frames the head. (Join of the collar to the back part of the neckline is hidden with a filling of fine material.) Sleeves, accompanied by the epaulette and the hanging open sleeve, are similar in cut to the men's and terminate in single or double cuffs. Skirts, less flared than the previous fashion, are open down the C.F. and fastened at intervals with rosettes and brooches. The pleated frounce, of the same material as the skirts, is frequently undecorated and cut separately.

Stockings — similar to the previous fashion.

Shoes — with wedge soles.

Head dress — similar to men's.

Hair — brushed up and away from the forehead to extend over pads to form a dome or egg shape. Hair styles are stark, simple and unornamented or very elaborate, exaggerated and artificial — tied and arranged in little sections with ribbons, rosettes, brooches, etc. The hairline is softened by back combing and frizzing.

Accessories — (used with little taste or discrimination) lace at neck, neckline and wrists. Hair ornaments, elaborate necklaces, pendants, bracelets, earrings, rosettes and bows of ribbons — decorative or functional. The fan, larger and composed of as many as a dozen ostrich feathers, hangs from a ribbon attached to the waistline. A piece of decorated, very fine material is frequently knotted and swagged about the upper part of one arm. Gloves — with or without gauntlet.

Notes on patterns: Men

Doublet — (add button fastening to C.F.s.) Ease the top surface front waistline to the front waistline of the lining. Tabs and fronts of the doublet require extra stiffening and whaleboning. Sleeve head should tightly fit the armhole.

Small slops — add extra stiffening to waist edge of the body parts, bullet-pleat and set to the lower edge of the waistband. (For theatre purposes a soft hip pad could be worn to give extra width at the hips.)

Hat — stiffen the crown either with a papier mâché foundation or by wiring the seams of the eight sections and inserting an interlining of light padding.

Notes on patterns: Women

Corsets — (lace at C.B. and bone throughout). Adapt bodice pattern by adding tabs.

Farthingale wheel — similar in construction to the previous pattern. The V point of the waistband is severely shortened to raise the front of the wheel to a much higher position.

Gown — the bodice, with C.F. edge to edge fastening, is lightly boned throughout. The epaulette should be sewn to roll away from the armhole to give height to the shoulder point. The small collar band requires stiffening to support the wired standing collar — darted to fit the neckline of the bodice. Insert whalebones in the darts to act as stiffeners to hold the collar up all round. A second collar of lace lies over the surface concealing the darts. Pleat the skirts to a waistband (C.F. opening). The frounce, composed of two thicknesses of material, is pleated along the waist edge and sewn to the waistband of the skirts proper or attached to its own waistband. (To achieve the formal appearance of the frounce lightly tie-catch each pleat.)

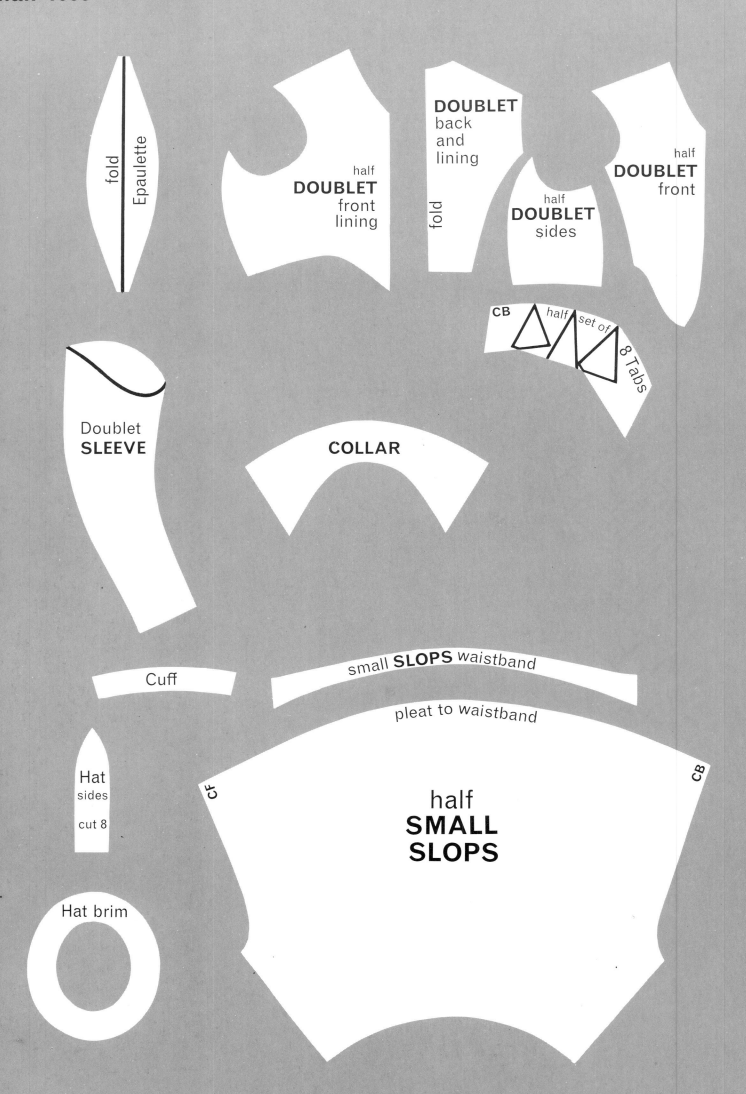

fold

Epaulette

half **DOUBLET** front lining

DOUBLET back and lining

fold

half **DOUBLET** sides

half **DOUBLET** front

CB half set of 8 Tabs

Doublet **SLEEVE**

COLLAR

Cuff

small **SLOPS** waistband

pleat to waistband

Hat sides cut 8

CF

CB

half **SMALL SLOPS**

Hat brim

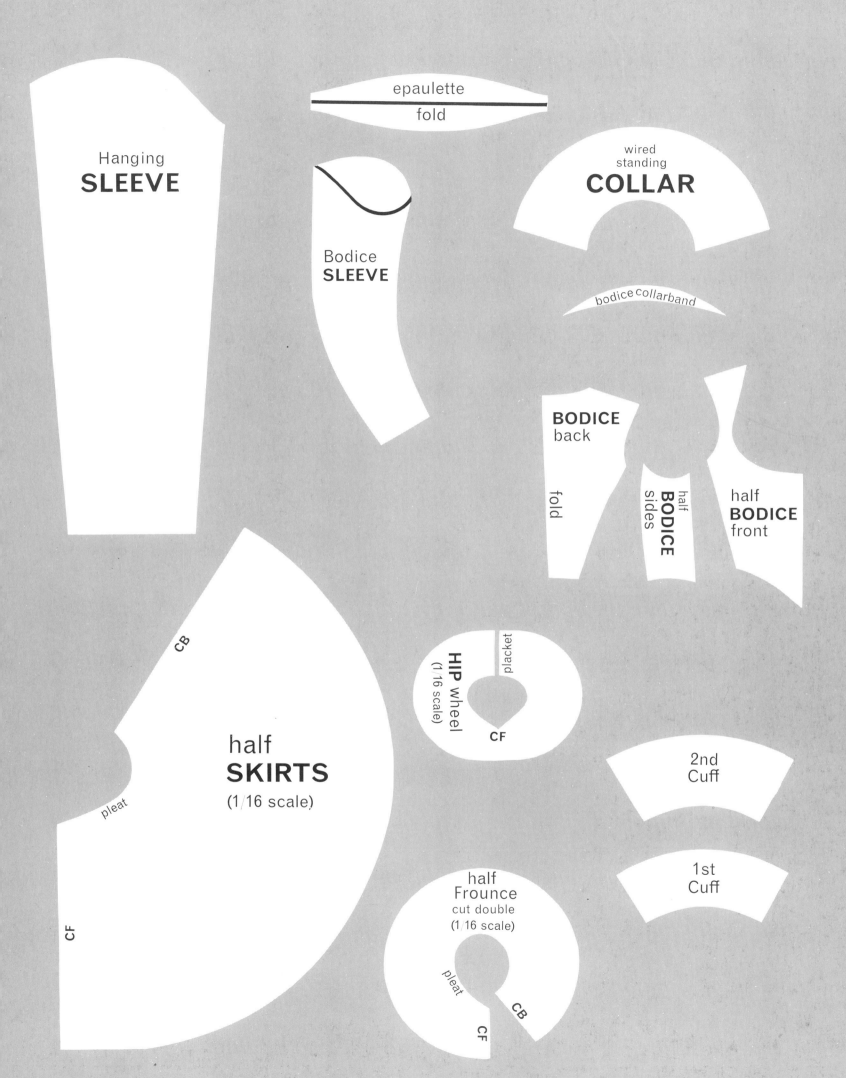

Hanging
SLEEVE

epaulette
fold

Bodice
SLEEVE

wired
standing
COLLAR

bodice collarband

BODICE
back

fold

half
BODICE
sides

half
BODICE
front

CB

half
SKIRTS
(1/16 scale)

pleat

CF

placket

HIP
wheel
(1/16 scale)

CF

2nd
Cuff

1st
Cuff

half
Frounce
cut double
(1/16 scale)

pleat

CB

CF

1610 James I

Fabrics: A return to finer and softer materials.

Colours: Similar to the previous fashion. Materials are frequently light in tone and decorated with dark embroidery.

Decoration: Rich embroidery, using motifs based on plant and flower forms, ranging from the very delicate and realistic to the bold and highly stylised. Bows, rosettes, ribbons and lace.

Padding and restriction, men: The doublet with high V-shaped waist is boned and stiffened — the sleeves and trunk-hose lightly padded.

Padding and restriction, women: Corsets narrow the waist and show signs of shaping to increase the size of the bosom. The farthingale disappears but the bum roll is retained as a foundation to keep the skirts, forming a soft bell shape, away from the body.

Movement, men: Natural and less awkward.

Movement, women: Swifter, less restricted and decidely more natural.

Men

General characteristics: Less eccentric in proportion and style. The doublet, trunk hose, and the Venetians or canions, match in fabric, colour, and decoration.

Under garments — similar to the previous fashion.

Doublet — high waisted, with diminutive peascod belly, and with all the seams braided. Epaulettes follow the slope of the shoulders. Lightly padded sleeves terminate in short cuffs. A series of overlapping tabs edge the waistline. The supportasse, two or more layers of standing ruff, and a falling band (darted to fit shape of the neck) are all tied, and set to a neckband.

Trunk hose — (heavy bombasting disappears) pleated and gathered to the breeches or Venetians.

Cloak — similar to the previous fashion.

Stockings — worn over the breeches or Venetians and cross gartered.

Shoes — similar to the previous fashion with a wedge sole or heel. The latchets are fastened with ribbon ties.

Hats — broad brimmed, undecorated, high-crowned hats.

Hair — ear length, cut full at the sides and back, softly waved, and brushed back from the forehead. Beards and moustaches (of various shape) will continue to be worn until the end of this century.

Accessories — gloves, broad ribbons worn around the neck holding miniatures, lockets, etc. Narrow waist belts of leather or ribbon.

Women

General characteristics: The waist higher, the sleeves less tightly fitting (frequently open and fastened at intervals with bows or rosettes), the skirt round in form and open down the C.F.

Under Garments — chemise rarely seen. The bum roll, fastened to the tabs of the corset, is worn under several petticoats.

Gown — the bodice, similar in shape to the previous fashion, is buttoned through at the C.F. Epaulettes emphasise narrow sloping shoulders. The standing ruff and supportasse are fastened to a neckband. The sleeve is composed of an inner sleeve, an open sleeve and a hanging sleeve (reaching the ground) — the open sleeve terminating above the wrist in near elbow-length double or treble cuffs. Open, pleated, skirts clear the ground.

Stockings — similar to the men's.

Shoes — a heavy small heel supports the foot, and a large rosette, frequently decorated with sequins, covers the latchet fastening.

Hair — softly and loosely brushed away from the forehead with the back hair arranged in a bun. Jewelled ornaments, feathers, rosettes, etc., continue to decorate the hair.

Hats — lace caps or broad-brimmed, high-crowned black hats (similar to men's).

Accessories — jewellery and body ornaments. A charming fashion is the securing of the finger ring to a narrow black cord, passing the cord up the back of the hand and tying it about the wrist to form a bracelet. The folding fan of wood, paper, or leather replaces the stick fan.

Notes on patterns: Men

Doublet — make up as in previous patterns. The falling collar is darted at the neck edge (for theatre purposes, instead of tying around the neck, sew to the lower edge of the ruff neckband).

Ruff — 3 tiers (worn with a small supportasse). Each tier, $2\frac{1}{2}$ inches wide (unfolded) and 80 inches long, is set in $1\frac{1}{2}$ inch pleats, with a depth of 1 inch, to overlap each other and give a distance at the neck edge of $\frac{1}{2}$ inch between each pleat (32 pleats in all). Mount finished ruff on $\frac{3}{4}$ inch wide neckband.

Venetians and trunk hose — the trunk hose, interlined and not padded, are pleated and gathered to the Venetians around the lower edge of the waistband and around the hips.

Hat — basically similar in construction to the previous pattern.

Notes on patterns: Women

Corset — bone throughout and back-lace.

Under petticoat — gather with drawstring.

Top petticoat — gather with drawstring. Gathering should be arranged at the sides and back, leaving the front to fall straight.

Gown — add a C.F. buttoned fastening to the bodice. The armhole should be small and tightly fitting. The under sleeve is gathered at the head and at the wrist to the sleeve proper, which is left open down its length and secured with ribbon ties. The epaulettes, separate tabs folded back on themselves, are cut to follow the line of the armhole. Skirts are arranged in small bullet pleats and set to a narrow waistband — fastening at the C.F. The standing ruff is composed of three tiers, set in box pleats, and like the supportasse, fastened down the C.F. or C.B.

Lace — for theatre purposes, the very rich lace can be simulated by painting the negative pattern of the lace on to linen in a similar colour to the garment worn beneath.

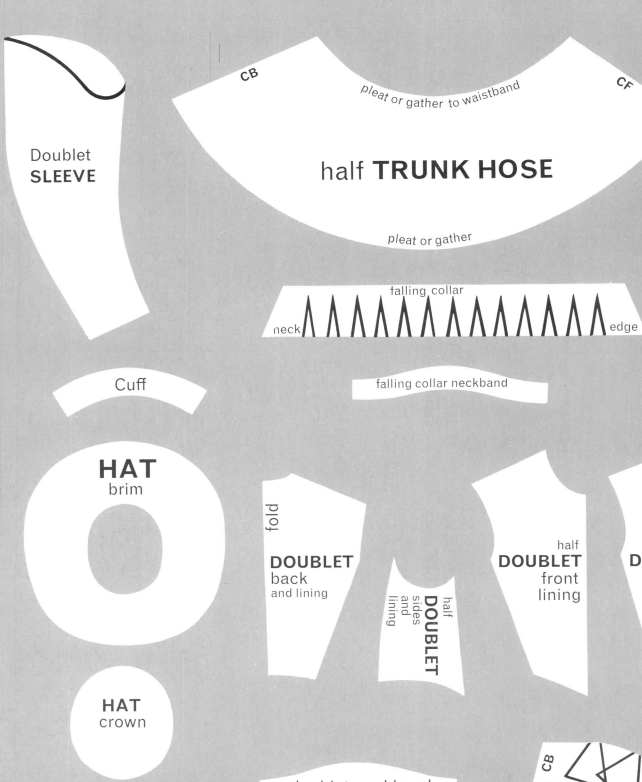

Doublet **SLEEVE**

half **TRUNK HOSE**

CB

CF

pleat or gather to waistband

pleat or gather

falling collar

neck

edge

falling collar neckband

Cuff

HAT
brim

fold

DOUBLET
back
and lining

half
DOUBLET
sides
and
lining

half
DOUBLET
front
lining

half
DOUBLET
front

HAT
crown

CB

half set
of 8
Tabs

doublet neckband

Hat
sides
cut 8

armhole edge
Epaulette

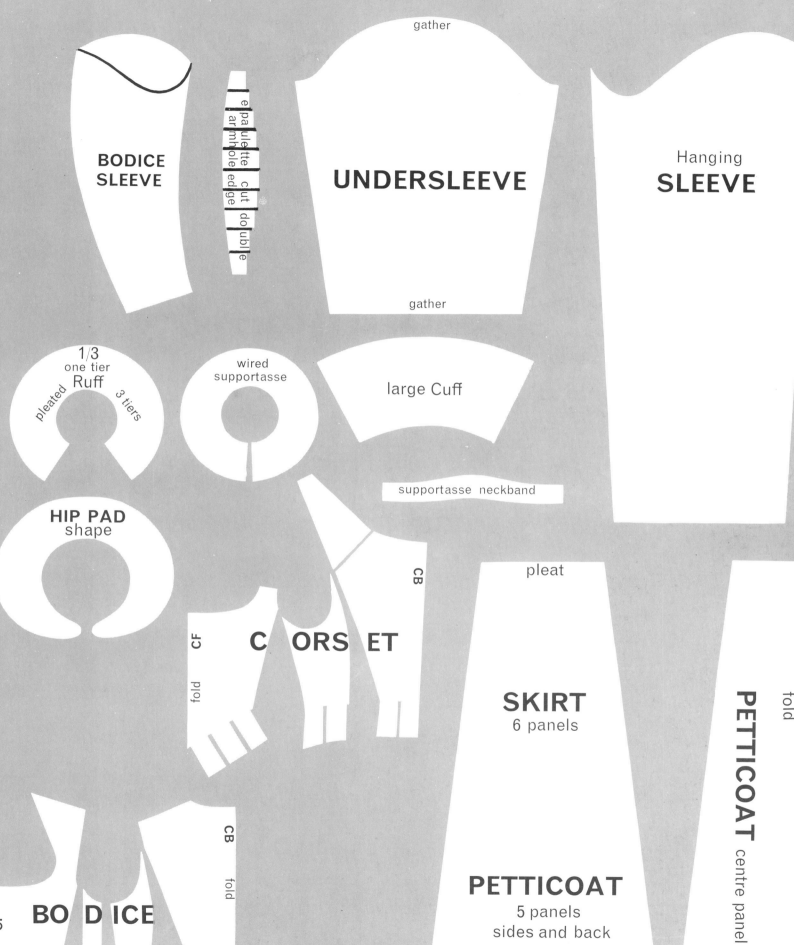

BODICE SLEEVE

epaulette cut double : armhole edge

UNDERSLEEVE

gather

gather

Hanging SLEEVE

1/3 one tier Ruff

pleated 3 tiers

wired supportasse

large Cuff

supportasse neckband

HIP PAD shape

pleat

CB

CF

fold

C ORS ET

SKIRT
6 panels

PETTICOAT
centre panel

fold

CB

fold

CF

BO D ICE

PETTICOAT
5 panels
sides and back

1620 James 1

Fabrics: Substantial and heavy cloths, velvets, silks and taffetas. Gold and silver lace.

Colours: Dark, rich and sombre.

Decoration: Black and coloured embroidery of more modest and conservative design. Very rich lace magnificently displayed — standing collar, ruffs, deep cuffs, women's caps, neckline edgings, etc. Braids.

Padding and restriction, men: Triangles of buckram or pasteboard, stiffening the doublet fronts, form a vertical ridge to the body when the doublet is buttoned up. The armhole, scooped to form a deep curve, restricts the movement of the arm.

Padding and restriction, women: Small boned corsets and a hip pad.

Movement, men: The figure is rigid from the head to the waist — standing collar and supportasse, stiffened doublet, tight armholes and sleeves. The high curved heel of the shoe, placed well under the foot, determines posture and walk.

Movement, women: Decorous. The small pointed heel of the shoe determines posture and walk.

Men

General characteristics: Small tight body parts, very large bloomer-like trunk hose.

Doublet — narrow waisted, forming a deep point at the C.F., and edged with a series of overlapping tabs. Epaulettes are shaped to fit the small armhole. The lower half of the tight-fitting sleeve is covered by a very deep lace cuff. The punto-in-aria lace is repeated in the semi-circular standing collar — displayed on its supportasse.

Trunk hose — large and baggy, gathered in above the knees and laced to the waistline of the doublet.

Cloak — near circular and knee length.

Stockings — elaborately embroidered clocks, with designs based on plant and flower forms, decorate the inside and outside of the leg.

Shoes — the curved stocky heel, set well under the foot, supports the shoe (embroidered and decorated). The front is cut away to form a narrow tongue. Latchets, fastening the shoe, are covered by enormous and elaborate rosettes (sometimes of gold or silver lace and sprinkled with sequins).

Hats — similar to the fashions of the last 20 years.

Hair — brushed back from the forehead to the nape of the neck and dressed to give width to the temples and sides of the head.

Accessories — walking sticks, deep gauntlet gloves — braided and fringed, lockets, finger rings. Very large, swagged and richly decorated garters knotted below the knee.

Women

General characterictics: A simple, modest and domestic costume enriched by magnificent lace and rich embroidery — a small, loose-fitting, buttoned-through bodice or coat worn with full pleated skirts.

Under garments — similar to the previous fashion.

Bodice — terminates a little below natural waistline at the C.F. in a gently curved point. Godets, inserted at intervals around the waistline, give the bodice a skirted and high-waisted appearance. The deeply scooped out armholes are small and covered by close-fitting epaulettes. These little coats are frequently made in linen and covered with black or coloured embroidery. Punto-in-aria lace, edging the very deep cuffs of the narrow sleeves, also edges the low curved neckline. The series of falling ruffs are fastened high at the back of the neck — the band ties brought forward over the chest, knotted, and tucked into the neckline of the bodice front.

Skirts — ankle length and heavily pleated to a waistband. The skirt is usually of a plain fabric decorated with horizontal bands of braiding and embroidery.

Stockings — similar to men's.

Shoes — similar to men's.

Hair — softly brushed back over a crescent pad and coiled into a bun at the back of the head.

Hats — starched lace caps, placed well on the back of the head.

Accessories — worn with discretion. Lace edged handkerchiefs are carried for display.

Notes on patterns: Men

Doublet — the fronts should be very stiffly interlined and whaleboned. Position and sew the epaulettes to roll over the top part of the arm and to snugly fit the armhole.

Standing collar — the collar and the supportasse are attached to a collar band (worn under the neckband of the doublet). To control the angle of the supportasse, the radial wires should continue through into the depth of the collar band.

Trunk hose — (add C.F. fastening), gather and/or set in pleats at the leg openings and around the waist edge, to the foundation.

Notes on patterns: Women

Petticoats — cut full, gather with a drawstring at waist, or set in pleats to a waistband.

Bodice — (add C.F. buttoned fastening), godets are inserted at A. B. and C. to form the high flared skirt.

Skirts — (add C.B. or C.F. placket), bullet-pleat to a waistband.

Falling collar — three collars are gently gathered or pleated to the top edge of the neckband and tied or hooked and eyed together at the back.

Cap — (starch, and if necessary wire the brim) gather the crown to the brim — the crown should be cut to give minimal gathering.

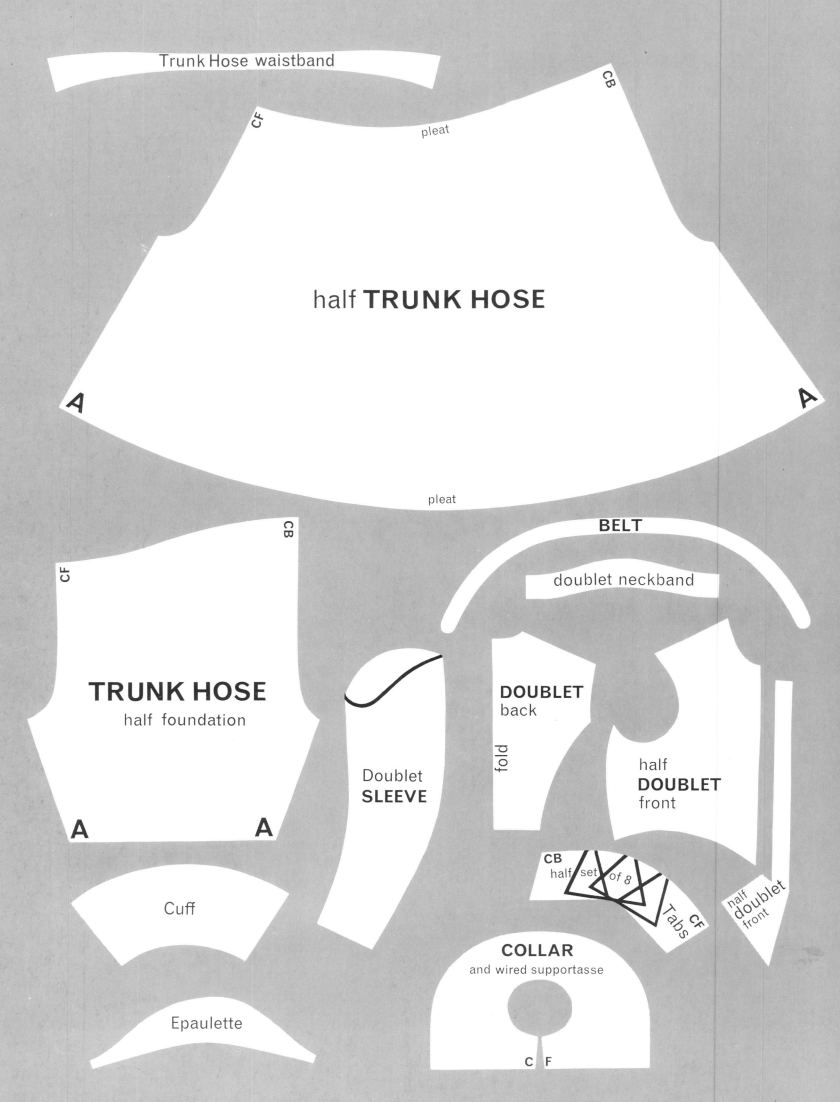

Trunk Hose waistband

CF

CB

pleat

half **TRUNK HOSE**

A

A

pleat

CB

CF

BELT

doublet neckband

TRUNK HOSE

half foundation

DOUBLET
back

half
DOUBLET
front

fold

Doublet
SLEEVE

A

A

Cuff

CB
half

set of 8

CF
Tabs

half
doublet
front

Epaulette

COLLAR
and wired supportasse

C F

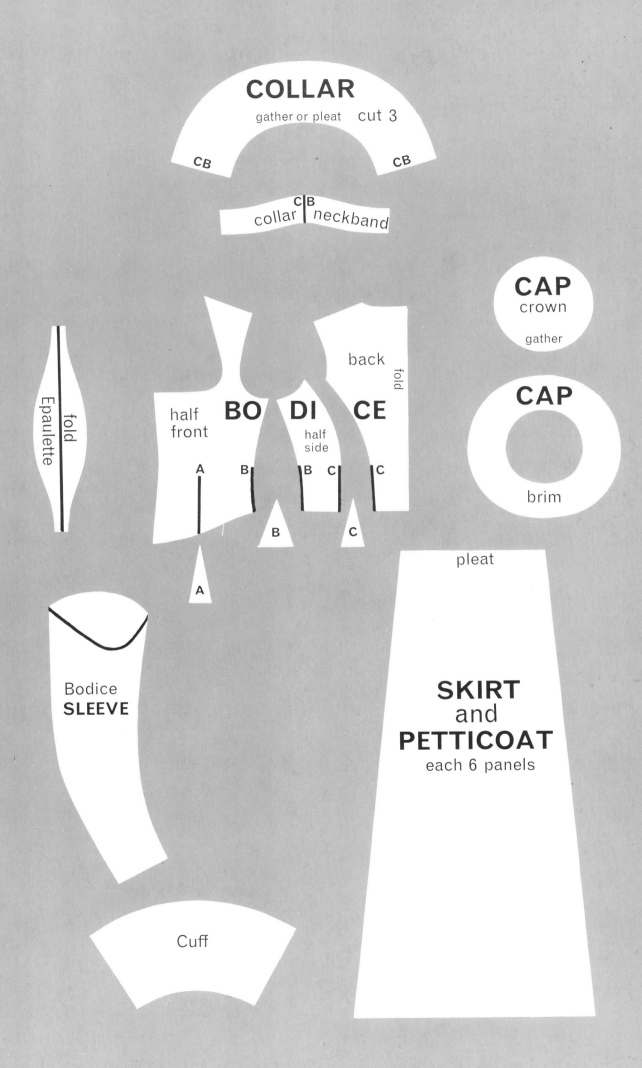

COLLAR
gather or pleat   cut 3
CB   CB

CB
collar | neckband

fold
Epaulette

half
front

BO DI CE

half
side

back
fold

CAP
crown
gather

CAP

brim

A   B   B   C   C

B   C

A

pleat

Bodice
SLEEVE

SKIRT
and
PETTICOAT
each 6 panels

Cuff

1625 Charles I

Fabrics: Similar to the previous fashion.

Colours: Similar to the previous fashion.

Decoration: Elaborate fastenings of laces, ribbons and rosettes. Braids of varying width, are liberally used to edge, stripe, and cover the seams of most garments.

Padding and restriction, men: Similar to the previous fashion.

Padding and restriction, women: A small, short, boned corset or under bodice with deep skirts and a pointed stomacher front. The corset is cut to reveal and push the bosom high up onto the chest. The sleeves (virago), are heavily bombasted and stuffed.

Movement, men: Similar to, though less mannered than, the previous fashion.

Movement, women: the heavy ground-length skirts, heavily bombasted sleeves, and the very short-waisted bodice, dictate decorous and formal movement. The baring of the arms almost to the elbow point, and the removal of the ruff from the neck, indicates a desire to focus attention on these parts of the body.

Men

General characteristics: A more dignified, substantial, and manly fashion.

Under garments — similar to the previous fashion.

Doublet — very high waisted, stiffened, braided and slashed. Large overlapping tabs, forming a skirt, are attached to the V-shaped waistline. Epaulettes, following the slope of the shoulders, conceal the join of the armhole to the sleeve. The sleeves are slashed, to reveal the shirt or an inner lining. A deep cuff of lace is worn at the wrist. The belt curves to follow the shape of the waist. Ribbon ties surrounding the waistline, either support the cloak bag breeches, or secure the tabs to the doublet. The set of ruffs, with stiffening and supportasse removed, fall in a soft, thick collar about the neck.

Cloak bag breeches — heavily pleated, melon shaped, gathered in above the knees, and either buttoned through or open on the outside of the legs to reveal the inner lining. Bows or ribbon ties edge the leg openings.

Cloak — similar to the previous fashion.

Stockings — looser in fit and gartered below the knee.

Shoes — similar to the previous fashion, more natural in shape and decorated with smaller, less ornate rosettes.

Hats — broad brimmed hats with tallish crowns trimmed with one or more large ostrich feathers.

Hair — shoulder length, centrally parted and brushed away from the forehead. Small beards and moustaches.

Accessories — similar to the previous fashion.

Women

General characteristics: High waisted, with broad shoulders formed by the large melon-shaped sleeves and the wide standing collar (rebato). Bulky skirts give a full, rich, rounded shape to the figure.

Under garments — chemise, corset, and numerous petticoats. The petticoats are possibly laced or hooked and eyed to the under side of the corset at the waistline — the top petticoat richly decorated with rows of braiding.

Gown — square necked, short waisted, and open down the C.F. to reveal the corset to which it is fastened (hooks and eyes). The pleating of the skirts to the waistline is covered by a sash. The sleeves are partially hidden by short open top sleeves fastened together on their lower edges with ribbon ties. The square neckline is covered by a tucked or pleated yoke (pinned to the fronts and back of the bodice), to which is fastened the wired rebato or standing collar. This collar, darted and shaped along its inner edge to take the curve of the neckline, together with the treble cuffs, is edged in narrow pointed lace.

Stockings — similar to the men's.

Shoes — similar to the men's.

Hair — elaborately parted across the front of the head and on either side above the ears — the back braided and arranged in a bun and the sides frizzed and curled to form spaniels' ears. The front hair is brushed forward, from the parting running across the forehead, into a short crimped fringe. Ornaments, ribbons, pearls, jewels, etc. decorate the hair.

Hats — rarely seen. Kerchiefs, of fine white lawn, tie under the chin.

Accessories — tight pearl necklaces and bracelets. Rich pieces of jewellery fastened to the costume with ribbons. Rosettes. The folding fan. Black patches decorate the face. A face mask is carried when travelling abroad — usually black, supported on a stick, or held to the face by means of a button, placed inside the mask and clasped between the teeth.

Notes on patterns: Men

Doublet — (add C.F. buttoned fastening). Stiffen body parts and tabs. The puffings of white material, protruding through the body and sleeve slashings, are sewn to the inside of the garment and pulled through.

Cloak bag breeches — (add C.F. buttoned fastening) the foundation controls length and pleating at knee and waist. The sides of the breeches can be closed or buttoned through with the last few buttons left open to reveal the lining (for theatre purposes braces should be worn to support the breeches).

Falling collar — three tiers of softly pleated fabric set to a neckband with C.F. or C.B. fastening.

Notes on patterns: Women

Petticoats — gather by means of a drawstring to the waistline, or hook and eye to the inner waist edge of the under bodice or corset.

Under bodice — (laced at C.B.) bone throughout, placing heavier boning down the stomacher front. The skirts should be stiffened.

Gown — lightly bone the open bodice. The skirts are pleated, then gathered or eased to the waistline of the bodice. The large virago sleeve is sewn to the foundation, to control the puffs, with the cavities between the two surfaces heavily padded. The open top sleeve is gathered to the head of the virago sleeve. The entire sleeve is then eased into the armhole. (It is advisable to tie-catch the many tiered lace cuffs, at intervals, to the sleeve).

Collar and yoke — the yoke is finely tucked, and the wired collar darted along its neck edge — the darts should be carefully positioned, and, if necessary, boned to achieve the stand and angle of the collar away from the neck edge of the yoke. The yoke should be firmly pinned to the back of the bodice, stretched over the shoulders, and pinned at the C.F. and on either side of the bodice front neckline.

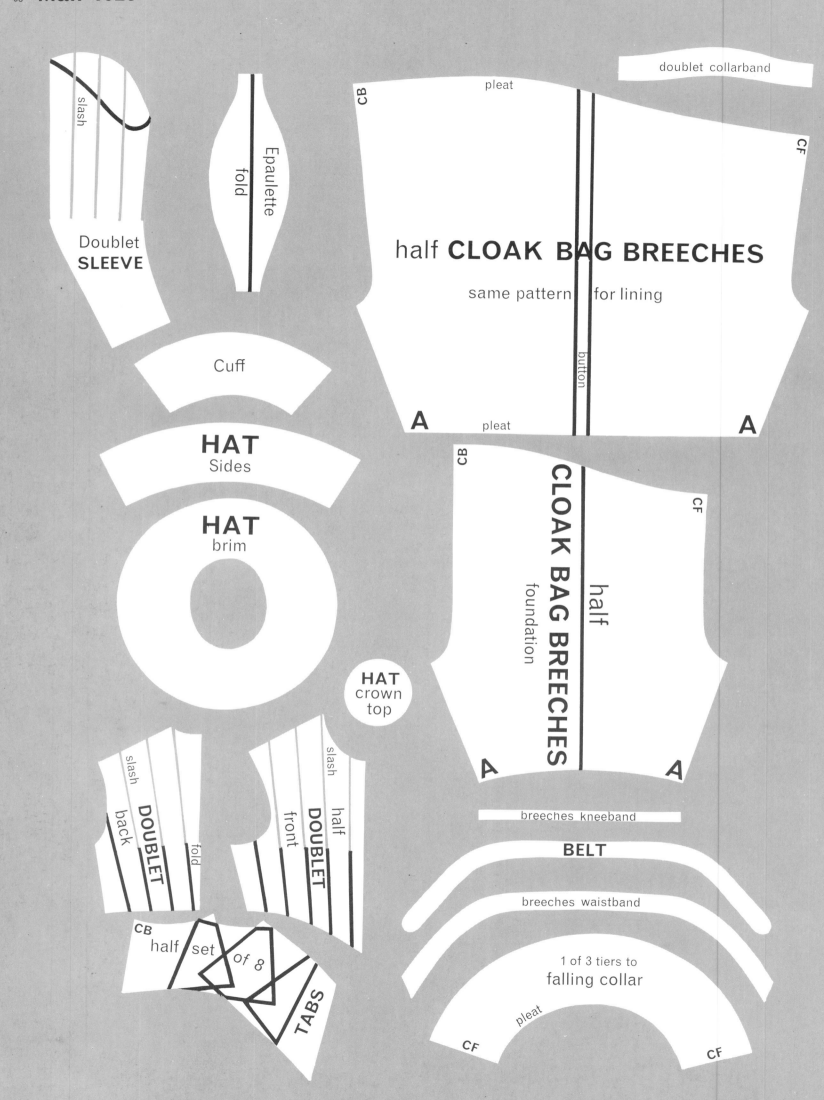

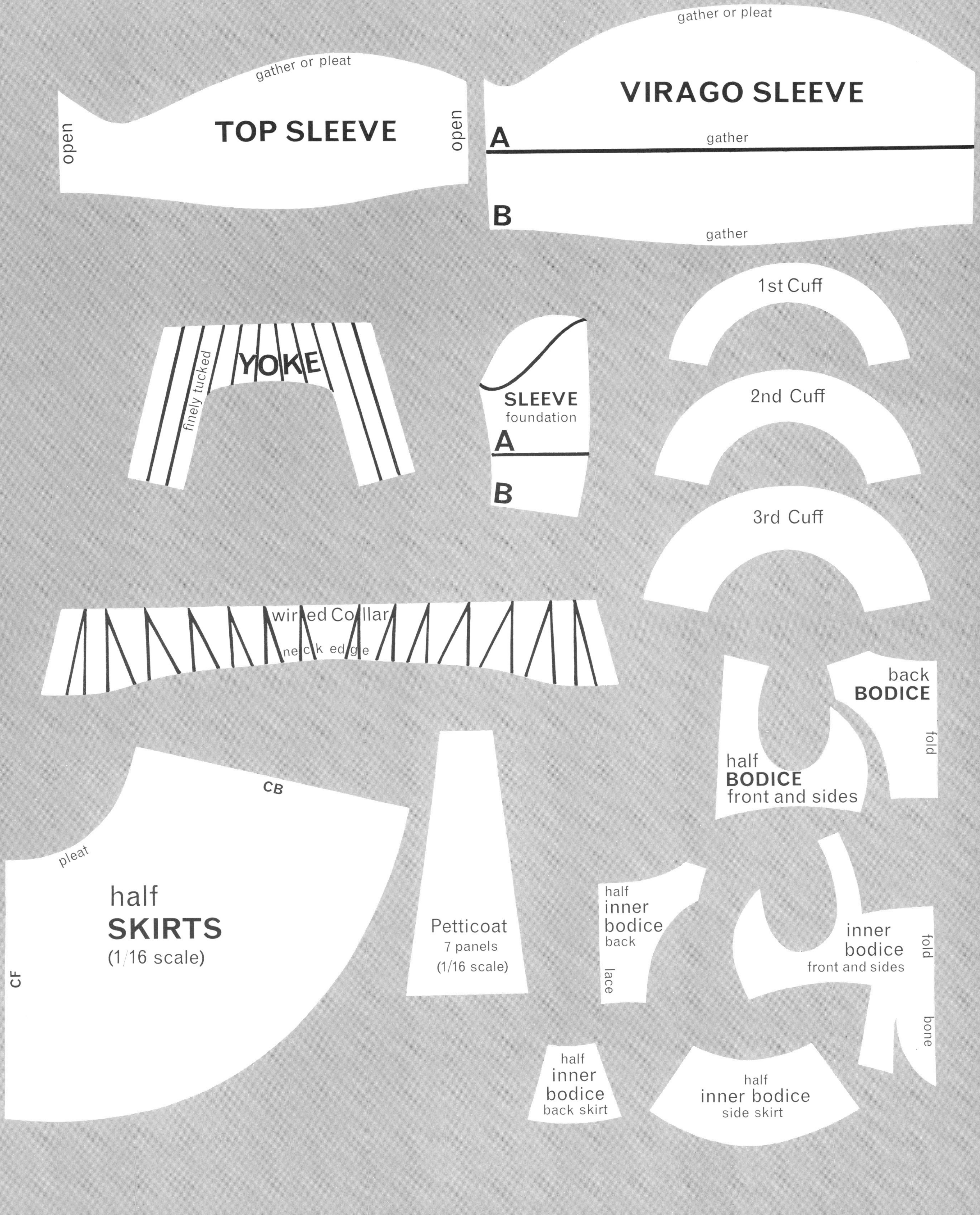

gather or pleat

TOP SLEEVE

open

open

gather or pleat

VIRAGO SLEEVE

A

gather

B

gather

1st Cuff

2nd Cuff

3rd Cuff

finely tucked

YOKE

SLEEVE
foundation

A

B

wired Collar

neck edge

back
BODICE

fold

half
BODICE
front and sides

CB

pleat

half
SKIRTS
(1/16 scale)

CF

Petticoat
7 panels
(1/16 scale)

half
inner
bodice
back

lace

inner
bodice
front and sides

fold

bone

half
inner
bodice
back skirt

half
inner bodice
side skirt

1635 Charles I

Fabrics: Softer and much lighter in weight. Unpatterned taffetas, silks, satins, velvets and cloth.

Colours: Subtle reds and pinks, mauves, honey, silver, soft greens and blues, deep plums, etc. Black very fashionable (costume always relieved by white lace or linen at the throat and wrists).

Decoration: Used with discretion — braiding, buttoning, delicate pricking and slashing. The rich geometric patterns, formed by the magnificent lace, develop into stylised floral designs. Lace, which has to be eased onto the linen areas of the collar or cuffs, is frequently of "bobbin" because of its greater softness and its ability to gather.

Padding and restriction, women: Similar to the previous fashion (without padding and bombast).

Movement, men: The use of soft materials, and the lack of boning or bombasting in the construction of clothes, creates a very elegant and beautiful costume for man to wear and display.

Movement, women: Similar to preceding fashion. With the costume now made in soft materials, a graceful gliding movement is adopted with the back arched, and the stomach thrust forward to lead the walk. Arms curve away from the body and come to rest on the front part of the skirts.

Men

General characteristics: Short hip-length coat, high-waisted long-legged breeches, and a cloak of matching colour and fabric. Long curled hair and broad brimmed hats.

Under garments — the shirt is cut full to pouch at the waistline and to fill out the open sleeves of the coat.

Coat — narrow shouldered, gently waisted (high), and usually buttoned at the throat. Full, open sleeves terminate in one or more cuffs. A deep falling collar, covering the shoulders in very large points or scallops of punto-in-aria lace, is tied high under the chin.

Spanish breeches — hooked to the coat lining or self-supporting with buttoned C.F. opening. Long, narrow and tubular in form. They terminate below the knee where they are trimmed with ribbon loops. Braid and buttons decorate the outside of the leg.

Cape — circular.

Stockings — usually wrinkle about the legs.

Shoes — similar to the previous fashion, a narrow square toe with higher heavier heel. High boots of soft leather — the tops pulled well down to form very deep cuffs about the lower part of the knee. Large instep decorations (butterfly shape) cover the fastening of the spurs. Boot hose, with a deep border of lace, are worn to protect the under stockings from dirt.

Hats — similar to the previous fashion.

Hair — much longer, curled and waved to fall about the shoulders. A single lock of hair is frequently tied with a ribbon bow or rosette. A short fringe covers the forehead. The beard covers a small area of the chin immediately under the lower lip. The moustache is brushed up at the sides.

Accessories — the sword (carried by gentlemen until the latter half of the 18th century). Gloves, walking canes.

Women

General characteristics: A soft, youthful, and graceful costume based on the style of the previous fashion.

Under garments — similar to the previous fashion.

Gown — the full skirts are closed, cut with a train, and possibly secured to the waistline of the corset. The join of the deep tabs to the waistline of the open bodice is covered by a half belt of ribbon ending in large rosettes. The front edges of the bodice are firmly secured to the sides of the decorated stomacher. Full sleeves, a little below elbow in length, are set with deep, large, lace-edged cuffs. The low square neck, formed by the sides of the bodice and the stomacher top, retains the collar of the previous fashion — unstiffened to fall over the shoulders and down the back (whisk). In addition a folded neckerchief, with a deep border of lace, is draped over the shoulders and fastened to the fronts of the short bodice.

Stockings — similar to the previous fashion.

Shoes — similar to the previous fashion.

Hair — similar in style to the previous fashion, curled and arranged in pretty, soft, snake-like ringlets. Ribbons and ropes of pearls decorate the thick coil of plaited hair — positioned high on the back of the head.

Hats — similar to the previous fashion.

Accessories — ropes of pearls at the throat, wrists, and looped across the bodice front — secured with ribbon ties and jewelled ornaments. Fans and little mirrors suspend from cords or ribbons attached to the waistline of the corsets. Gloves cover the lower part of the arm to disappear under the cuff of the sleeve.

Notes on patterns: Men

Shirt — use pattern of 1690 for body parts and neckband. The sleeve requires a wrist placket and wristband.

Falling collar — the lace edging is eased to the collar which should be darted to fit the shape of the neck and shoulders. The collar is attached to a collar band and tied with strings, down the C.F. edges.

Coat — add C.F. buttoned fastening to upper parts of chest and neck band.

Spanish breeches — form a C.F. buttoned opening.

Cape — adapt curve of neck and revers if a buttoned front is required.

Boot hose — for theatre purposes, substitute with tubes ending in deep lace cuffs.

Hats — adapt pattern of 1680.

Notes on patterns: Women

Short corset — lightly bone throughout, and lace down the C.F.s. The stomacher, fastened to the front, requires heavy boning.

Petticoat — cut full, with the sides and back slightly flared. Pleat, then gather to a narrow waistband and hook and eye to the waist edge of the corset.

Gown — hook and eye sides of the bodice to the sides of the stomacher. Bullet-pleat head of sleeve to armhole. The skirts should be pleated then gathered to a narrow waistband with a C.F. or side fastening. The waistband is hooked and eyed, or laced, to the waist edge of the corset.

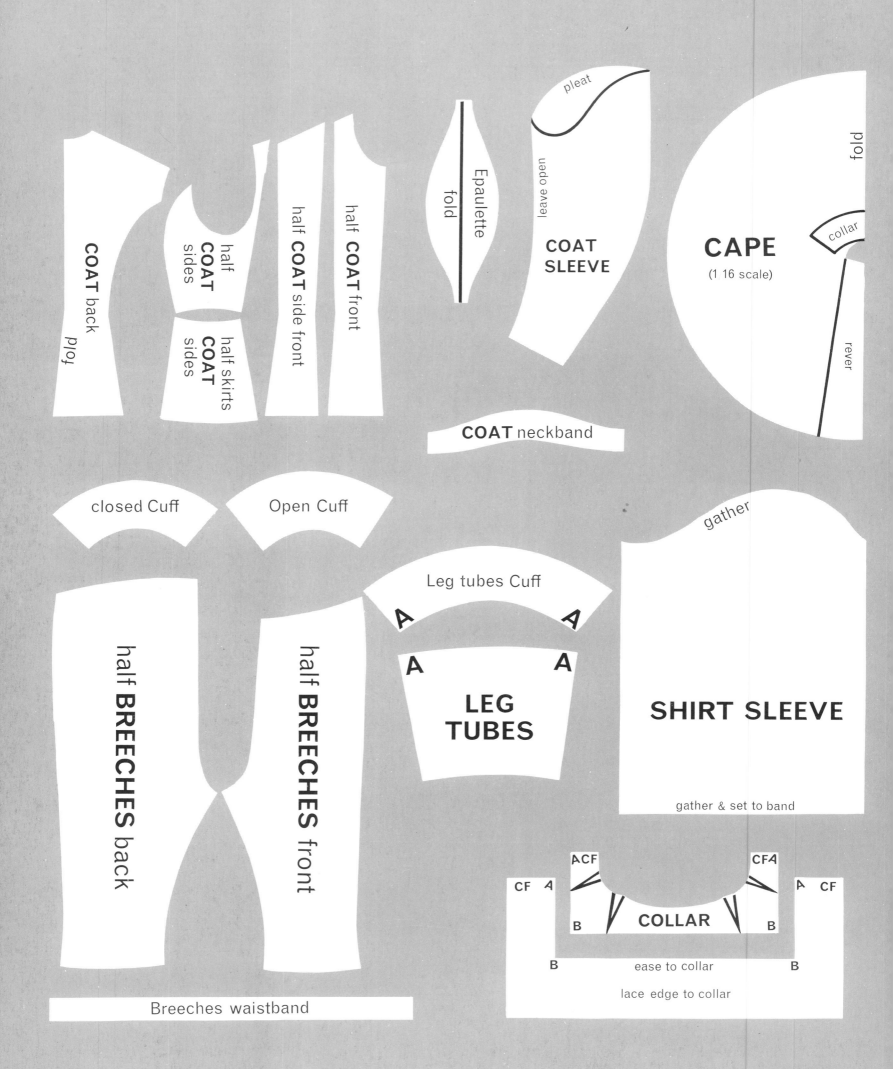

COAT back

fold

half **COAT** sides

half **COAT** sides

half skirts

half **COAT** side front

half **COAT** front

Epaulette

fold

pleat

leave open

COAT SLEEVE

CAPE

(1 16 scale)

fold

collar

rever

COAT neckband

closed Cuff

Open Cuff

Leg tubes Cuff

gather

A

A

A

A

LEG TUBES

SHIRT SLEEVE

half **BREECHES** back

half **BREECHES** front

gather & set to band

ACF

CFA

CF A

A CF

B

B

COLLAR

B

ease to collar

B

lace edge to collar

Breeches waistband

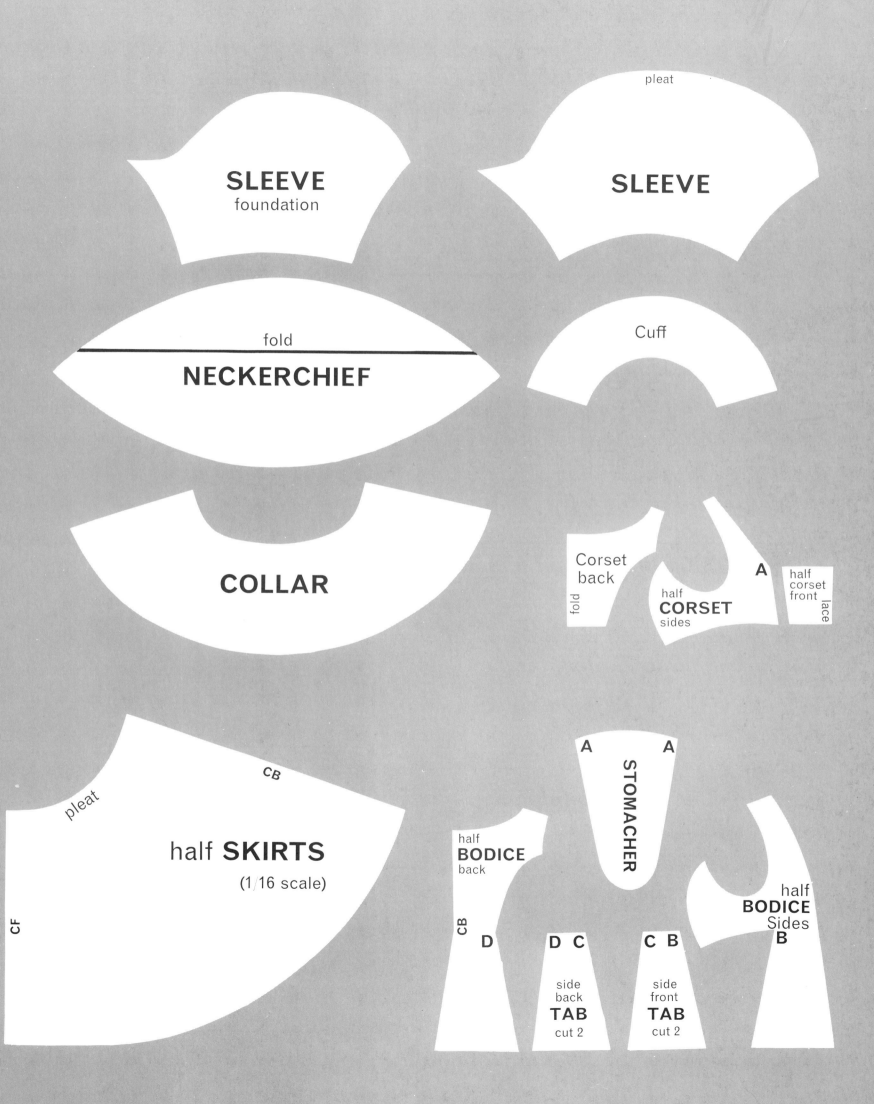

1665 Charles II

Fabrics: Taffetas, velvets, silks and satins — some substantial, others soft and capable of being finely pleated.

Colours: Similar to the previous fashion.

Decoration: Rose point lace of scrolling, baroque forms (formal floral designs), the outline of the forms padded to give relief as rich as carved ivory. Often more than 100 yards of ribbon edge and decorate the costume.

Padding and restriction, women: Corsets, heavily busked and boned and with a long stomacher point, are constructed to emphasise large rounded bosoms and narrow waists. A small and tight armhole severely restricts the movement of shoulders and upper arm. A bum roll or hip pad is secured to the series of tabs at the waistline.

Movement, men: The mass of ribboning, the elaborate sleeves of the shirt, together with lace frills, flounces and ruffles, dictate flamboyant gesture and movement to set off a very showy wardrobe. The art of dancing and deportment, part of man's education, influences behaviour and is seen in the studied turn of the leg, point of the toe, play of the hands, etc., — a fashion to continue in modified or exaggerated forms throughout this and the following century.

Movement, women: Corsets straighten and hollow the back. The arms curve away from the body, and rest on the hip pad. Skirts, extending into a train at the back, dictate a curved line of walk (full semi-circle) when turning about.

Men

General characteristics: An eccentric and complex fashion which, when taken to excess, becomes effeminate, ill-proportioned and ridiculous.

Under garments — similar to the previous fashion. The shirt is very full, particularly the sleeves which are puffed, ribboned and frilled. The falling band, with a deep edging of lace, and set in pleats at the C.F., covers the chest and shoulders. It is attached to a neckband and fastened with strings.

Coat — resembles a short-sleeved bolero with the fronts buttoned together at the neck.

Petticoat breeches — constructed either as a flared and heavily pleated short skirt, or as very wide short trousers, and attached to an under pair of tight-fitting breeches (self-supporting) which cover the knee. The hem, waistline, and sides of the skirt, are all decorated with row upon row of ribbon loops.

Cape — circular, with revers and a flat collar.

Stockings — wrinkle about the leg. Wide frills (canons), gathered to the tops of the stockings, cover the garters.

Shoes — similar to the previous fashion.

Hats — a broad-brimmed hat, the brim often turned up in front, trimmed with a standing cluster of ostrich feathers.

Hair — centrally parted, with or without a fringe, falls about the shoulders onto the chest and back. The small, divided moustache and the tiny chin beard are both still very fashionable.

Accessories — similar to the previous fashion.

Women

General characteristics: Low decolletage, deep lace collar, firmly corseted, long-waisted body, and full skirts.

Under garments — a chemise, low necked and gathered with a drawstring about the shoulders, is worn under the corset. The full sleeves are gathered in with drawstrings to form frills about the elbows. A hip pad assists the bulk of petticoats to spring out from the waistline.

Gown — the bodice is frequently built onto the corset and laced down the C.B. A deep lace collar edges the low neckline. The cuffed, short sleeve, similar to the previous fashion, reveals the gathered chemise sleeve worn beneath. Skirts, separate from the bodice, are richly pleated and open down the front.

Stockings — similar to the previous fashion.

Shoes — similar to men's.

Hair — dressed in an exaggerated style based on the previous fashion with the side hair, held out by combs and pads, falling to the shoulders in a mass of ringlets and curls.

Hats — similar to the previous fashion.

Accessories — fans, ropes of pearls, ribbons. Earrings, pendants, and dress ornaments of silver or gold set with precious stones — real and imitation.

Notes on patterns: Men

Shirt — develop the width of the body parts of the shirt pattern of 1690 to give extra fullness. The sleeve is placed on a foundation to form two large puffs. Add a wrist placket.

Falling collar — make up as in the previous pattern forming a pleat on either side of the C.F.

Coat — add buttoned fastenings to the sleeves and front.

Petticoat breeches — (form a C.F. opening with concealed fastening) heavily pleat the petticoat breeches to the waistline of the under breeches and set to the waistband. (Under breeches may require knee plackets at outside leg.)

Cape — adapt previous patterns.

Hat — adapt pattern of 1680 developing the height of the crown and narrowing the brim.

Notes on patterns: Women

In future all corsets should restrict the measurement of the natural waist unless otherwise stated.

Corsets — heavily bone throughout and back-lace. The shoulder strap will require adjustment, in length and angle, in relation to the slope of the shoulder.

Chemise — adapt previous patterns to give extra width. Cut neckline in a wide deep curve and insert a drawstring.

Hip pad — lightly pad and add strings to tie about the waist.

Under petticoat — make up in heavy calico and insert a drawstring at the waist.

Top petticoat — bullet-pleat to narrow waistband allowing the pleating to commence away from the C.F.

Collar — cut to fit the shape and slope of the shoulders and fasten at the C.F. (For theatre purposes it is advisable to attach the collar to the neckline of the bodice.)

Gown — the bodice (waist edge indicated at LB on the pattern) should be mounted onto the corset. The armhole is extended by a narrow strip of material to which the sleeve is pleated. The skirts are bullet-pleated to the top edge of a narrow waistband — fastening at the C.F. (The skirts are worn under the stomacher and bodice front, but over the tabs at the bodice back — side seams of the bodice should be left open $\frac{1}{2}$ inch at the waist edge to assist the skirts to pass over and neatly cover the back tabs.)

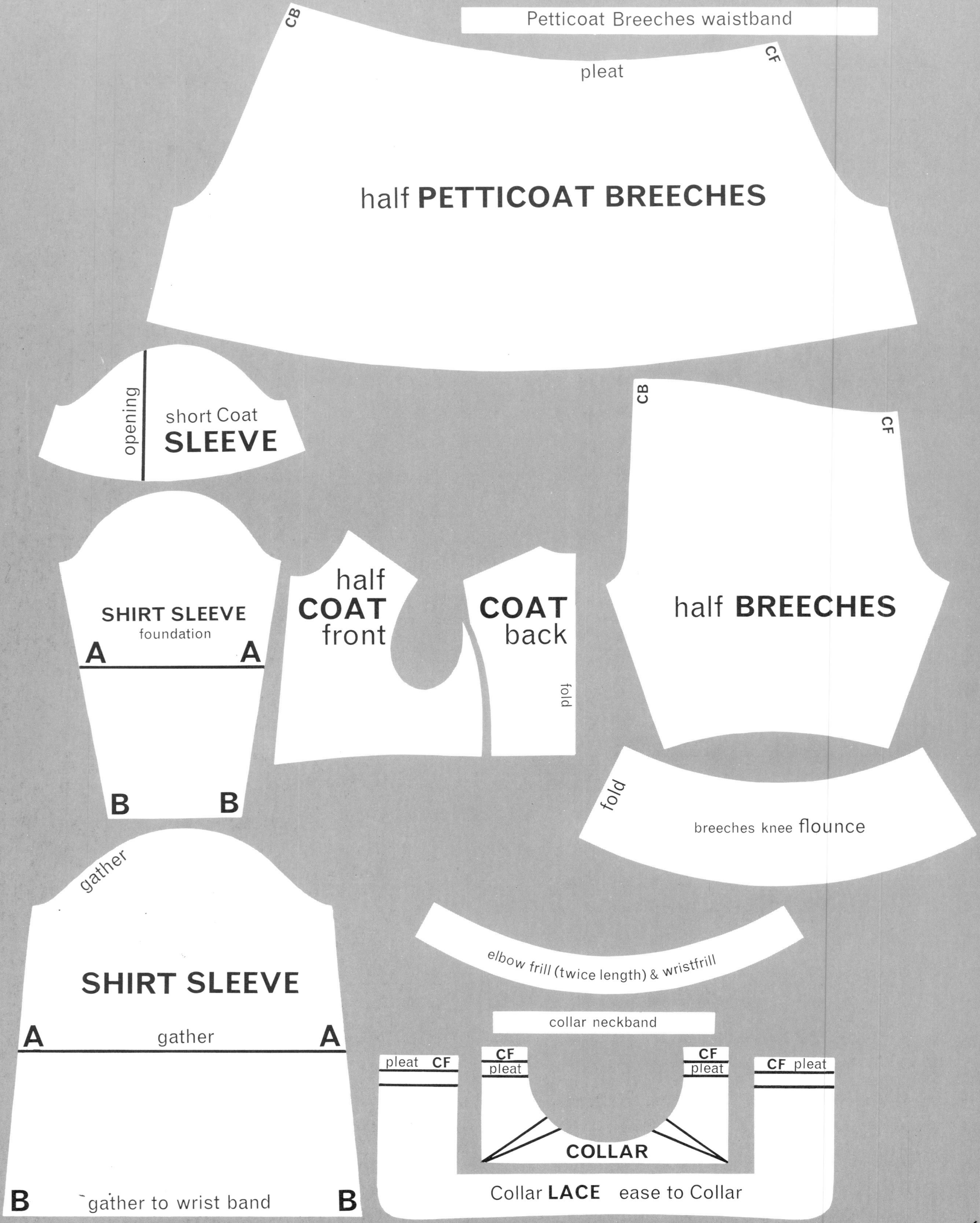

Petticoat Breeches waistband

pleat

CB

CF

half **PETTICOAT BREECHES**

opening

short Coat
SLEEVE

CB

CF

half **BREECHES**

SHIRT SLEEVE
foundation

A   A

half
COAT
front

COAT
back

fold

B   B

fold

breeches knee flounce

gather

elbow frill (twice length) & wristfrill

SHIRT SLEEVE

collar neckband

A   gather   A

pleat **CF**

CF
pleat

CF
pleat

CF pleat

COLLAR

B   gather to wrist band

B   Collar **LACE**   ease to Collar

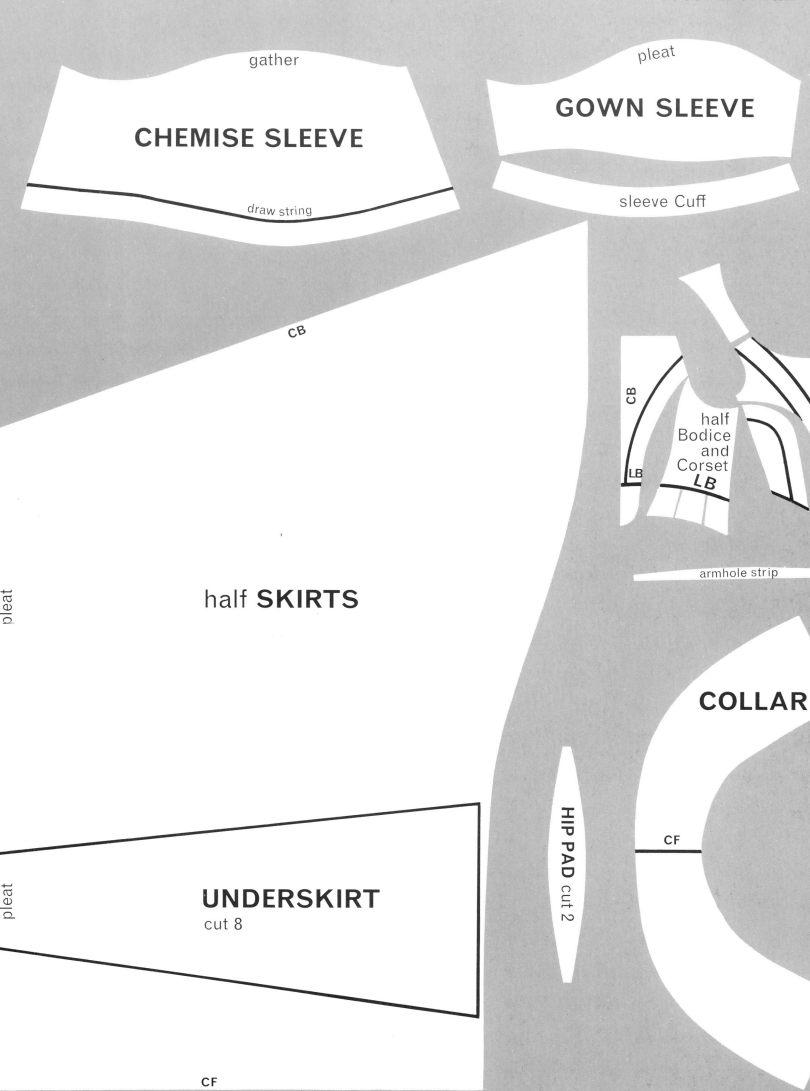

gather

CHEMISE SLEEVE

draw string

pleat

GOWN SLEEVE

sleeve Cuff

CB

half SKIRTS

pleat

CB

CF

half
Bodice
and
Corset
LB

LB

LB

armhole strip

COLLAR

pleat

UNDERSKIRT
cut 8

HIP PAD cut 2

CF

CF

CF

1675 Charles II

Fabrics: Heavy silks, satins, brocades, velvets, cloths etc., worn by men. Women favour similar fabrics of lighter weight.

Colours: Darker, richer colours worn in preference to the delicate and sweeter colours of the previous fashion.

Decoration: Similar to the previous fashion with a more moderate use of ribbon ties, bows, and loops.

Padding and restriction, women: The corsets, long and narrow waisted, emphasise the roundness of the breasts and hips by tight lacing. A hip pad holds out the petticoats and skirts.

Movement, men: Quiet, dignified and conservative. The long wig restricts head and neck movement.

Movement, women: Corseting and the fullness of the back parts of the skirts dictate upright carriage and assured movement.

Men

General characteristics: A short-sleeved, knee-length coat, shirt and neck cloth, breeches, shoes, stockings and hat, establishes the composition of men's dress to the present day.

Under garments — similar to the previous fashion.

The neck cloth or cravat replaces the falling band. Always of white, it is placed centrally at the throat with the ends taken around to the back of the neck, crossed over, then brought forward to the front again, where they are knotted or tied in a bow at the throat.

Coat — the C.B. and side seams of the skirt, left open to form vents, are set with buttons and buttonholes. The fronts of the coat, with pockets placed low on the skirts, are buttoned through to the waist, then left open to fall away over the breeches. The short sleeve terminates in a cuff and a fall of lace.

Breeches — low cut at waist, self-supporting, and gathered into bands just above the knee.

Stockings — gartered below the knee.

Shoes — less exaggerated shape based on the previous fashion.

Hats — broad brimmed and high crowned — decorated with a feather or ribbons.

Heads — the wig (generally adopted by 1700), is centrally parted, richly curled or straight, with or without a fringe, and dressed to fall over either shoulder onto the chest, and to cover the neck and upper back of the wearer.

Accessories — walking canes, gloves and sword — frequently suspended from a shoulder belt or baldrick.

Women

General characteristics: Long narrow bodice with deep V-shaped waist and low circular neckline. Full skirts, worn over hip pads, are looped up about the hips to give a backward thrust to the costume.

Under garments — similar to the previous fashion.

Gown — (fastening at C.F. usually indicates that the bodice is separate from the corset). The short sleeve, ending in a cuff, reveals the gathered chemise sleeve. Skirts, less bulky than the previous fashion, are open down the C.F., looped up on either hip and fastened with ribbons. (Back and side fullness will soon develop into the large hooped skirts of the 18th century.)

Stockings — similar to the men's.

Shoes — similar to the previous fashion. Elegant and narrower in cut.

Hair — arranged in a similar manner to the previous fashion, centrally parted, tightly curled about the ears, with one or more long locks of hair brought forward and displayed on the shoulder. The fringe disappears.

Hats — similar to the previous fashion.

Accessories — ribbons, bows, pearls, jewels. The large folding fan, imported from the East, is a very fashionable and much prized addition to the toilette.

Notes on patterns: Men

Shirt (use pattern of 1690 for body parts). The sleeve is attached to a foundation to control puffs at AA and BB. Form wrist plackets.

Neck cloth — a strip of soft linen, approximately 7 feet in length and 8 inches wide.

Breeches — form knee and C.F. buttoned plackets.

Baldrick — make up in two thicknesses of leather, adding a buckle and attachments to secure the front to the back (X to X). The sword is slotted through the three loops formed at A, A, A.

Hat — make up in very heavy fabric, or stiffen and wire.

Notes on patterns: Women

Corset — adapt bodice pattern forming tabs around the waistline. Heavily bone and lace at the C.B.

Chemise — construct as in previous pattern.

Hip roll — construct as in previous pattern.

Petticoats — construct as in previous pattern.

Gown — lightly bone bodice throughout and fasten down C.F., adding a narrow frill to the neck edge. The sleeve is placed to the narrow armhole strip with its front seam open to expose the chemise sleeve. Skirts are finely bullet-pleated to the *top* of a waistband — fastening at the C.F. Ribbon ties, threaded through eyelet holes worked in the skirt, secure and control the draping and looping up of the two front edges. To increase the spring of the skirts out from the waistline, fold back the waist edge from nothing at the C.F.s to 3 inches at the C.B. before pleating.

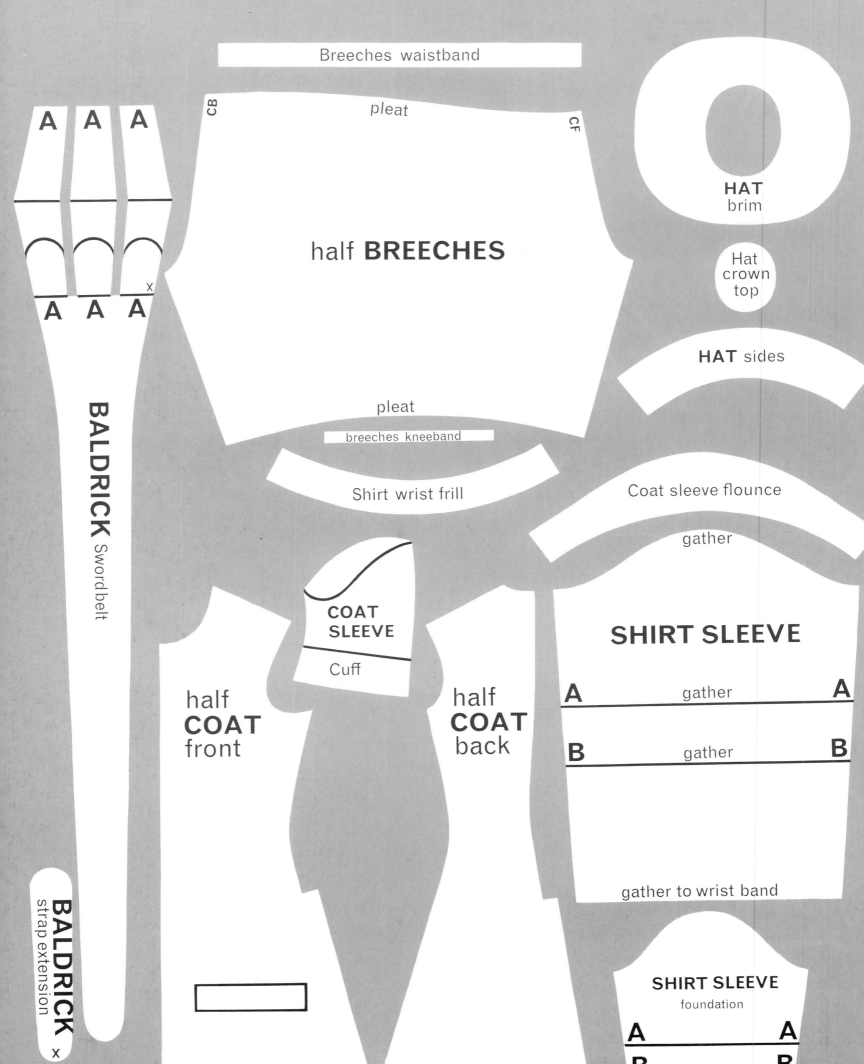

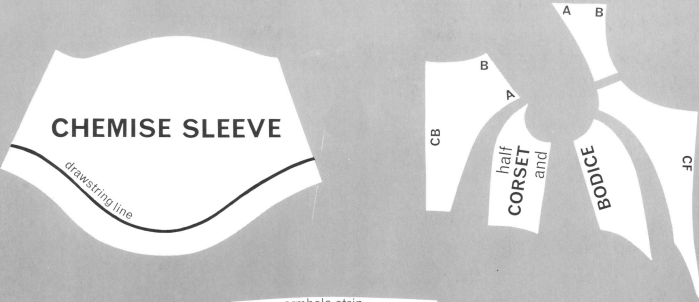

CHEMISE SLEEVE

drawstring line

B

CB

B

A

half CORSET and

BODICE

A B

CF

armhole strip

GOWN SLEEVE

GOWN SLEEVE flounce

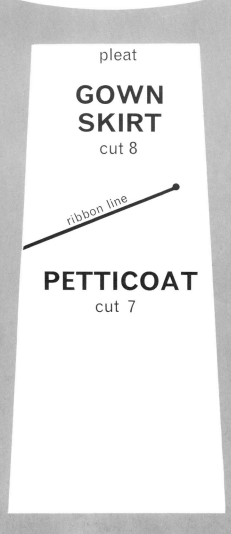

pleat

GOWN SKIRT

cut 8

ribbon line

PETTICOAT

cut 7

1690 William and Mary

Fabrics: Men — stout satins, cloths, silks and velvets. (The art of tailoring, commencing at about this date, requires fabrics that will mould, stretch and shrink to the shape of the body.) Women — similar or of lighter weight. Lace, usually gathered, is finer and softer with a much smaller design (*point de neige* — snow flake).

Colours: Large range of beige, yellows, reds, browns, peach and greys.

Decoration: Stripes — embroidered, woven, or applied (braids). Profusion of buttons and buttonholes on men's costume. Bunches of ribbon.

Padding and restriction, men: Possibly a light pair of stays, or back of waistcoat laced, to narrow the waist and body. Flared skirts, cuffs, and chest parts are interlined and stiffened with parchment, boning and buckram.

Padding and restriction, women: Similar to the previous fashion.

Movement, men: Length of wig, increase in width of skirts, falls of lace at wrists and throat, influence movement and behaviour in order to display and "show" the costume to advantage. Arms, turned out and curved, are kept away from the body — dictated by the tight armholes and narrow shoulders of the coat. Weight is thrown onto one leg with the feet placed in the open T position. Movement of the neck and head is controlled by the wig.

Movement, women: Similar to the previous fashion — formal and upright. The high lace cap (fontage) controls movement of the head.

Men

General characteristics: The science of tailoring and the fit of clothes becomes increasingly more important. (As tailoring improves, decoration will disappear.) Suit consists of coat, matching waistcoat and breeches.

Under garments — similar to the previous fashion. The knotted neck cloth, forming a jabot, is often accompanied by a multiple bow of ribbons placed beneath it. Shirt wrist frills cover most of the hand.

Coat — narrow shouldered, low waisted and knee length. Buttoned only at the waist. Side and back vents, decorated with buttons and buttonholes, are left open to give free passage for the sword — now placed on hangers and attached to a belt under the waistcoat. Elbow-length sleeves terminate in deep cuffs. Pockets, functional or decorative, always appear on the front part of the skirts.

Waistcoat — similar in cut to the coat, with narrow sleeves.

Breeches — cut to terminate above the knees, and with a C.F. buttoned opening.

Stockings — worn over the breeches and gartered below the knee.

Shoes — the heel is higher than the previous fashion. The latchets neatly buckle over a high stiffened tongue.

Hats — the brim of the hat, braided and edged with feathers, is formed into a triangle by turning it up (cocking) into three sections — held in position with straps.

Hair — the full-bottomed wig is back combed, frizzed, or loosely curled. The hair on either temple, divided by the central parting, is curled and arranged high to form horns.

Accessories — lace handkerchief, sword, gloves, snuff box, watch, walking stick.

Women

General characteristics: The hips and the back are strongly accentuated by the looping up and tying back of the top skirts.

Under garments — the lace frills, attached to the chemise sleeves, are fuller and longer at the back of the arm. The C.F. of the corsets is straight and rigid (whalebone, horn, or wooden busks). A small bum roll, fastened under the tabs, helps the backward thrust of the skirts. Petticoats, flared and pleated at sides and back, are less full and often made of the same material as the gown — a drawstring fastens them at the waist.

Gown — pleated or gathered open skirts, cut with a train, are attached to the waistline of the bodice. The front edges are looped up and pinned to the C.B. of the bodice waistline to reveal the front and sides of the petticoat. The bodice, fastening down the C.F., is sometimes cut to reveal the V point of the corset at the front waistline. The short sleeves are cuffed, and gathered or pleated to the armhole.

Stockings — similar to men's.

Shoes — neater in fit, with a pointed toe. Upper parts of leather or embroidered fabric.

Hair — centrally parted and arranged in high curls on either side of the forehead. The back hair forms a bun and loose curls, which are brought forward and displayed on the shoulder.

Hats — (fontage) a cap of lace or linen shaped to fit the back of the head, with a series of pleated frills sewn to the face edge — these frills develop into streamers (lappets) to fall down the back or onto the chest. The frills are kept upright or angled forward by a wire frame (commode).

Accessories — ribbons, earrings, necklaces. The fan. Black patches continue to decorate the face which is powdered (white) and rouged.

Notes on patterns: Men

Stays — small pair of lightly-boned stays should be worn to narrow and lengthen the waist.

Shirt — (extend at A to the required length) add wrist plackets and frills to the sleeves.

Coat — stiffen fronts, skirts and cuffs.

Waistcoat — stiffen skirts.

Breeches — adapt pattern of 1705 terminating the breeches above the knee (form C.F. buttoned opening).

Hat — stiffen and wire. The folding back of the brim should be curved and not angular at the three points.

Notes on patterns: Women

Corsets — heavily bone throughout and lace at C.B. Worn over the petticoats.

Hip pad — cut from the pattern of 1705, adding strings to secure at the waist.

Chemise — construct as in previous pattern.

Under petticoats — pleat, then gather on a drawstring to the waist.

Top petticoat — pleat at sides and back, then gather on a drawstring to the waist (gathering and pleating should commence well away from the C.F.).

Gown — (the striped fabric, of the gown illustrated, is embroidered and not woven to enable the stripes to pass up the bodice and across the chest to the shoulder points). The bodice, fastened down the C.F., is gathered up on either shoulder point with ribbon ties. Gather sleeve to armhole. The front skirts are looped up and fastened A to A at the C.B.

Fontage — the pleated front edge is supported from behind with a structure of wire or stiffened net. The edges marked X on the lappet patterns, are sewn to the lower side edges of the cap. Firmly secure cap to the sides of the head.

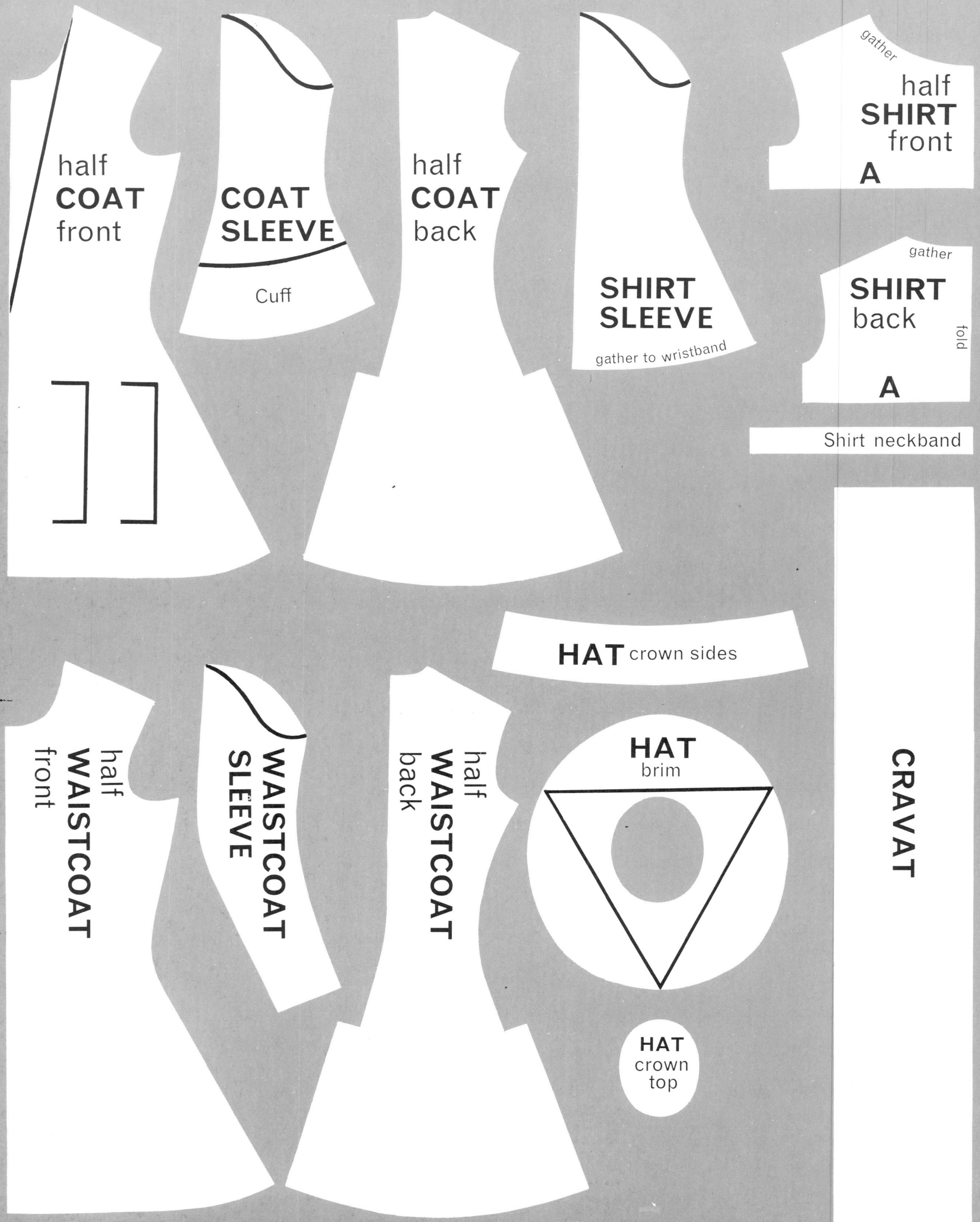

half
COAT
front

**COAT
SLEEVE**

Cuff

half
COAT
back

**SHIRT
SLEEVE**

gather to wristband

gather

half
SHIRT
front

A

gather

SHIRT
back

fold

A

Shirt neckband

HAT crown sides

half
WAISTCOAT
front

**WAISTCOAT
SLEEVE**

half
WAISTCOAT
back

HAT
brim

HAT
crown
top

CRAVAT

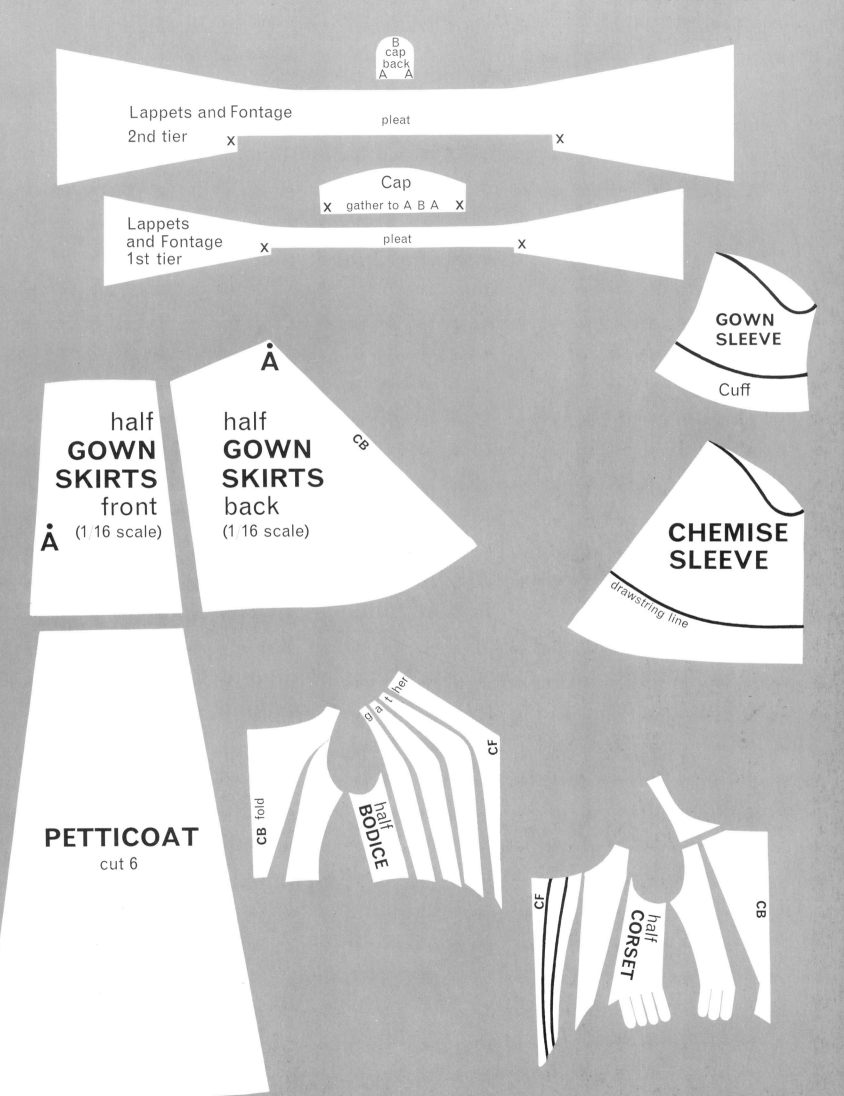

B
cap
back
A A

Lappets and Fontage
2nd tier
X
pleat
X

Cap
X gather to A B A X

Lappets
and Fontage
1st tier
X
pleat
X

**GOWN
SLEEVE**

Cuff

Ȧ

half
**GOWN
SKIRTS**
front
(1/16 scale)

Ȧ

half
**GOWN
SKIRTS**
back
(1/16 scale)

CB

**CHEMISE
SLEEVE**

drawstring line

PETTICOAT
cut 6

CB fold

g a t h e r

half
BODICE

CF

CF

half
CORSET

CB

1705 Anne

Fabrics: Heavier and richer than previous fashion. Fur used as trimming.

Colours: Rich and intense. Black, reds, purples, golds, etc.

Decoration: Embroidered or woven large florid scrolls, developed from highly stylised plant forms, make all-over repeating patterns or are used to edge borders of coat, cuffs, waistcoat, pocket flaps, etc. Elaborate metallic braids, fringing, and tasselling.

Padding and restriction, men: Similar to the previous fashion.

Padding and restriction, women: Similar to the previous fashion with a larger bustle extension.

Movement, men: An extravagant development of the previous fashion with the arms held up and away from the body to support and display the mighty cuffs of the sleeves. A hand is usually placed on the hip or "plays" the lace of the cravat, while the other arm, bent, is placed behind the back. An age of formality and baroque flamboyance — the bow, taking of snuff, carrying of the hat, etc.

Movement, women: The heavily-boned corset, bustle and train of the skirts, and high fontage, determine a decorous and straight carriage. Behaviour is as formal as the men's.

Men

General characteristics: Similar to the previous fashion. Skirts are heavily flared, cuffs very large, and the wig dressed full and high on top.

Under garments — similar to the previous fashion. A long neck cloth (Steinkirk) is loosely knotted at the throat, with the ends pinned to the upper part of the coat or passed through one of the buttonholes (name derived from the Battle of Steinkirk, 1692).

Coat — the immensely large skirt flares are set into pleats on either hip, with deep flapped pockets placed low on either side of the fronts. The sleeves, extending almost to the wrist, end in large cuffs.

Waistcoat — full-skirted without sleeves.

Breeches — fit more closely the shape of the leg. They are buckled and buttoned below the knee.

Stockings — worn under the breeches.

Shoes — similar to the previous fashion.

Hats — larger.

Hair — the wig, with high curled horns, is fuller and longer at the fronts and the back where it almost reaches the waist. The face, clean shaven, is often painted.

Accessories — similar to the previous fashion. Large fur muffs carried.

Women

General characteristics: The narrow body parts of the gown, open in front, reveal the pointed, decorated stomacher. The bunched-up skirts extend into a long train at the back.

Under garments — similar to the previous fashion. Flared petticoats, flat in front, develop into pleats at the sides and back to form a bell-shaped foundation for the skirts. The top petticoat is richly decorated.

Gown — the open fronts of the bodice are hooked and eyed to the sides of the stomacher. The richly pleated or gathered looped up skirts are cut with a long narrow train behind. Sleeves terminate at the elbow in turned back cuffs. Revers edge the entire length of the C.F. edges of the gown, to form a flat collar or yoke at the back of the neck. The small corseted waist is emphasised by a narrow belt worn at natural waist level.

Stockings — similar to men's.

Shoes — similar to the previous fashion.

Hair — dressed in a similar style to the previous fashion, is neater, and characterised by the two large curls set high on either side of the centre parting.

Hats — the fontage, changing its shape, is composed of a larger gathered cap, edged with a narrow frill to form lappets. A series of tall, erect, stiffly pleated pieces of linen or lace, one, two or three in number and resembling organ pipes, decorate the top of the front edge.

Accessories — long gloves, fans, earrings. Pearl necklaces worn tightly around the throat. Aprons of fine muslin and lace. Narrow stoles and muffs of fur.

Notes on patterns: Men

Stays — refer to notes of 1690.

Shirt — use the pattern of 1690.

Cravat — fine linen strip 7 to 8 feet in length and 8 inches wide.

Coat — stiffening should be added to the fronts, cuffs and skirts. Extra strengthening is required at the hip points and C.B. to take the weight of the skirts.

Waistcoat — stiffening should be added to the skirts, with the addition of whalebone or buckram at the sides. Form openings on the side and back seams of the skirt in relation to the side and back vents of the coat.

Notes on patterns: Women

Corset — heavily bone throughout and lace at the C.B. The corset is worn over the top petticoat.

Hip pad — lightly pad and attach strings for fastening.

Chemise — construct in the manner of the previous pattern. Add a foundation to the sleeve to control the gathering at the elbow.

Petticoats — make of heavier material but construct as in previous pattern.

Gown — lightly bone the bodice. The skirt is bullet-pleated to the waistline, with the fronts folded back to continue into the revers and collar of the bodice. Skirts are looped up to fasten A to A at the C.B. (fold back top edge of the skirts, graduating from nothing to 3 inches at the C.B. before pleating, to increase the spring of the skirts out from the waistline). Interline revers and cuffs.

Fontage — gather the crown of the cap X to X, joining it to the central gathered part of the lappets, which forms the narrow frilled edging. A wired foundation angled forward, or upright, but never backwards, supports the three tiers of stiffly pleated lace or linen.

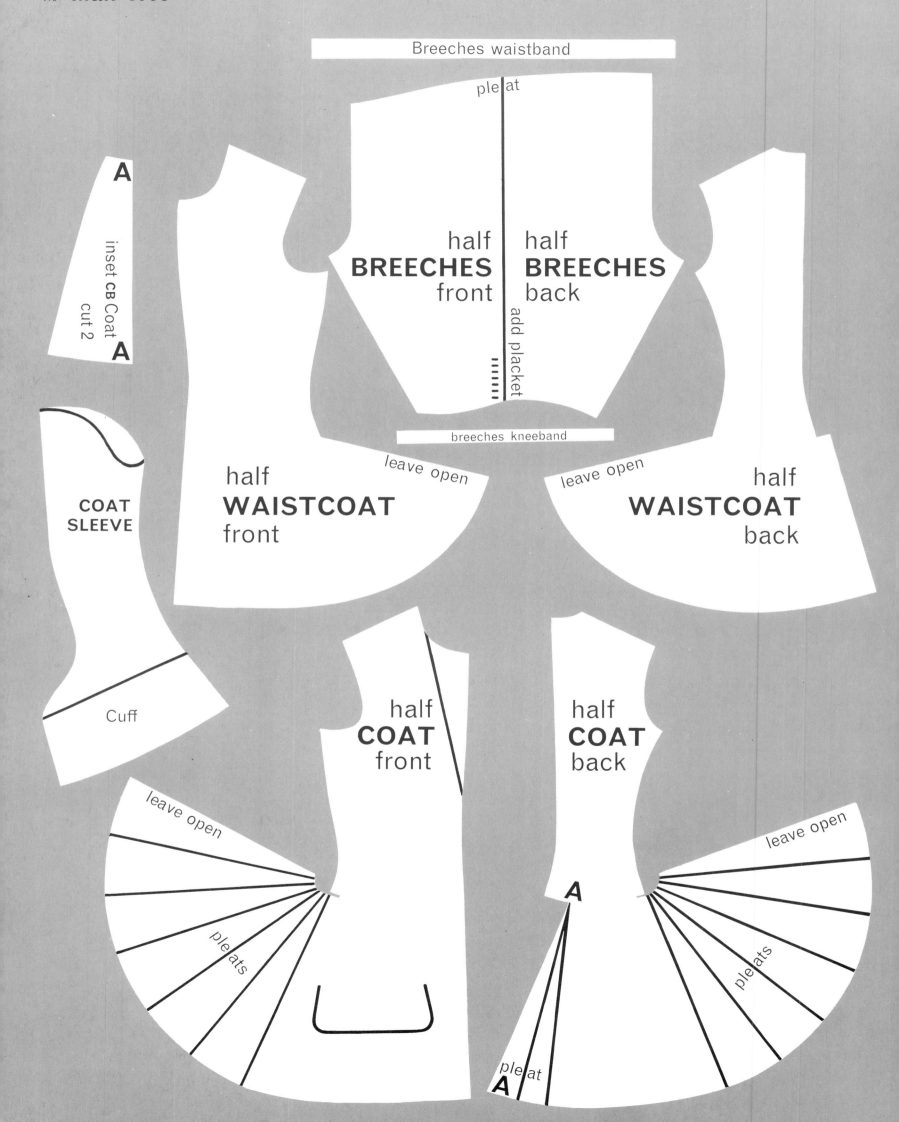

Breeches waistband

pleat

A

inset **CB** Coat cut 2

A

half **BREECHES** front

half **BREECHES** back

add placket

breeches kneeband

COAT SLEEVE

Cuff

half **WAISTCOAT** front

leave open

leave open

half **WAISTCOAT** back

half **COAT** front

half **COAT** back

leave open

pleats

leave open

pleats

A

pleat

A

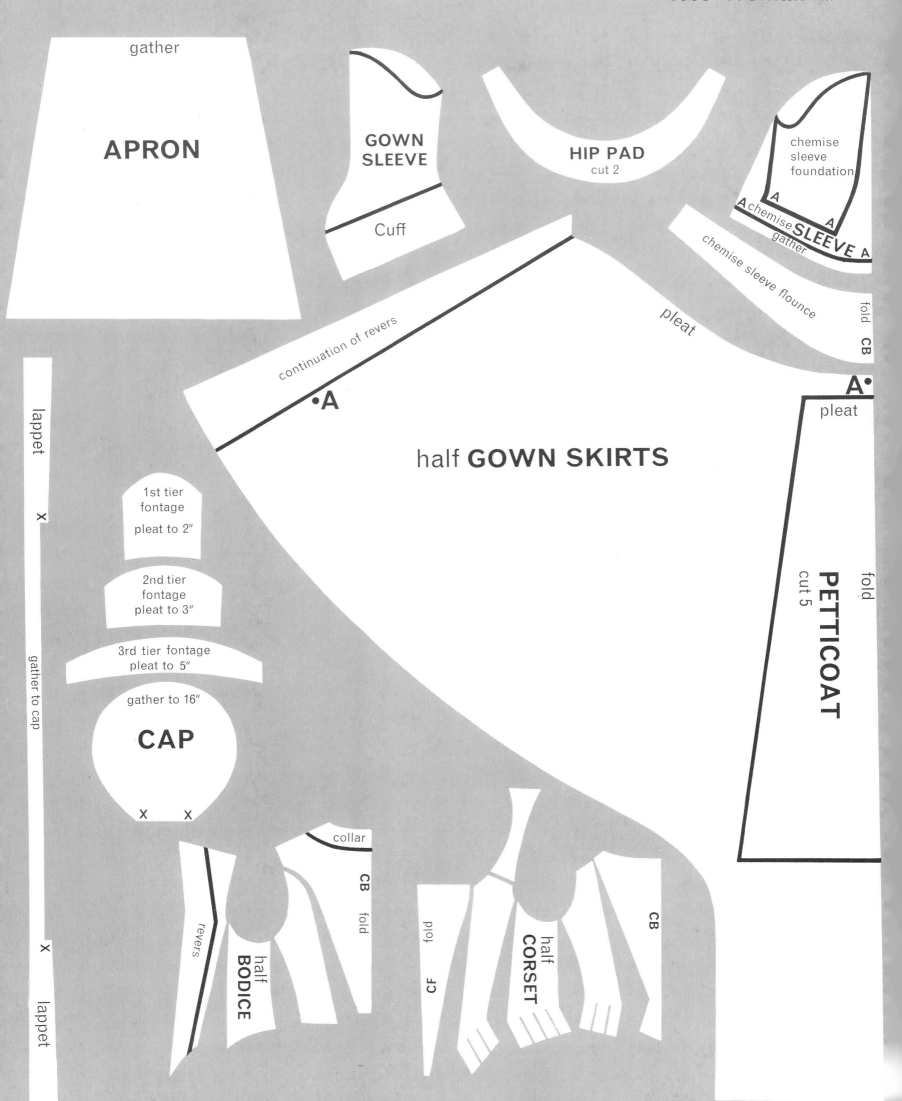

APRON

gather

GOWN SLEEVE

Cuff

HIP PAD
cut 2

chemise sleeve foundation

A chemise SLEEVE A
gather

A

chemise sleeve flounce

fold CB

pleat

A•

continuation of revers

•A

half GOWN SKIRTS

pleat

fold PETTICOAT cut 5

lappet

x

gather to cap

1st tier fontage
pleat to 2"

2nd tier fontage
pleat to 3"

3rd tier fontage
pleat to 5"

gather to 16"

CAP

x   x

collar

CB fold

revers

half BODICE

CF fold

half CORSET

CB

x

lappet

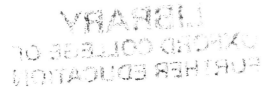

1720 George I

Fabrics: Men — cloth, plush, velvet, silk and satin. Fur trimmings. Women — soft silks, satins, damask, chintz. Printed, painted, or plain Indian cottons.

Colours: Wide variety of colours, usually of a light or middle tone.

Decoration: Large buttons and buttonholes (men) and modest use of ribbons (women).

Padding and restriction, women: Tight, narrow, back-laced corsets. A hooped dome-shaped skirt (cupola) supports the petticoats and gown.

Movement, men: Relaxed and "casual" interpretation of the previous fashion.

Movement, women: Youthful, lyrical and feminine. The full, flowing gown of soft material contrasts strongly with the previous formal and matronly fashion. Graceful and speedier movement.

Men

General characteristics: Similar to the previous fashion — the coat and waistcoat somewhat looser in cut and with an absence of heavy stiffening.

Under garments — similar to the previous fashion.

Coat — left unbuttoned down the fronts.

Waistcoat — considerably shorter in length than the coat, and left unbuttoned to the waist. Two flapped pockets are placed on either side of the skirt fronts.

Breeches — similar to the previous fashion, cut full in the seat. Small horizontal pockets (fob), placed in the waistband, are positioned on either side of the C.F. buttoned opening.

Stockings — of worsted or silk. Ribbed and in various colours, worn over the breeches, and gartered below the knee.

Shoes — similar to the previous fashion.

Hats — similar to the previous fashion, occasionally trimmed with feathers, and worn well back on the head.

Heads — faces throughout this and the first half of the following century are usually clean shaven. The full-bottomed wig is sometimes shorter and less formal — long bob covers the neck, a short bob exposes it.

Accessories — similar to the previous fashion.

Women

General characteristics: A very simple, loosely-fitting closed robe or gown (sack) worn over a hooped underskirt and the corsets.

Under garments — a calico underskirt extended into a bell shape by graduated hoops of whalebone or metal, set into casings. The corsets, with a shorter stomacher front, severely restrict the body. The low square neckline, edged in a frill of muslin, is cut to expose a full rounded bosom. Chemise. Petticoats.

Gown (sack) — set in deep box pleats to a neckband or yoke. It forms a large flowing bell from shoulders to hem. The back pleats are sewn down to shoulder level, the front pleats converge to a point in front, with the opening tied with ribbons. Loose sleeves, pleated into the armholes, terminate below the elbow point in cuffs (unstiffened and softly pleated up the width of the cuff at inner arm) to reveal the puff and narrow frill of the chemise sleeve worn beneath.

Stockings — white stockings very popular.

Shoes — similar to the previous fashion but with massive heels and pointed toes.

Hair — simply dressed, is loosely brushed back from the forehead and temples to form a bun or cluster or ringlets at the back.

Hats — a small cap with a frilled border, decorated with a tie of ribbons at the C.B., is worn square on the top of the head.

Accessories — absence of heavy jewellery — a ribbon tied about throat replaces the necklace. Large folding fans, small muffs.

Notes on patterns: Men

Similar in construction to the previous pattern. Stiffening should be replaced with interlinings of lighter weight.

Breeches — terminate the pattern above knee point and omit the knee bands. The small strip placed on either side of the C.F.s is cut double. The breeches are attached to the waistband at the back and sides — from the side front darts. The C.F. opening is fastened with buttons, the size of the waist adjusted by lacing at the C.B.

Hat — the crown is similar to the pattern of 1690.

Notes on patterns: Women

Corset — adapt pattern for 1785. The boned stomacher is tied or hooked and eyed to the front. A narrow frill of lace edges the neckline.

Chemise — construct as in previous patterns.

Cupola — a calico skirt 120 inches around, with bone or steel hoops set at intervals in casings, to form the bell shape. The skirt, fitting the waist by means of a drawstring, terminates a little below knee in length.

Petticoats — construct as the cupola omitting the boning.

Gown — (to control the waistline and set of the gown, ribbons are attached to points A at the side seams to tie in front about the waist). The fullness of the skirts at the waist sides is formed by arranging the material in pleats to radiate from points A. The back pleats, sewn down two or three inches, are set to the yoke (cut double). The front pleats, set to the shoulder seams (controlled in width by ribbon ties), are caught down at the C.F. waistline. Ribbons, sewn to the fronts, tie across the stomacher. The gown can be worn with a narrow belt.

Cap — gather by means of a draw ribbon to fit the shape of the head.

119

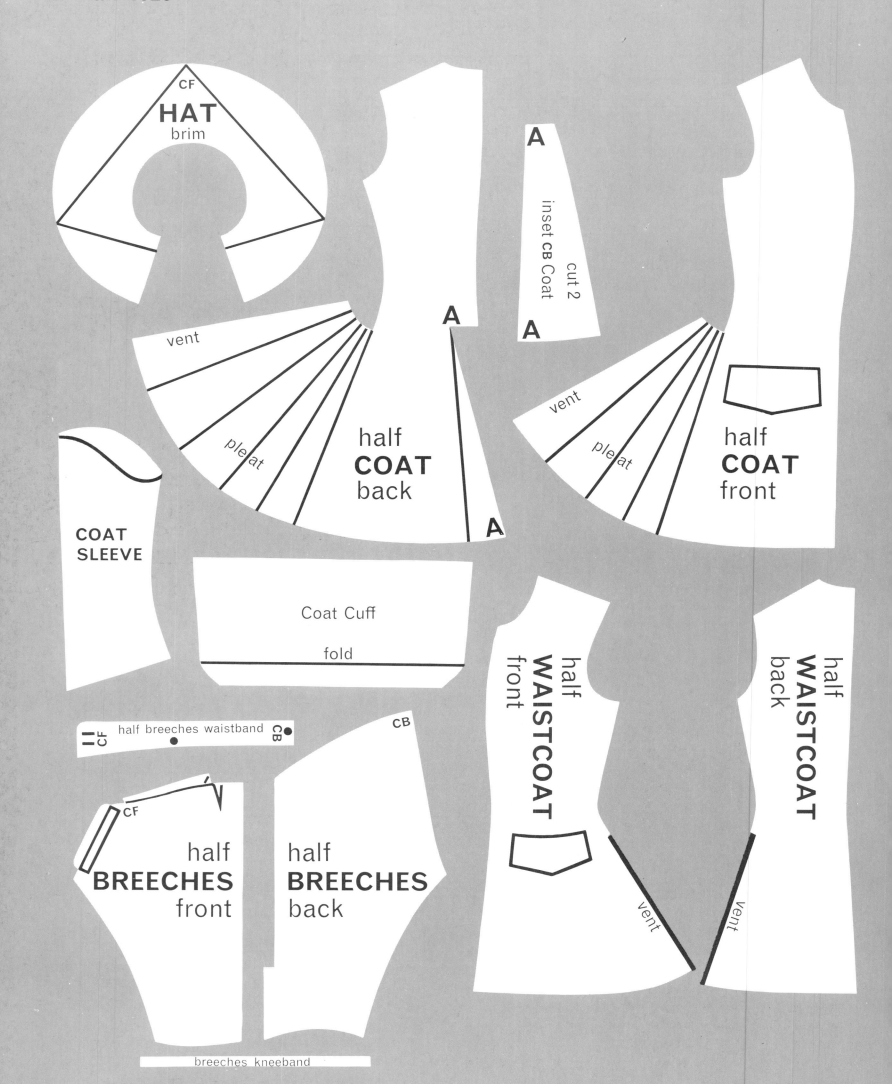

HAT brim
CF

A
inset **CB** Coat
cut 2
A
A

vent
pleat
half **COAT** back
A

vent
pleat
half **COAT** front

COAT SLEEVE

Coat Cuff
fold

half breeches waistband
CF
CB

CF
half **BREECHES** front

half **BREECHES** back

half **WAISTCOAT** front

half **WAISTCOAT** back
vent
vent
CB

breeches kneeband

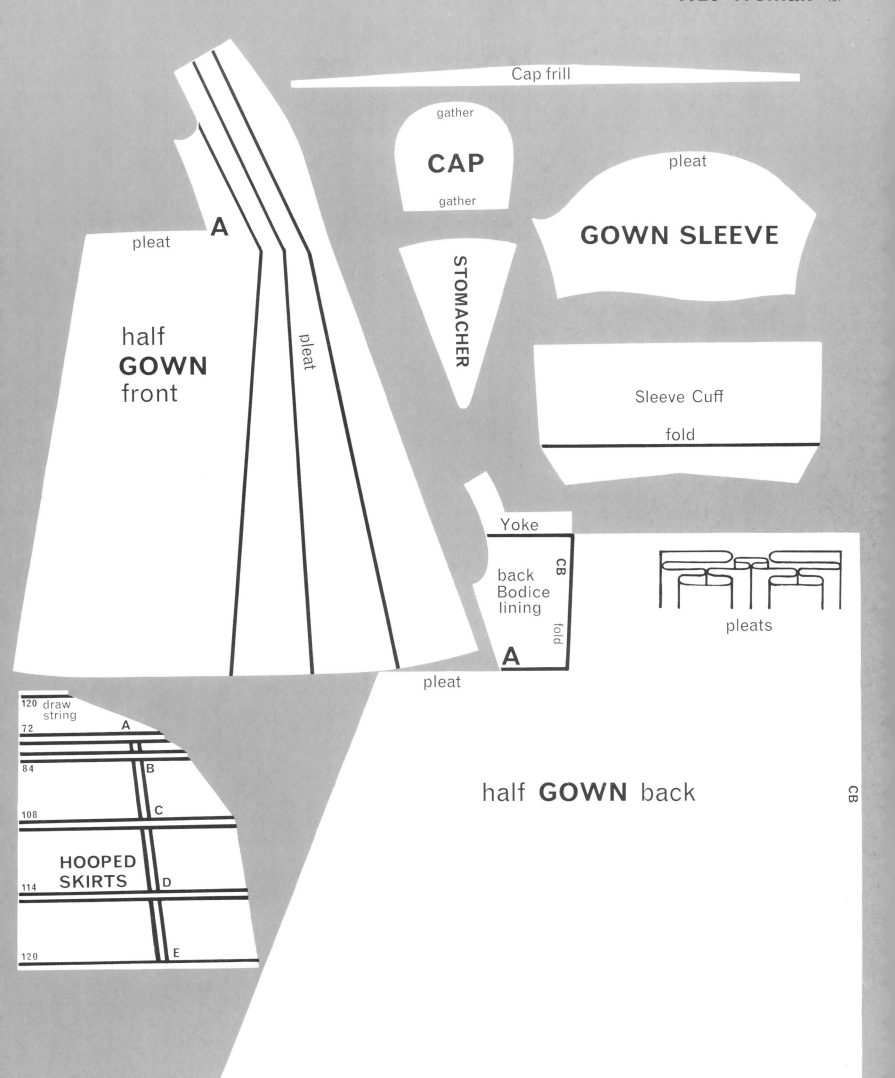

Cap frill

gather

CAP

gather

pleat

GOWN SLEEVE

pleat

A

half
GOWN
front

pleat

STOMACHER

Sleeve Cuff

fold

Yoke

CB

back
Bodice
lining

fold

A

pleat

pleats

120 draw
string

72

A

84

B

108

C

**HOOPED
SKIRTS**

114

D

half **GOWN** back

CB

120

E

1740 George II

Fabrics: Similar to the previous fashion. Muslins, often embroidered in white, for aprons, neckerchiefs, caps, trimmings, etc.

Colours: Brighter, lighter and more intense. Brilliant yellow very fashionable.

Decoration: Men — fabrics woven in small geometric patterns. Buttons, buttonholes and braiding. Embroidery covers the front edges and pocket flaps of the waistcoat. Women — quilting of petticoats in small geometric designs. A freedom of design in East Indian cottons, influences all European textile design.

Padding and restriction, men: A return to stiffening and interlining, particularly the fronts and sides of the coat and waistcoat skirts. A pair of stays, or lacing at the back of the waistcoat, narrows the waist.

Padding and restriction, women: Similar to the previous fashion. The hooped underskirt, flatter at front and back, extends the skirts well out from the hips.

Movement, men: Very formal and elegant behaviour — less extravagant than the mode of 1700.

Movement, women: Practical and unaffected. Arms, curving away from the body, rest on the side extensions of the skirts.

Men

General characteristics: Clothes are more formal. The style of the wig radically changes. The shirt front, exposed by the open waistcoat, sports a frill or ruffle. The stock replaces the cravat.

Under garments — the sleeves of the full shirt are gathered and set to a wristband with deep lace ruffles. The stock, of linen or cambric and folded to form a high neckband, is stiffened and buckled behind. It covers the neckband of the shirt, and is usually worn with the "solitaire" — a length of black ribbon placed over the stock and tied in a bow at the throat.

Coat — fronts curve away to expose the waistcoat. The side flares of the skirts, set out by whaleboning and stiffening, are *very* full and arranged in pleats. Pleats are also placed on either side of the C.B. vent. Pockets rise to hip level and the large cuff, originally closed (Boot sleeve), is open and falls away at the back.

Waistcoat — of different material from the coat. Short backed, and buttoned through from low chest to low waist. The skirts are very strongly flared and stiffened, with flapped pockets positioned higher on the fronts than those of the coat.

Breeches — similar to the previous fashion. The breeches do not necessarily match the fabric of the coat.

Stockings — similar to the previous fashion.

Shoes — toes are more rounded, the tongue much shorter and covered by a small square or oblong buckle. The low heel is frequently red.

Hats — usually black, similar to the previous fashion, and carried (not worn) in the crook of the arm.

Hair — hair or wig centrally parted, brushed well back over pads to form a large roll on either temple, frizzed and curled at the ends. The back hair (queue) is enclosed in a square black bag, which is tied with ribbon and/or secured to the back part of the solitaire. (Wigs of human and animal hair, with feathers sometimes used for the foretop.)

Accessories — similar to the previous fashion. Gloves, with or without gauntlets. Elegant walking canes.

Women

General characteristics: Simple, boned, open bodices laced across the front, with the full extended skirts set to the waist edge, at the sides, in large pleats — the skirts clear the ground.

Under garments — similar to the previous fashion (petticoats arranged and adapted to the shape of the hooped skirt).

Open robe — the fronts, from hem to nape of neck, are bordered with sewn-down revers (robings). The bodice is cut with a narrow back — the open fronts held in place with ribbon ties or lacing, the gap filled with a neckerchief. Narrow sleeves, fitting the armhole, are similar to the previous fashion.

Stockings — similar to the previous fashion.

Shoes — similar to the previous fashion.

Hair — dressed in a similar style to the previous fashion.

Hats — starched caps with gathered crowns, edged in a frill to surround the face, tie under the chin (mob cap). A large flat straw hat (bergère), tied with ribbons under the chin, is worn with the mob cap when travelling abroad.

Accessories — aprons, neckerchiefs, elbow length gloves or mittens, muffs. Very large, up to 24 inches across, folding stick fans.

Notes on patterns: Men

Shirt — similar in construction to previous fashion with the addition of a pleated or gathered ruffle of lace or linen at the C.F. neck opening.

Stays — lightly bone and back-lace to restrict the shape of the waist.

Stock — make in very fine linen or lawn. Gather at either end to tapes, or to a strap and buckle.

Coat — a return to heavy interlining. Strips of whalebone down each pleat, assists the skirts to swing out and away from the body — strengthening is necessary at the hip points to support the weight of material. Lightly pad chest and shoulders to give a rounded form to the upper body parts. The cuff, left open to fall away at the underarm, is held up and secured to the sleeve proper with buttons or by tie-catching.

Waistcoat — the size of the waist is adjusted by back lacing.

Breeches — use previous pattern.

Black bag and solitaire — the black bag is secured around the queue by means of a black draw ribbon (tied in a formal bow at the nape of the neck) and/or the solitaire, which is attached to the top of the bag, brought forward around the stock, and tied in a bow at the throat. Where the solitaire is inserted to draw up the bag, instead of the ribbon, a false bow is sewn to the top edge of the bag.

Hat — similar in construction to previous patterns.

Notes on patterns: Women

Corsets — adapt pattern for 1785.

Chemise — construct as in previous patterns.

Hooped underskirt — use previous pattern. The shape of the skirt, flat front and back and oval in plan, is adjusted by a series of tapes sewn to points A. B. C. D. and E. at front and back sides. When the tapes are tied together A to A, B to B etc., they automatically control the width of the skirts from front to back.

Petticoats — use previous pattern. The top petticoat is cut with a central front panel shaped to lie flat.

Robe — cut lining of the back bodice to fit the corseted figure. Pleatings at back and front, are sewn down to waist level. The back yoke is cut double. (The back pleats, as late as the 70's, are alternatively sewn down as far as the waistline or allowed to hang free. If the latter arrangement is required, the waistline should be controlled by the back bodice lining and a ribbon inner belt commencing from the side seams — see notes 1720.) The fronts of the bodice are held in place by a series of ribbons tied across the stomacher. The sleeve cuff is pleated in a similar manner to the previous fashion.

Cap — gather back of neck to 9 inches and insert a drawstring at A to tie under the chin.

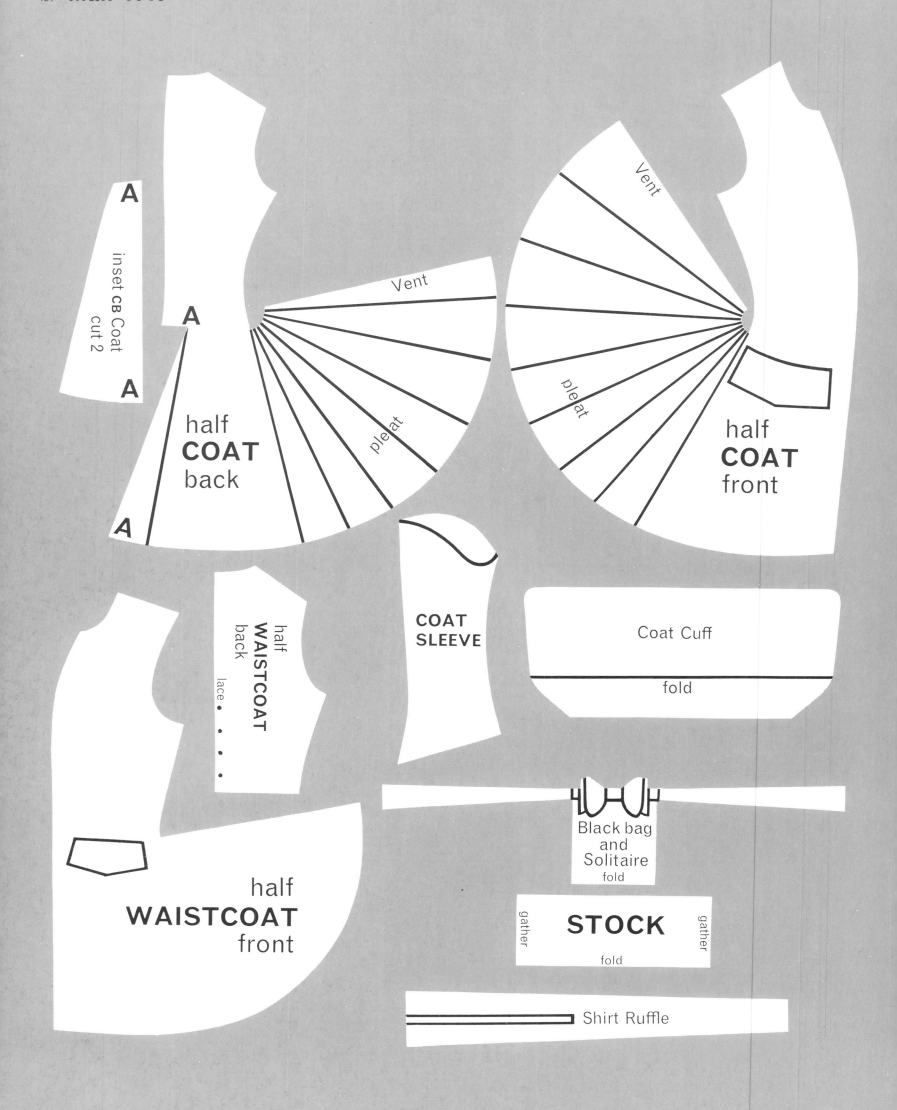

A

inset **CB** Coat
cut 2

A

A

half
COAT
back

A

Vent

pleat

Vent

pleat

half
COAT
front

half
WAISTCOAT
back

lace • • • • •

**COAT
SLEEVE**

Coat Cuff

fold

half
WAISTCOAT
front

Black bag
and
Solitaire
fold

gather   **STOCK**   gather

fold

Shirt Ruffle

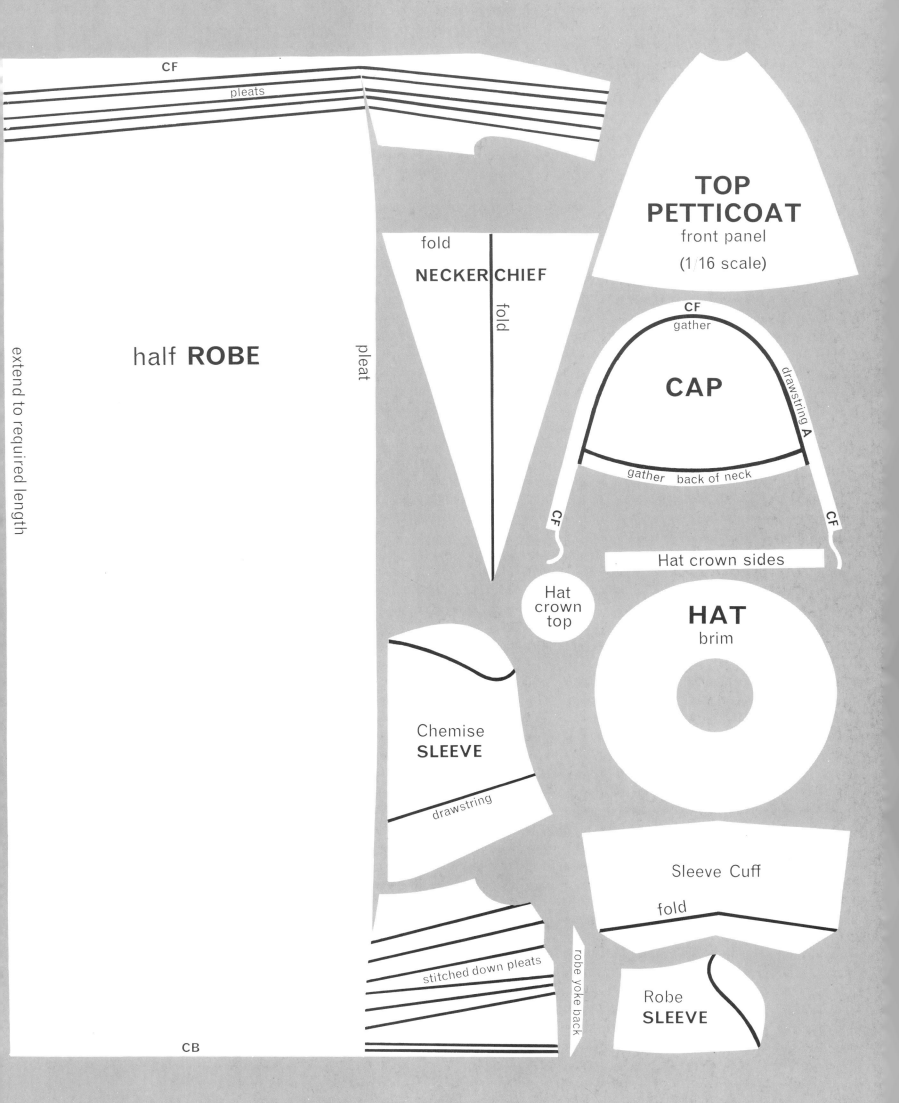

CF

pleats

TOP
PETTICOAT
front panel
(1/16 scale)

fold

NECKERCHIEF

fold

CF

gather

CAP

drawstring A

gather   back of neck

CF

CF

Hat crown sides

half ROBE

extend to required length

pleat

Hat
crown
top

HAT
brim

Chemise
SLEEVE

drawstring

Sleeve Cuff

fold

stitched down pleats

robe yoke back

Robe
SLEEVE

CB

1755 George II

Fabrics: Similar to the previous fashion.

Colours: Men prefer more subdued and darker colours, while women continue to wear bright, light and clear colours — yellow still very fashionable.

Decoration: Men — buttons and buttonholes, braiding, frogging and tasselling. Women — quilting, embroidery, woven and printed fabrics, in large all-over scrolling patterns, lighter and more frivolous in treatment than the baroque incorporating flower, plant, and bird forms. Ribbons, ruchings, fine lace.

Padding and restriction, women: Similar to the previous fashion. The hooped underskirt, now flat at the front and back, becomes so vast that the petticoats and the top skirt are carried and extended horizontally out from the waistline on either side, to then hang vertically down to the ground — some hooped underskirts are collapsible or hinged to permit the wearer to pass through doors.

Movement, men: Quiet, dignified and reserved. Behaviour less flamboyant and affected.

Movement, women: Elegant and assured. The small armholes and tight sleeves restrict the movement of the arms, which are held up and away from the body to display the deep lace flounces at the elbows. Every movement of the figure is controlled in order to avoid bounce, swing, or change of angle, of the great skirts.

Men

General characteristics: Coats continue to be cut away in the front, the skirts lose their flare at the sides. Breeches match the material of the coat. Waistcoats, of contrasting colour and material, are shorter in length

Under garments — similar to the previous fashion. The shirt sleeve, less full, has smaller wrist ruffles.

Coat — straighter in cut from shoulders to hem. The fronts, cuffs, and pocket flaps, are decorated with braid, buttons, tassels, and frogging.

Waistcoat — buttons and buttonholes stop at the low waist, from whence the skirts are cut away at an angle to reveal the breeches.

Breeches — similar to the previous fashion. The waist band has a buckle and strap at the back to adjust the breeches to the size of the waist. The front-buttoned fastening, no longer covered by the waistcoat skirts, is concealed by a flap (fall). Legs of the breeches, ending just below the knee, are open on the outside and buttoned.

Stockings — similar to the previous fashion. The breeches cover the tops of the stockings.

Shoes — similar to the previous fashion. The red heel disappears.

Hats — similar to the previous fashion.

Hair — the queue at the back is enclosed in the black bag. Front hair, brushed back from the forehead, forms a "foretop" or continuous roll from temple to temple. The hair on either side of the head is arranged in 2 or 3 horizontal rolls placed close together (Pigeon wings).

Accessories — similar to the previous fashion.

Women

General characteristics: Narrow, boned, open bodices, the front filled in with a richly decorated stomacher. Enormous open skirts, clearing the ground and sometimes cut with a train at the back, reveal the richly decorated petticoat beneath.

Under garments — similar to the previous fashion. Lace flounces, sewn to the sleeves of the robe, replace the full frilled sleeves of the chemise. Petticoats, with drawstrings to gather them at the waist, are adapted to fit the shape of the various hoops, hip extensions, bum rolls, etc.

Open robe — the narrow back is cut right through without a waist seam (en fourreau). The very elaborately arranged pleatings at the back, set to a little yoke, are sewn down to waist level, allowed to fall free, or both methods are employed on the same garment. The C.B. pleats free and the side pleats sewn down. Skirts are cut to fit the shape of the hooped under skirt, with the side seams carried out horizontally from the waistline and arranged in a fan of pleats over either hip. The tight-fitting sleeve ends at the elbow in a falling flared cuff — longer at the back than the front. A stomacher, usually decorated with a series of graduating bows (échelles) is pinned to the front of the corset to fill the gap formed by the open fronts of the bodice.

Stockings — similar to the previous fashion.

Shoes — toes are sharply pointed. The heel, high, slender and waisted. The upper parts made of kid, brocade, embroidered silk, etc.

Hair — arranged in a style very similar to the men's, with the back hair dressed in a bun, or a flat plait pinned to the top of the head.

Hats — when worn, are similar to the previous fashion.

Accessories — bracelets and collarettes of ruched and pleated ribbons. Earrings and small finger rings. Fans. Little bunches of flowers are often pinned to the corsage — moss roses, lilies of the valley, pinks, daisies, etc. The face is painted and powdered — white.

Notes on patterns: Men

Shirt — similar in construction to the previous pattern.

Breeches — use pattern of 1720. The breeches terminate below the knee with side buttoned openings and buckled knee bands.

Black bag and solitaire — similar in construction to previous pattern.

Coat — fitting should not be so restricted as in previous fashions

Notes on patterns: Women

Corset — adapt pattern for 1785.

Chemise — terminate sleeves above elbow.

Hooped under skirt — is attached to the waistline by means of drawstrings passed through the waist edge of sections A of the pattern. The angle of the skirts can be adjusted by altering the length of the pattern at BC. Heavy continuous boning is placed in the skirts at D E F G H and J. To control depth and shape of the skirt, attach sets of tapes at intervals down the length of the side seams, back and front, and tie off.

Petticoats — gather to the waist by means of a drawstring with little or no fullness at C.F. A drawstring is also placed along the seam AC to adjust the width of the petticoats to the width of the hooped under skirt. The sides are pleated or gathered AB to BA.

Robe — cut back bodice lining to fit the corseted figure. Skirts are sewn to the waistline, front and back sides, without fullness. Side seams continue out horizontally to the further points of the extensions, where the material is arranged in a fan of pleats (X to X). The pleats at the back, attached to a very narrow yoke or strip of material similar in cut to the previous fashion, are sewn down to waist level. Sleeves tightly fit the armhole. Ruchings of fine material cover the join of sleeve to falling cuff. A narrow frill of lace edges the neckline.

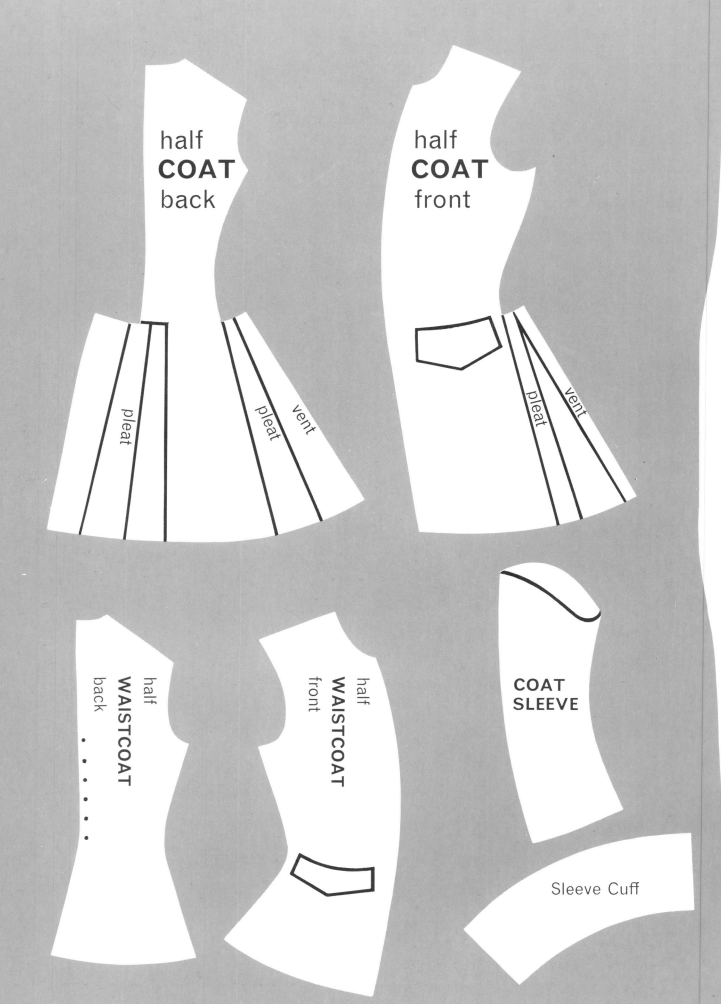

half
COAT
back

pleat

pleat

vent

half
COAT
front

pleat

vent

CRAVAT

half
WAISTCOAT
back

half
WAISTCOAT
front

**COAT
SLEEVE**

Sleeve Cuff

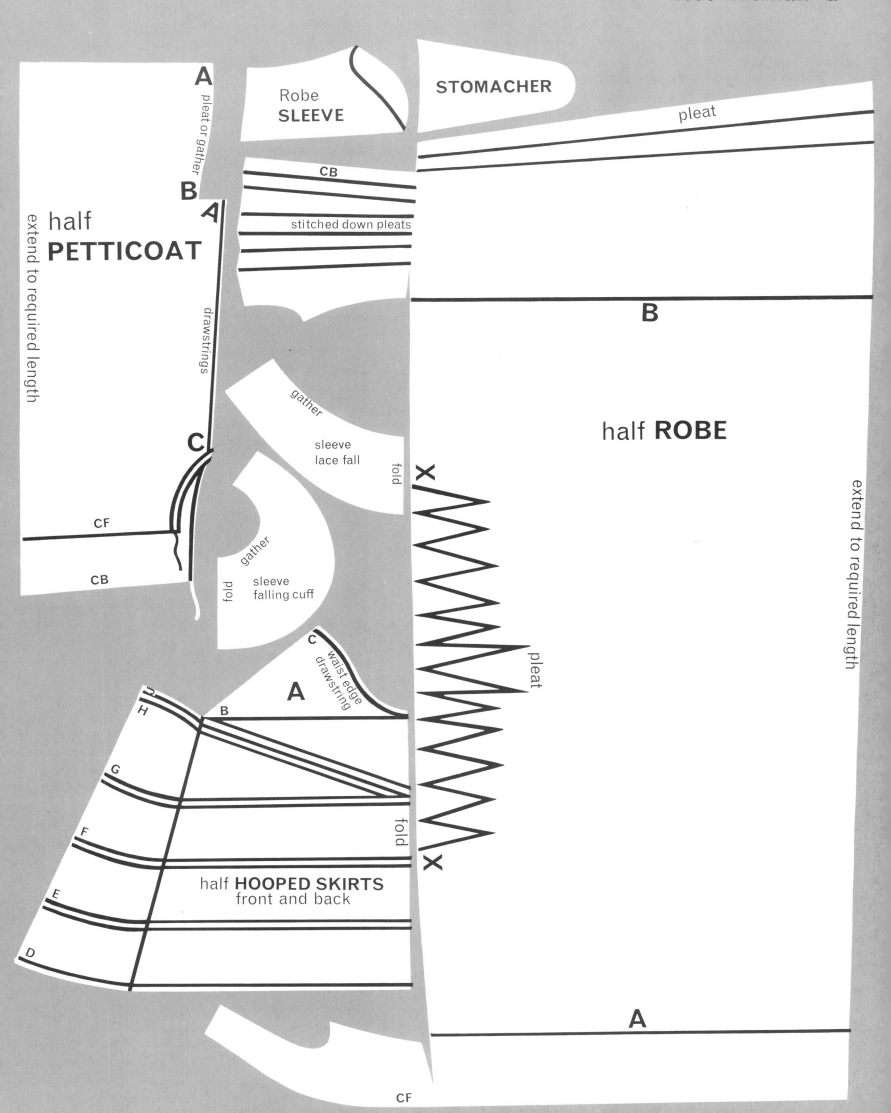

A

pleat or gather

half
PETTICOAT

extend to required length

Robe
SLEEVE

STOMACHER

pleat

CB

B

A

stitched down pleats

drawstrings

gather

sleeve
lace fall

fold

C

X

half **ROBE**

extend to required length

CF

gather

fold

sleeve
falling cuff

CB

B

C

waist edge
drawstring

A

H

B

pleat

G

fold

F

X

half **HOOPED SKIRTS**
front and back

E

D

A

CF

1770 George III

Fabrics: Similar to the previous fashion. Plain satins very fashionable. Fine muslins, gauze, tissues and lace used as trimmings on women's dress. Men for "undress" wear wool and cloth.

Colours: Men continue to wear subdued colours. Women show preference for pretty pinks, blues, greys and white, etc.

Decoration: Ornament, based on rococo forms — shells, plants, scrolls, and unsymmetrical and broken curves, etc., covers most of the women's costume in embroidery, quilting, sequins, ruchings, pleatings, and swags of material. Men confine decoration to the embroidered waistcoat, or to deep bands or richly embroidered edgings on both the coat and the waistcoat — fronts, pockets, cuffs, etc.

Padding and restriction, men: With the development of tailoring, moulding and fitting of the body parts is given greater attention — padding of chest and shoulders to give rounded and smooth form to the coat, etc. Extremists of fashion wear tight stays, and improve the shape of their legs with false calves.

Padding and restriction, women: Similar to the previous fashion. Skirts are very large — some hoops reaching a circumference of 8 yards. A bum roll extends the skirts out at the back.

Movement, men: Similar to the previous fashion.

Movement, women: Similar to the previous fashion. The very high hair style, or wig, severely controls all head and neck movement.

Men

General characteristics: Clothes are more tailored with the coat, waistcoat, and breeches frequently of the same material.

Under garments — similar to the previous fashion. The collar band of the shirt, stepped on either side of the neck, is seen above the stock.

Coat — curved and cut away in front, the skirts arranged in pleats on the side back seams and with a vent, without pleats, at the C.B. The closed cuff of the sleeve, considerably reduced in size, fits the shape of the arm.

Waistcoat — skirts are much shorter and cut away in the front to form a wide inverted V. Flapped side pockets are positioned a little below the natural waist. The neck edge is stepped and appears above the neckline of the coat.

Breeches — tighter and more elegant in cut. A fall covers the C.F. fastening. The leg openings, buttoned at the side, terminate in buckled knee bands.

Stockings — similar to the previous fashion.

Shoes — larger buckles cover most of the instep.

Hats — similar to the previous fashion.

Hair — wigs, powdered and dressed in a variety of ways, are based on the styling of the previous fashion.

Accessories — similar to the previous fashion. The snuff box, handkerchief and a pair of watches are indispensable parts of man's dress.

Women

General characteristics: Skirts are bulkier and very large, the wig or hair dressed very high on top of the head. Dress for evening or day wear becomes clearly defined — "dress" or "undress".

Under garments — similar to the previous fashion. Petticoats are cut very full and gathered.

Open robe — similar to the previous fashion. The robe is covered with ribbons, ruchings, etc., and laced across the stomacher. Deep lace falls (bobbin or very fine needlepoint), are gathered to the sleeve openings. Robings, of ruched muslin or silk, border the front edges from hem to C.B. The skirts are sometimes unattached in front and fastened under the bodice and stomacher with drawstrings, to give a neater and trimmer appearance to the waist.

Stockings — similar to the previous fashion.

Shoes — similar to the previous fashion. Shoes are buckled or fastened with ribbon ties.

Hair — extended with pads and artificial hair, and dressed with pomade and powder, rises to monstrous heights in gigantic rolls, plaits, loops, etc., arranged on the sides and at the back.

Hats — mob caps, increasing in size, are edged and decorated with ruchings, ribbons and frills. For formal and evening wear turbans, feathers, flowers, vegetables, fruit, jewels, ribbons, etc., decorate the hair.

Accessories — similar to the previous fashion.

Notes on patterns: Men

Breeches — the buttoned front fastening is covered by the fall. (B marked on the front pattern is attached to the front breeches to form the front fastening.) The fall is held up by two buttons attached to the waistband. The waist is adjusted at C.B. by lacing, or by a strap and buckle.

Notes on patterns: Women

Corsets — adapt pattern for 1785.

Chemise — similar in construction to the previous fashion.

Side extensions — increase the width of the hooped underskirt of the previous pattern, or construct out of metal and webbing (see diagram).

Petticoats — similar in construction to the previous pattern.

Robe — construct in a similar manner to the previous fashion, using section AB for the side skirts. The side front and side back skirts are gathered to the corresponding waistline of the body parts.

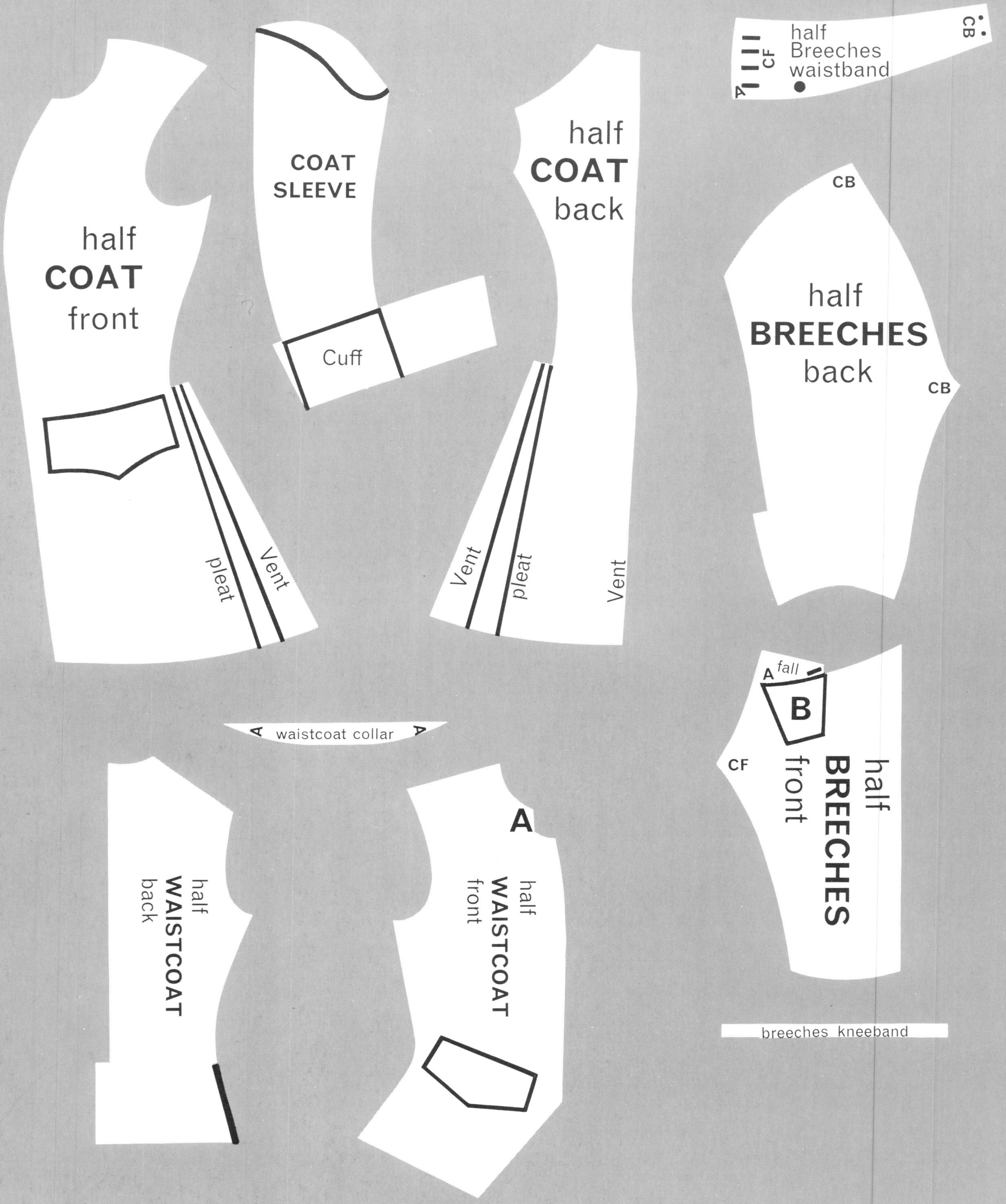

half
COAT
front

**COAT
SLEEVE**

Cuff

half
COAT
back

pleat

Vent

Vent

pleat

Vent

CB

half
**Breeches
waistband**

CF

A

half
BREECHES
back

CB

CB

A fall

B

CF

half
BREECHES
front

breeches kneeband

A waistcoat collar A

A

half
WAISTCOAT
back

half
WAISTCOAT
front

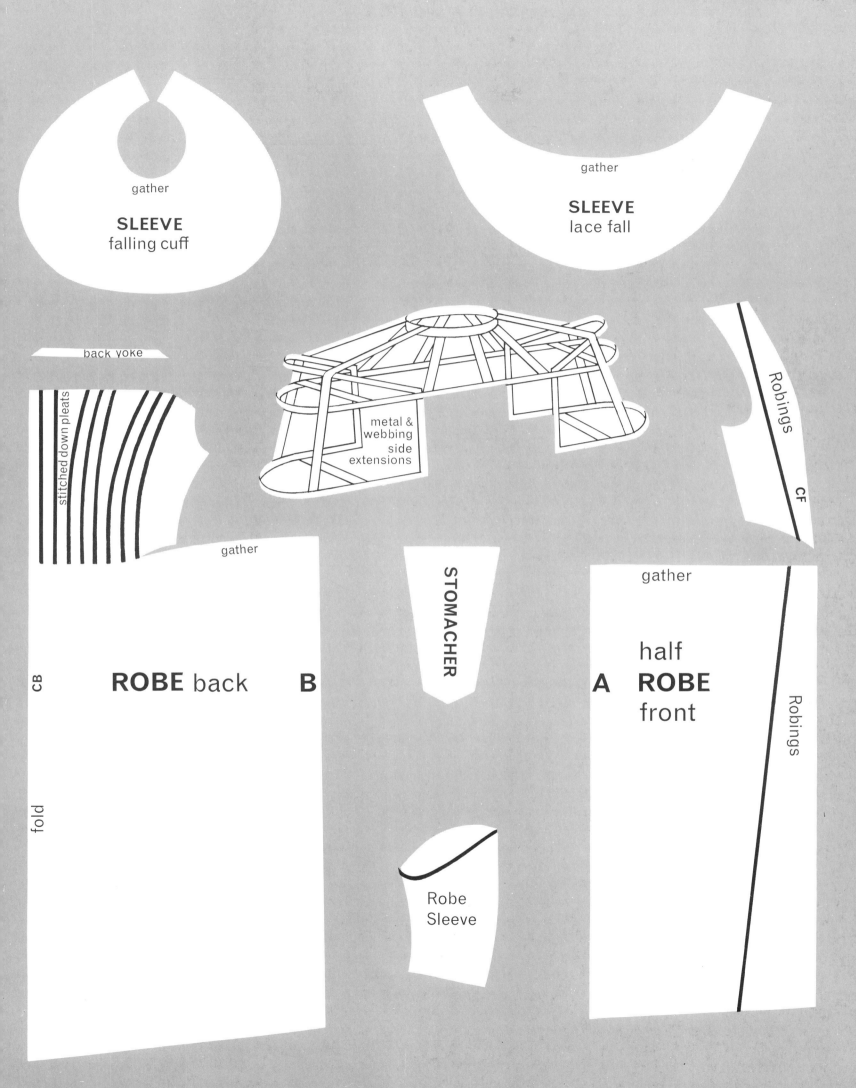

SLEEVE falling cuff

gather

SLEEVE lace fall

gather

back yoke

stitched down pleats

metal & webbing side extensions

Robings

CF

gather

CB

ROBE back **B**

STOMACHER

gather

A ROBE front

half

Robings

fold

Robe Sleeve

1780 George III

Fabrics: Similar to the previous fashion. Women favour cottons, muslins, chintz and light silks.

Colours: Similar to the previous fashion. Men continue to become more conservative in their choice of colours — browns, deep blues, dark reds and greens, grey and black.

Decoration: Similar to the previous fashion. Women particularly admire delicate embroidered sprig patterns and light stripes.

Padding and restriction, women: The corset lengthens to give a longer waist with deep points at back and front. The hooped skirts are frequently discarded and replaced with side buckets — extensions on either hip, of buckets made of calico and whalebones secured with tapes to the waist and hips. A bum roll — of calico stiffened with strips of whalebone and sewn up to form a long cylinder, is tied around the back waist to hold out the back skirts.

Movement, men: Similar to the previous fashion.

Movement, women: Very fashionable to appear youthful and countrified. The short skirts, and absence of hoops, permit speedier and more natural movement.

Men

General characteristics: Marked difference in clothes for "country", "dress", and "undress" wear.

Under garments — similar to the previous fashion. A knotted cravat is worn as an alternative to the stock.

Frock-coat — (undress) distinguishable from the coat because of its collar. The coat (dress) is worn only in the evenings and for formal occasions. The fronts of the frock-coat are cut away to reveal most of the upper parts of legs and thighs. Pleatings at the C.B. and on the side seams are optional. Large flat buttons decorate the fronts, and the wrist opening of the sleeves. The collar rises and falls close about the neck (stand-fall).

Breeches — become excessively tighter to fit the form of the leg and thigh. Made up in cloth, buckskin, cashmere, jersey cloth, etc.

Stockings — similar to the previous fashion.

Shoes — similar to the previous fashion. "Jockey boots", close fitting and ending below the knee in deep turned-down tops, are worn for undress and country wear.

Hats — cocked in a variety of ways — brim turned up only at the back, in the front, or at the back and front (bicorne). A flat topped hat with a flat or gently rolled brim, worn for country and casual wear.

Hair — wigs, resembling in character the previous fashions, are more loosely dressed.

Accessories — similar to the previous fashion.

Women

General characteristics: Countrified adaptation of the previous fashion with the open top skirts looped and bunched up at the sides and back to reveal the ankle-length underskirt.

Undergarments — similar to the previous fashion. The hooped skirts, if worn, return to the bell shape.

Open robe — (Polonaise) the long-waisted, boned bodice resembling the shape of the corset, is closed in front with lacing or hooks and eyes. The pleated back is replaced by a series of narrow panels tapered to fit the waist. The square or low curved neckline is filled with a folded square of muslin tied in front over the breasts. The sleeve tightly fits the armhole — radial darts, formed at the head of the sleeve, take up excess material. Darts, tucks, or pleats are also formed at the inner elbow to shape and curve the sleeve to fit the lower arm. Deep ruchings, covering the whole of the elbow joint, or narrow frills, terminate the sleeve. The gathered and bunched up skirts, bodice neckline, and underskirt, are all edged with pleatings. The front waist edges of the skirt are sometimes free from the bodice and placed on drawstrings — permitting the fullness to be arranged and adjusted to the shape of the side extensions. Underskirts are usually of the same fabric as the robe.

Stockings — with ankles revealed, stockings become more decorative — ribbed, striped, embroidered, etc.

Shoes — buckled high over the instep, pointed, with a slender heel placed well under the foot.

Hair — dressed in a similar manner to the previous fashion.

Hats — caps are large, or very small to perch on top of the head. The calache — a hood fastened under the chin and boned to keep it away from the face, is worn for out-of-doors. Flat straw hats.

Accessories — similar to the previous fashion. Little, prettily decorated parasols. Women imitate men by wearing a pair of fob watches and carrying tall walking canes.

Notes on patterns: Men

Cravat — a strip of linen approximately 5 feet long and 8 inches wide.

Coat — the sleeve, with a half cuff, has a buttoned wrist opening.

Breeches — use pattern for 1795.

Notes on patterns: Women

Corset — adapt pattern for 1785.

Chemise — similar in construction to the previous fashion.

Bum roll — attach strips of whalebone to the width of the fabric. Form into a cylinder and place on a drawstring.

Hip buckets — (make two) insert six strips of heavy whaleboning in casings to the side sections 1, 2, 3, 4, 5, 6. The base joins sides at A. B. and C. The inner side joins sides and base at D.D. AA, CC, and EE. Drawstrings, inserted in the top edges, fasten and control the buckets at the waist. Tapes are placed at D and A on the backs and E and C on the fronts, to further secure the buckets at hips and thighs.

Petticoats — gather with a drawstring at the waist. (The gathering is arranged in relation to the side buckets.)

Polonaise — bone bodice on all seams and fasten with hooks and eyes, or lacing, at C.F. The skirts, folded back along the top edge to increase their spring from the waistline, are sewn to the back waist edge but free in front. These two front sections are placed on drawstrings and tied under the bodice front (skirts stop at point B). The bunchings up of the skirts at the back are controlled by sets of tapes (sewn to points A on either side of the C.B.) which when tied, form loops to support the arrangement and depth of fabric.

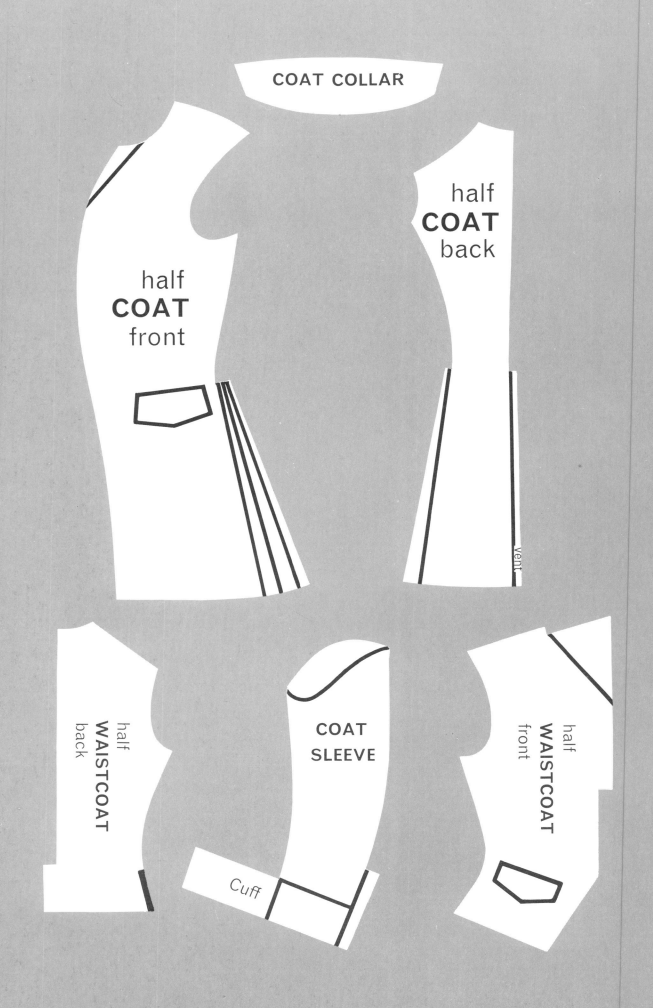

COAT COLLAR

half
COAT
back

half
COAT
front

half
WAISTCOAT
back

**COAT
SLEEVE**

half
WAISTCOAT
front

vent

Cuff

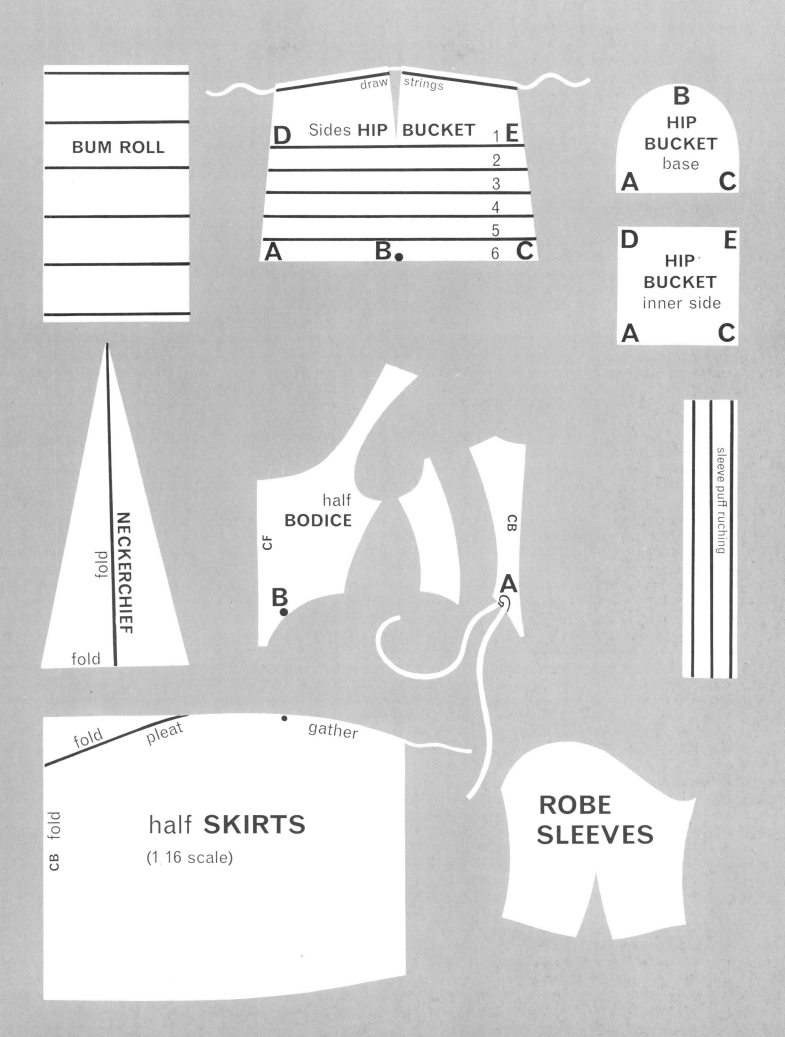

BUM ROLL

draw strings

D Sides **HIP** | **BUCKET** 1 E

2

3

4

5

A B. 6 C

B
HIP
BUCKET
base
A C

D **E**
HIP
BUCKET
inner side
A C

NECKERCHIEF

fold

fold

fold

half
BODICE

CF

CB

B.

A

sleeve puff ruching

fold pleat gather

CB fold

half **SKIRTS**

(1 16 scale)

ROBE
SLEEVES

1785 George III

Fabrics: Similar to the previous fashion. Striped fabrics very popular.

Colours: Similar to the previous fashion. Women favour white and bright colours — orange, scarlet, emerald green and bright blue, etc.

Decoration: Embroidered and woven stripes. Designs based on the antique (Greece and Rome), treated in a light and delicate manner, decorate edges, or form small scattered repeat patterns.

Padding and restriction, women: Hip buckets disappear. The bum roll remains to form a bustle. The long corsets are laced down back and front.

Movement, men: Similar to the previous fashion.

Movement, women: The back is straight with the head held high. The bosom is thrust forward to resemble a pouter pigeon — emphasised by the large puffed-out neckerchief. The pelvis tilts back to complement the line of the bustle. Compared to the formal behaviour of the lest hundred years, movement is relaxed and more natural.

Men

General characteristics: Very similar to the previous fashion. Cut of clothes gives a trim, straight, narrow line to the figure. The waistcoat terminates a little below natural waist.

Under garments — similar to the previous fashion. Linen at the wrist is reduced to a small pleated frill. Drawers of cotton, stockinette or wool, extend to the knee. They are open down the C.F., set to a waistband, and adjusted at the back with tapes, to fit the waist. Braces are introduced to support, and improve the hang of the breeches.

Frock-coat — similar to the previous fashion. The stand-fall collar is higher. Sleeves terminate in half cuffs with the wrist openings stepped and buttoned. Side seams curve from the lower back shoulders to almost meet at the C.B.

Waistcoat — similar to the previous fashion — pocket flaps disappear. Made of fancy and striped silks.

Breeches — similar to the previous fashion. White breeches very popular. A pair of watches or fobs are worn on either side of the small fall.

Stockings — white, coloured and striped.

Shoes — large buckles decorate the fronts.

Hats — similar to the previous fashion.

Hair — wigs, frequently unpowdered, and fuller at the sides, are crimped and curlier. The queue is usually turned up on itself and tied with narrow black ribbons (catogan).

Accessories — similar to the previous fashion.

Women

General characteristics: Large hats, puffed out bodice fronts (bouffant), and full skirts — extended out at the back into a train.

Under garments — chemise, corsets, gathered petticoats, and bum roll.

Open robe — the full open skirts are gathered to the waistline of the low, round-necked bodice. The fronts of the bodice, cut away at a sharp angle, are fastened to the corset. The tight sleeves, similar to the previous fashion, are longer and edged in short muslin frills. A full muslin or cotton underskirt, usually white, is worn under the robe. A large folded kerchief, covering the shoulders and crossing over the bosom, is tied at the small of the back. A wide ribbon or sash, placed about the natural waist, ties in a large bow at the back.

Stockings — generally white.

Shoes — similar to the previous fashion with a lower, smaller heel.

Hair — frequently curled all over, is dressed in a similar manner to the preceding fashion, but severely reduced in height on top. The sides are wider and fuller. The back is arranged in a long full queue, plaited, looped up and tied, or allowed to hang in a cluster of ringlets down the back.

Hats — very large brimmed hats handsomely trimmed with large feathers, ribbons, etc.

Accessories — bracelets and collarettes based on classical design, ribbons tied high about the throat, long gloves, watches. Large, elaborately trimmed muffs.

Notes on patterns: Men

Shirt — construct in a similar manner to the previous fashions but reduce the width of the sleeve and the depth of the wrist frill.

Stock — adapt pattern of 1740.

Breeches — use pattern for 1795.

Coat — the side vents are buttoned, or left open with decorative buttons sewn at intervals down the pleats.

Bicorne — the crown is flower pot or round in shape. The shaping and folding up of the brim, back and front, should form a subtle curve sweeping up from the sides to flatten at the C.F. and C.B.

Notes on patterns: Women

Corset — close bone throughout and lace at C.F. and C.B. The shoulder straps are adjustable (ribbon ties at the front) in relation to the slope and angle of the shoulders. (All bodices should be cut and fitted in relation to the corset.)

Bum roll — use pattern of 1780.

Chemise — similar to the previous fashion.

Petticoats — (worn under the corsets) cut full and gather at the waist with a drawstring.

Robe — the bodice, lightly boned throughout, is fastened at the fronts with hooks and bars to the corset. The sleeve should tightly fit the arm and armhole.

Hat — requires wiring and stiffening.

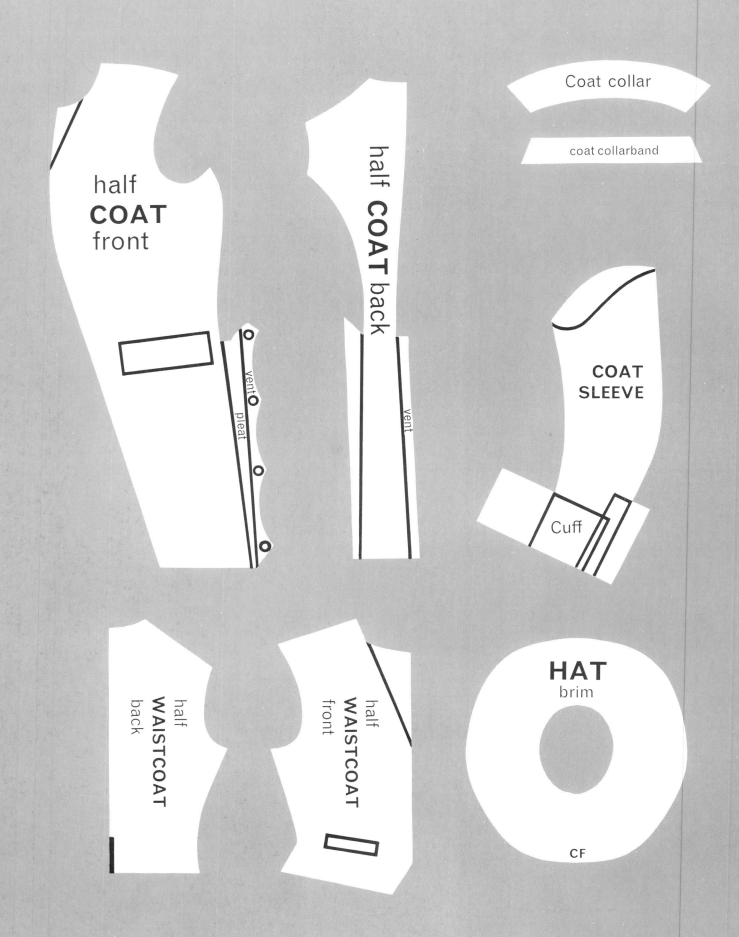

half **COAT** front

half **COAT** back

Coat collar

coat collarband

COAT SLEEVE

Cuff

vent

pleat

vent

half **WAISTCOAT** back

half **WAISTCOAT** front

HAT brim

CF

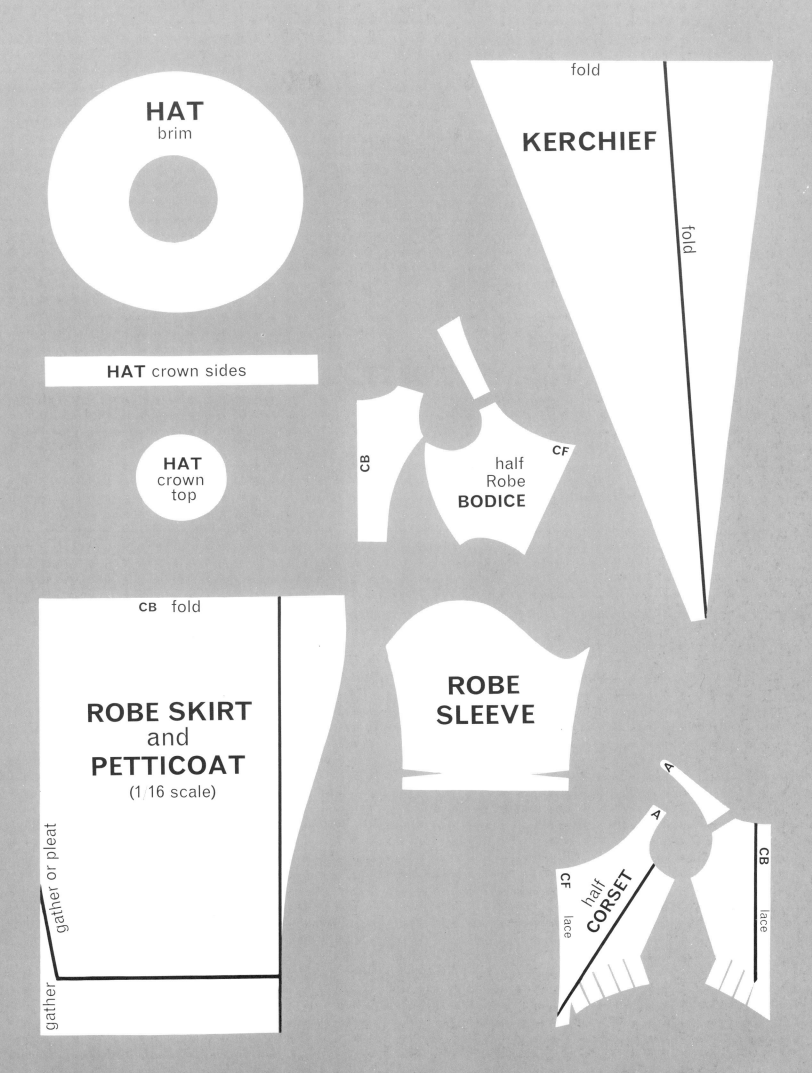

HAT brim

HAT crown sides

HAT crown top

KERCHIEF

fold

fold

CB

half Robe **BODICE**

CF

ROBE SKIRT and **PETTICOAT** (1/16 scale)

CB fold

gather or pleat

gather

ROBE SLEEVE

half **CORSET**

A

A

CF

lace

CB

lace

1795 George III

Fabrics: Cloths, wools, muslins, soft silks, calicos.

Colours: Similar to the previous fashion.

Decoration: Fabrics woven, embroidered, or printed in stripes — narrow, broad, decorated or left plain. Spots and formal small repeating patterns.

Padding and restriction, women: A small short corset and little bum roll. A series of cotton balls, sewn to the back tabs of the corset to thrust out the skirts gracefully from the high waistline, often replaces the bum roll.

Movement, men: Relaxed, easy and natural compared to the formal behaviour seen in previous fashions. The very high stand-fall collar and cravat limits the movement of head and neck.

Movement, women: The costume of light and soft material, without massive extensions or constriction, permits simple, natural and easy movement. Posture and deportment similar to the previous fashion.

Men

General characteristics: Youthful and boyish. The hips, stomach, thighs and legs, are totally exposed in front — encased in extremely tight-fitting breeches.

Under garments — similar to the previous fashion. The muslin cravat, carefully folded lengthwise, is passed twice around the neck and tied at the throat in a soft bow.

Frock-coat — comfortably fits the shoulders and chest, and falls straight down the back and front with little or no signs of waisting. Short, square-cut, open fronts develop into wide rolled lapels and a stand-fall collar — stiffened to stand high about the neck and the sides of the face. The skirts (tails) commence well back on the sides of the body. Sleeves are tighter in fit with half cuffs following closely the shape of the sleeve. Large flat buttons decorate the sleeve and the back and front openings of the coat.

Waistcoat — waist length, double breasted with high lapels, welted pockets, and decorated down the front with two rows of large flat buttons. The waistcoat is frequently striped.

Breeches — (usually white) terminate well below the knee where they are buttoned and tied with ribbons at outer leg. Cut full and high at the back, with the front-buttoned opening covered by a small fall, the breeches are set to a deep waistband.

Stockings — fancy knit.

Shoes — low square heel, fronts cut away, with toes no longer round but pointed. Ribbons replace the buckle.

Hats — flower-pot shaped with a tall crown and smallish brim. A broad hat band and buckle trim the crown.

Hair — (wigs disappear) natural hair is arranged in loose short curls at the sides and back of the head. The front hair, curled high, begins to form a small fringe.

Accessories — similar to the previous fashion. Elegant walking canes.

Women

General characteristics: Similar in cut to the previous fashion, but with a very high rounded waist.

Under garments — chemise, soft full petticoats and short corset.

Open robe — made in light-weight cottons, muslins and silks. Bodice fronts fasten edge to edge, or are double breasted. The skirts commence well away from C.F. to reveal the full gathered muslin petticoat worn beneath. A long muslin scarf, placed about the shoulders and crossed over the bosom to fall down in front, is secured by the waist ribbon.

Stockings — similar to the previous fashion.

Shoes — narrow and slender in shape with a very low heel and a square toe.

Hair — dressed "déshabille" in wild snake-like curls and ringlets, is based on the style of the previous fashion.

Hats — straw, low-crowned hats with large brims — a folded muslin kerchief or scarf is placed over the hat and tied under the chin. Turbans. Trimmings of ribbons and tall feathers.

Accessories — a reticule to hold handkerchief, purse, bottle of scent, etc., becomes an indispensable part of dress. Muffs, small fans, scarves, and long gloves.

Notes on patterns: Men

Shirt — the sleeve terminates in a wristband, pleated frill, and placket.

Waistcoat — form-welted pockets.

Breeches — (no inside leg seam) cut on cross. Welted pockets are placed above the buttons, supporting the fall, on either side of the C.F. Lacing or a buckle and strap, positioned at the C.B. of the waistband, adjusts the breeches to the size of the waist. The outside leg openings are buttoned and draw ribbons are inserted into the knee bands. Braces should be worn.

Hat — the crown is blocked or constructed in sections — wired and stiffened.

Notes on patterns: Women

Short corset — bone throughout and lace at front and back. Pom-poms are sewn to the waistline of the back sections to help support and thrust out the back skirts. As an alternative, a small bum roll (use pattern for 1805) is sewn to the inside edge of the waistline of the robe. The shoulder straps are adjustable (ribbon ties at the front) in relation to the slope and angle of the shoulders.

Petticoats — (muslin or soft cotton) gather at waistline with a drawstring.

Under gown — (add placket and hook and eye fastening at C.B.). The skirts are gathered to the waist edge of the bodice (with or without short sleeves). The bodice is gathered at the front and back waist edge, and neckline.

Robe — (C.F. edge to edge fastening). Lightly bone bodice. Skirts are gathered to the bodice commencing at A on either side of the C.F. The sleeve should tightly fit the arm and armhole.

Hat — make in straw.

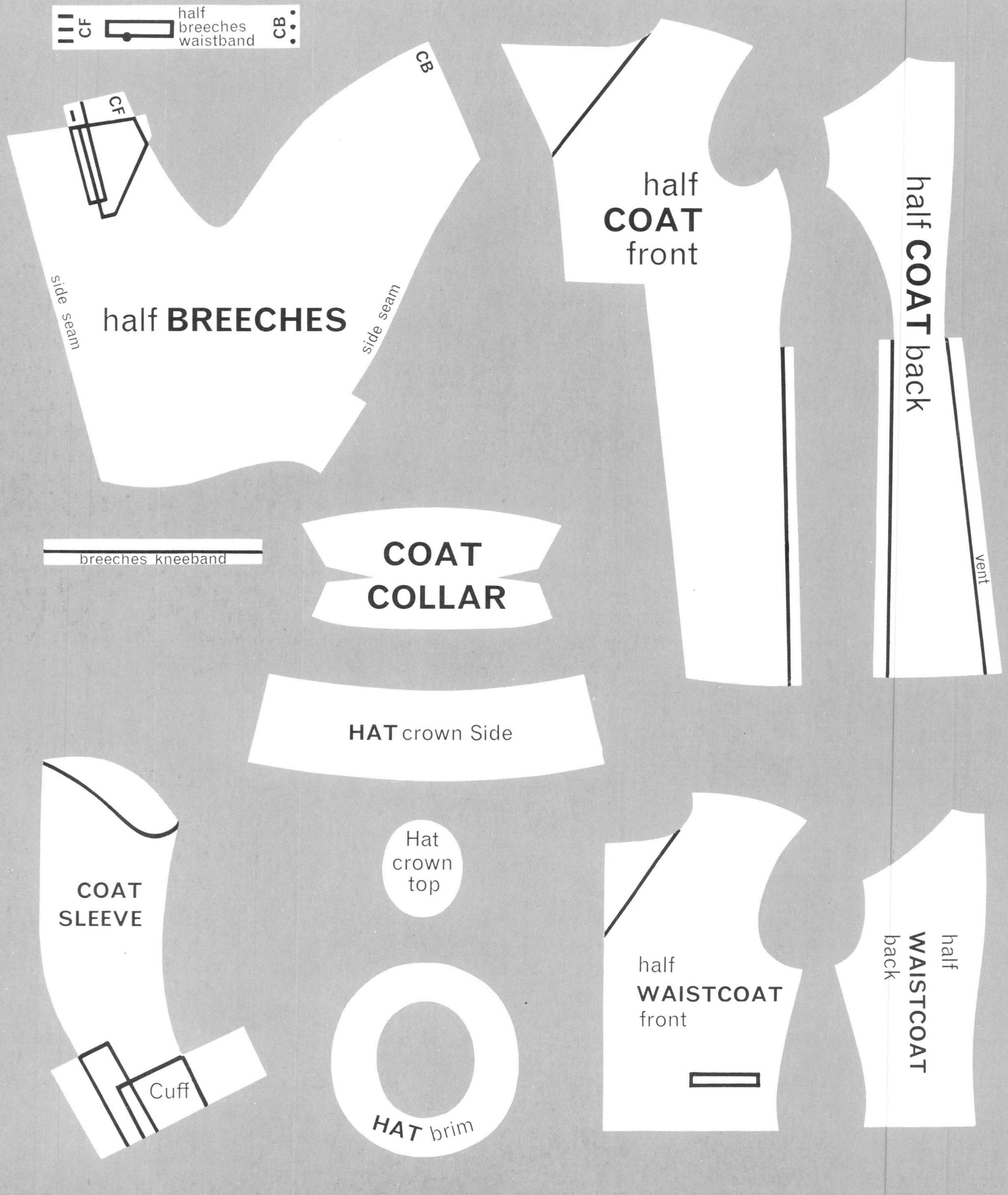

CF half breeches waistband CB

CB

CF

half **BREECHES**

side seam

side seam

breeches kneeband

half **COAT** front

half **COAT** back

vent

COAT COLLAR

HAT crown Side

Hat crown top

COAT SLEEVE

Cuff

HAT brim

half **WAISTCOAT** front

half **WAISTCOAT** back

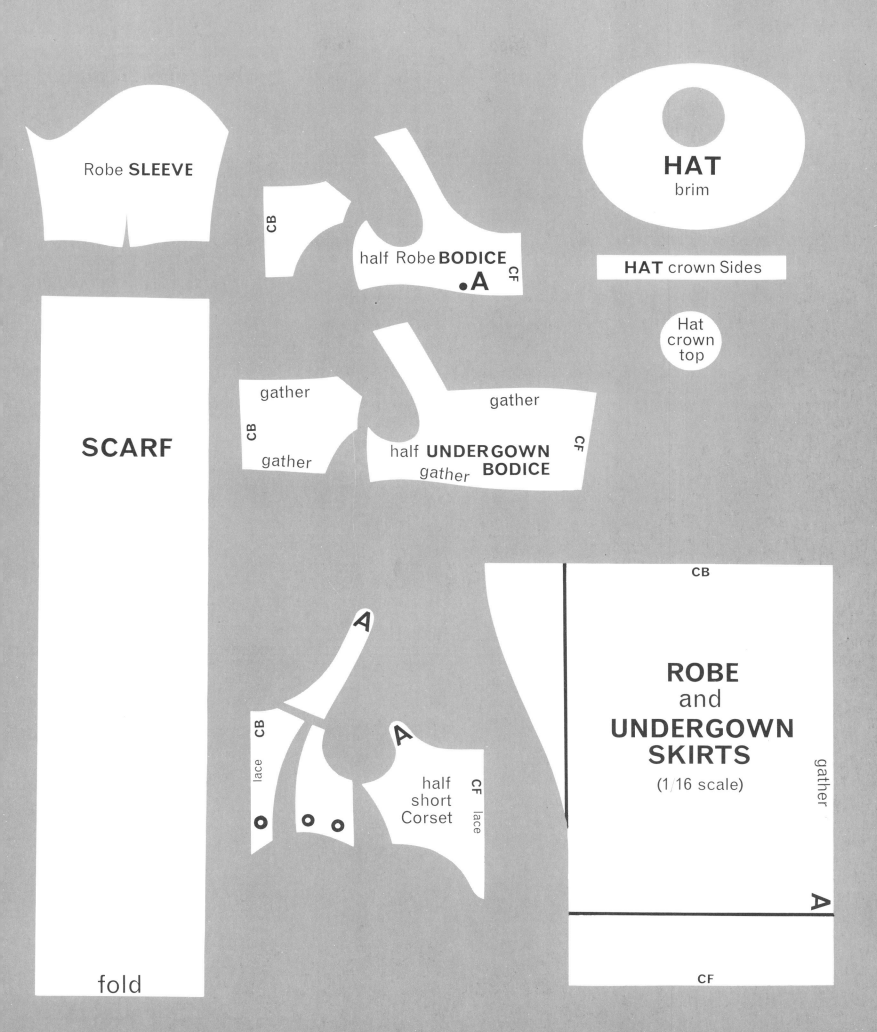

Robe **SLEEVE**

CB

half Robe **BODICE** .**A** CF

HAT
brim

HAT crown Sides

Hat
crown
top

SCARF

gather
CB
gather

gather
half **UNDERGOWN**
BODICE CF
gather

A

CB
lace
half
short
Corset
A
CF
lace

CB

ROBE
and
UNDERGOWN
SKIRTS
(1/16 scale)

gather

A

CF

fold

1805 George III

Fabrics: Similar to the previous fashion.

Colours: Very conservative. Men prefer dark blue, black or bottle green for the coat, and white for the breeches. Women universally wear white (classical dress). Touches of colour are introduced in the trimmings and accessories.

Decoration: Almost a total absence of decoration in both men's and women's dress. Women aim for simplicity and men concentrate on cut and tailoring, achieving exquisite taste in line and proportion.

Padding and restriction, men: Stays, back-laced, worn to reduce the waistline.

Padding and restriction, women: Artificial bosoms sometimes worn to improve shape and size of the natural breasts. A small corset is sometimes worn to emphasise the high waist.

Movement, men: Very assured, upright yet relaxed. The chest is thrust forward and the stance draws attention to the shape of the leg.

Movement, women: (classical). A gliding liquid progression of movement based on antique statuary. The thin, almost transparent, little white muslin or cotton dress reveals the unrestricted form of the figure beneath.

Men

General characteristics: A development of the previous fashion with fastidious attention paid to cut and detail.

Under garments — similar to the previous fashion. The folding, starching and pleating of neck linen becomes an art. The high-standing, stepped collar of the shirt appears well above the cravat or stock, which is frequently made up in linen, stiffened from behind (with a shaped piece of buckram or pasteboard) and buckled at the back.

Frock-coat — double breasted and usually worn buttoned. It is cut to reveal the waistcoat and an expanse of the shirt front. Wide revers develop into an M-cut high rolled collar. Sleeves, gathered and padded at the armhole, are close fitting and without cuffs.

Waistcoat — (seen below the fronts and at neck edges of the coat), single breasted, with a stepped stand collar, and lapels that stand away from the chest.

Pantaloons — (worn with high boots) similar in cut to the breeches (skin tight), they extend to the ankles where the side seams are open (buttoned fastening) for the purpose of pulling on.

Stockings — usually white.

Shoes — similar to the previous fashion. Calf-length boots, with curved tops terminating in a tassel at the C.F., are very popular for out-of-door wear (Hessians).

Hats — similar to the previous fashion. Collapsible bicornes (*Chapeau Bras*), the shape resembling a crescent, are carried or worn on formal occasions.

Hair — dressed in the "Brutus crop". It is cut fairly short and curled particularly in the front where it rises high to form a negligently arranged fringe. The sides are brushed forward over the temples and cheekbones.

Accessories — similar to the previous fashion. A series of fobs and watches hang from one of the fob pockets of the breeches.

Women

General characteristics: Very high waisted, with a tiny bodice and tubular skirt — with or without a train.

Under garments— frequently not worn, with flesh coloured tights often taking their place.

Round gown — (frock) back fastened, ground length, with low neck, and short or long sleeves. The little bodice is attached to the skirts, which are flat in front and gathered at the back. Edges and openings of the gown are bordered in the classic manner — key patterns, flowing ivy, honeysuckle, etc., or with simple bands. Ionic fastenings very popular.

Stockings — white or flesh colour.

Shoes — flat and pointed with thin soles. Classical cross gartering, lacing the shoe to the foot, frequently extends to as high as the knee.

Hair — dressed in the Grecian manner with bunches of small curls and ringlets arranged over the forehead, temples, and at nape of the neck. The rest of the hair is combed back and formed into an elaborate bun or cluster of curls placed high on the back of the head.

Hats — mob caps. A wide variety of hats of fabric or straw, including turbans and military helmets, worn for out-of-doors. Veils.

Accessories — shawls and scarves, small and large, fringed, patterned, or plain. Reticules, small folding fans, long or short sticked parasols, walking canes, wrist-length gloves. Very little jewellery is worn during the day.

Notes on patterns: Men

Shirt — the collar should be stepped in front and cut high enough to cover the lower jaw bone.

Neck cloth or cravat — an isosceles triangle (50 to 60 inches along its base and 10 to 12 inches in height) of fine muslin. To wear, first reduce the width to $3\frac{1}{2}$ inches by pleating, then centralise the strip to the throat, passing the ends around to the back of the neck, crossing them over, and then bringing them forward again to be tied in a bow at the pit of the throat.

Coat — pad shoulders, chest, and the tops of the sleeves. The buttoned opening at the wrist is usually left undone.

Pantaloons — (no inside leg seam) cut on cross. Form outside buttoned openings at the ankles.

Notes on patterns: Women

Bum roll — fasten to the inside edge of the back waistline of under gown.

Under gown — (add placket at C.B., with hook and eye fastening). The skirt, sewn to the sleeveless bodice, is gathered or pleated at the back.

Gown — (add placket at C.B., with hook and eye fastening). The front of the bodice is gathered along the neck edge (to a very narrow edging approximately 12 inches long) and at the waistline. The skirts, at the back, are gathered and left open with the edges held together at intervals by ribbon ties. The sleeve, gathered to the armhole, is also fastened at the outside arm with ribbons.

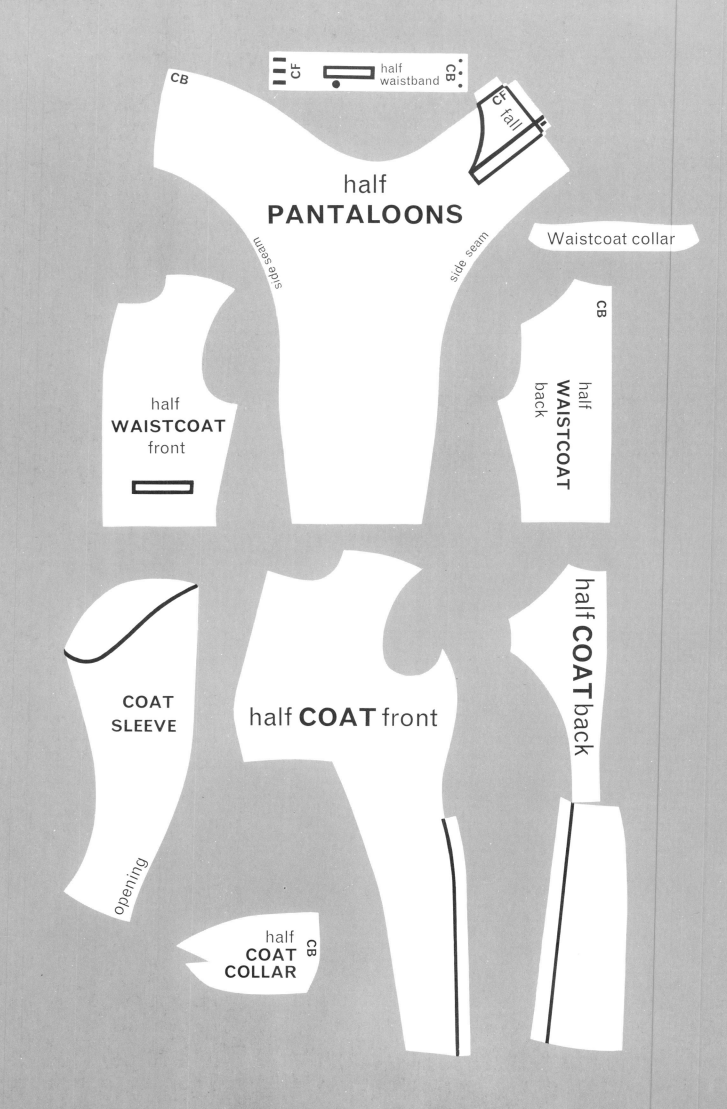

CB

CF half waistband CB

CF fall

half **PANTALOONS**

side seam side seam

Waistcoat collar

CB

half **WAISTCOAT** front

half **WAISTCOAT** back

COAT SLEEVE

half **COAT** front

half **COAT** back

opening

half **COAT COLLAR** CB

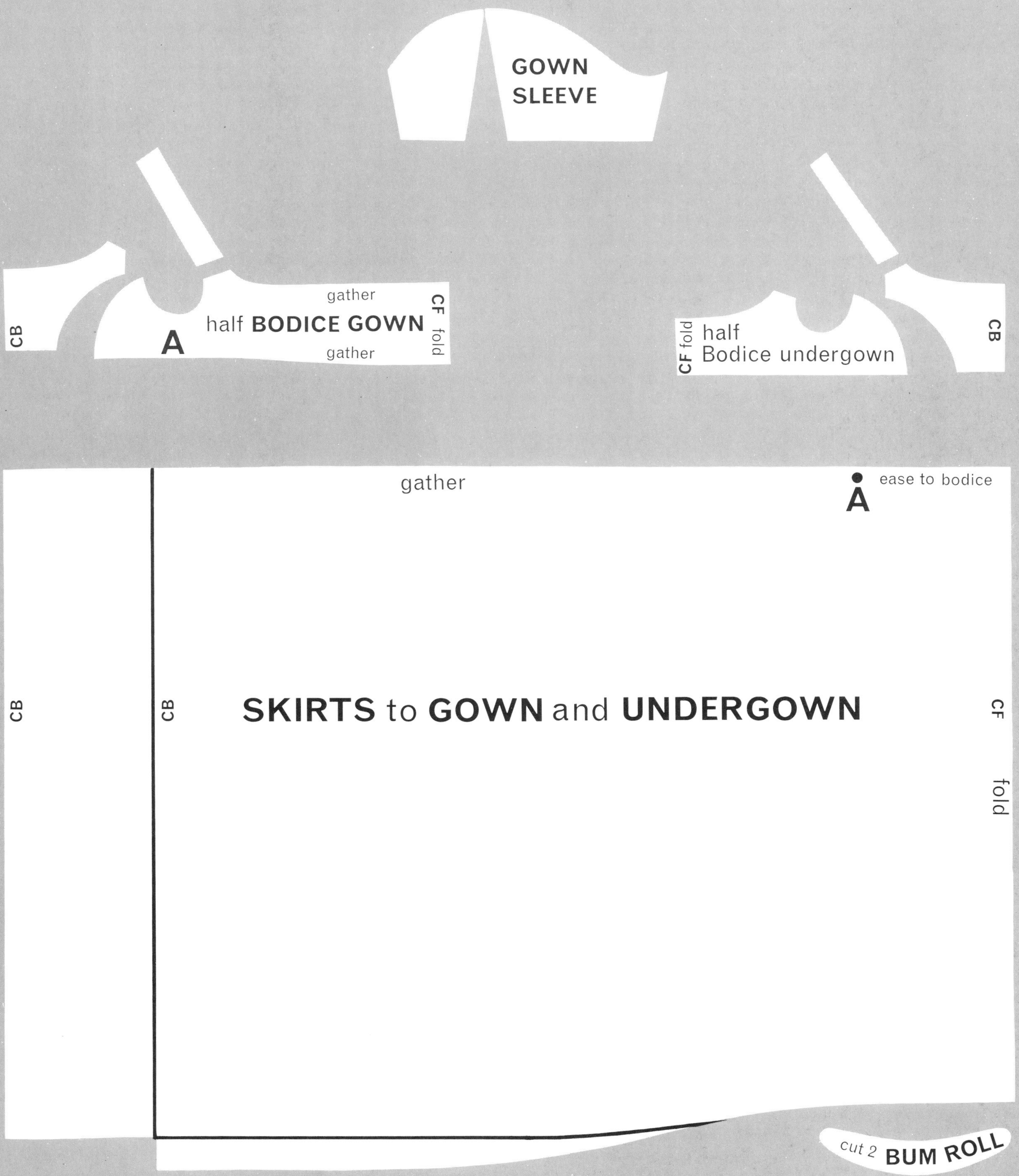

GOWN SLEEVE

CB

gather

A half **BODICE GOWN** gather

CF fold

CF fold half Bodice undergown CB

gather ● ease to bodice

A

CB

CB

SKIRTS to GOWN and UNDERGOWN

CF

fold

cut 2 **BUM ROLL**

1815 George III

Fabrics: Similar to the previous fashion. Women continue to wear cambric, poplin and muslin — frequently embroidered with small sprig patterns.

Colours: Though white is still universally worn by women, soft and light colours such as pinks, blues, yellows and greens steadily gain favour. Men continue to wear light-coloured (usually white) pantaloons or breeches, light waistcoats, and dark coats.

Decoration: Men's clothes show an absence of decoration other than in the embroidered or woven fabric (striped) of the waistcoat. The most noticeable feature of decoration in women's dress is the elaborate trimming, originally a simple band or frill, of the hem of the skirt. Often some 20 inches in depth, it is composed of three-dimensional applied ornament, puffs, swags, ruchings, frills, artificial flowers, ribboning, etc.

Padding and restriction, men: Boned stays are worn to force out the chest and restrict the waist and upper abdomen.

Padding and restriction, women: Small, lightly boned under bodices or corsets are sometimes worn. A bum roll or little bustle thrusts out the skirts at the back.

Movement, men: Though similar to the previous fashion men affect a casual "negligent and poetical" appearance.

Movement, women: Small, prim, nimble and mincing, far removed from the breadth of 18th-century bravura, formality and elegance, The arms hang naturally at the sides of the body. At times the bustle, if large, dictates an affected form of posture — thrusting out the posterior and bending the body forward from the waist up — "the Grecian Bend".

Men

General characteristics: The coat front waistline is lower, the shoulders rounded, and the tails smaller and shorter — above knee in length and with a C.B. vent. Pantalons replace the breeches.

Under garments — similar to the previous fashion. The cut of the under drawers is basically the same as the breeches.

Tail coat — usually single breasted with wide lapels and a deep collar (M-cut), the fronts rarely buttoned together. The coat is cut with a seam at the waistline, the side back seams almost meeting at the C.B. waist. The sleeves, gathered to the armhole, taper to the wrist where they extend over the hand to cover the knuckles.

Waistcoat — (single breasted) square cut with a stepped standing collar, very tight in fit, and buttoned to reveal an expanse of shirt front frilling.

Pantaloons — (curved fall) cut with a high waist, pleated on either side at the front, and sufficiently short in the leg to reveal the ankle and an expanse of sock — the outside leg openings frequently left unbuttoned. Pantaloons are cut loose for day wear but tight for evening dress. Made in jersey cloth, drill, etc.

Socks — (replace stockings) generally white. Plain, ribbed, embroidered or striped.

Shoes — heelless, elegant little slippers with a very low vamp.

Hats — (black, browns, greys) the beaver — a tall crowned hat with concave sides and a curling brim. Later, often made in silk, it becomes known as the chimney pot, pot, silk, or top hat.

Hair — thick at the back and nape of the neck, the hair is dressed high at the front in a similar manner to the previous fashion with the sides brushed forward over the temples and cheeks.

Accessories — short gloves, walking canes, fobs, watches, umbrellas, etc.

Women

General characteristics: The waistline is high. The dress, tubular in form, is decorated in "the Gothic manner" — puffs, bows, lace, rosettes, ruffs, ruffles, etc. The skirt, flat in front, flared at the sides and gathered at the back, stands away at the hem to terminate well above the ankles.

Under garments — a simple under gown or chemise, and drawers — separate legs attached to a waistband, or similar in cut to the men's under drawers.

Dress — (C.B. fastening) a narrow waistband frequently joins the skirt to the bodice, which is cut with a long sloping shoulder line, a low or high neck, and small armholes. The sleeves, usually puffed at the head, terminate well below wrist in length. A variety of short jackets, shawls, wrappers and coats are worn with these dresses. The example shown (Spencer) is similar in cut to the dress bodice but made in heavier material, with a high standing collar, C.F. fastening, waistband, and long sleeves.

Stockings — similar to the previous fashion.

Shoes — narrow, pointed toed slippers, heelless, with a very low vamp.

Hair — centrally parted and curled or waved on either temple. The back hair is braided and arranged in a bun placed high on the back of the head.

Hats — richly trimmed turbans, berets, and tall crowned bonnets with the brim open or closed. Mob caps, covering the hair and framing the face, (tying under the chin) are worn for indoors.

Accessories — large costly (also cheaper imitations) Kashmir shawls and scarves. Reticules, tubular purses of knitted silk, tall stick parasols, umbrellas, short gloves. Small fans carried in the evening.

Notes on patterns: Men

Shirt — adapt collar pattern for 1825 or 1830.

Cravat — see previous patterns.

Coat — use padding to mould and curve the shoulder line and upper chest. Lightly pad or interline head of sleeve.

Waistcoat — make up to fit tightly and restrict the waist.

Pantaloons — for extra fullness at waist, open up and extend the width of the front pattern.

Notes on patterns: Women

Chemise — similar in shape to the dress (without sleeves), or cut to hang loose from the shoulders.

Dress — (add C.B. placket) skirts are eased at the front and gathered or pleated at the back to a narrow waistband (attached to the bodice). A small, lightly-stuffed pad should be sewn to the back waistline edge of the bodice to gently thrust out the skirts.

Spencer — (concealed hook and eye front fastening) use light padding to mould and curve the shoulder line and upper chest. Ease the fronts of the body parts to the waistband, forming a small pleat or dart on either side under the bust. The sleeve is composed of a long under sleeve and a short top puffed sleeve (A). The standing collar requires stiffening.

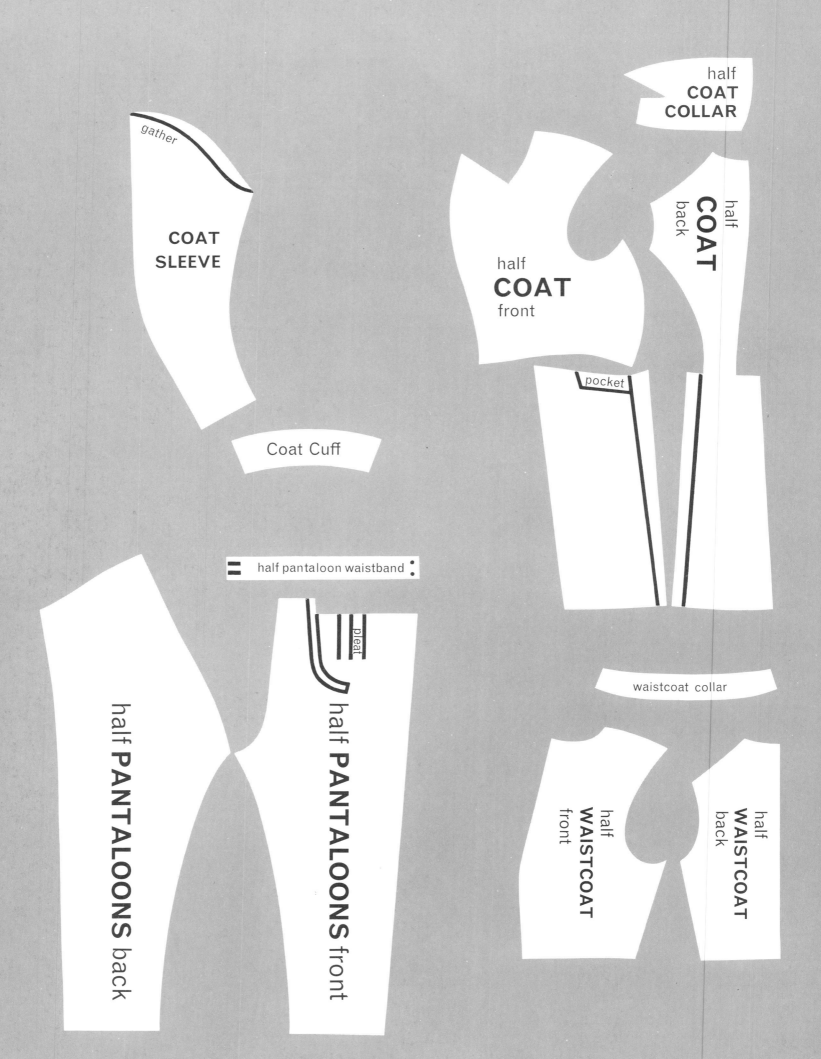

half
COAT
COLLAR

half
COAT
back

half
COAT
front

COAT
SLEEVE

gather

pocket

Coat Cuff

half pantaloon waistband

waistcoat collar

pleat

half PANTALOONS back

half PANTALOONS front

half
WAISTCOAT
front

half
WAISTCOAT
back

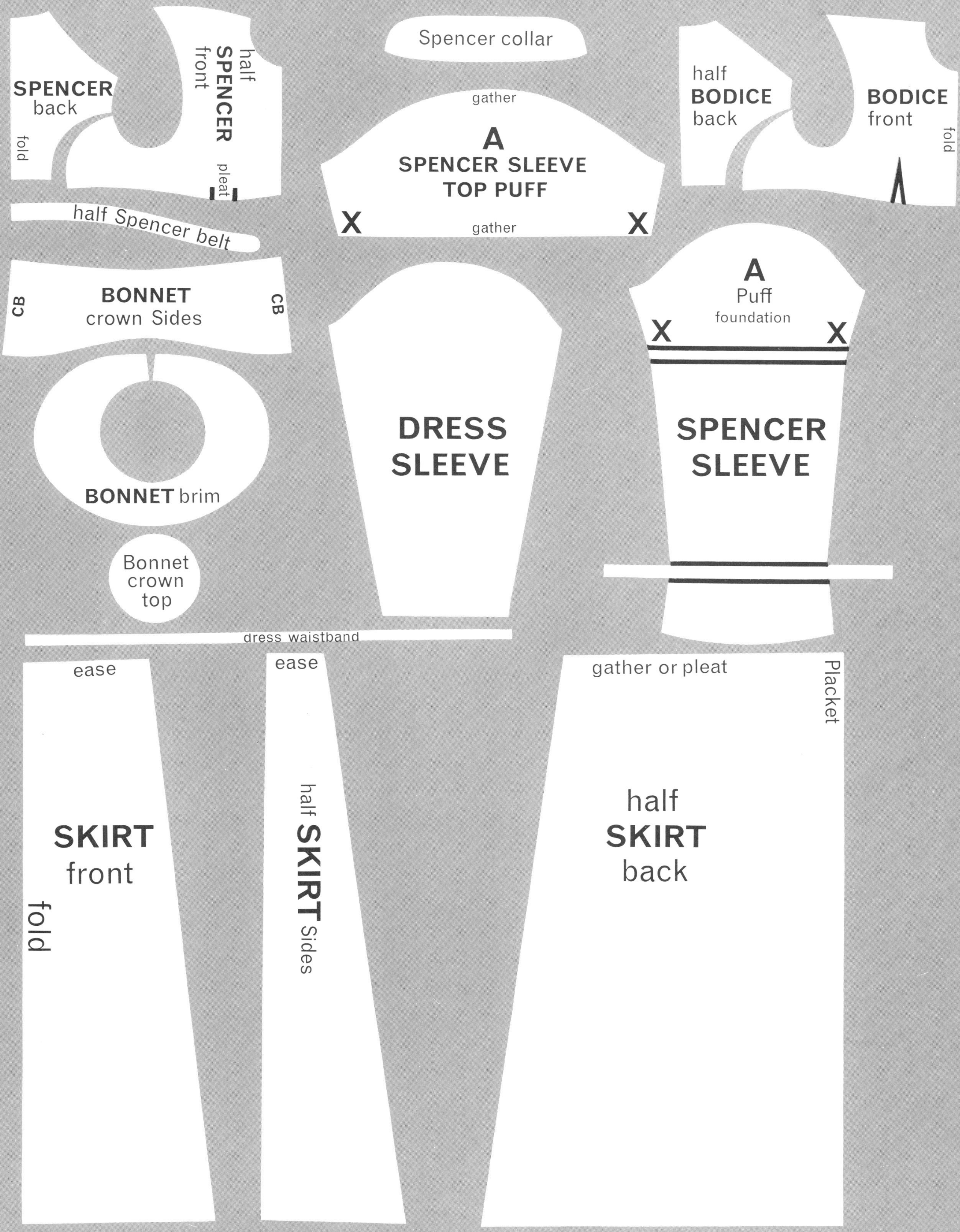

SPENCER back

fold

half **SPENCER** front

SPENCER pleat

half Spencer belt

Spencer collar

gather

A
SPENCER SLEEVE TOP PUFF

X   gather   X

half **BODICE** back

BODICE front

fold

CB   **BONNET** crown Sides   CB

BONNET brim

Bonnet crown top

DRESS SLEEVE

A Puff foundation

X   X

SPENCER SLEEVE

dress waistband

ease   ease   gather or pleat   Placket

SKIRT front

fold

half **SKIRT** Sides

half **SKIRT** back

1825 George IV

Fabrics: Season and occasion determine weight and choice of fabric. Men's coats and trousers are usually of cloth. Women — heavier materials such as silks (including wild silk), and light-weight cloths. Cottons, muslins, poplins, etc., are still very fashionable. Chintzes on dark and light grounds.

Colours: Women — noticeable increase in choice of colours, including lilacs, pinks, amber, Indian red, browns and black as an alternative to white and pastel shades.

Decoration: Various military campaigns influence decoration — frogging, fur trimming, braiding, cut, etc. Women's dresses trimmed and decorated with ornament borrowed or adapted from peasant wear (particularly Spanish), costumes of the 16th and 17th centuries, and medieval art (Gothic). Fabrics are frequently striped and checked in intermingling colours of all sorts and tones.

Padding and restriction, men: Similar to the previous fashion.

Padding and restriction, women: Similar to the previous fashion. Corsets, to support the bust and narrow the waist, reappear.

Movement, men: Somewhat economic, staid and formal with little or no sign of "fancy manners".

Movement, women: Commencement of the "age of politeness". With the adoption of a more sensible form of dress, complimenting all age groups, deportment in general is quiet and reserved. Movement is natural and unhampered by restriction.

Men

General characteristics: Similar to the previous fashion. Waistlines are lower. For day-wear a dark cloth coat, coloured silk waistcoat, and white moleskin or cloth trousers — covering the top of the boot and loose in cut. For evening dress, a black or dark blue coat, black pantaloons, trousers or breeches, and a black or white waistcoat.

Under garments — similar to the previous fashion. The stock, shaped in buckram or leather, boned and covered with fabric, buckles at the back of the neck — "Royal George" stock of black velvet and black satin very fashionable. The collar, often 4 or 5 inches high and visible above the stock, is attached to the shirt.

Polish coat — a top coat seamed at the waist, double breasted, usually frogged and with toggle fastenings. The skirts, with C.B. vent, are flared, with pockets placed in the side back seams. Cuffs, and the tall stand-fall collar are usually of contrasting material.

Cossacks — full trousers (with a small fall) pleated to a waistband. The legs are stretched and kept taut by single or double straps fastening under the boot. C.F.s of the leg openings are cut away to take the shape of the foot.

Socks — similar to the previous fashion.

Shoes — low-heeled, low-vamped slippers with rounded toes. Soft leather, square toed, heeled boots.

Hats — similar to the previous fashion. The sides of the crown are straighter and the brim narrower.

Hair — similar to the previous fashion.

Accessories — similar to the previous fashion.

Women

General characteristics: Dress is determined by occasion and the time of day. Morning and day dresses prohibit the exposure of throat, bosoms and arms. Waistlines are lower and round. The bodice, with a long shoulder seam sloping to a small armhole, is usually cut or decorated to form a V-pointed front. Skirts, neatly joining the waist, are ankle length and flared at the sides and back.

Under garments — similar to the previous fashion. A petticoat attached to a simple sleeveless bodice. A camisole or under bodice. Longer drawers.

Pelisse gown — (C.F. fastening to hip level) the cut is neat and tailored in comparison to the last fashion, with the skirt fullness confined to the back. Decoration on the bodice, together with the elaborate puffs at the head of the sleeves, emphasises the sloping shoulder line. The skirt, hem and fronts, is usually decorated with ornament of similar design. A narrow waistband joins the skirt to the bodice.

Stockings — silk.

Boots and shoes — simple slippers with a single thickness of leather for the heel. Narrow boots barely covering the ankle, of cloth, leather or silk, are laced at the side.

Hair — similar to the previous fashion, fuller at the temples, with the bun arranged in a more elaborate knot.

Hats — elaborate indoor caps, framing the face, are richly trimmed with frills and ribboning. Outdoor hats with larger brims, usually open, are decorated with feathers, flowers, streamers and ribbons — embroidered, striped, checked, and multicoloured.

Accessories — wide variety of shawls, capes, scarves, etc. Short gloves, large muffs and reticules. Jewellery is usually confined to evening wear — "antique" necklaces, bracelets, and brooches.

Notes on patterns: Men

Cossacks — for extra fullness extend the width of the patterns.

Notes on patterns: Women

Corsets — if worn, use 1830 pattern.

Chemise — adapt gown pattern omitting the sleeves.

Petticoat — (with or without bodice) similar in cut to the gown. The skirts are stiffened from hem to knee, with rows of closely placed piping or cords.

Pelisse Gown — (C.F. fly fastening to hip level). The collar and belt are attached. The sleeve is similar in construction to the previous fashion with the addition of an ornamental top — caught at each point to the armband terminating the puff. The sleeve is left open at the wrist. Three or more box pleated frills, forming a ruff, are sewn to the neck band.

Hat — make up on a wire or cane foundation. The puffed crown is separated from the brim by a narrow stiffened band.

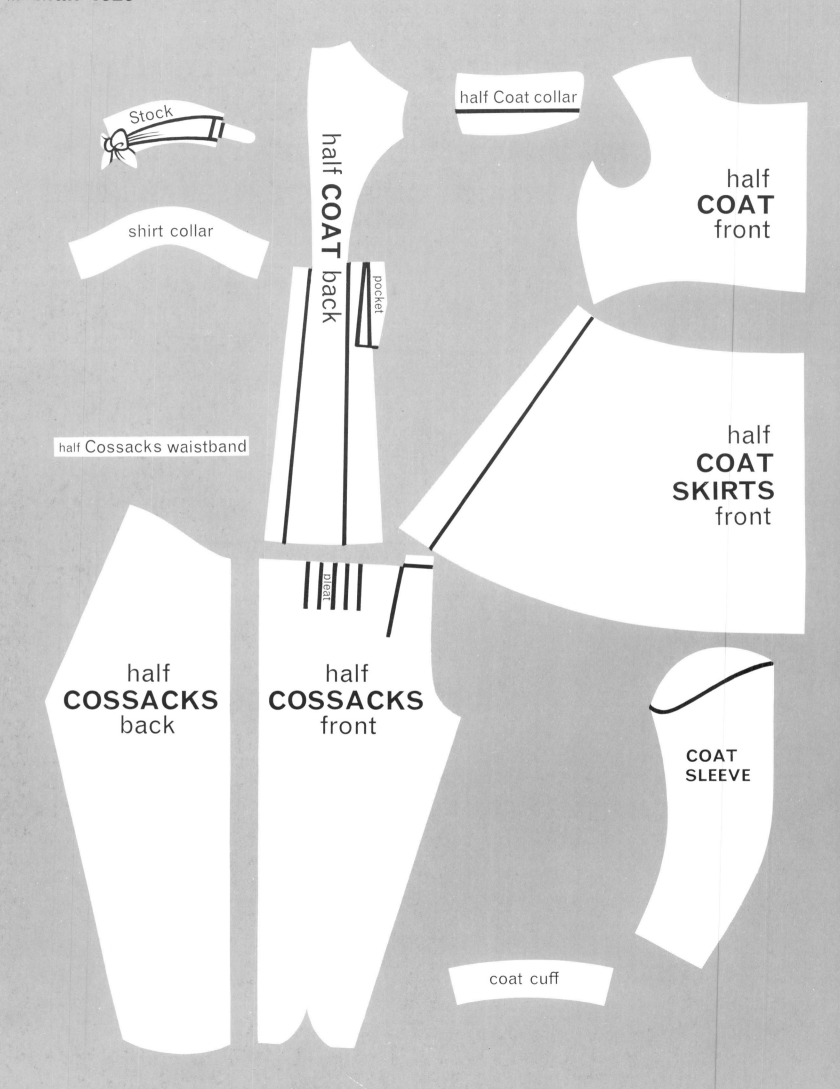

Stock

shirt collar

half Coat collar

half **COAT** back

pocket

half Cossacks waistband

half **COAT** front

half **COAT SKIRTS** front

pleat

half **COSSACKS** back

half **COSSACKS** front

COAT SLEEVE

coat cuff

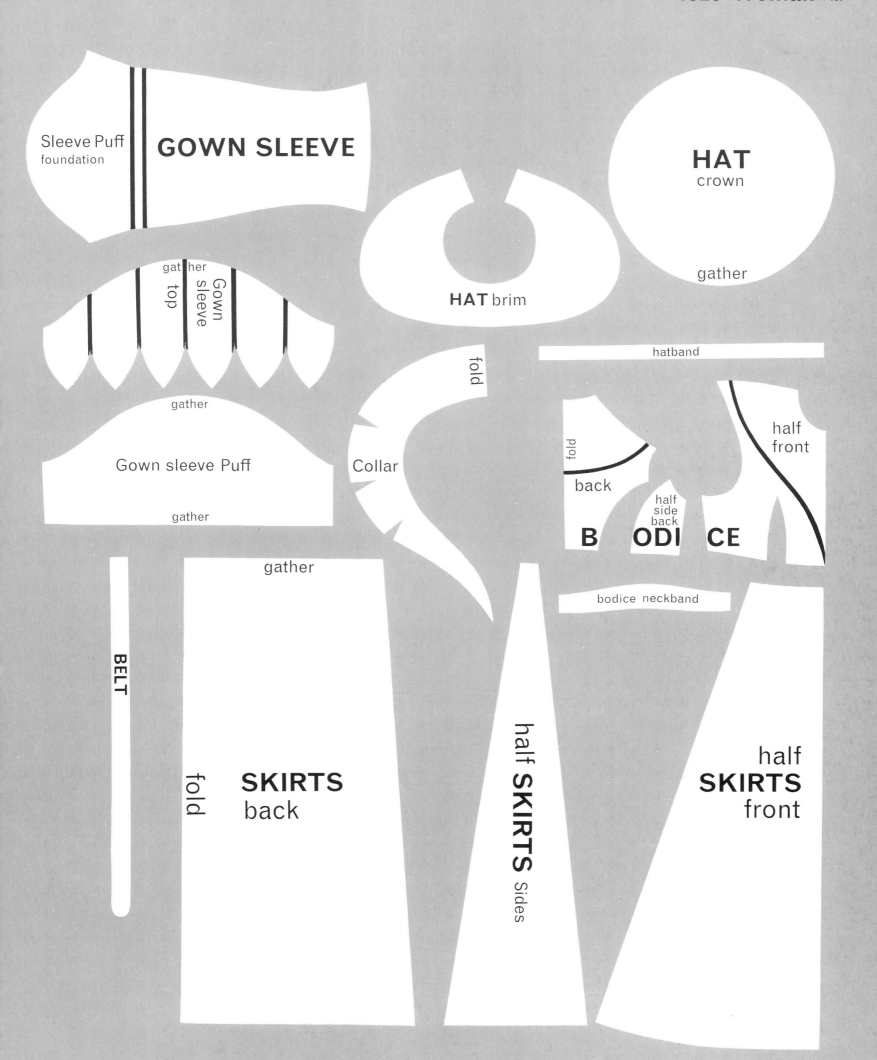

1830 William IV

Fabrics: Women — ginghams, foulards, chintzes, woven or printed fabrics on a black ground, or materials similar to the previous fashion. Blond lace, bobbin, machine-made net (with lace patterns embroidered onto the net) for trimmings and accessories — collars and cuffs, shoulder capes and scarves, aprons, etc.

Colours: Men's choice of colours grows steadily more conservative. Women show preference for darker, richer and more intense colours — sage green, plum, old rose, amber, tobacco browns, etc.

Decoration: Similar to the previous fashion. Dress fabrics, and the silk waistcoats worn by the men, are patterned — floral, complex checks, stripes, sprigs, etc. Dresses are trimmed with pleatings, frillings, braiding, lace and embroidery.

Padding and restriction, men: A pair of tightly-laced stays emphasises the fashionable small waist. Heads of sleeves, chest parts of coat and waistcoat — padded.

Padding and restriction, women: A tiny waist and rounded bosom is formed by the corset which is boned on all seams and laced back and front. The sleeves are extended out by cane constructions or pads of feathers attached to the tops of the low positioned tight armholes. Pads, varying in size, fastened to the waist edge of the dress, thrust out the skirts at the back.

Movement, men: The fashionable small waist, sloping shoulders, and thrusting out of the chest, indicates showier movement, affected elegance, and taut and arrogant deportment. The back is straight and the head held very high.

Movement, women: Somewhat frivolous and less staid than the previous fashion.

Men

General characteristics: The coat and waistcoat are cut and padded to give a full-bosomed, wasp-waisted line to the figure. Lapels are long and wide, the shoulders rounded and sloping. Skirts and tails are short. The coat is dark, the trousers usually light, the waistcoat of some fancy material — frequently black.

Under garments — similar to the previous fashion. The shirt is often cut without frillings or pleatings at wrists and chest. As an alterntive to the stock, a cravat of black silk or satin is worn about the throat — crossed over the chest and puffed out to hide the shirt.

Tail coat — seamed at the waist, single breasted, and rarely fastened. The tails, with C.B. vent, commence well on the sides of the front. The sleeves, padded and cut to give height at the shoulders, are tight in fit to terminate well below the wrist with the outside seam left open.

Waistcoat — tightly fitting, with a small pointed waist, and cut low in front to reveal an expanse of shirt or cravat. Single breasted with lapels and rolled collar.

Trousers — (small fall or fly fastening) the pleatings at the front disappear. Cut to fit the upper parts of the legs they are looser from the knees down. Buckled straps, placed under the instep, hold the trousers taut.

Socks — white or black.

Boots and shoes — similar to the previous fashion.

Hats — the top hat, sometimes made in straw, is taller and straighter. For country wear hats are frequently low crowned and broad brimmed.

Hair — thick and luxuriant in cut with centre or side parting. When centrally parted the hair at the sides and temples, curled and waved, is often dressed to extend to the outer point of each eye (aggravators). Sideboards are thick and curly. Very small, neatly trimmed moustaches and beards.

Accessories — similar to the previous fashion.

Women

General characteristics: The shoulders are long and sloping, the waistline lower. Skirts are full and wide at the hem. Very large hats and sleeves.

Under garments — similar to the previous fashion. Bust improvers, bum roll, and several gathered petticoats.

Dress — a lightly boned and tightly fitting bodice — collars, shoulder capes, pelerines of cambric or muslin edged with frillings of lace, etc., shoulder extensions, and gigantic sleeves, emphasise the width of the shoulders. The sleeves narrow to fit the lower arm and wrist, where they terminate in turned-back cuffs or frills. Gathered or pleated skirts, very full and ankle-length, are flared at the sides and back. A wide buckled belt is worn with the dress.

Stockings — similar to the previous fashion.

Boots and shoes — black or white square toed boots, or slippers with ribbon ties.

Hair — centrally parted, curving down over the forehead, and arranged in a cluster of curls about the temples and ears. The back hair is arranged in an elaborate knot placed high on the top of the head. The Apollo knot — a false loop of hair wired to make it stand, is secured to the existing bun.

Hats — very large wide-brimmed hats with soft or stiff crowns, berets, turbans, and bonnets — closed or open and worn with a veil. Rich trimmings of feathers, flowers, satin ribbons and lace. Large lace and muslin caps, worn under the hat or in the home, are elaborately trimmed with frillings, streamers, rosettes and ribbons.

Accessories — gloves — wrist length for day wear, long for the evening. Net or knitted mittens. Reticules, fringed parasols of watered silk, umbrellas.

Notes on patterns: Men

Stays — bone on all seams and lace at the C.B.

Shirt — similar to the previous fashions, or use pattern for 1843. The collar (separate) fastens with stud or button at the C.F. and C.B.

Coat and waistcoat — chest and shoulders require padding to increase the size of the chest and to round the shoulders. Cut waistcoat and coat to fit the figure tightly.

Trousers — cut with a front fall or fly fastening, with curved pockets placed well forward from the side seams.

Cape — extend the pattern at AA to form the long under cape. Line B indicates the termination of the front edges of the shorter cape.

Notes on patterns: Women

Corsets — bone on all seams. Lace back and front. Insert A (2 on either side of the C.F.) for bust fullness.

Chemise — cut to hang loose from the shoulders or adapt dress pattern.

Petticoat — cut straight, or with flares at sides and back. Gather to a waistband or place on a drawstring.

Dress — (C.B. hook and bar fastening) the skirts, 11 feet plus in circumference, are cartridge pleated to the bodice waistline. (See 1843 pattern notes for method of pleating.) The fullness can be distributed all round or concentrated on the side fronts and back. To reduce the quantity of material at the waist edge the side and back panels of the skirt can be flared. Line the sleeves with a light but stiff fabric, and gather or cartridge-pleat the head to fit the armhole. To extend the sleeves out from the armholes insert light cane constructions or feather pads. Form wrist plackets.

Pelerine — fastened at the throat and tucked into the belt, it is edged with a frilling of lace.

Hat — construct on wire or cane foundation.

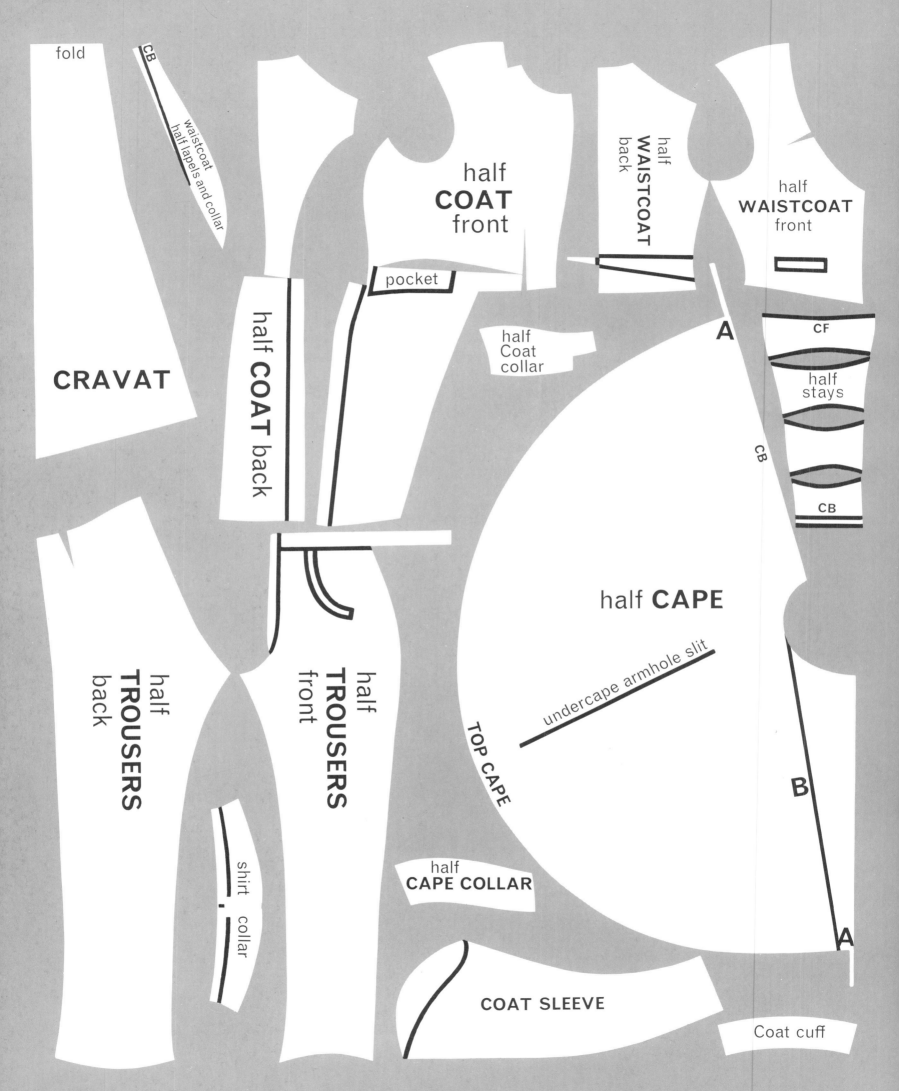

fold

CB

waistcoat half lapels and collar

half
COAT
front

half
WAISTCOAT
back

half
WAISTCOAT
front

CRAVAT

half **COAT** back

pocket

half
Coat
collar

A

CF

half
stays

CB

CB

half **CAPE**

half
TROUSERS
back

half
TROUSERS
front

TOP CAPE

undercape armhole slit

B

shirt   collar

half
CAPE COLLAR

A

COAT SLEEVE

Coat cuff

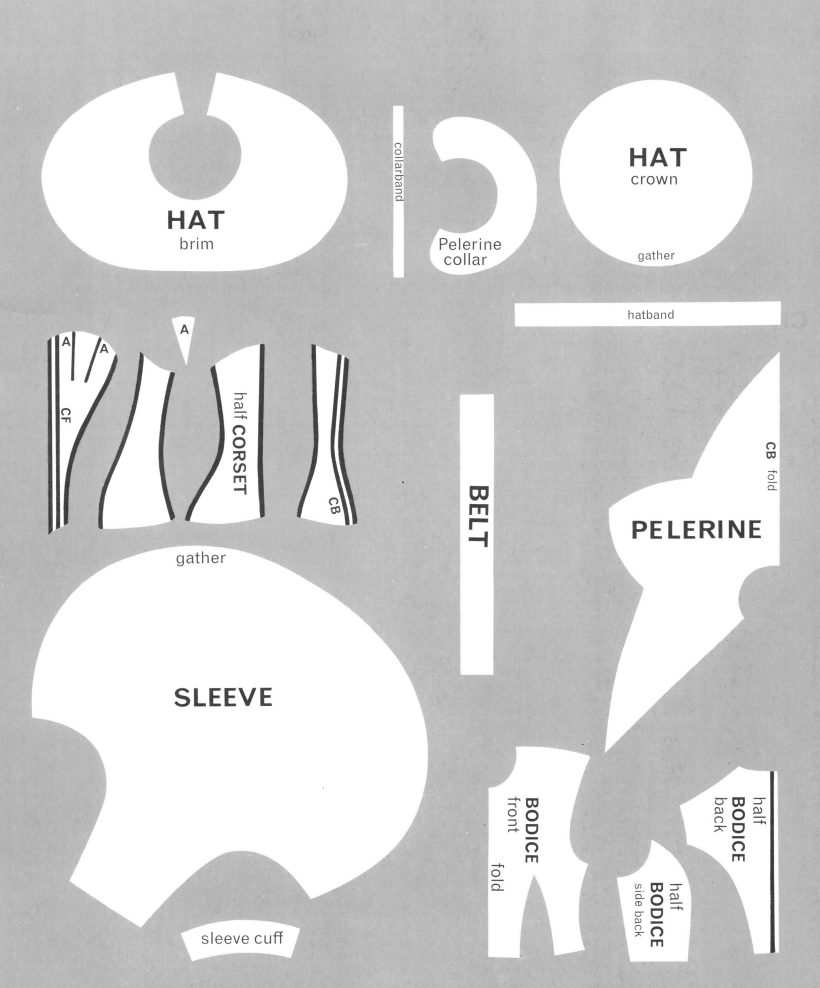

HAT brim

collarband

Pelerine collar

HAT crown

gather

hatband

A

A A

CF

half **CORSET**

A

CB

gather

BELT

PELERINE

CB fold

SLEEVE

sleeve cuff

BODICE front

fold

half **BODICE** side back

half **BODICE** back

1843 Victoria

Fabrics: Women — wools, taffetas, cottons, soft and crisp silks — shot and watered. 18th-century dresses are unpicked and made up in the current style and the fabrics imitated and copied. Black lace.

Colours: Women — softer and more subdued colours.

Decoration: Women — quieter and smaller patterns echo the general trend towards daintiness and sweetness — sprigs, chintzes, floral patterns, stripes and checks. Silk fringing, Piping, tucking, pleating and ruching.

Padding and restriction, men: Modification of the previous fashion.

Padding and restriction, women: The tight-fitting tapered bodice with a small pointed waist, has a curved and rounded shoulder line with very low-placed tight armholes. Corsets are essential as foundations to these bodices — it is from this date that the art and science of corsetry really commences. The full skirts are held out by as many as six or more petticoats.

Movement, men: Showiness and flamboyance is disappearing in favour of solidarity, simplicity and conservatism. The stance is upright. The hands are frequently held behind the back over or under the skirts of the coat, or placed in the trouser or waistcoat pockets. The weight of the body is thrown more evenly onto both legs. Manner and behaviour is contrasted sharply with the growing passive role demanded and expected of women in society.

Movement, women: Demure and quiet, gentle and gliding. Absence of bold or vigorous movement.

Men

General characteristics: Less exaggerated and flamboyant in cut and styling. The waistline is lower and neckwear more modest. The frock coat, single or double breasted, is longer. Trousers are tight.

Under garments — shirts, with tucked fronts, back yokes, and cuffed sleeves, are frequently coloured and striped (pink or blue) but always worn with a white collar (sometimes turned down) which is now separate from the shirt. Long drawers replace the knee-length under drawers and an under vest is worn. The black cravat is narrower and ties in a wide bow at the throat.

Frock-coat — (tail coat worn in the evenings) the body parts are cut in six pieces. The skirts, with C.B. vent, are gently flared with pockets placed in the side back seams. Sleeves, fitting the armhole, are cuffed.

Waistcoat — similar to the previous fashion, but more conservative in the choice of fabric.

Trousers — (frequently checked) a front fly fastening replaces the fall. The legs are narrower and tighter from the knee down.

Socks — similar to the previous fashion.

Boots and shoes — boots, frequently made of cloth with patent leather toe caps, are ankle length with side lacing and square toes. A row of mother of pearl buttons decorates the front of the boot. Little low-heeled slippers, with low vamps and flat bows, are worn in the evening.

Hats — the top hat is worn well on the back of the head. The crown is broader, the wider brim curves up at the sides to dip down at the C.F. and back.

Hair — the style, though similar to the previous fashion, is less exaggerated. The sideboards are longer and often cover the jaw bone.

Accessories — similar to the previous fashion.

Women

General characteristics: Sloping shouldered, heart-shaped, tightly fitting V-waisted bodices with narrow sleeves. The ground-length skirts, forming a soft bell shape, are cut full all round.

Under garments — similar to the previous fashion.

Chemisette — of soft or fine material, sleeveless, waist length, and open on the side seams. The front and back waist edges are placed on drawstrings. It is worn under the dress to partially fill the low neckline.

Dress — much fine sewing and hand work is put into the construction of these dresses — minute pleatings, tucking, insertions, smocking, shirring, piping, etc. The skirts are cartridge-pleated to the bodice waistline, the hem decorated with a series of flounces.

Stockings — (black or white) rarely seen.

Boots and shoes — heels reappear. Side lacing of the boot is replaced with V-shaped elastic inserts (feet are hidden by the skirts).

Hair — centrally parted, curving down over the forehead to form clusters of very long ringlets arranged over the ears. The back hair is dressed high on top in a bun or knot.

Hats — smaller bonnets, framing the face, are tied under the chin with long ribbons. Flowers, frillings, ribboning and lace, decorate the inside and the outside of the brim. Veils. Indoor caps, worn on the back of the head, are also prettily trimmed with streamers and frillings.

Accessories — capes, shawls, cloaks and mantles. Scarves, little black silk afternoon aprons, chatelaines of cut steel, small parasols. Closely-fitting short gloves.

Notes on patterns: Men

Shirt — adapt collar from the previous pattern.

Notes on patterns: Women

Corset — adapt pattern of 1830.

Petticoats — 10 feet plus in circumference with an inserted drawstring at the waist.

Dress — (form C.B. placket running through the bodice into the skirts) lightly bone bodice seams. The deep pleated edging to the neckline is formed by shaped strips of material cut double and on the cross. Sew up and attach to the lines indicated on the patterns, with the lower edge of each strip overlapping by $\frac{1}{4}$ inch. The sleeve, with triple puffs at the head, requires a wrist placket, narrow wristband, and frilled edging. Pleating of the skirts to the waist edge of the bodice is formed by folding the waist edge of the material back, arranging it in close cartridge pleats, and sewing the top fold of each pleat *only* to the bodice waistline (a narrow piping hides join of skirts to bodice). A fine layer of wadding interlines the back skirts from waist to knee (see pattern). Flared flounces, decorating the skirt at A.A.A., are stiffened with cords placed in the hems.

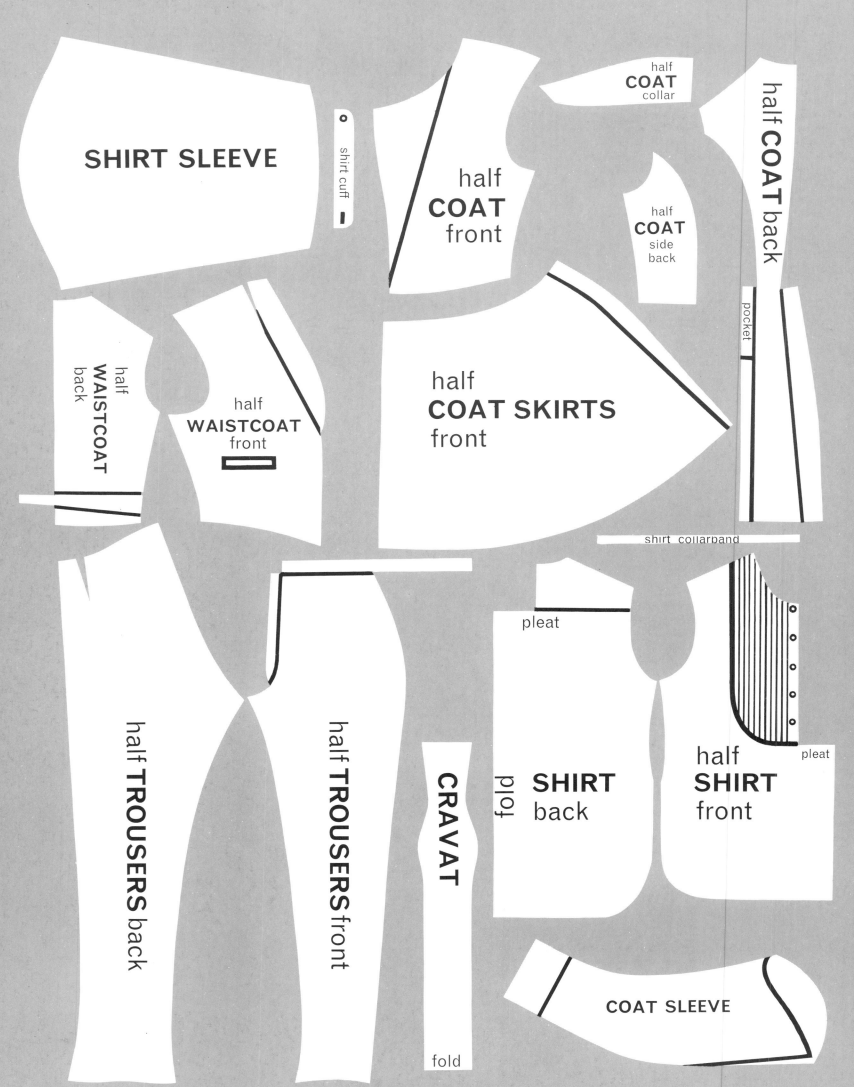

SHIRT SLEEVE

shirt cuff

half **COAT** collar

half **COAT** front

half **COAT** side back

half **COAT** back

pocket

half **WAISTCOAT** back

half **WAISTCOAT** front

half **COAT SKIRTS** front

shirt collarband

pleat

pleat

half **TROUSERS** back

half **TROUSERS** front

CRAVAT

fold **SHIRT** back

half **SHIRT** front

COAT SLEEVE

fold

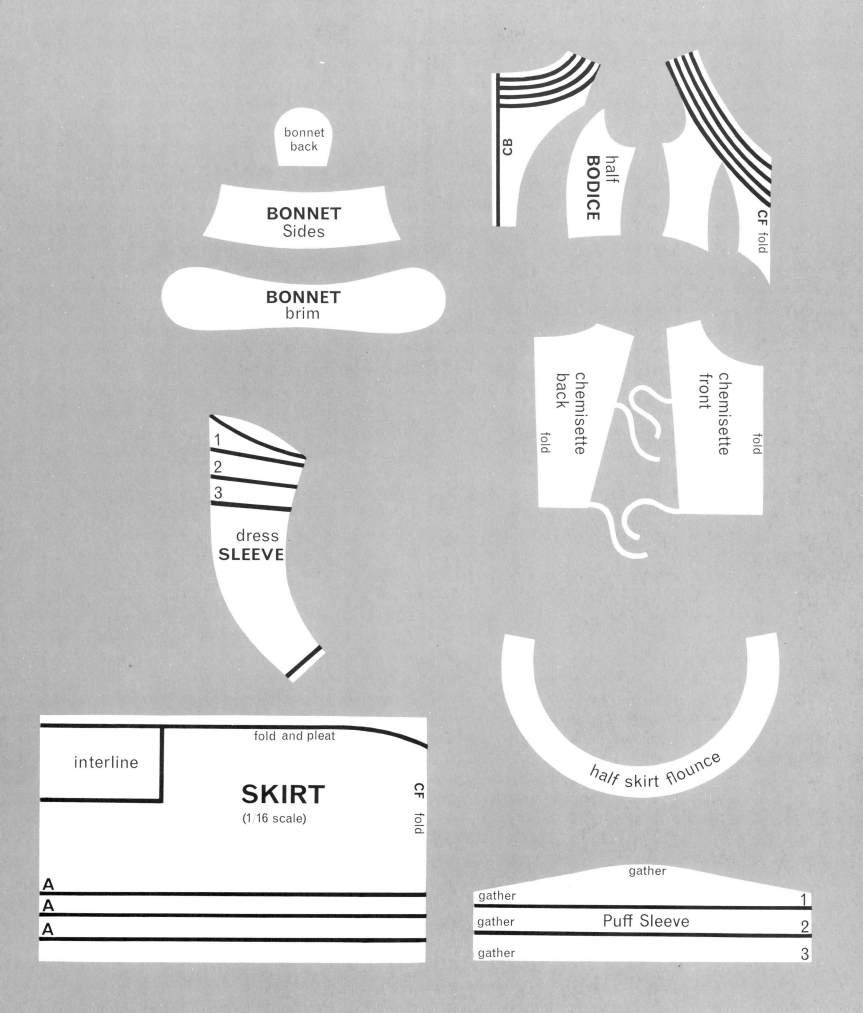

bonnet back

BONNET Sides

BONNET brim

CB

half **BODICE**

CF fold

chemisette back

fold

chemisette front

fold

1
2
3

dress **SLEEVE**

half skirt flounce

fold and pleat

interline

SKIRT
(1/16 scale)

CF fold

A
A
A

gather

gather

gather

gather

Puff Sleeve

1

2

3

1853 Victoria

Fabrics: Similar to the previous fashion.

Colours: Lighter, softer colours for spring and summer wear, darker amd more sombre colours for autumn and winter. Men are wearing trousers of darker colours, often similar in tone and of the same fabric as the coat.

Decoration: Similar to the previous fashion. Fabrics specially printed, embroidered or woven for the flounces of the larger crinoline skirts, give horizontal emphasis to the dress.

Padding and restriction, women: Similar to the previous fashion. The corsets, laced back and front, are shorter in length. The fuller, larger skirts require a vast number of petticoats to extend them — flounces on the petticoats are reinforced with horsehair and stiffened with piping placed in the hems.

Movement, men: Becomes increasingly more conservative.

Movement, women: Similar to the previous fashion. A swift, small, gliding walk, the feet rarely if ever revealed, with the hands demurely held together. The posture, though straight, is relaxed.

Men

General characteristics: A wide variety of top garments for day wear. Cut is generally looser and less restrictive than previous fashions.

Under garments — similar to the previous fashion. The shirt collar is lower. The narrower cravat ties in a smaller bow at the throat.

Riding coat — (many coats are seen of similar shape — Surtout, Newmarket, Cutaway, Shooting coat and, by the 80s., the morning coat worn as an alternative to the frock coat). Shorter in length than the frock coat, the skirt fronts are curved and cut away.

Waistcoat — (made of cloth) longer in the waist and cut to form a triangular notch at the C.F. waistline.

Trousers — similar to the previous fashion. Peg-topped trousers, wide at the hips and close-fitting at the ankles, are very popular. The trouser legs are frequently decorated with a broad stripe on the outer seam. The strap under the foot disappears.

Socks — similar to the previous fashion.

Boots and shoes — similar to the previous fashion. V-shaped elastic insertions replace the side lacing. Laced "Oxonian" shoes occasionally worn.

Hats — the top hat (proportion and shape changing yearly) is replaced by the bowler (black, brown or grey) for more informal wear.

Hair — parted centrally or on the side, less flamboyantly curled or waved, and frequently dressed with Macassar oil. Side whiskers and neatly trimmed moustaches.

Accessories — similar to the previous fashion.

Women

General characteristics: Though basically similar to the previous fashion the line is simpler, neater and more flowing. The bell-shaped skirts are larger.

Under garments — similar to the previous fashion. Drawers are elaborately trimmed with ribbons and edgings of broderie anglais.

Dress — skirts are tiered and flounced. The bodice is high necked, finishing with a flat collar. The sleeves, tightly fitting the armhole, are full at the wrist where they are gathered into a narrow band.

Pardessus coat — seamed to fit tightly over the bodice, it terminates at the waist or develops into flared skirts — hip to knee in length. The sleeves, tightly fitting the armholes, are three-quarter length and bell shaped (pagoda sleeve).

Shoes — similar to the previous fashion.

Hair — (grown very long) smoothly dressed, centrally parted, curving down over the forehead to below the ears, where it is looped up, often in braids, to meet the bun placed high on the back of the head.

Hats — bonnets are smaller with brim and crown made all in one. They are elaborately and delicately trimmed with lace, ribbons, flowers and small feathers. Indoor caps of squares and triangles of lace, trimmed with streamers and ribbons, are worn on top of the head.

Accessories — similar to the previous fashion. Large brooches worn at the throat.

Notes on patterns: Men

Shirt — use pattern of 1843. The collar is starched and fastened to the shirt with back and front collar studs.

Cravat — adapt pattern of 1843.

Notes on patterns: Women

Corset — black lines indicate the positioning of whalebones. Lace back and front.

Petticoats — add flounces, stiffened with interlining and with cords placed in the hems.

Dress — (form C.B. placket running through the bodice into the skirts). Lightly bone the bodice seams. A second layer of fabric forms the gathered front and back of the bodice. Cut the head of the sleeve to tightly fit the armhole. Form wrist plackets. Arrange the waist edge of the skirt into tiny cartridge pleats and attach to the bodice — see notes for 1843. A,A,A, marked on the skirt pattern indicates the positioning of the flounces — gathered, deep enough to overlap each other, and in circumference at least twice the measurement of the skirt.

Pardessus coat — (fronts fastened with ribbon ties) the sleeve should tightly fit the armhole to give an unbroken curved line from the neck through the shoulder into the sleeve.

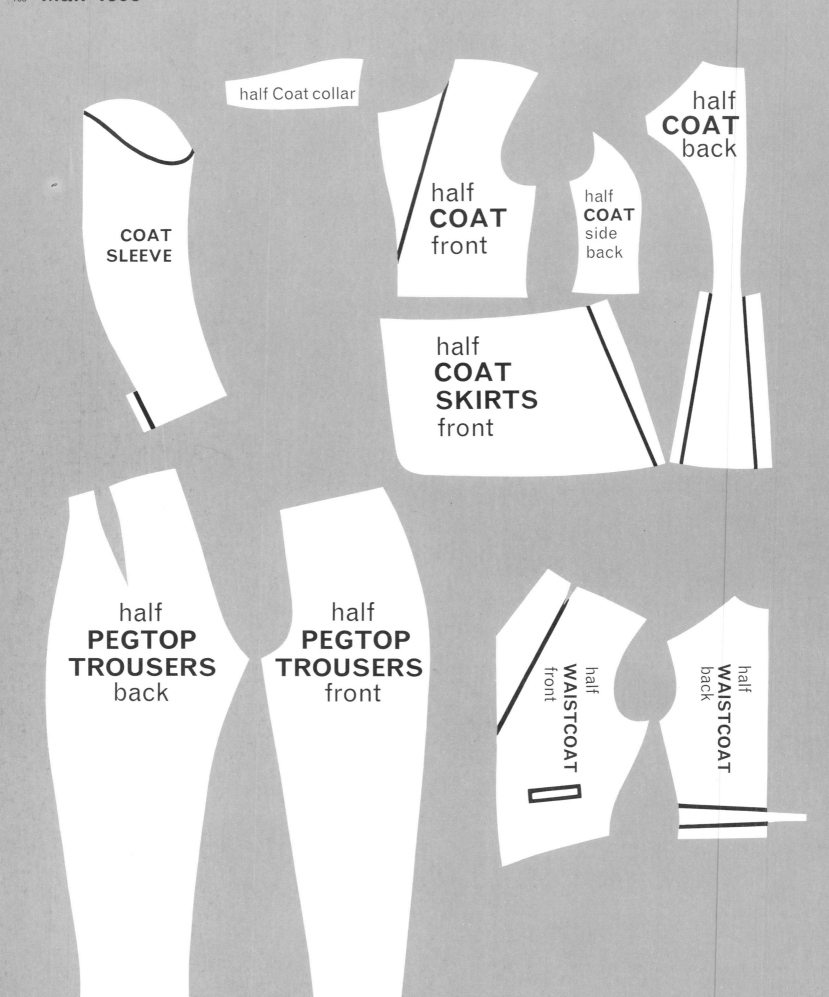

half Coat collar

COAT
SLEEVE

half
COAT
front

half
COAT
side
back

half
COAT
back

half
**COAT
SKIRTS**
front

half
**PEGTOP
TROUSERS**
back

half
**PEGTOP
TROUSERS**
front

half
WAISTCOAT
front

half
WAISTCOAT
back

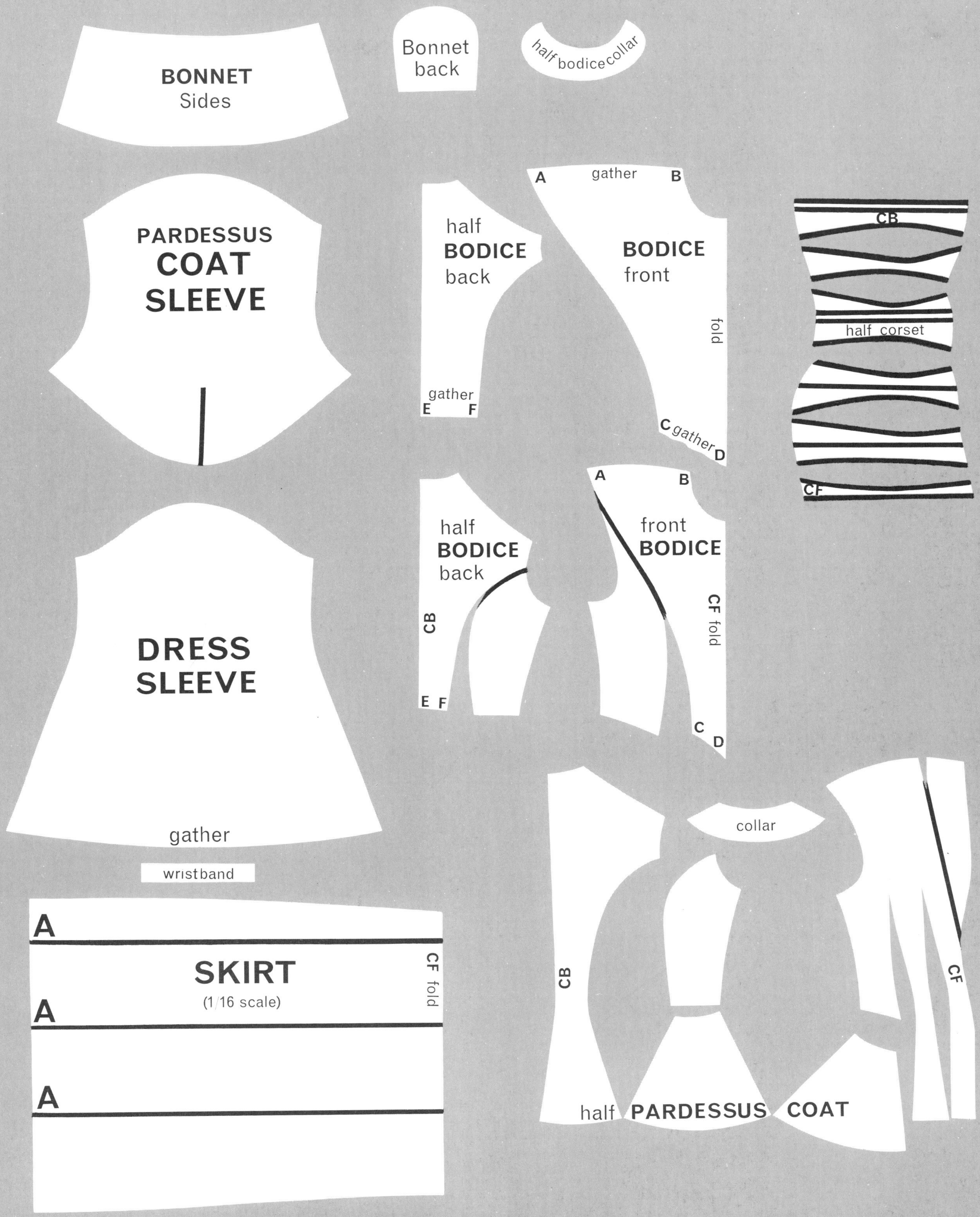

BONNET
Sides

Bonnet
back

half bodice collar

PARDESSUS
COAT
SLEEVE

half
BODICE
back

gather

E   F

A   gather   B

BODICE
front

fold

C gather D

CB

half corset

CF

DRESS
SLEEVE

half
BODICE
back

CB

E F

A   B

front
BODICE

CF fold

C   D

gather

wristband

A

A

SKIRT
(1/16 scale)

A

CF fold

collar

CB

CF

half **PARDESSUS** **COAT**

1863 Victoria

Fabrics: Women — wide choice of fabrics including alpaca, poplins, wools, taffetas, rich silks, and opulent velvets and satins.

Colours: With the appearance of analine dyes, women select brilliant and very sharp colour combinations in daring schemes such as purple with cerise, and veridian with royal blue. Black or dark colours are generally worn by women over 40 — the conventions of mourning dictate that all relations, even young children, wear total black for as long as a year. Jewellery also black — jet.

Decoration: Women show preference for plain flat trimmings of darker colours based on stripes and classical motifs — key patterns, etc. Where all-over floral patterns are used the designs are larger, richer, and very bold.

Padding and restriction, women: The crinoline (constructed of calico and extended by whalebones or flexible steels) replaces the numerous petticoats required to hold out the skirts. Small corsets, very tightly laced, severely restrict the size of the waist.

Movement, men: Formal, very conservative, staid, stiff and self-consciously dignified.

Movement, women: The crinoline is a very difficult skirt to control — the wearer adopting a gliding walk, with perfect balance, to prevent the great skirts from swinging or bouncing. The back parts of the crinoline are lifted prior to sitting down. Young children are given instruction in deportment — back board, book on head, etc.

Men

General characteristics: The narrow-waisted, sloping-shouldered fashions, characteristic of the past 40 years, are replaced by a broader, looser style. A three-piece lounge suit, of the same material, is worn as an alternative to the frock-coat. Knickerbockers for country wear.

Under garments — similar to the previous fashion. The starched collar, separate from the shirt is sometimes turned down (Shakespeare) and worn with a broad tie.

Frock-coat — broad, squarer-shouldered, with narrower collar and lapels. The waistline is low. A flapped breast pocket appears on the left side. The edges of the coat are frequently braided.

Waistcoat — V-cut at C.F. waist, buttoned high, with small lapels and collar. Welted or flapped pockets are placed a little above the waistline on either side of the front. The waistcoat frequently matches the material of the trousers.

Trousers — looser and baggier in cut.

Socks — similar to the previous fashion.

Boots and shoes — similar to the previous fashion.

Hats — similar to the previous fashion.

Hair — centre or side parting. Combed smooth across the forehead, with the hair cut thick at the sides to join up with the side whiskers — trimmed in a variety of styles and sometimes grown very long and full.

Accessories — similar to the previous fashion. Watch, fob and chain are regularly carried in the waistcoat pockets, with the chain looped through a buttonhole at the C.F.

Women

General characteristics: The waistline is higher. Bodices are form fitting with very small waists, dropped shoulder line and fancy armholes. The pagoda sleeves increase in size. The cupola form of the skirt, extended by the crinoline, grows to gigantic proportions and develops a strong backward thrust by 1863.

Under garments — similar to the previous fashion. With the addition of the crinoline, many petticoats are dispensed with. Petticoat and drawers are often of red flannel.

Dress — bodices and skirts are frequently separate, a blouse sometimes replacing the bodice. The bishop sleeves, fitting a tight armhole and full at the wrist, are often false when worn with the pagoda sleeve. The skirts are double and triple pleated to a waistband or to the bodice. Hems, sometimes gathered up on the side seams, are decorated with flat bands of trimming.

Pardessus coat — similar to the previous fashion with skirts heavily flared at the sides and back.

Stockings — coloured — frequently matching the red of the petticoat.

Boots and shoes — heeled with pointed toes, the upper parts perforated with ornamental holes to reveal the coloured stockings. Boots are taller and cover the ankle.

Hair — (very thick, long and luxuriant) centrally parted, it is waved and loosely drawn back to cover the ears, and arranged either in a very large chignon at the nape of the neck, a large bun, cluster of ringlets, or formed into massive looped-up braids securely held with pins and combs. Snoods are frequently worn.

Hats — richly trimmed with feathers, flowers, ribbons, jet, lace, embroidery, buckles, etc. Mandarin hats, pork pie hats with a snood at the back, felt hats with low crowns and curling brims. Diadem bonnets, worn on the back of the head and tied with broad ribbons under the chin. Shallow-crowned straw hats with large brims curved to dip down at the back.

Accessories — similar to the previous fashion.

Notes on patterns: Women

Corsets — adapt pattern of 1853.

Crinoline — the pattern is slightly shaped at the C.F. (flare or dart). Pleating, to the waistband, commences from point A on either side of the C.F. Graduated whalebones or steels, placed into casings, determine the shape of the silhouette. The pattern shown, with approximate measurement of hoops, is for the crinoline with strong back thrust and flat front.

Petticoats — use the pattern for the crinoline omitting the casings and hoops.

Blouse — (form C.B. fastening). The head of the sleeve should be cut to tightly fit the armhole. Form wrist plackets.

Skirt — attach to waistband in small single, double, or triple pleats, commencing from point A on either side of the C.F. A tightly-fitting belt, with a buckle fastening, is worn with the blouse and skirt.

Pardessus coat — it is preferable, in the cutting of the very long shoulder line and the dropped armhole, to model than flat cut the patterns. The fronts, at the waistline, are fastened with linked buttons. The head of the pagoda sleeve is attached to the lining of the coat to follow the natural line of the armhole.

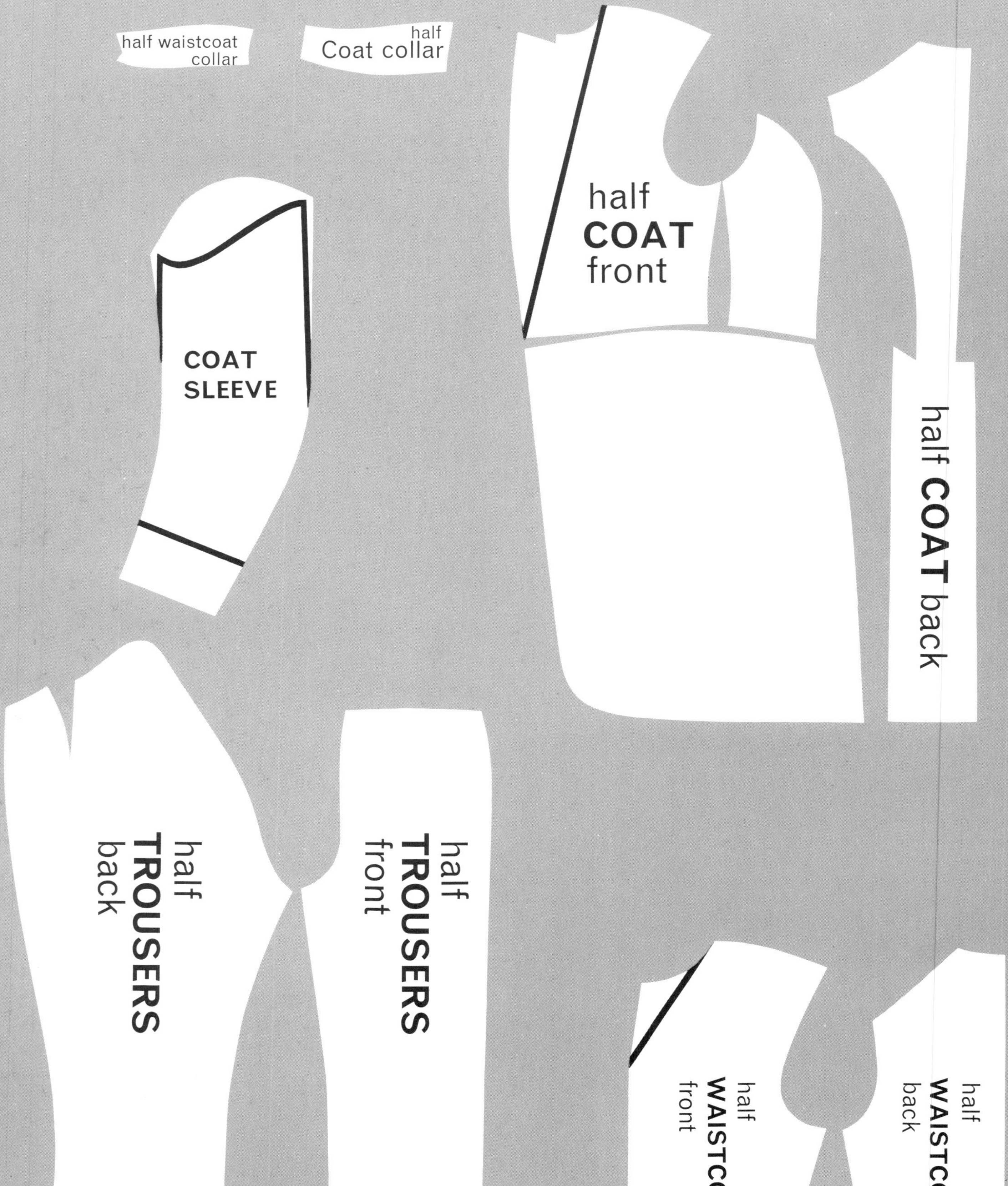

half waistcoat collar

half Coat collar

COAT SLEEVE

half **COAT** front

half **COAT** back

half **TROUSERS** back

half **TROUSERS** front

half **WAISTCOAT** front

half **WAISTCOAT** back

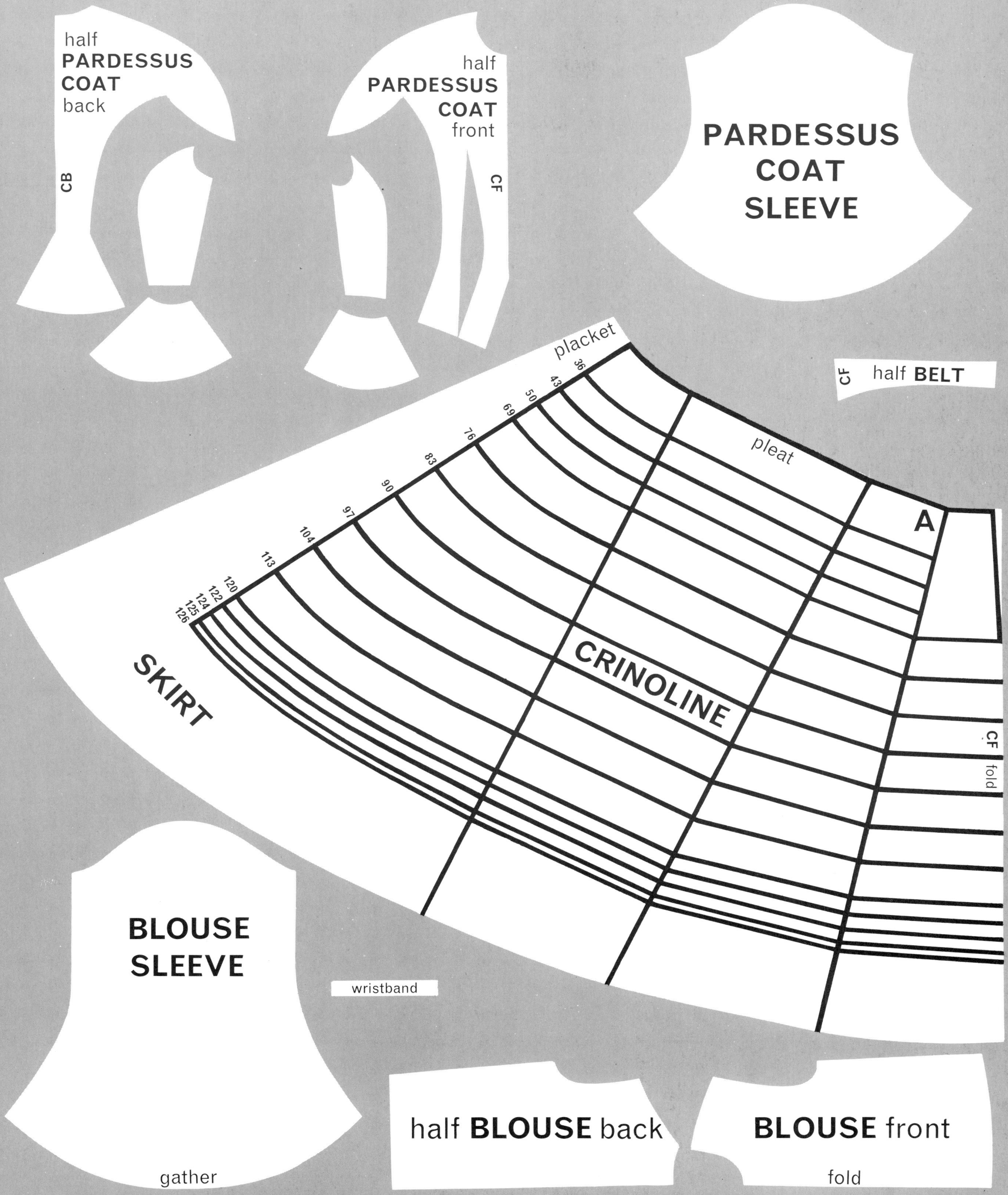

half
**PARDESSUS
COAT**
back

CB

half
**PARDESSUS
COAT**
front

CF

**PARDESSUS
COAT
SLEEVE**

placket

36
43
50
69
76
83
90
97
104
113
120
122
124
125
126

pleat

A

CF half **BELT**

SKIRT

CRINOLINE

CF fold

**BLOUSE
SLEEVE**

wristband

half **BLOUSE** back

BLOUSE front

gather

fold

1870 Victoria

Fabrics: Women — materials are lighter in weight. Shot silks, muslins, foulards, moiré, cashmere, chintzes and sateens.

Colours: Women — light and pastel colours influenced by the late 18th century. Men — black predominates.

Decoration: Women — fabrics are striped, spotted or decorated with small sprig patterns. Dresses trimmed with flat braiding, piping, scalloping, bows, flounces, etc. Men's waistcoats made up in spotted or fancy materials.

Padding and restriction, women: A small crinoline, bell-shaped and flat in front, with a very large bustle (of calico and whalebone or flexible steels) attached to the back, extends the skirts well out and up from the waistline — the wearer no longer stands in the centre of a circle but in the front of an ellipse. Longer corsets control and round the stomach and hips.

Movement, men: Similar to the previous fashion.

Movement, women: The high-heeled shoes and bustle dictate posture — from the waist up the body leans forward, from the waist down the posterior is thrust out (emphasising the bustle) to form the popular "Grecian bend" or "S" curve — the top of the S commencing at the forehead with the last curve of the S passing over the bosom and through into the bustle. Walk is spirited and bouncy.

Men

General characteristics: Well-tailored and elegant formal clothes. Coats are cut looser around the armholes.

Under garments — similar to the previous fashion. Shirt collars worn straight up, turned down or winged. Ties are loosely knotted, formed into a bow, or drawn through a seal ring. Cravats very fashionable.

Frock-coat — (knee length, double breasted) flatter collar, lapels frequently faced in silk, C.B. vent with a button positioned on either side at the waistline.

Waistcoat — (double breasted) low buttoned with wide lapels.

Trousers — narrowish.

Socks — similar to the previous fashion.

Boots and shoes — similar to the previous fashion.

Hats — similar to the previous fashion.

Hair — closer cropped, with less flamboyant whiskers and beards. The hair is sometimes centrally parted from the forehead to the nape of the neck.

Accessories — gloves always worn with formal clothes.

Women

General characteristics: The waist is high, the bodice form fitting. The skirt extends out at the back over the large bustle. Style imitates the middle and latter part of the 18th century — looping up of top skirts to form panniers, delicately patterned fabrics, ribbons, etc. Dolly Varden hats tip down well over the forehead.

Under garments — bustle, small crinoline (steels or whalebone placed chiefly at the back) drawers, petticoats, camisole and chemise.

Dress — (skirts and bodice separate) the bodice is usually V-necked, lightly boned and fastened down the C.F. A basque, arranged in pleats at the back to accommodate the bustle, hides the join of skirt to bodice. The sleeves, decorated with a flounce at elbow and wrist, tightly fit the arm. Two skirts are usually worn (both flounced), the underskirt developing into a short train, the top skirt gathered up at the sides to form an apron or pannier at back and front. A belt is frequently worn.

Stockings — white or coloured, embroidered or striped. Wool or cotton for day wear, silk for evening.

Boots and shoes — (high heels) buttoned or elastic sided boots with broad square toes. Fronts of shoes decorated with buckles or hard or soft ribbon bows.

Hair — centrally parted and dressed to reveal the ears. The chignon placed high at the back of the head, is arranged in a cluster of long curls. The front hair is frizzed or prettily curled to form a fringe.

Hats — little straw hats or diadem bonnets with long ribbon ties. Trimmings of flowers, ribbons, lace, etc.

Accessories — small muffs, elaborately trimmed parasols, gloves, handbags. Tortoiseshell combs for the hair, large earrings, cameo brooches, etc.

Notes on patterns: Women

Corsets — adapt pattern of 1853.

Small crinoline — gather to a waistband adding a side placket, or insert a drawstring arranging most of the fullness to the sides and back. Whalebones (X), placed in casings, determine the shape and size of the crinoline.

Bustle — (make up in very heavy calico) the top edge H to H is pleated or gathered to the waistband (H to H). The size, angle, and shape, is formed by heavy pieces of whalebone (X) set into casings — the measurements given, form a very large bustle. The sides (A) are also stiffened with whalebone. Make up the pleated flounce in stiffened material, with a heavy cord placed in the hem. Two flaps (G) attached to the sides, with eyelet holes worked on the free edges, are laced together at the back — this lacing controls the spring of the bustle out from the back waistline. Tapes attached to the sides are tied in front at low waist and hip level. The waistband is fastened at the C.F. with hooks and eyes.

Petticoats — adapt crinoline pattern omitting the whalebone and casings.

Bodice — (C.F. buttoned fastening) match front skirt darts to bodice front darts. B.B. sewn to D.D. forms the skirt side seam, and E.E. to C.C. a pleat to the side of the C.B. Lightly bone bodice darts and seams. The flared skirts to the bodice should be cut in relation to the size and shape of the crinoline and bustle.

Skirts — (form side placket) attach both skirts to the waistband, with pleating or gathering commencing from E and F. Add flounces and gather up the side seams of the top skirt to form a front and back apron. Cut the skirt patterns in relation to the shape and size of the crinoline and bustle.

fold frockcoat collar

half Side back

half Double-breasted **FROCKCOAT** front

half Double-breasted **FROCKCOAT** back

half Double-breasted **FROCKCOAT** skirts

half **WAISTCOAT** front

fold or seam

WAISTCOAT back

Double-breasted **FROCKCOAT SLEEVE**

fold waistcoat collar

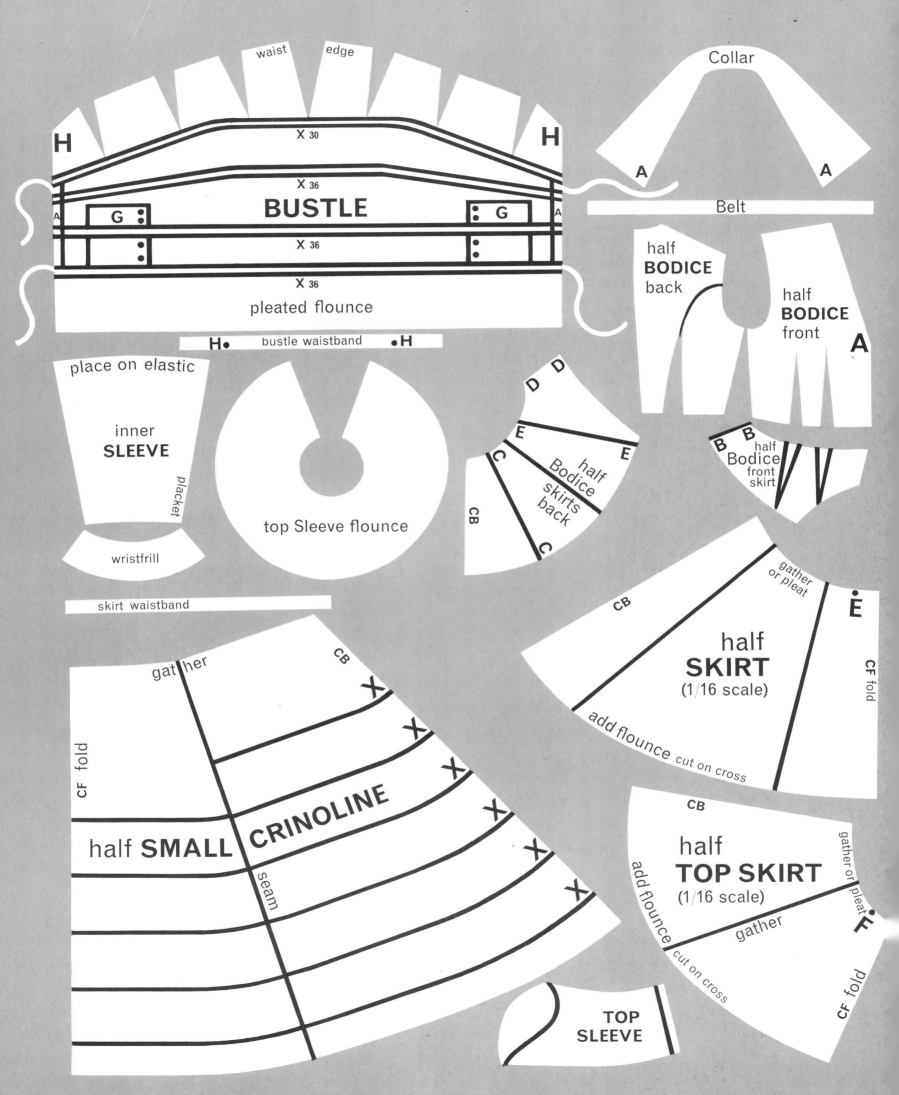

1876 Victoria

Fabrics: Women — cashmere, serge, twill, poplin, satin, velveteen, heavy silks, Scotch plaids.

Colours: Women — dark and sombre.

Decoration: Two or more different materials make up the dress. Prevalence of braids, deep fringes, ribbons, pleatings, ruchings and elaborate flounces (often of a striped material, pleated to show only one colour). Velvet used as a flat trimming on wool and silk dresses.

Padding and restriction, women: The long cuirass-shaped corset extends to well below the hips. The crinoline is discarded. The smaller bustle (or steel half hoops with horsehair or crinoline flounces) follows the curves of back and waist to reach its largest dimension at the hips. The petticoat, cut narrow at the front and sides, forms a train at the back (gathered at the waistline and reinforced with a series of stiffened flounces). Front and sides of the skirt give the appearance of being wrapped around the figure, the skirts being tied back by inside sets of tapes placed at intervals down the side seams. Every device is employed to emphasise the small waist, long body and roundness of hips and bosom.

Movement, men: Similar to the previous fashion.

Movement, women: The walk is severely restricted to small steps by the tight front and sides of the skirts. Movement of the body, carriage upright with shoulders well back, is also restricted by the long, boned corset.

Men

General characteristics: Similar to the previous fashion. Shoulders are square and padded.

Under garments — similar to the previous fashion. Combinations worn.

Inverness coat — cut straight from the shoulders, double breasted, with arm length cape and storm collar. Mid-calf in length.

Hats — the tall "square" bowler frequently replaces the top hat.

Hair — clipped beards and turned-down moustaches. Whiskers are short, or very long and combed out (Piccadilly weepers).

Women

General characteristics: "Woman seems to be standing in front of her dress." The silhouette emphasises a series of long, uninterrupted sinuous curves. The dress, very close-fitting and form-revealing in front, is subtly extended out at the back into the bustle and train (heavily and richly complex in cut and decoration). Hair is dressed to echo the bustle and train.

Undergarments — similar to the previous fashion, but adapted to suit the new style. The chemise is narrower, the top bordered with insertions and edgings, and darted, pleated, or with gussets added, to neatly fit under the bodice.

Dress — (separate bodice and skirt) the seams of the bodice are lightly boned, the neck is high or V-shaped. Sleeves are narrow, wrist length, and trimmed in a similar manner to the neckline with frills or pleating at the wrist. Fastened down the C.F., the long bodice is modestly trimmed in comparison to the elaborate fantasy of loops, bows, braids, flounces and fringes which decorate the back of the skirt and train. Construction and fastening of the skirt is very complex, being composed of so many different pieces — aprons, drapings, linings, stiffenings, appendages, etc.

Stockings — coloured to match the dress.

Boots and Shoes — similar to the previous fashion.

Hair — (false hair worn) the style like the dress is excessively complicated. The effect is to enlarge the size of the head, particularly at the back, with a heap of highly placed ringlets or curls or with an elaborately plaited chignon. The top and side hair is waved, the fringe frizzed or curled.

Hats — (hats for informal wear, bonnets for formal occasions) very small, tipped forward or clinging on behind as best they can.

Accessories — similar to the previous fashion. Outdoor mantles of varying length fit the figure behind falling loose in front.

Notes on patterns: Women

Corsets — heavy black lines indicate the positioning of the whalebones.

Bustle — sew up the foundation, gather up the back section, and place to the waistband A to A. The bustle, with whalebones (X) set into casings, is sewn down to the foundation on the side back seams D.E., and gathered at the waist edge to the waistband. Attach pleated or gathered stiffened flounces (5 to 6 inches in depth) to the bustle at 1, 2, 3, 4, 5, 6, 7. The waistband is fastened at the C.F. with hooks and eyes.

Petticoats — adapt under skirt pattern inserting a drawstring at the waist, and adding a pleated flounce to the hem.

Bodice — (form C.F. hook and eye fastening) bone all seams. Cut all patterns, particularly from the waist down at the back, to closely fit the form and shape of the curves of the bustle.

Skirts — (under skirt and top skirt are both sewn to a waistband with a placket formed either at the side or at the C.B.). The skirt patterns should be cut in relation to the size of the bustle. The pleated flounces are sewn to the under skirt at B.B. and at C.C. The top skirt, sewn to a foundation to control the draping, has inside sets of tapes sewn to the side seams (G.F.) — these tapes, tied together under the skirts at the back, determine the clinging front skirt silhouette. The bustle back, set into pleats or gathered at the waist edge and from F to H to the foundation, is interlined with a thin but stiff material — the arrangement of the puffings, pleatings, etc., controlled by tie-catching. H to J is left open to form the fish tail. (The patterns given for the pleated flounces need to be opened up at regular intervals and extended — in relation to the width of pleats required.)

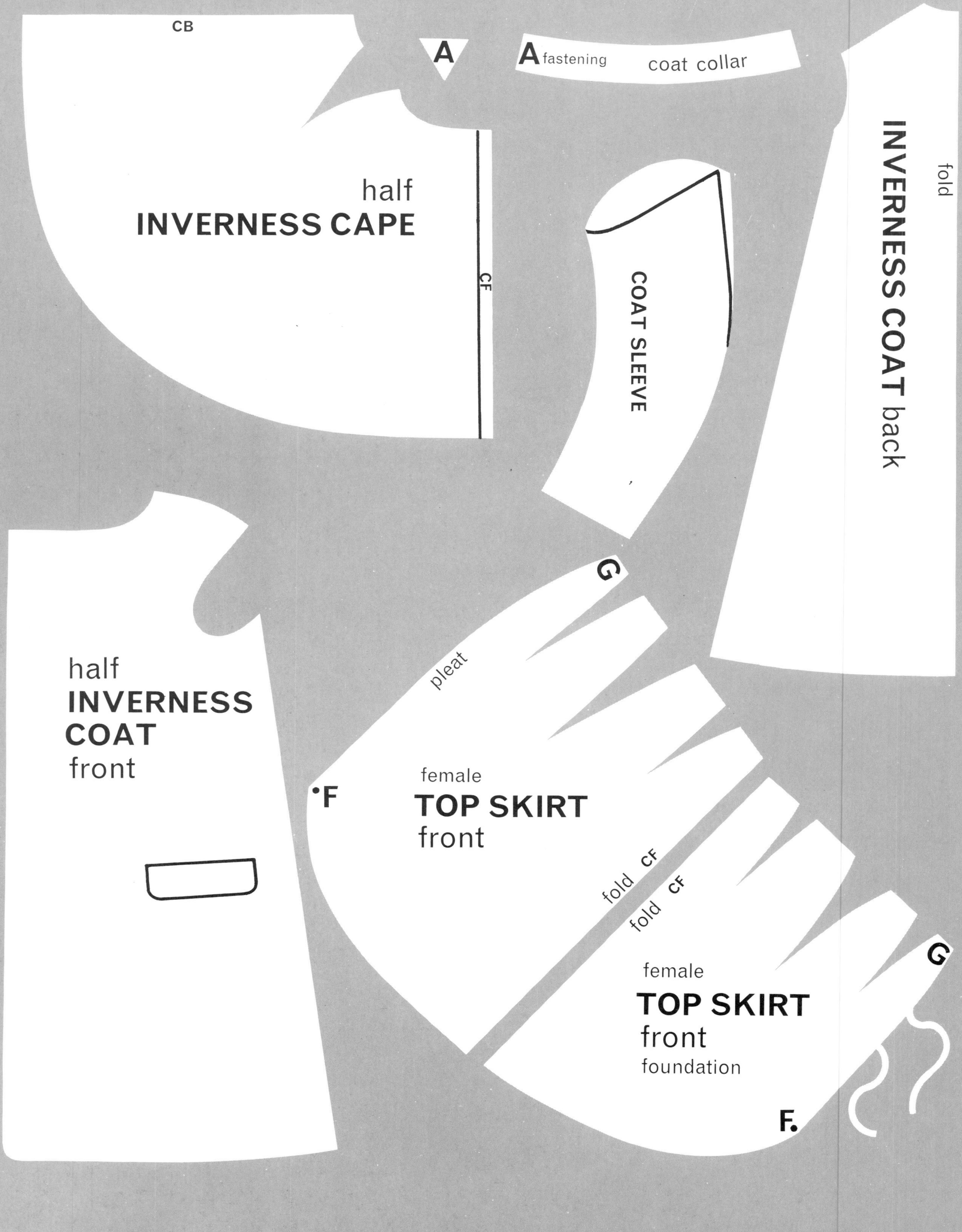

CB

A

A fastening   coat collar

half
INVERNESS CAPE

CF

COAT SLEEVE

INVERNESS COAT back

fold

CF

G

half
**INVERNESS
COAT**
front

pleat

female
TOP SKIRT
front

•**F**

fold **CF**

fold **CF**

female
TOP SKIRT
front
foundation

G

F.

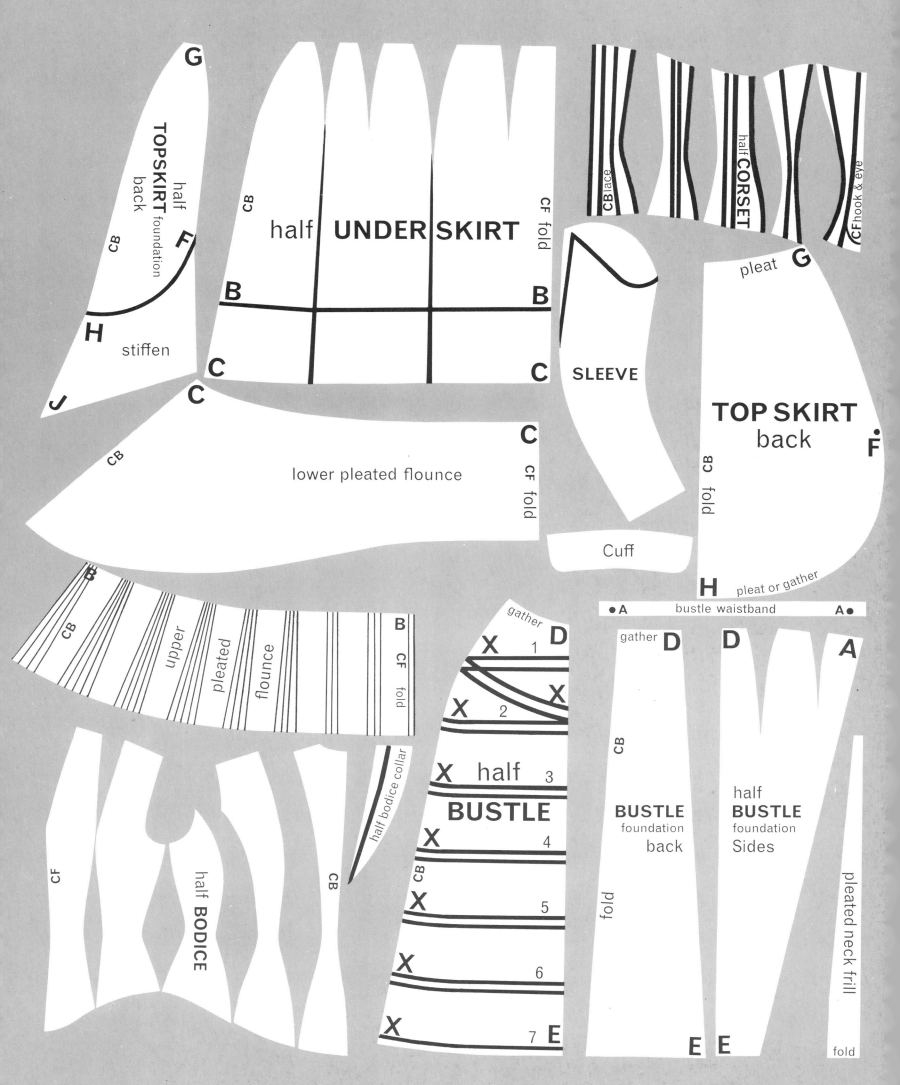

G

TOPSKIRT half back foundation

CB

F

H

J

stiffen

CB

CF fold

half **UNDER SKIRT**

B B

C C

C

lower pleated flounce

CF fold

CB lace

half **CORSET**

CF hook & eye

G

pleat

SLEEVE

TOP SKIRT back

CB fold

F

H pleat or gather

Cuff

● A bustle waistband A ●

B

CB

upper pleated flounce

B

CF fold

half bodice collar

CB

CF

half **BODICE**

gather

X 1 D

X

X 2

X half 3

BUSTLE

X 4

CB

X 5

X 6

X 7 E

gather D D A

CB

BUSTLE foundation back

fold

half **BUSTLE** foundation Sides

pleated neck frill

E E

fold

1880 Victoria

Fabrics: Men — checks, plaids and rougher textured fabrics for country and less formal wear.

Women — similar to the previous fashion. Silk or wool jersey very fashionable. Fur trimmings, mantles, and coats.

Colours: Women — soft autumn tints, greys, pinks, maroon, many greens including sage, bottle green and khaki. Peacock blue.

Decoration: Women — heavy applied decoration disappears. The dress is made of two or more different materials, one figured, one plain, one of bright colour, the other quiet, etc.

Padding and restriction, men: Coats have padding in the front, at the back and around the armhole. Shoulders are held out by small triangular pads.

Padding and restriction, women: The bustle is discarded. The corset still encases the body to well below hip level. Skirts are cut very narrow all round. Excessively tight sleeves and armholes. The entire dress is restrictive and uncomfortable. (Dressing gowns worn whenever possible.)

Movement, men: Similar to the previous fashion.

Movement, women: The tightly tied-back skirt, long boned bodice and high pointed heels make walking almost an impossibility — minute steps. Arms are so restricted, by the tightness of the sleeves, that they cannot be raised above the head or bent at the elbow to blow the nose!

Men

General characteristics: Three-piece lounge suits very popular. All coats are buttoned high.

Under garments — similar to the previous fashion.

Lounge suit — (matching coat, waistcoat and trousers) the single-breasted coat, cut fairly straight with little indication of waisting or flaring of skirts, is four buttoned, the collar and lapels narrow. Pockets are positioned on either hip and on the left breast. A ticket pocket is frequently placed above the right hip pocket. The waistcoat is single breasted and high buttoned.

Socks — similar to the previous fashion.

Boots and shoes — similar to the previous fashion. Spats in light colours.

Hats — similar to the previous fashion. Straw boater for the seaside. Deer stalker or cap for country wear.

Hair — cut to reveal the natural shape of the head, parted on one side, and short at the back. Young men sport a drooping moustache, without the beard.

Accessories — similar to the previous fashion.

Women

General characteristics: All garments fit close to the figure and are cut as narrow as possible to give a long thin silhouette. The method of making, fastening, draping and getting into, very complex.

Under garments — chemise seamed to fit the figure. Combinations are now worn. Petticoats are restricted to the barest minimum.

Dress — high necked with a stand-up collar (trimmed with frillings, lace, or jabot). The top half, extending to well below hip level, is button through or cut away in front to reveal a "waistcoat". Sleeves are similar to the previous fashion. The foundations of all skirts, back and front, are cut as narrow as possible (particularly at the knees). The top skirt, forming a tightly swathed apron front, develops at the back into a series of hanging pouches. The underskirt is flared from the knees down at the sides and back where it forms a short train — visible areas of the under skirt are always arranged in pleats.

Stockings — similar to the previous fashion.

Boots and shoes — high slender heels.

Hair — (dressed to reveal ears and neck) waved or curled in front, the back coiled loosely into a large bun.

Hats — larger, and worn square on top or at the back of the head. Ribbons tied in a large bow under the chin help secure the bonnet.

Accessories — buttonless gloves are always tucked under the sleeve. Very elaborate muffs decorated with birds' wings, parasols with large china or crystal handles. Purses — sometimes attached to a waistbelt. Small earrings and brooches.

Notes on patterns: Women

Corsets — use pattern of 1876.

Petticoat — adapt under skirt pattern. The back train of the top petticoat should be set with flounces.

Bodice and waistcoat — (make up separately, or as one with the front edges of the bodice sewn or fastened down to the waistcoat), all bodice patterns should be cut from measurements taken from the corseted figure. Lightly bone seams and darts. Form buttoned fastening down C.F. of the waistcoat. The back skirts of the bodice form a large flared box pleat.

Skirts — (under skirt and top skirt are both sewn to a waistband with a placket formed at the side or at the C.B.). The under skirt, partially cut on the cross, is set into pleats from A. down. The top skirt, sewn to a foundation to control the draping and back pouches, is constructed in a similar manner to the previous fashion with the side seam tapes tied very tightly at the back to achieve the wrapped and clinging effect at the front. The back part of the skirt forms two hanging pouches — sewn up on the sides, interlined, and gathered or pleated to the foundation at C. and at the waist edge. The front draping and swathing of the skirt is controlled by tie-catching.

Charcteristics: Three piece lounge

[...] popular. All coats buttoned high

Similar to the previous fashion

[...]tching Coat; waistcoat + trousers.

Single-breasted Coat, cut fairly

[...]ght. with

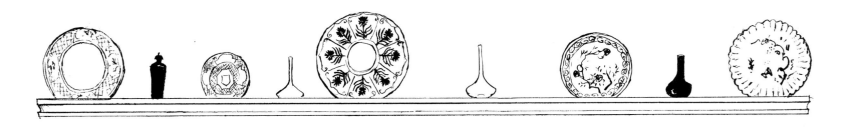

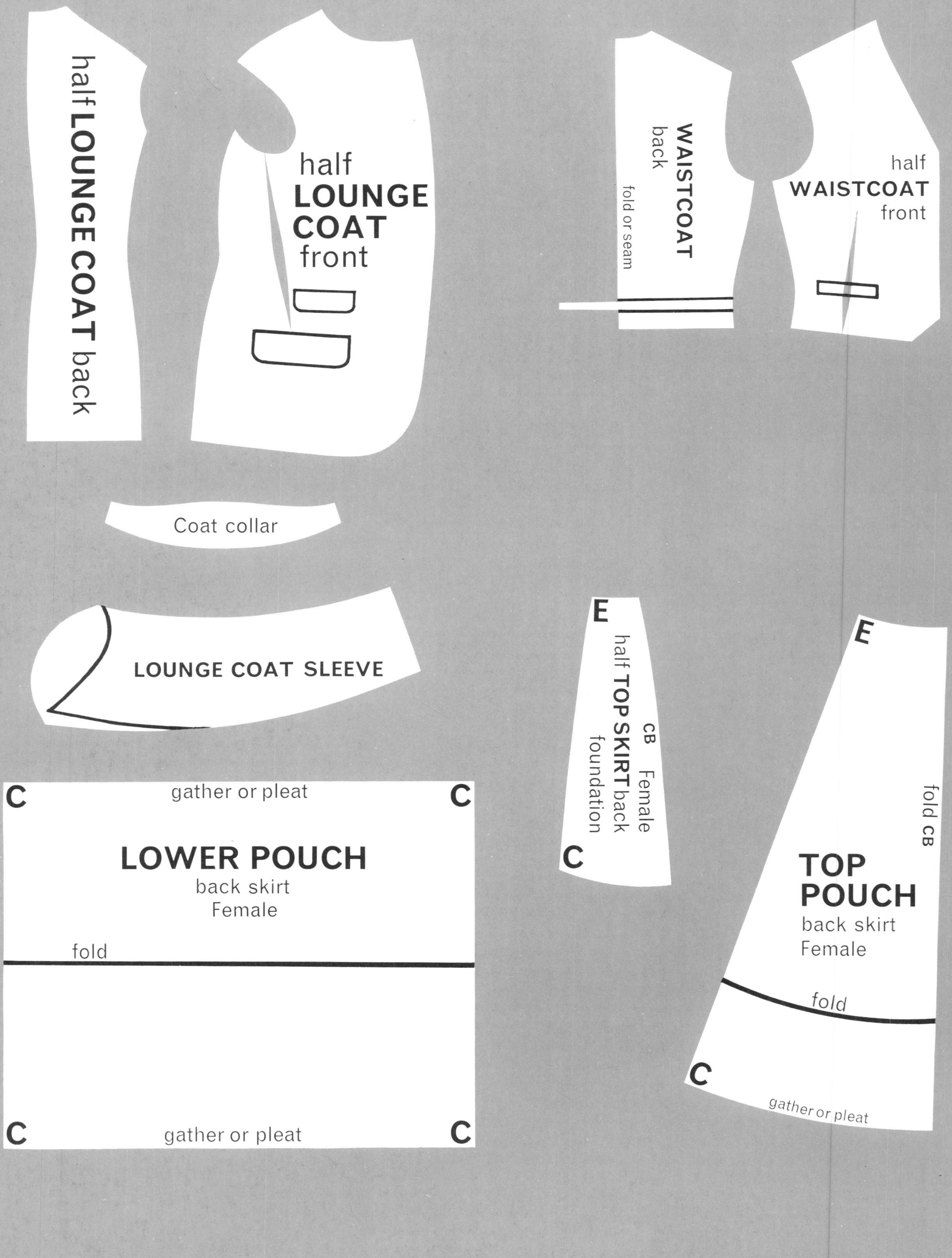

half **LOUNGE COAT** back

half **LOUNGE COAT** front

WAISTCOAT back

fold or seam

half **WAISTCOAT** front

Coat collar

LOUNGE COAT SLEEVE

E

half **TOP SKIRT** back foundation

CB Female

C

E

fold CB

TOP POUCH back skirt Female

fold

C

gather or pleat

C gather or pleat C

LOWER POUCH back skirt Female

fold

C gather or pleat C

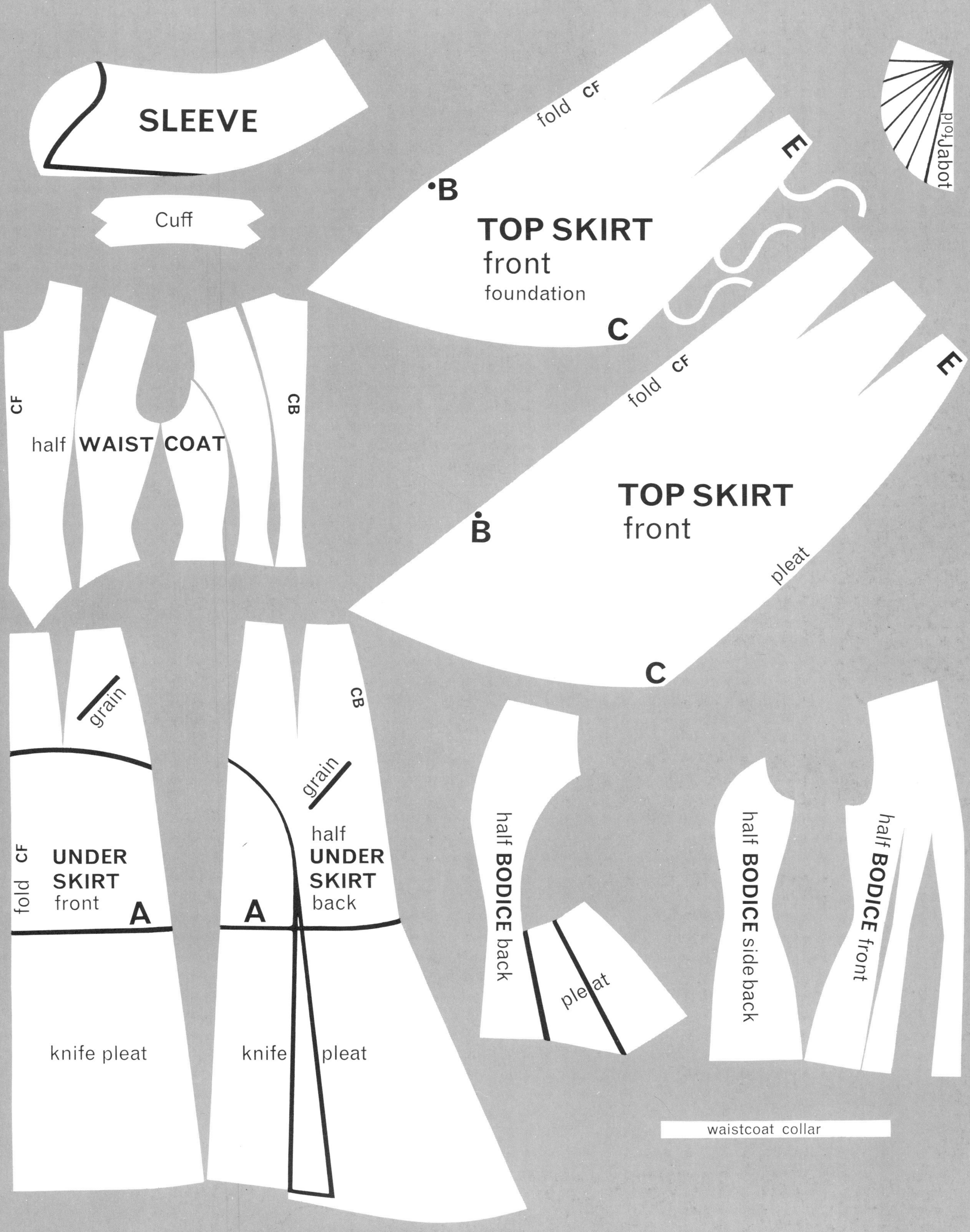

SLEEVE

Cuff

fold **CF**

·B

TOP SKIRT
front
foundation

E

C

jabot

E

fold **CF**

CF

half **WAIST COAT**

CB

TOP SKIRT
front

Ḃ

pleat

C

grain

CB

grain

CF
fold

**UNDER
SKIRT**
front

A

half
**UNDER
SKIRT**
back

A

knife pleat

knife pleat

half **BODICE** back

pleat

half **BODICE** side back

half **BODICE** front

waistcoat collar

1886 Victoria

Fabrics: Women — wool and cloth, tweed and cheviots for tailor-mades; foulards, heavy silks and velvets for more dressy occasions. Mantles, top coats and trimmings of Canadian beaver, astrakhan, moleskin, sealskin, sable, blue fox. Men — serge, twill, flannel, tweeds, checks and stripes for informal, summer, and country dress. Evening waistcoats of white pique or silk.

Colours: Women — browns, maroons, lichen green, petunia, sunflower yellow, maize, deep strong blues.

Decoration: Women — frogging, large buttons, pleating, applied bands of material of the same colour as the dress but of a different richer texture (satin, ottoman silk, velvet, fur, etc.). Cut velvet and figured materials based on formalised plant forms. Novelty stripes.

Padding and restriction, women: The corset is shorter. Large bustles, similar to the style of the 1870s, of more complex structure reappear, thrusting the back skirts out at a right angle from the natural waistline. Extremely tight sleeves from the elbows down.

Movement, men: Similar to the previous fashion.

Movement, women: Rigid upright and never alluring. The bustle gives a solemn majesty to the carriage. Walking and "striding out" is no longer hampered by tight skirts — the skirts are now cut full all round, just above ground in length, and without a train.

Men

General characteristics: Similar to the previous fashion.

Under garments — similar to the previous fashion.

Covert coat — (frequently seen with a velvet collar) short fly-fronted overcoat with strapped seams. Cut with a whole back with short vents in the side seams.

Trousers — legs are wider and gently flared from the knees down (spring bottoms). Trousers occasionally turned-up.

Socks — similar to the previous fashion.

Boots and shoes — Oxford shoes worn for summer wear with fancy socks.

Hats — bowler with curled brim very popular.

Hair — similar to the previous fashion.

Accessories — similar to the previous fashion.

Women

General characteristics: Essentially matronly with a minimum display of physical charms. The waistline returns to the natural position. The form of the lower part of the body is concealed by an oppressively heavy skirt which is thrust out at the back by the large bustle extension — severe and lacking any quality of enchantment or frivolity. The head of the sleeve is gathered or pleated and puffed up. Hats are loaded with birds, parts of birds, animals, buckles and formally arranged ribbons and bows.

Under garments — suspenders, replacing garters, are buttoned to the corset. Two petticoats close fitting in front, and flared, gathered, and flounced at the back, are usually worn (of flannel or quilted silk). Drawers or knickerbockers with knee bands are trimmed with lace. A bust bodice laced front and back and boned on either side of the lacings, is worn as a device to support the breasts.

Dress — the boned bodice, with stiff upright military collar, is seamed to spread out from the natural waist to form a V in front, and arranged in complex flares and pleats at the back to take the form of the bustle. The bag plastron of one or more pouches replaces the waistcoat front. Sleeves are three-quarter or full length. Hooks and eyes or lacing fastens the bodice at the C.F.s. Panniers and draperies give way to gathered or pleated skirts with front and back aprons (flat in front, pleated at sides and back).

Stockings — ribbed, black, or in every imaginable colour.

Boots and shoes — high buttoned boots and laced-up shoes. Large buckles decorate the fronts of shoes.

Hair — dressed neatly and close to the head. The forehead is covered by a curled, crimped or waved fringe. The ears are exposed and the back hair is swept up to form a plaited chignon or bun, placed high on the top of the head.

Hats — (heavily trimmed), very much larger and taller with the brim turned up in front. Most hats are worn on the back of the head and secured with hat pins.

Accessories — similar to the previous fashion. Boas of fur or feathers. Mantles slit up at the back to let the bustle peep through, elbow-length capes, long full-length yoked capes, jackets.

Notes on patterns: Women

Corsets — use pattern for 1892.

Bustle — adapt pattern of 1870, adding if necessary, extra whaleboning and several stiffened flounces.

Petticoats — cut full, insert a drawstring at the waist edge with the gathering concentrated away from the front. Finish the hem with a deep pleated flounce.

Bodice — (lightly bone darts, seams, and standing collar), the bodice plastron front is darted, then pleated at waist edge, shoulder seams, and neck edge. It is then mounted to the foundation which is sewn to the inside of the bodice front at one side and fastened with hooks and eyes to the other. The collar, on the fastening side, is joined to the neck edge with hooks and bars. Gather head of sleeve to armhole. The bodice back skirts should be cut to follow the shape of the bustle — interline and set the hem in flutes (by radial stitching from waistline to hem and with tie-catching) to resemble the edge of a figure 8 ruff.

Skirts — (in the initial stages of making up, cut back skirts considerably longer than ground length — petticoats and bustle should be worn when the length of hem, even all round, is finally determined). The skirt, front and back aprons, and bustle swag, are all eased to a waistband — with a placket formed on one side at D. Extend the skirt and back apron patterns to form pleats, with the waist edge darted all round to closely fit the figure and shape of the bustle. The apron front is arranged in pleats at the sides (D. to C.) to form the swagged effect. Make up back apron from patterns 1 and 2 — cutting away the fronts to form the zig-zag hemline (see pattern). The bustle swag is interlined, closely pleated at the sides (X.X.) and at the waist edge — the join of the bustle swag to the back waistline of the skirt is frequently concealed by a large flat bow.

Hat — wire and/or stiffen, and turn brim up to an acute angle in front.

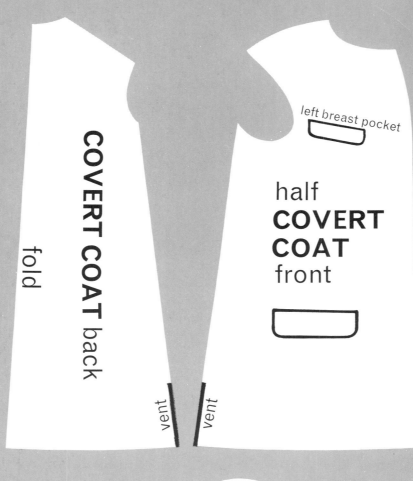

COVERT COAT back

fold

half
COVERT COAT front

left breast pocket

vent vent

COAT SLEEVE

Coat collar

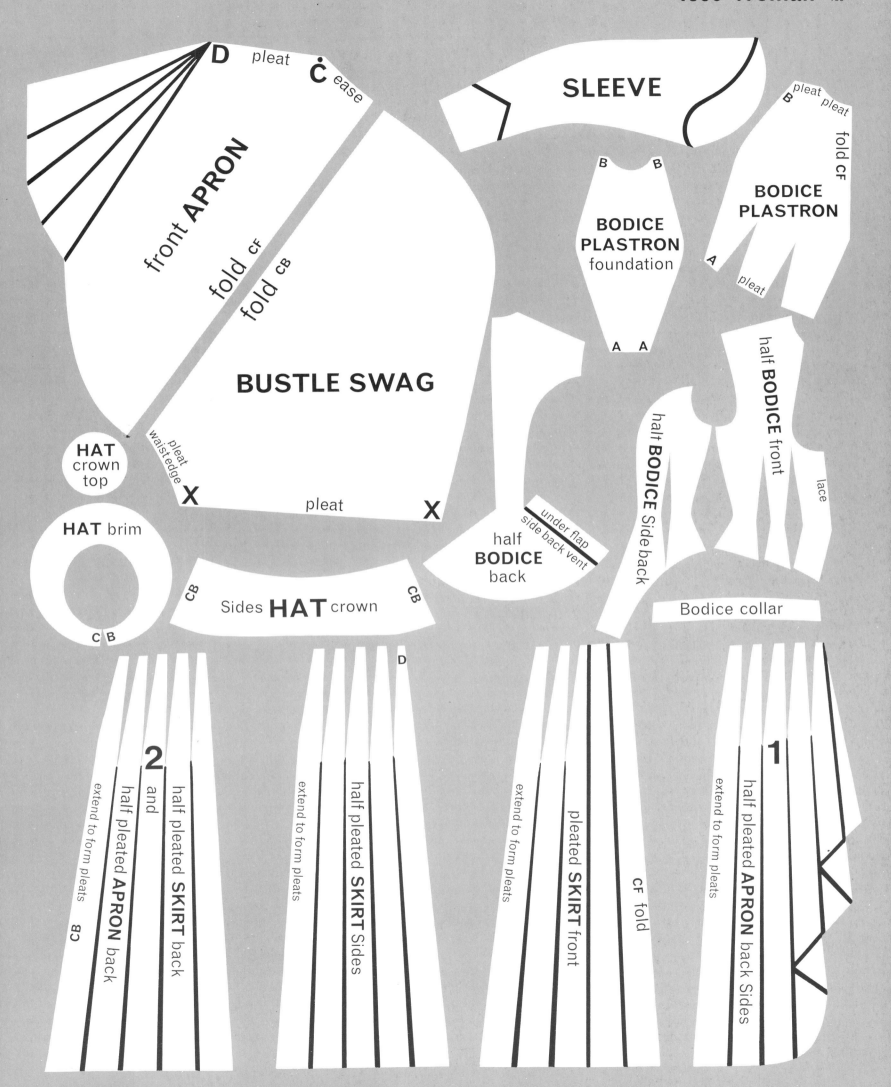

front **APRON**

D pleat Ċ ease

fold cf

fold cb

BUSTLE SWAG

pleat waistedge

X pleat X

HAT crown top

HAT brim

C B

CB Sides **HAT** crown CB

SLEEVE

B B

B pleat pleat

fold cf

BODICE PLASTRON

BODICE PLASTRON foundation

A

A A

pleat

half **BODICE** front

half **BODICE** Side back

lace

half **BODICE** back

under flap

side back vent

Bodice collar

2

extend to form pleats

half pleated **APRON** back

and

half pleated **SKIRT** back

CB

extend to form pleats

half pleated **SKIRT** Sides

D

extend to form pleats

pleated **SKIRT** front

cf fold

1

extend to form pleats

half pleated **APRON** back Sides

1892 Victoria

Fabrics: Similar to the previous fashion.

Colours: Men — white flannel trousers and dark coats for country wear (summer). Women — yellow very dominant, particularly for evening wear. Reds, heliotrope, pinks, lichen green, fawn — all very discordant.

Decoration: Women — simple in comparison to the previous 20 years. Edgings (particularly around the hem), flat braids, frogging. Decoration is mainly concentrated on the upper half of the dress.

Padding and restriction, women: Corsets are very tightly laced (average 22 inches, with tight lacing producing waists of under 16 inches!). The gored petticoat is set with stiffened flounces at the back.

Movement, men: Similar to the previous fashion.

Movement, women: The upper part of the body is severely restricted by the length and very tight lacing of the corsets. Skirts permit a lengthy stride.

Men

General characteristics: Square-shouldered, straight-waisted silhouette. Frock coat and top hat for formal occasions, lounge suit for ordinary wear. Trousers are looser in cut (young men wear permanent turn-ups). Very long, almost ankle-length, overcoats.

Under garments — shirts are buttoned through the C.F.s.

Country wear — (Norfolk jacket, knickerbockers, deerstalker hat, woollen stockings, high buttoned boots and mid-calf gaiters), the high buttoned, single-breasted jacket is sometimes cut with a yoke. The pleats are either laid on (fake) or cut in one with the fronts and the back. Slots formed on either side of these pleats hold the belt in place. Patch pockets with flaps are positioned on either hip. The knickerbockers, cut full and longer than ordinary breeches, terminate below the knee where they are pleated into deep knee bands, (outside leg opening and fastening).

Hair — parted in the middle, at the side, or brushed straight back. Walrus moustaches, and clipped side whiskers grown to link up with the moustache.

Women

General characteristics: Dress is basically simple. Skirts are practical and very much alike — straight and flat in front, gored and pleated at the sides and back. The shoulder line is broader, the top of the sleeves larger. Hair is dressed to follow the shape of the head.

Under garments — similar to the previous fashion. Combinations of natural wool, muslin, or silk, decorated with bands of lace, insertions and coloured ribbons. Petticoats, no longer of flannel but silk and prettily trimmed, follow closely the cut of the skirt — pleated or gored with a drawstring behind,

Country wear — (skirt and tie, waistcoat, hip-length or longer tailored coat, and skirt), the shirt, with high starched collar, is similar to the men's. The waistcoat, often double breasted, and cut with a collar and broad lapels, forms a sharp V point at the C.F. waist. The single-breasted coat, with side and back skirts flared and frequently set in pleats, closely fits the figure. The lapels are wide. The Head of the "Leg of mutton" sleeve is pulled out and *not* up. The pleats, forming the back and sides of the skirt, are controlled or sewn down to hip level (inside sets of tapes, sewn to the side seams, help to flatten the front silhouette).

Stockings — similar to the previous fashion.

Boots and shoes — (very high heels), a long pointed toe ceases to permit small feet to be a prominent feature.

Hair — (Greek style) usually waved, the hair is drawn back, revealing the ears, into a small and neat bun or plait placed high at the back or on top of the head. The forehead is covered with a mass of small curls.

Hats — (veils, drawn in under the chin by a string, cover the face or are so short they barely reach the nose), hats, large or small, perch on top of the head. Secured with large pins they are made up in every material imaginable. Upright trimmings of feathers, flowers, lace and ribbons.

Accessories — similar to the previous fashion.

Notes on patterns: Women

Corsets — thick black lines indicate positioning of whalebones.

Petticoats — adapt under skirt pattern, insert a drawstring — placing all the fullness to the sides and C.B.

Under skirt — (form placket at side seam), gather sides and back and sew to the waistband. Gathered flounces are positioned at X.

Shirt — cut with bishop sleeves, full front (buttoned through) and full back — gathered to a narrow yoke. The stiff collar is separate.

Skirt — the skirt, attached to a half lining and a waistband (with side-back or side-front placket), is set into pleats — a large inverted box pleat placed on either side of the front followed by a series of knife pleats terminating in a box pleat at the C.B. The pleats are sewn down to hip level.

Waistcoat — (double breasted), lightly bone all darts.

Coat — lightly bone all darts and seams. Lightly pad and interline shoulders and fronts to achieve a rounded form, and add stiffening to the heads of the sleeves. The back skirt is set in a wide box pleat — finished off with embroidered arrow heads.

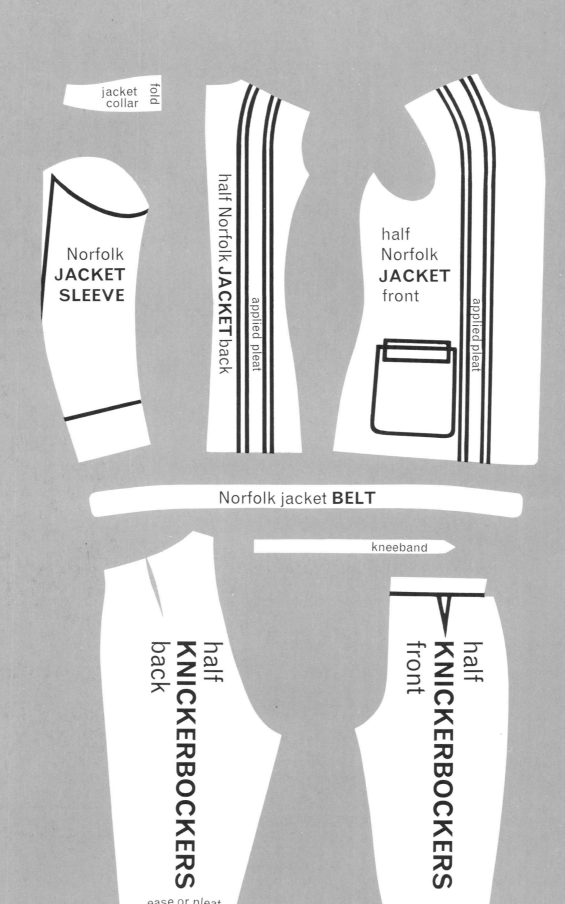

jacket collar fold

Norfolk **JACKET SLEEVE**

half Norfolk **JACKET** back applied pleat

half Norfolk **JACKET** front applied pleat

Norfolk jacket **BELT**

kneeband

half **KNICKERBOCKERS** back

ease or pleat

half **KNICKERBOCKERS** front

ease or pleat

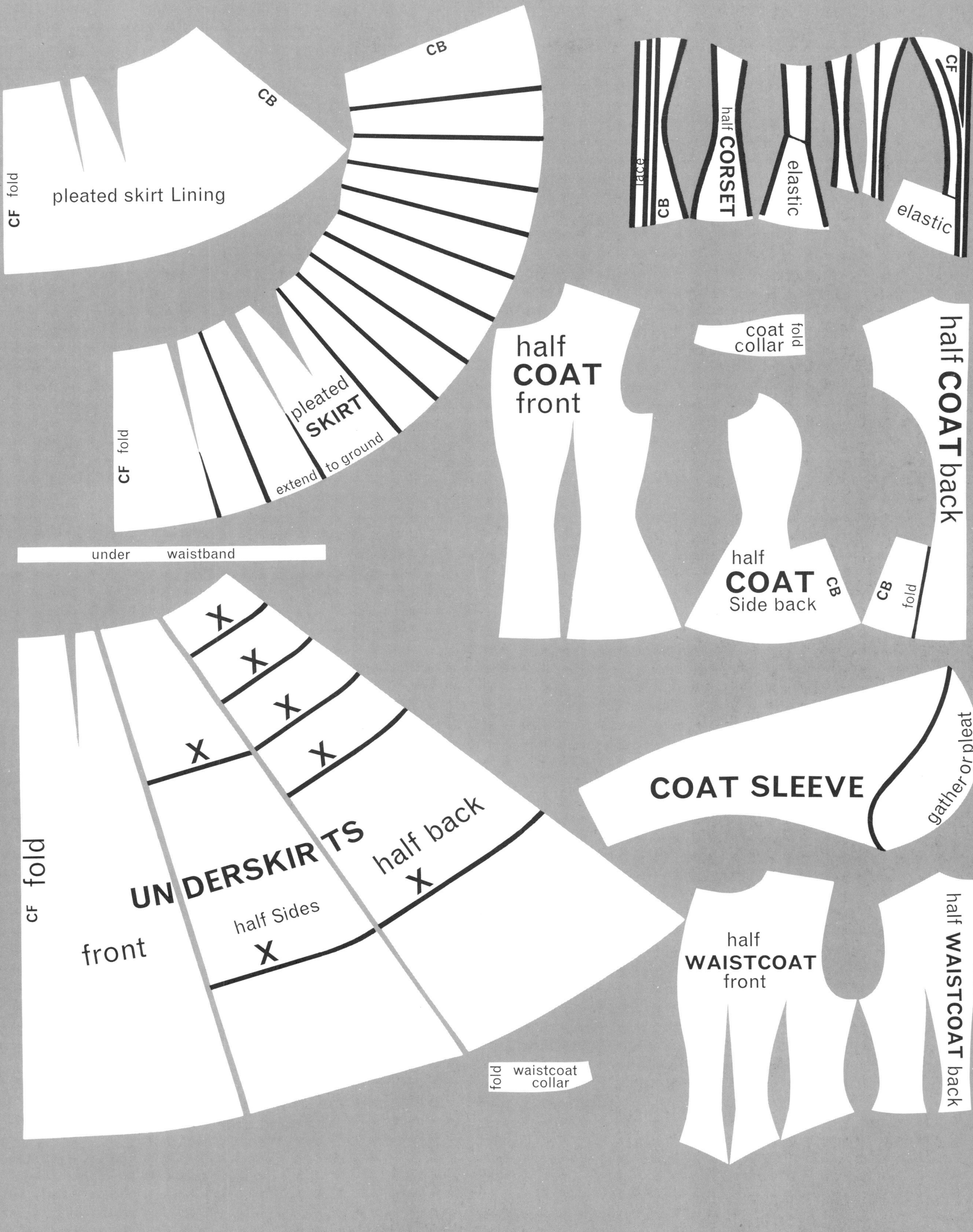

CB

CB

CF fold

pleated skirt Lining

CF fold

pleated
SKIRT

extend to ground

under waistband

X
X
X
X
X
X

cF fold

UNDERSKIRTS

half back

X

half Sides

X

front

fold waistcoat collar

lace

CB

half **CORSET**

elastic

CF

elastic

coat collar fold

half
COAT
front

half **COAT** back

half
COAT
Side back

CB

CB fold

COAT SLEEVE

gather or pleat

half
WAISTCOAT
front

half **WAISTCOAT** back

1896 Victoria

Fabrics: Women — materials are prettier, more feminine and lighter in weight.

Colours: Women — vivid, garish and very startling.

Decoration: Women — concentrated on the bodice, coat, or blouse. Bows, lace, novelty ribbons, flowers, elaborate braidings (Art Nouveau influence), tucks and pleatings, etc.

Padding and restriction, women: The corsets, cut low in front, are very beautifully made up in brocades, silks and satin. The silk petticoat is cut tight to knee level from whence it flares out to the hem. A series of graduated flounces increases the flare and gives a rustling sound to the walk. Very high standing collars are boned. Tops of sleeves are held out by layers of eiderdown, stiffened muslin, or small steels.

Movement, men: Formality and decorum is at times self-conscious and very mannered.

Movement, women: The walk, more like a glide, is swift and direct with a pelvic roll due to the tightness of the skirts from waist to knee. The head is held very high.

Men

General characteristics: Similar to the previous fashion. The Frock coat is longer with a shorter waist. Increasing variety of more informal clothes — dinner jackets, blazers, etc.

Under garments — similar to the previous fashion. Shirt collars are very high — winged, standing, or turned down.

Informal lounge coat — cut straight with three button fastening. Patch pockets on either hip and on the left breast.

Waistcoat — in white, plaid, or bright colours, single breasted, sometimes cut with a stepped standing collar.

Trousers — similar to the previous fashion.

Socks — black.

Boots and shoes — patent leather with tops of kid or cloth. Spats. Patent leather pumps with pointed toes worn with evening dress. Shoes are sometimes white for summer wear.

Hair — similar to the previous fashion. The younger man favours a smoothly shaven face, innocent of moustache and side whiskers.

Hats — similar to the previous fashion. Homburgs for informal wear.

Accessories — handkerchief placed in the breast pocket of the coat. Pince-nez, monocles, gloves of leather or chamois, walking canes, cigarette case, card case, cuff-links, watch and chain, etc.

Women

General characteristics: Similar to the previous fashion. To be tall and slim is the aim of every woman. Enormous gathered or pleated tops to sleeves, collars, revers, and decoration, give breadth to the bosom and shoulders, and emphasise the very small V-shaped waist. Blouses are very fashionable (a boned wide belt hides the join of skirt to blouse). Hair is dressed fuller to support the hats.

Under garments — similar to the previous fashion, elaborately and prettily trimmed with lace, flounces, ribbons, etc. Drawers are cut very wide at the leg. Due to the shortness of the corset front, a bust bodice or improver is worn.

Blouse — (C.F. bodice fastening, C.B. collar fastening), high necked. Cut full with a jabot or frilled front. The sleeves are enormously large at the top but tight from the elbows to wrist (wrist placket and frill).

Coat — seamed to closely fit the corseted figure, the waistline develops into a flared skirt or basque. Upstanding collar and very wide lapels. Huge leg-of-mutton sleeves.

Skirt — cut with 7 gores, flat in front, and flared at the sides and back from hips to ground (flares stiffened with lining).

Stockings — similar to the previous fashion.

Boots and shoes — boots in half kid and half leather, button or lace. Shoes have little pointed toes, and Louis heels positioned low under the instep. Day shoes are laced, the lacing hidden by a flap. Buckles.

Hair — always waved, fuller and looser and carried out over a pad or frame from forehead to ears. The bun is placed high on the top of the head. Hair is brushed back from the forehead and sides, the ears partially or completely covered.

Hats — sit on top of the head. Brims are wider and often turn up at the back. Exuberance of very elaborate trimmings — whole birds, stiff bows, wings, accordian pleated chiffon, buckles, every imaginable flower and feather. Toreador hats, small homburgs, very tiny bonnets and toques.

Accessories — ostrich feather and fur boas three yards long, handbags, parasols, umbrellas, small muffs, etc. Large fans for evening wear.

Notes on patterns: Women

Corsets — use pattern of 1892.

Petticoat — adapt skirt pattern. Several deep flounces, flared and gathered, should be sewn to the hem.

Skirt — set to a waistband.

Blouse — the collar (boned or wired, and with a C.B. fastening), is joined to the neckline on one side with hooks and bars, buttons and buttonholes, or very small press studs. The blouse fronts are buttoned.

Coat — (lightly bone all seams to just below waist level), the upper part of the sleeve should be interlined and, if necessary, held out with a crescent-shaped piece of buckram, lightly boned and sewn into the armhole. Stiffen the collar.

Belt — (fasten at C.B. or C.F.), stiffen with pieces of whalebone placed at C.F., side fronts, sides, side backs and C.B.

Hat — stiffen and/or wire brim.

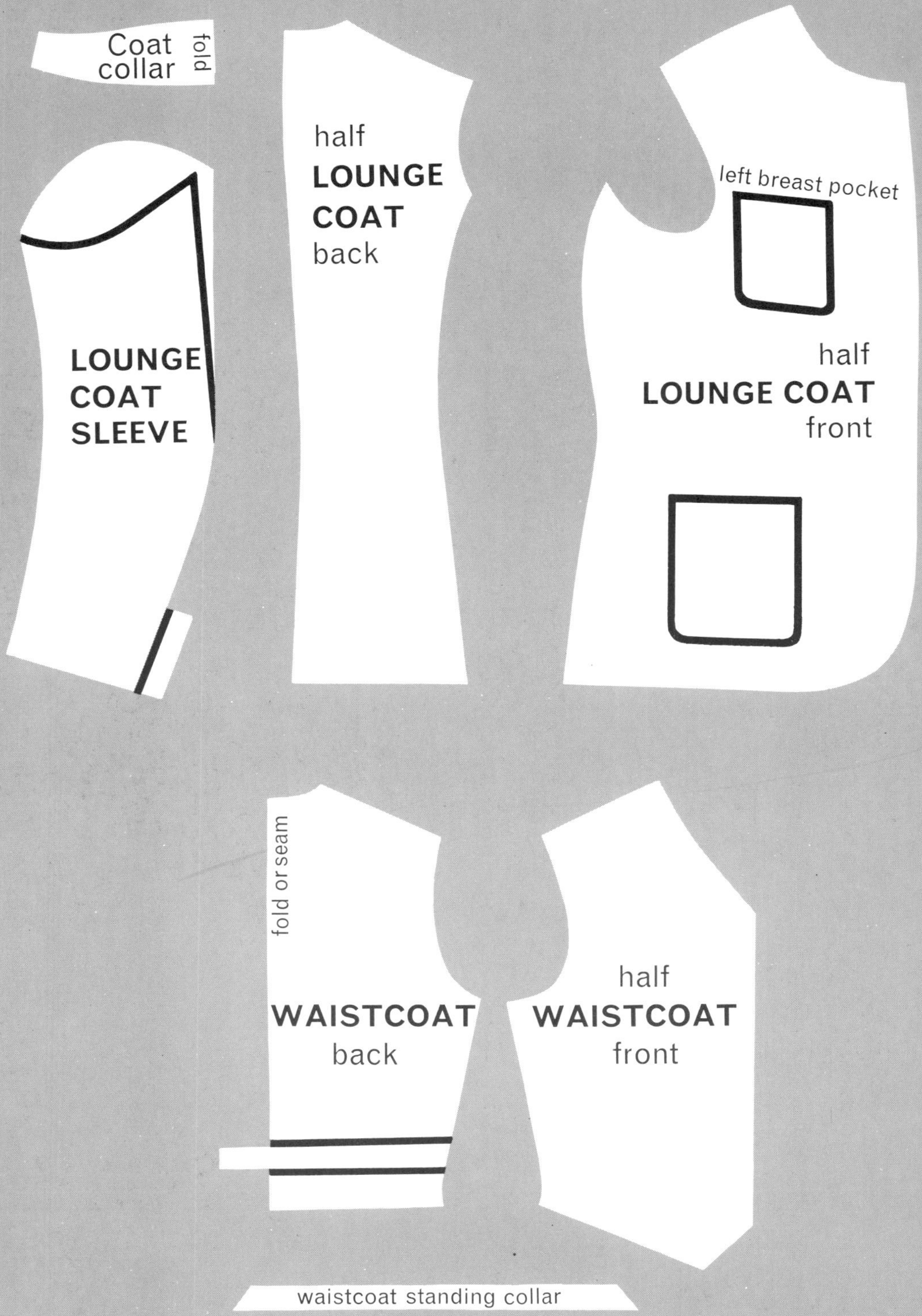

Coat collar fold

half **LOUNGE COAT** back

LOUNGE COAT SLEEVE

left breast pocket

half **LOUNGE COAT** front

fold or seam

WAISTCOAT back

half **WAISTCOAT** front

waistcoat standing collar

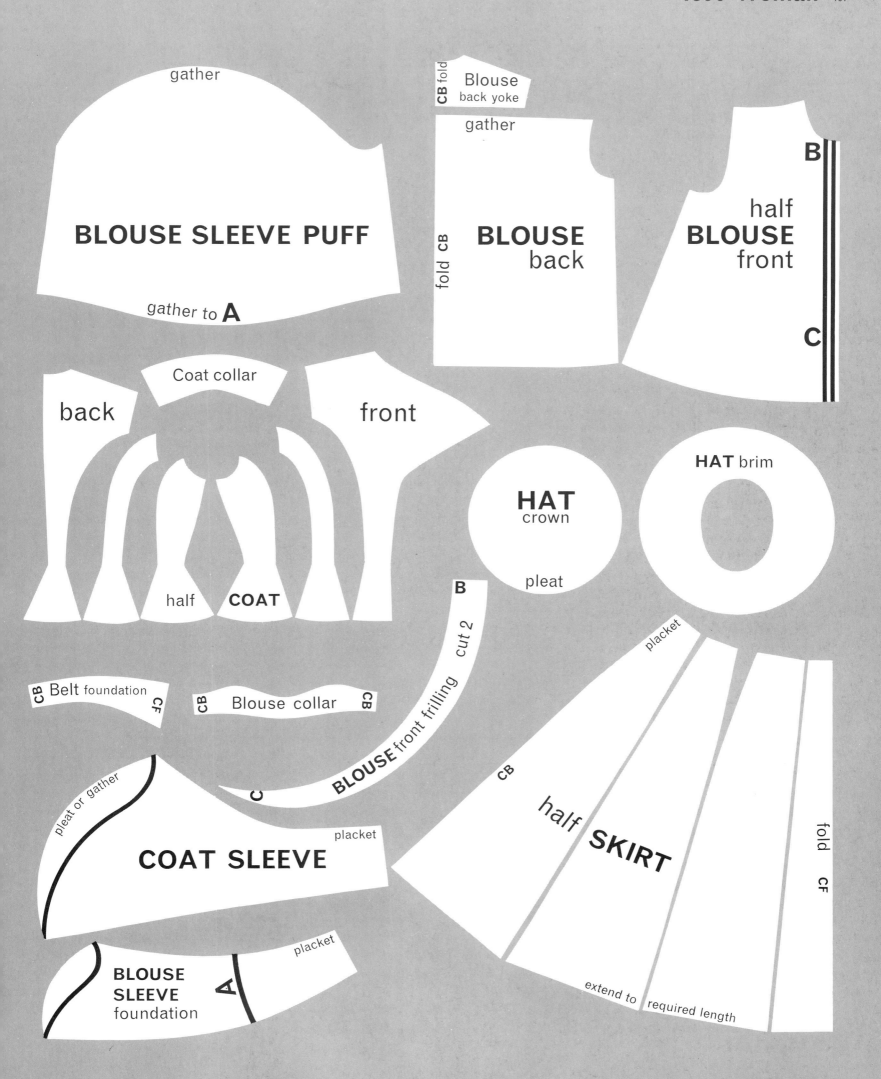

1900 Victoria

Fabrics: Women — soft, very feminine materials such as silky alpacas, mohairs, lawn, chiffon, muslin, clinging velvets, artificial silk, etc. Lavish use of lace. Firm fabrics for tailormades.

Colours: Men — black and white for evenings. Blue and white, black, dark blue, grey and white mixture, blue or grey with white pin stripe for day wear. Silver grey for summer. Women — harmonious or monochromatic schemes heightened with vivid touches of strong colour (particularly red).

Decoration: Women — embroidery, bead embroidery, spangles, insertions of lace, hand-painted materials, frills, braiding, soft pleating, etc.

Padding and restriction, women: Similar to the previous fashion. Hips and busts are accentuated as much as possible to produce an hour-glass silhouette (padding or artificial hips and busts worn). The petticoat is heavily and richly trimmed on its hem with flounces to assist the skirt to kick out from below knee to hem. ("Skirts grow tighter round the hips monthly.")

Movement, men: Similar to the previous fashion. All relationships between human beings have their rules of behaviour, from the relaxed to the most rigid formalities, demanded by society.

Movement, women: The carriage of the figure tilts forward from the waist up. The head is held high (stiff boned collars). Walking, extremely restricted by the tight skirts, is similar to the previous fashion. Woman uses her arms freely in a sensuous and expansive manner — she also enjoys posturing and posing, frequently taking the weight of the body on one leg with the hands coming to rest on the thrust-out hip.

Men

General characteristics: Proportions and subtle changes in style occur yearly.

Under garments — similar to the previous fashion. White bow tie worn with full evening dress, black bow tie worn with dinner jacket. Starched front to shirt for evening dress, shirt with a soft pleated front sometimes worn with the dinner jacket.

Full evening dress — (tailed coat, white waistcoat, trousers), the coat requires great skill in cutting and making to achieve perfect fit and balance. It is never buttoned up. The lapels are faced with silk, the tails fit close to the sides of the figure. The waistcoat, single breasted, cut very low in front with curved lapels, is sometimes made up in satin or brocade, with buttons of jade, onyx, lapis lazuli, etc. — with cuff-links and shirt studs to match. Trousers are somewhat narrower than for day wear.

Socks — black silk for evening. Patterned, striped or spotted for casual wear.

Boots and shoes — (round toes), high laced shoes for winter wear. Oxfords for summer in black, tan or white. Light coloured spats.

Hair — similar to the previous fashion. Older men wear small waxed, close clipped, or walrus moustaches, and clipped beards.

Hats — similar to the previous fashion.

Accessories — similar to the previous fashion. Cuff-links, signet ring, watch, etc.

Women

General characteristics: Line is more willowy, slender, and essentially feminine. The shape of the bosom is hidden by a loose pouched front. The small waist is strongly accentuated by a V-pointed belt, or the shaped waistline of the bodice. Sleeves are bell or bishop shaped or closely fit the entire arm. Skirts, cut to produce a concave front and flared hem, are gored to cling very closely to the figure. Hats and hair styling increase the size of the head.

Under garments — similar to the previous fashion. Beautiful materials and elaborate trimmings.

Evening dress — (made up in pre-pleated material with C.B. fastenings), the cut of the bodice, with low plunging décolletage, emphasises the width of the shoulders and obliterates the shape of the bosom. The skirt develops into a train at the back. The join of skirt to bodice is hidden by a deep, boned belt.

Stockings — day stockings of black, brown or scarlet. Some in black lisle thread with fronts worked in brilliant colours. White stockings worn with white shoes for summer wear.

Boots and shoes — excessively pointed toes.

Hair — fuller at the sides, higher on the top, and always waved.

Hats — very large with the brim turned down in front and up at the back, or turned up at the side and worn tilted. Halo hats with upturned brims, wide toques with veils, straw sailor hats. A galaxy of trimmings, including fancy cock feathers, cherries, nuts, flowers, tulle, lace and ribbons. Hats made up in gathered chiffon blended in many shades (white to cream to yellow to orange to chocolate).

Accessories — much jewellery is worn including finger rings, large drop earrings, bracelets, dog collars and hair ornaments. Full-length gloves always worn with evening dress.

Notes on patterns: Women

Corset — adapt pattern for 1906.

Petticoat — flounces should commence from the knees down.

Dress — (entire dress sunray pleated), the bodice is mounted to the foundation with the waistline fullness, gathered all round, chiefly concentrated at the front. The arm straps follow the line of the neckline embroidered bands (back and front). The angled shoulder straps, supporting the dress, terminate in bows and streamers. The skirt, eased to the bodice waistline, is very gently held in from the thighs down by the two lower embroidered bands which are cut slightly smaller in circumference than the relative circumference measurement of the skirt. Form a hook and bar placket at the C.B. running from the neckline down to 10 inches below the waist level.

Belt — construct in a similar manner to the previous fashion with a C.B. or C.F. fastening.

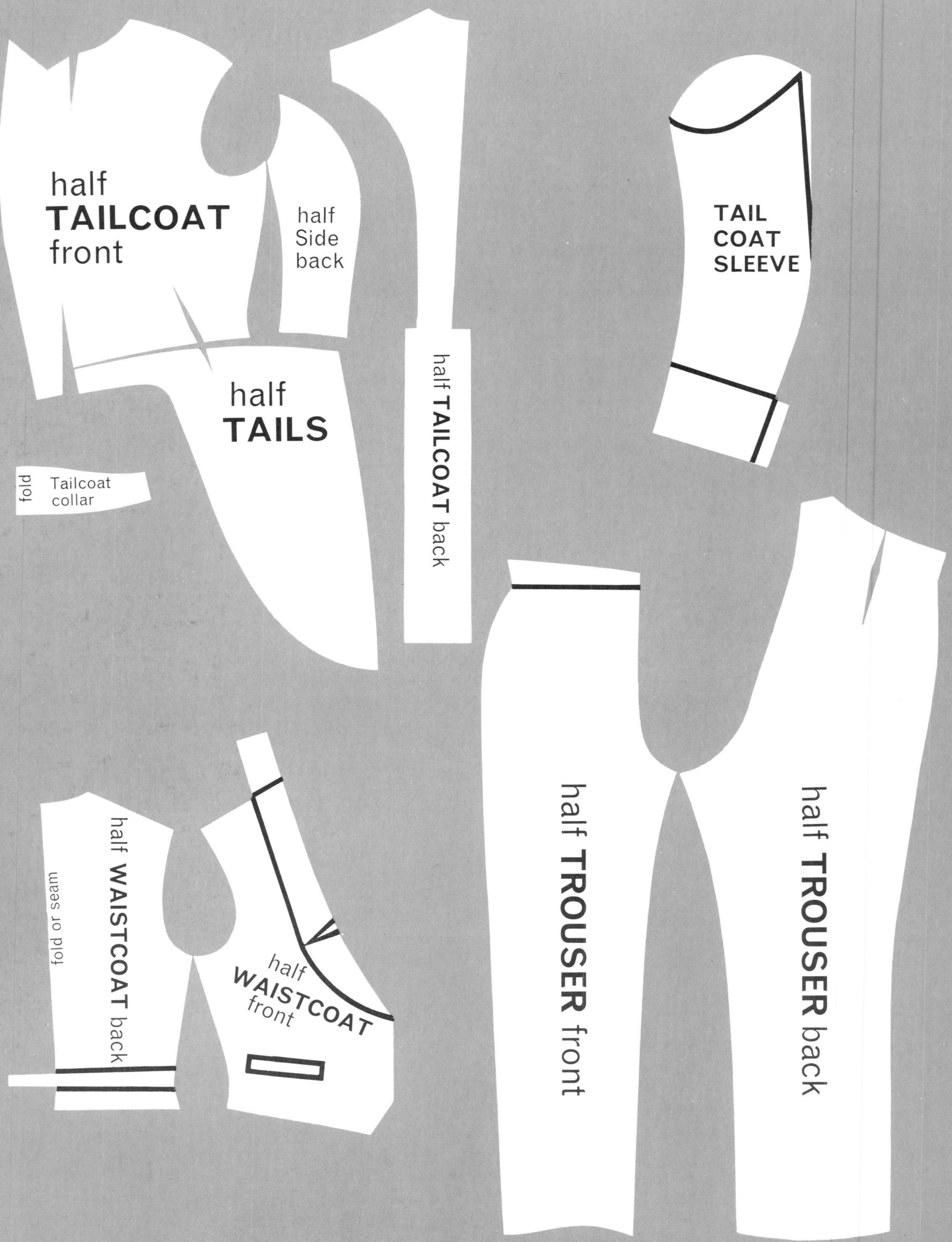

half
TAILCOAT
front

half
Side
back

half
TAILS

fold Tailcoat
collar

half **TAILCOAT** back

**TAIL
COAT
SLEEVE**

fold or seam

half **WAISTCOAT** back

half
WAISTCOAT
front

half **TROUSER** front

half **TROUSER** back

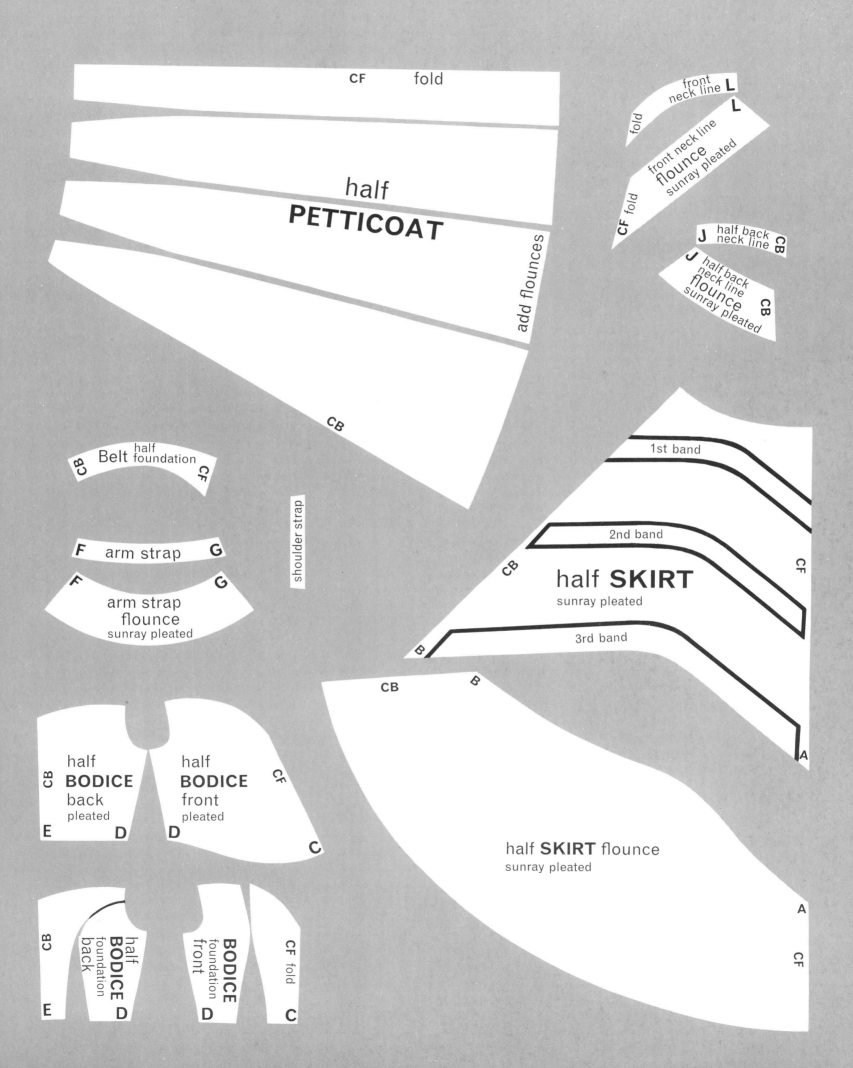

CF fold

half
PETTICOAT

add flounces

CB

front neck line **L**

fold

L

front neck line
flounce
sunray pleated

CF fold

J half back neck line **CB**

J half back neck line
flounce
sunray pleated **CB**

1st band

2nd band

CB half **SKIRT**
sunray pleated **CF**

3rd band

B

A

CB **B**

half **SKIRT** flounce
sunray pleated

A

CF

CB Belt half foundation CF

shoulder strap

F arm strap **G**

F **G**
arm strap
flounce
sunray pleated

CB half
BODICE
back
pleated

E **D**

half
BODICE
front
pleated

CF

D

C

CB half
BODICE
foundation
back

E **D**

BODICE
foundation
front

D

CF fold

C

1906 Edward VII

Fabrics: Women — wide range of fabrics used including transparent and semi-transparent materials. Faille, ottoman silk (glossy and ribbed), painted satins, velvets, woollens in shadow checks and phantom stripes. Coffee-coloured guipure lace.

Colours: Women — pastel shades replace the blacks worn for the mourning of Queen Victoria. Dim greys, mauve, greens, ivory and beige.

Decoration: Women — age of feathers, frills and pleats, and elaborate and finely made lingerie and blouses. Strappings, insertions, pipings of contrasting colour or texture, embroidery, sequins for evening wear. Embroidered "arrow heads" finish off pleats and pockets. Buttons.

Padding and restriction, women: The corset is straight fronted, longer below the waist and shorter above, to form a long sloping bustline and round waist. (Very tiny waists no longer so fashionable.) Collars, held up by wire foundations or supports, are extremely high.

Movement, men: Rules of behaviour somewhat less rigid.

Movement, women: Similar to the previous fashion. Restrained and less flamboyant.

Men

General characteristics: Styling, length and cut of clothes dependent upon occasion — formal, town casuals, summer wear, shooting, fishing, tennis, etc.

Under garments — similar to the previous fashion.

Morning coat — (worn in preference to the Frock coat at all the most fashionable functions and important occasions), cutting and construction requires great skill to achieve the perfect fit. The waist is close fitting, the hips rounded (addition of a thin layer of wadding). The skirts, cut away in front, are separated at the C.B. by a vent (2 C.B. waist buttons). For dress occasions made up in black, though dark grey, and for summer wear light shades of grey, are acknowledged as correct.

Waistcoat — (accompanying the Morning coat it is always white or grey), single breasted.

Trousers — (pressed to give a crease down backs and fronts of legs), fuller in the leg. Grey and black striped trousers worn with the Morning coat.

Socks — similar to the previous fashion.

Boots and shoes — similar to the previous fashion.

Hair — fuller at the temples or cut short. A side parting is more popular than the central.

Hats — top hat always worn with Morning coat. Caps, some with large peaks, for sports and country wear.

Accessories — similar to the previous fashion, walking sticks.

Women

General characteristics: More matronly in style. The heavy pouch, formed by the front of the bodice or blouse, gives the impression that the bosom has been thrust forward and dropped to the waistline — accentuated by the positioning of the belt. The width of shoulders and roundness of hips is no longer emphasised. Many dresses cut "Princess" style — seamed and fitted right through without a waist seam.

Under garments — similar to the previous fashion. Wide legged knickers, French drawers with frothy silk flounces, bust bodices.

Blouse — (C.F. bodice fastening, C.B. collar fastening), frequently cut with a yoke, with jabot front and bishop sleeves.

Bolero coat — cut square and left open in front. Bell-shaped sleeves, elbow or wrist length, tightly fit the armhole.

Skirt — (concealed side or C.B. fastening) ground length, with or without a short train, the skirt is cunningly gored and set into pleats. The pleats are top stitched to below hip level and controlled by a tight hip-length inner lining to emphasise the fashionable slim silhouette.

Stockings — similar to the previous fashion.

Boots and shoes — similar to the previous fashion.

Hair — fluffy looking and back combed, rolled up from the back and puffed forward over the forehead and eyes. (False fringes, pieces, pads and frames to increase size.)

Hats — large and wide brimmed. Tricornes, toques. Veils very fashionable.

Accessories — parasols to match the ensemble. Small or large handbags of cut steel, gold mesh, or bead work, with metal mount and chain. Large ostrich or sable stoles. Fine gloves. Bar pins worn at the throat, fob watches pinned to the lapel of the coat, ivory or metal bangles, longish delicate necklaces and beads, etc.

Notes on patterns: Women

Corsets — thick black lines indicate positioning of whalebones.

Petticoats — adapt pattern of 1900.

Blouse — (if pin-tucked or pleated fronts and backs are required, open up and extend the width of the patterns), the fronts are buttoned through — the collar fastens at the C.B. (see 1896 notes). Angled whalebones or wired supporters at the sides and back, hold up the collar. Cut wristbands double, form wrist plackets, and fasten with cufflinks, buttons, or hooks and eyes. The jabot, sewn to either side of the C.F. opening, is set in small pleats radiating from point A.

Bolero — (interline fronts and back), neck, fronts, and sleeve edgings, are applied and top stitched. Gently pad to round the head of the sleeve.

Skirt — (sewn to a waistband with concealed placket formed at the side or C.B. — and with a tight half lining, or inside sets of tapes sewn to the side seams for tying at the back). The skirt should be shaped to snugly fit the waist and hips. Each pleat, sewn down to just above knee level, is finished off with an embroidered arrowhead. The arrangement of pleats terminate at the C.B. in an inverted box pleat.

Hat — the hat brim, wired, stiffened and shaped, is sewn to a shallow crown — stiff, or soft and beret-shaped.

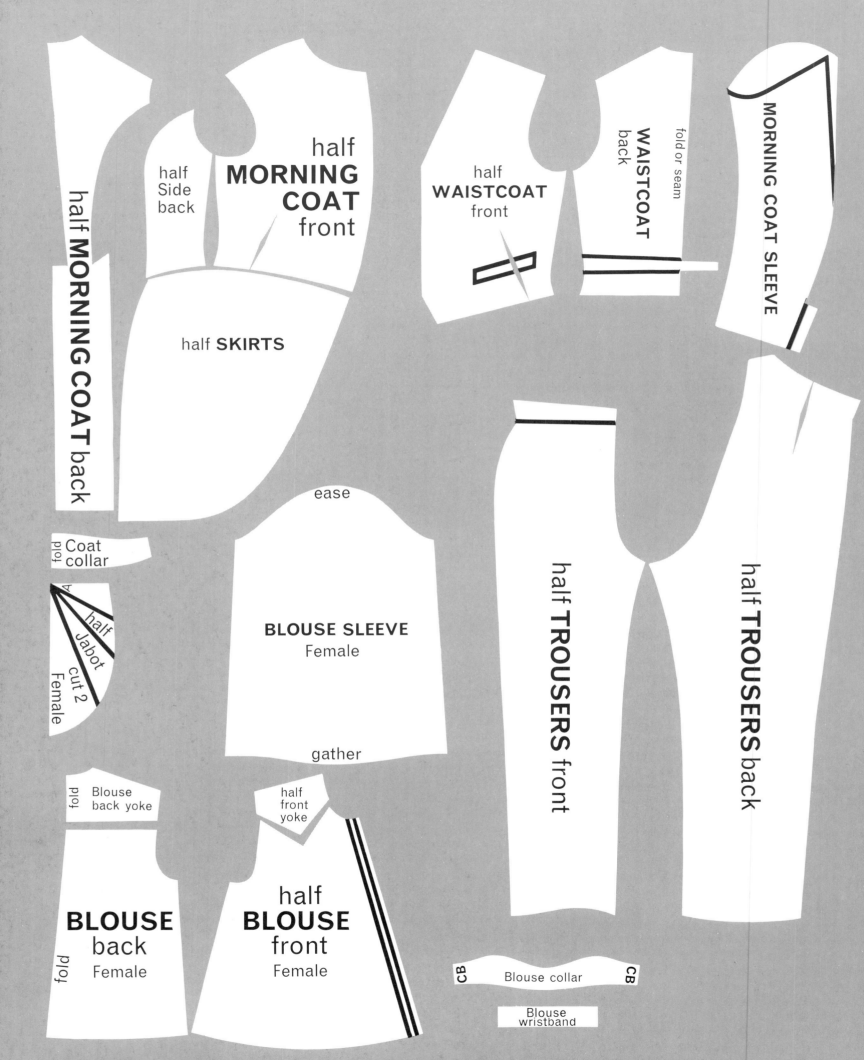

half Side back

half **MORNING COAT** front

half **MORNING COAT** back

half **SKIRTS**

fold Coat collar

A half Jabot cut 2 Female

half **WAISTCOAT** front

WAISTCOAT back

fold or seam

MORNING COAT SLEEVE

ease

BLOUSE SLEEVE Female

gather

fold Blouse back yoke

half front yoke

half **TROUSERS** front

half **TROUSERS** back

BLOUSE back Female

fold

half **BLOUSE** front Female

CB Blouse collar CB

Blouse wristband

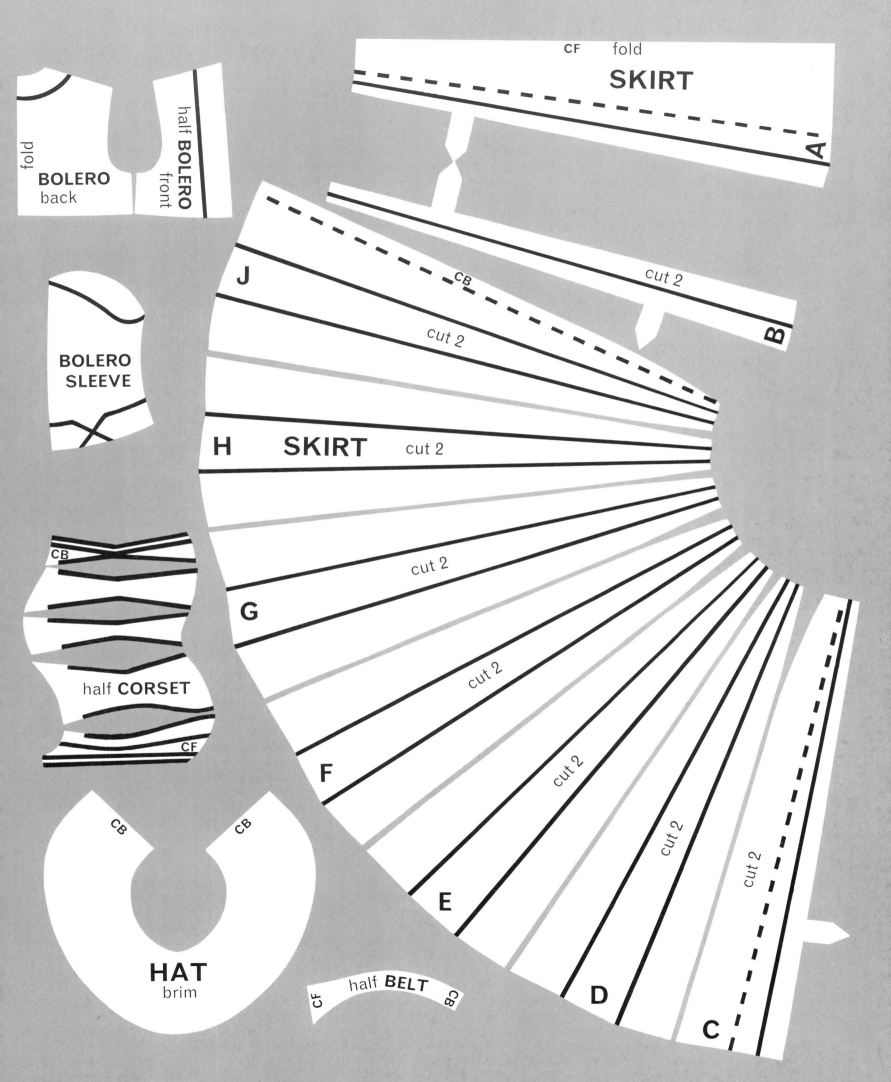

1911 George V

Fabrics: Women — rough hair cloths, supple satins, raw silks, velvet, georgette, crepe. Linen for suits.

Colours: Women — subdued colours such as maize, shell pink, silver, brown, sulphur, apricot, champagne and tobacco. White with black pin-stripe broadcloth, black and white plaids.

Decoration: Women — embroidered Italian cut work, Irish crochet, diamanté, artificial flowers, buttons in all sizes, braiding, silk tassels, bugle headwork. Fur pelts for all kinds of trimmings. Elaborate sashes.

Padding and restriction, women: Similar to the previous fashion. The excessively long sheath-shaped corset with a short top is constructed to produce long slim hips.

Movement, men: Similar to the previous fashion.

Movement, women: The ankle-length straight skirt determines a short tripping step.

Men

General characteristics: Similar to the previous fashion. Elegant or very formal clothes give way to the lounge suit and more casual wear. Sweaters, cardigan jackets, turtle neck sweaters, V-necked pullovers for country, weekend and leisure wear.

Under garments — similar to the previous fashion. Shirt collars are high, stiff and turned down.

Paletot coat — (sporting top coat), below knee length, with close-fitting back and straight hanging fronts. Front fly fastening.

Waistcoat — some are cut with collar and lapels. A light coloured waistcoat is occasionally worn with the lounge suit.

Trousers — ankle-length when worn with turn-ups.

Socks — brightly coloured for casual wear.

Boots and shoes — similar to the previous fashion. Young men prefer the shoe to the boot.

Hair — similar to the previous fashion.

Hats — similar to the previous fashion.

Accessories — similar to the previous fashion. Umbrellas.

Women

General characteristics: Less matronly. The style is basically vertical and tubular with a high positioned waistline ("Directoire" or "Empire" dresses). Mannish tailormades still very popular. Hats of monstrous size.

Under garments — similar to the previous fashion.

Blouse — (C.B. fastening) cut full, sometimes with a cross-over front, and with a high or V-shaped neckline. The sleeves, tightly fitting at the wrist, are frequently cut in one with the bodice.

Skirt — (side fastening), ankle length, straight, and high waisted. A belt or wide sash is positioned at the natural waist.

Coat — (three-quarter length), sometimes cut with a short bodice front, the skirts of the coat hang straight in front, fit the sides of the figure, and semi fit the back. Sleeves are narrow. The deep collar, cuffs and fronts, are decorated with elaborate braiding and frogging.

Stockings — black or in the same colour as the dress.

Boots and shoes — long slim foot with Louis or Cuban heel. Patent leather with tops of white, grey, or biscuit coloured buckskin.

Hair — dressed low with a central parting and combed back in loose full waves over the ears — pads or frames worn to give added width. The back hair is swept up, braided or coiled, to give weight to the back of the head.

Hats — "Helmet", "Coal-scuttle", "Bee-hive", "Cake-tin" or "Mushroom" shapes of gargantuan size. Trimmings, particularly side ornaments, are large and very beautiful — enormous flowers, ospreys, aigrettes, ostrich plumes, swathings of velvet, rosettes, etc. Extravagant veils.

Accessories — are all large. Handbags, satchel-shaped with very long strap or cord, made up in tooled leather, tapestry work or alligator skin. Enormous muffs and stoles of fox, wolf, lynx or marten. Rolled umbrellas. Long necklaces.

Notes on patterns: Women

Corsets — thick black lines indicate positioning of whalebones.

Petticoat — lengthen and adapt pattern for 1914.

Blouse — (C.B. hook and bar fastening), sew down front shoulder tucks 4 inches. Form wrist plackets with hook and bar fastenings. Stiffen collar with angled whalebones or wire supporters at the sides and back.

Skirt — (form placket and lightly bone all seams to 4 to 6 inches below waist level). Section A. is tucked horizontally at the hem to reduce it to the same length as the rest of the skirt. The back of the skirt forms a box pleat, the side fronts form open inverted box pleats. Pleats should be sewn down to well below hip level.

Coat — stiffen collar, fronts, and cuffs. The two side back pleats are folded towards the C.B.

Hats — the very large hats, constructed on a wire foundation, are secured to an inner shape or crown, made up to sit on the top of the head.

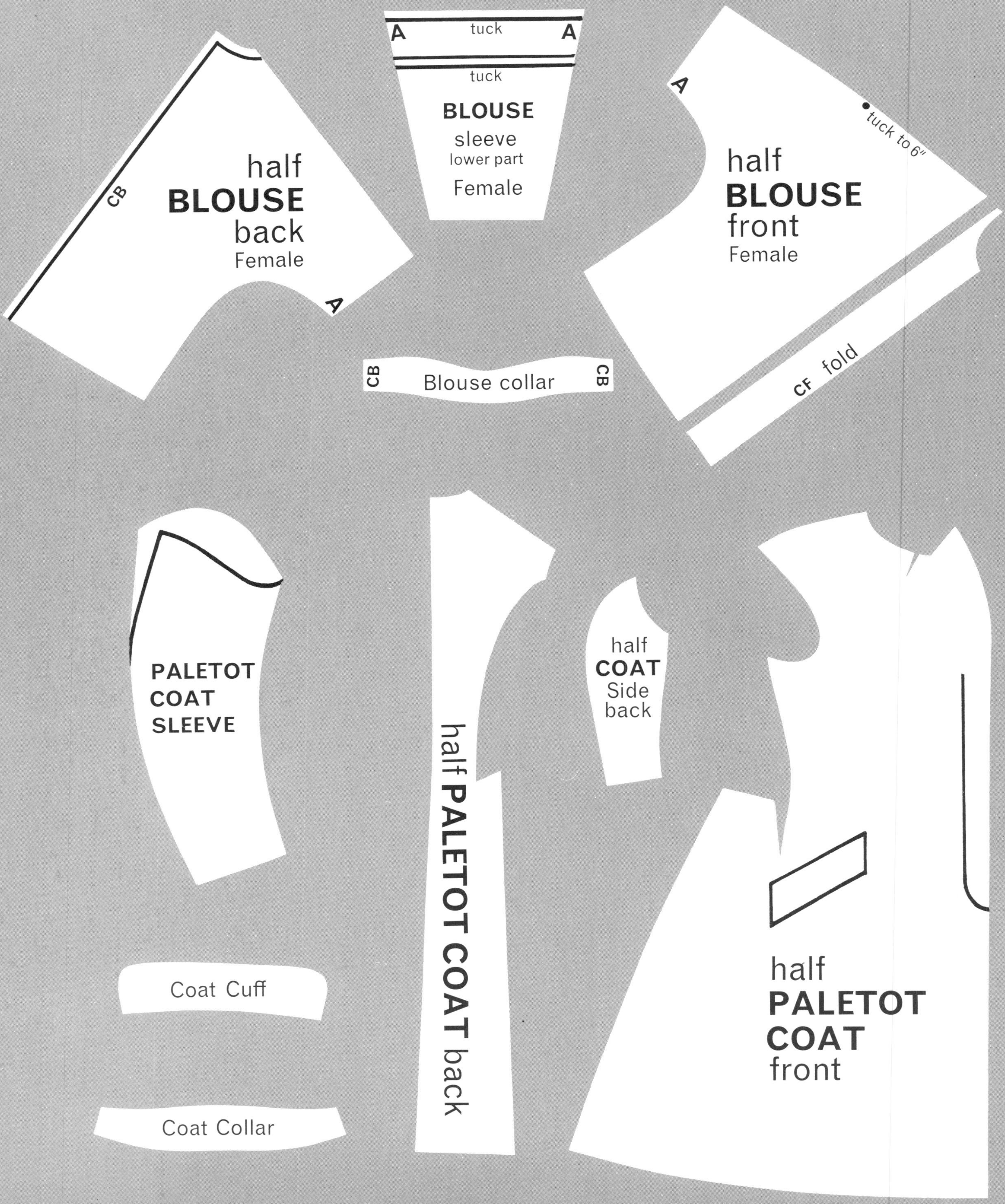

A tuck A

BLOUSE
sleeve
lower part
Female

half
BLOUSE
back
Female

CB

A

half
BLOUSE
front
Female

•tuck to 6"

CF fold

CB Blouse collar CB

**PALETOT
COAT
SLEEVE**

half
COAT
Side
back

half **PALETOT COAT** back

Coat Cuff

half
**PALETOT
COAT**
front

Coat Collar

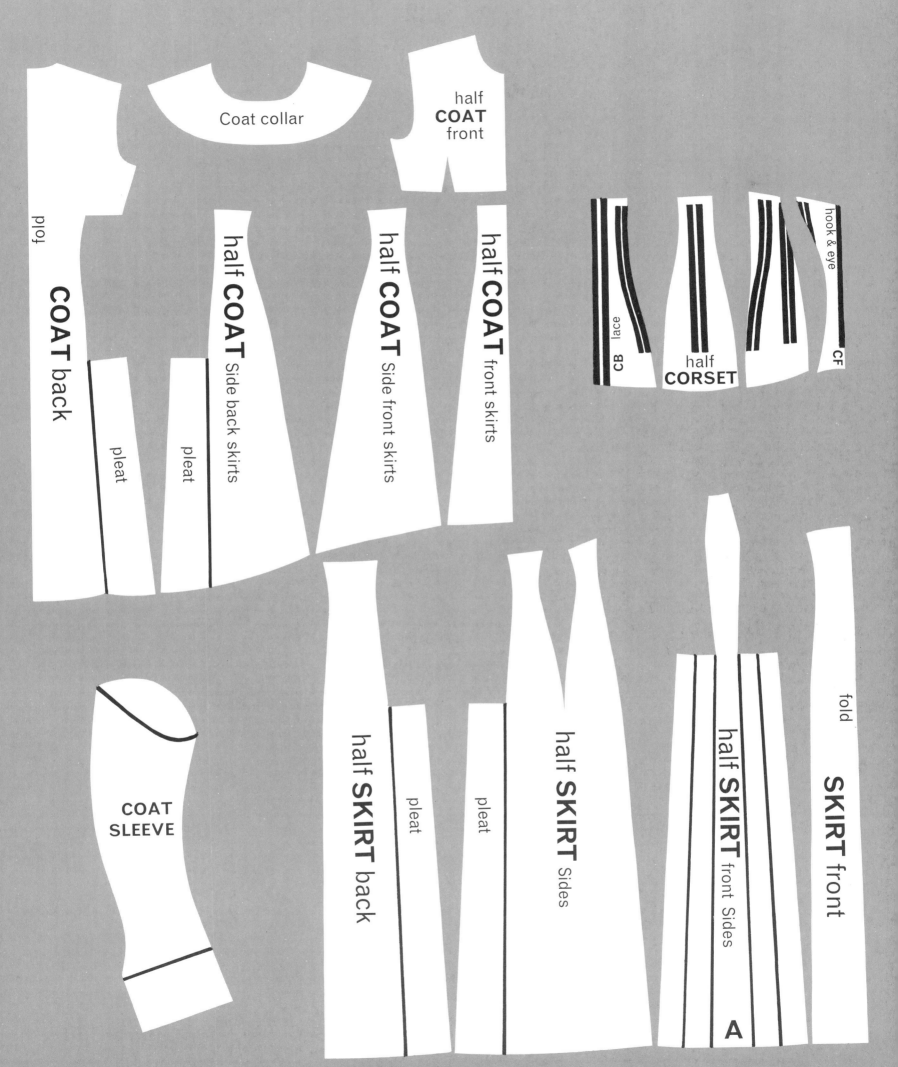

Coat collar

half **COAT** front

fold

COAT back

half **COAT** Side back skirts

half **COAT** Side front skirts

half **COAT** front skirts

pleat

pleat

CB lace

half **CORSET**

hook & eye

CF

COAT SLEEVE

half **SKIRT** back

pleat

pleat

half **SKIRT** Sides

fold

half **SKIRT** front Sides

SKIRT front

A

1914 George V

Fabrics: Women — brocades, velvets, chiffons, marquisette, ninon, tulle, georgette. Hop sack and serge for tailormades. Knitted jumpers.

Colours: Men — soft and sombre browns and greens for country and casual wear. Women — black, orange, jade, cerise, royal blue and violet very fashionable. Schemes of colour are violent and strong.

Decoration: Women — dress is strongly influenced by Bakst's designs for Diaghilev's production of "Scheherazade" — exotic draperies, floating panels, sashes, wool embroidery, tassels, fringing, large patterns of peasant or Eastern origin, embroidered plaques, fur edgings, braid and buttons. Smocking.

Padding and restriction, women: The long boned corsets are no longer worn. Some skirts measure as little as 18 inches around the hem.

Movement, men: Very relaxed and natural in comparison to the previous fashions.

Movement, women: Walking, resembling a sack race, is severely restricted by the "Harem", "Hobble", "Lampshade" or "Peg-top" skirts.

Men

General characteristics: The three-piece lounge suit is now worn by most men for day time and business wear. The Frock coat is still worn by elderly gentlemen and some professional classes, the Morning coat for only the most important functions.

Under garments — shirts are white, or striped and coloured, with stiff or soft, white turned down collars. Narrow ties. Vest and underpants, or combinations.

Three-piece lounge suit — the coat is gently waisted, the lapels long, the sleeves frequently cuffed. The waistcoat is single breasted, and the trousers, with crease down front and back of the legs and with deep turn-ups, are cut looser and fuller in the seat and waist.

Socks — similar to the previous fashion.

Boots and shoes — similar to the previous fashion.

Hats — Homburg or trilby hats with widish brims are very popular.

Accessories — similar to the previous fashion.

Women

General characteristics: (less distinction between dresses for particular functions or times of day). High waisted, and very tight in the skirt from knee down to the ankle-length hem. Skirts are frequently designed to wrap over in front and button at the side. Sleeves, with deep armholes, or cut in one with the body parts (Magyar, dolman or kimono), tightly fit the arms from elbow to wrist. Hair is smoothly dressed to follow the shape of the head. Tall pot-shaped hats.

Under garments — (reduced to minimum), silk tight-fitting combinations, narrow jersey silk petticoats, knickers or cami-knickers (combination of camisole and knickers), a simple brassiere or bust bodice.

Dress — (waistcoat, skirt, tunic coat and sash), the waistcoat with Medici collar and V-shaped neck is buttoned through the C.F.s. The wrapped skirt, with concealed right fastening, is cut to drape diagonally across the body from left waist to right hip and knee. The tunic coat is gathered in and held at the waist by a highly-placed made-up sash (fastening in line with the wrapover edge of the skirt).

Stockings — pale coloured silk with openwork fronts.

Boots and shoes — (Louis heel), bronze kid, grey suede, patent leather, brocade for evening. Large oval or square buckles. Fancy buttoned tops to boots. Spats.

Hair — flatter on top, smoother at the sides. Hair is arranged in big waves across the forehead and built out behind in a loose bun, braids, or cluster of curls. Deep bandeaux or narrow fillets are worn, particularly in the evenings.

Hats — deep wide crowns, brimless or with brims almost non-existent on one side and very broad on the other (turned up acutely to follow the angle of the crown). Upright arrangements of stiff feathers or waxed ribbons decorate the side. The crown is usually swathed with a broad piece of soft velvet or some other kind of rich material.

Accessories — similar to the previous fashion. Jewellery of bizarre, oriental or barbaric design. Long bead necklaces, slave bangles, pendant earrings, large rings. Long military style capes. Furs.

Notes on patterns: Women

Foundation garment — adapt corset of 1911 or use a ready-made firm, elastic or cloth, boned girdle.

Petticoat — add ribbon shoulder straps and form a side placket.

Skirt — (lightly bone darts and side seams to 4 to 6 inches below waist level, or stiffen waist edge with a piece of boned petersham), line throughout or face waist edge, fronts, and hem. Sew down commencement of pleats, 2 to 3 inches at waist edge on the left side — the visible folded edges of the pleats placed upwards. Form fastening at O. by securing the right front skirt to the left front skirt to the length of the dart with hooks and eyes, and fastening the edge of the right front skirt to well below the length of the dart on the left front skirt (X), also with hooks and eyes and/or buttons and buttonholes.

Waistcoat — (the fronts are buttoned), lightly stiffen and face collar.

Coat — make up foundation. Attach top part of the coat to the foundation — gathering or pleating the waist edge of the coat to the waist edge of the foundation (A). The skirts, fitting the waist edge, should be interlined with a thin but firm fabric. The deep belt, tightly fitting the waist, is stiffened, fastened on the left side, and finished off with a made-up tie with hanging ends. The belt is slotted through narrow straps positioned and sewn to the side seams at waist level on the coat.

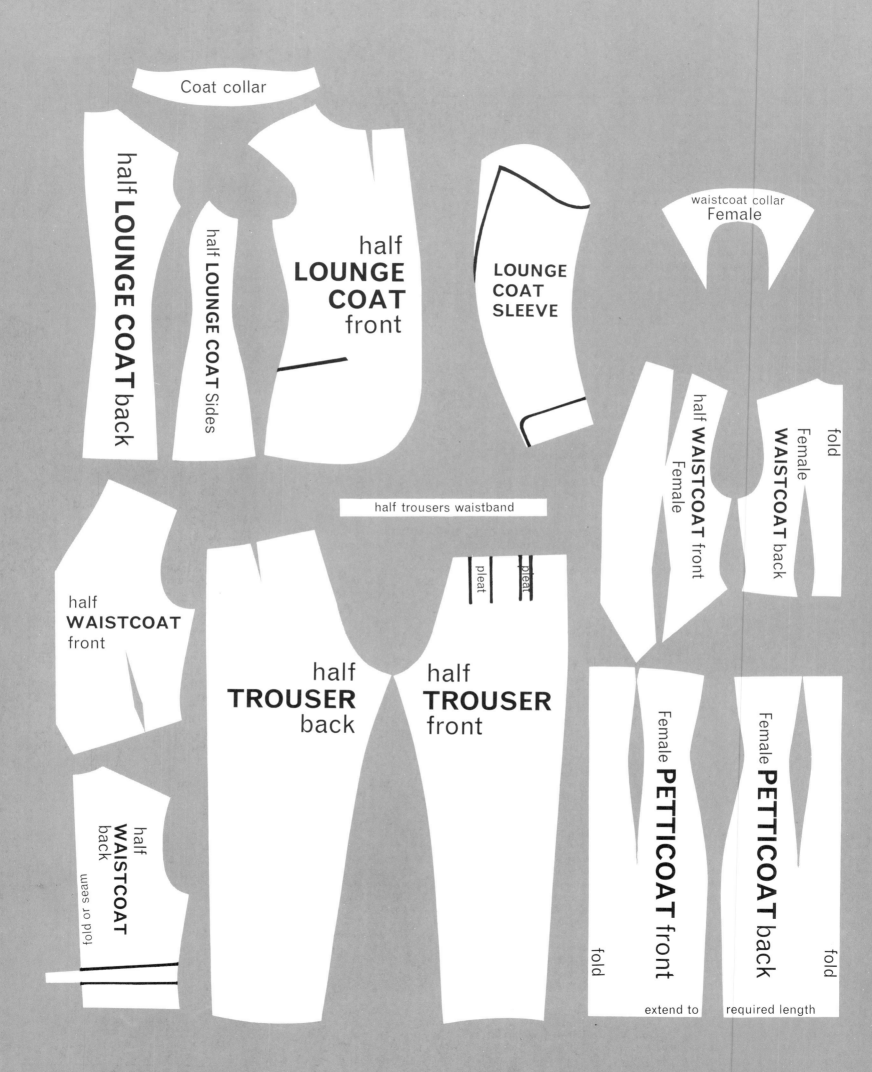

Coat collar

half **LOUNGE COAT** back

half **LOUNGE COAT** Sides

half **LOUNGE COAT** front

LOUNGE COAT SLEEVE

waistcoat collar Female

half **WAISTCOAT** front Female

fold Female **WAISTCOAT** back

half trousers waistband

pleat

pleat

half **WAISTCOAT** front

half **TROUSER** back

half **TROUSER** front

half **WAISTCOAT** back

fold or seam

Female **PETTICOAT** front

Female **PETTICOAT** back

fold

fold

extend to   required length

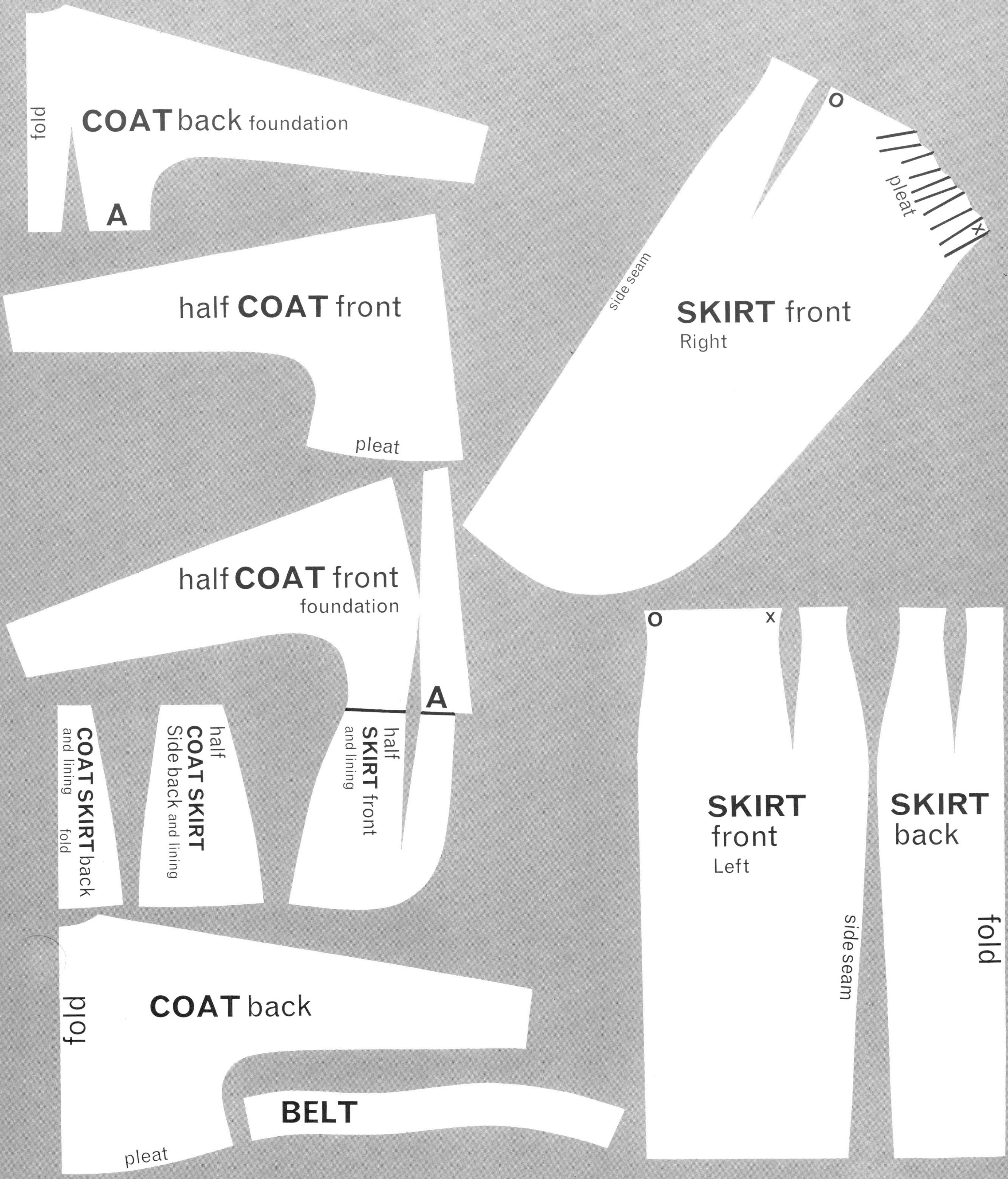

COAT back foundation

fold

A

half COAT front

pleat

half COAT front foundation

A

COAT SKIRT back and lining fold

half COAT SKIRT Side back and lining

half SKIRT front and lining

COAT back

fold

BELT

pleat

SKIRT front
Right

side seam

o

pleat

x

o   x

SKIRT front
Left

SKIRT back

side seam

fold

1920 George V

Fabrics: Woven — velvet, georgette, shantung, velvet brocade, serge, rough checks, gabardine, gold and silver lace, diaphanous net, knitted wear.

Colours: Women — khaki, browns, dull yellows, beige, greys, navy blue, etc. for day wear. Brilliant colours for evening wear.

Decoration: Women — embroidered, printed or painted fabrics influenced by Chinese, Japanese and Russian art. Striped fabrics. Bead embroidery, tassels. Jewelled shoulder straps and gold embroidery for evening wear.

Padding and restriction, women — a waistless girdle or lightly boned corset tends to flatten the bust and hips.

Movement, men: Relaxed and natural.

Movement, women: Relaxed and natural.

Men

General characteristics: Double-breasted lounge suits worn for formal wear, single breasted for the country.

Under garments — similar to the previous fashion. Bow ties for day wear in striped, paisley, or spotted patterns.

Top coat — well below knee in length, loose fitting with raglan or fitted sleeve. Double- or single-breasted, with wide collar and revers.

Socks — similar to the previous fashion.

Boots and shoes — boots are rarely worn by the younger man. Spats.

Hair — similar to the previous fashion. Short back and sides.

Hats — Homburg, trilby and bowler (city or business wear). Caps with large peaks and full crowns for sports, motor car driving, and week-end wear.

Accessories — similar to the previous fashion.

Women

General characteristics: Straight silhouette. All garments are loose and easy fitting. Skirts are barrel shaped and a little above the ankle in length. The waistline drops to below the natural waist. Hats have wide brims.

Under garments — similar to the previous fashion, of crêpe-de-chine, lawn, silk and Viyella. Princess slip or vest frequently replaces the chemise.

Blouse — (side fastening at hip) cut full in the body and gathered to a wide, low-placed waist-band. A wide, flat turned-down collar and revers edge the V-shaped neckline (a soft scarf is loosely knotted under the collar and revers). The sleeve is gathered at the wrist into a deep, loosely fitting cuff.

Skirt — (supported by a straight fitting, sleeveless top of thin silk), made up in four pieces and eased, gathered, or lightly pleated, at the waist.

Coat — (three-quarter or hip length), single breasted, flared, and arranged in soft pleats at the sides and back, the low waistline controlled by a loose half belt. The front edges form long narrow revers, the collar lies flat. Sleeves are loose in fit and bell shaped.

Stockings — similar to the previous fashion. Black for day wear, coloured for the evening.

Shoes — court shoes, or with fronts laced, or fastened over the vamp with simple or elaborate straps. Large buckles still fashionable. Spats and close-fitting gaiters.

Hair — parted on the side, bobbed and waved. The hair is brought forward well onto the cheeks.

Hats — of all shapes and sizes, and pulled well down over the eyes. Picture hats with drooping brims. Hats with stiff crowns with brims larger at the sides or at the front. Toques, sailor hats, large tam o'shanters, pirate pull-on stocking caps. Crowns are swathed, and decorated with flowers, bunches of fruit, or cut-felt motifs.

Accessories — Spanish shawls, Japanese sun-shades. Long necklaces of large amber or stone beads strung on a knotted cord. Long pearl necklaces. Wrist watches and vanity cases. Large fans of ostrich plumes or peacock feathers for evening wear.

Notes on patterns: Women

Foundation garment — use ready made-up boned girdle or adapt corselet pattern for 1926.

Petticoat — adapt pattern of 1914.

Blouse — cut waistband, collar, cuffs, and C.F. panel, double. Form a buttoned opening from A. to B. on the C.F. panel and a placket on the left side seam — the waistband fastening with buttons and buttonholes.

Skirt — (form a placket at the side), attach narrow shoulder straps to the skirt top. As an alternative place the skirt to a petersham waistband.

Coat — A. marked on the front of the coat indicates the positioning of the commencement of the belt.

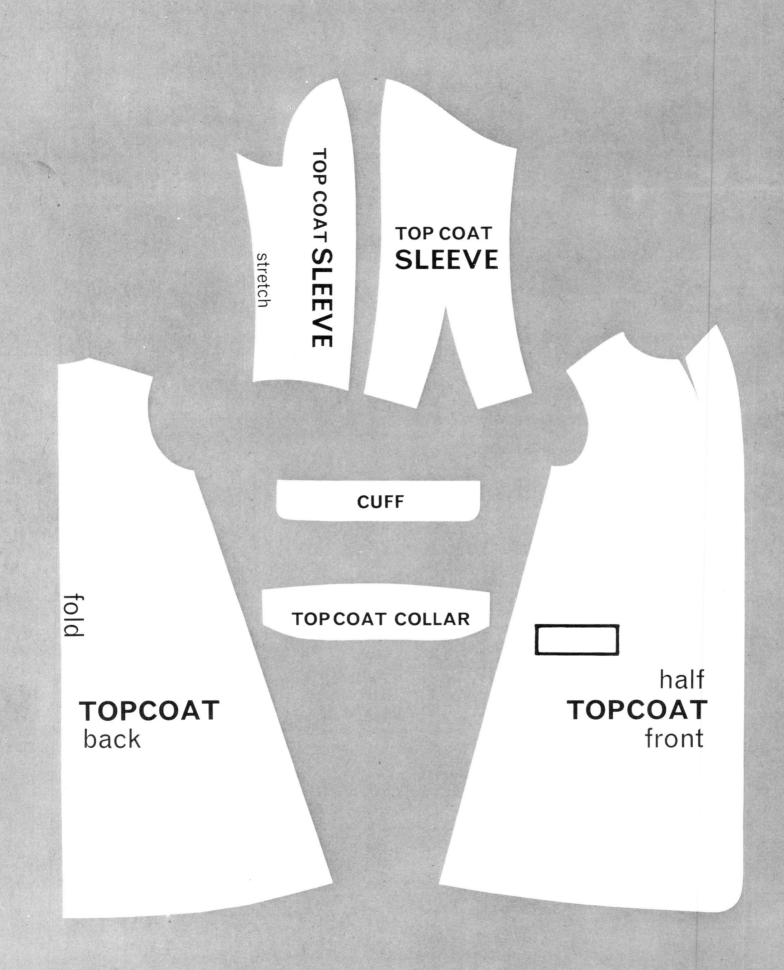

TOP COAT SLEEVE

stretch

TOP COAT SLEEVE

CUFF

fold

TOP COAT COLLAR

TOPCOAT back

half **TOPCOAT** front

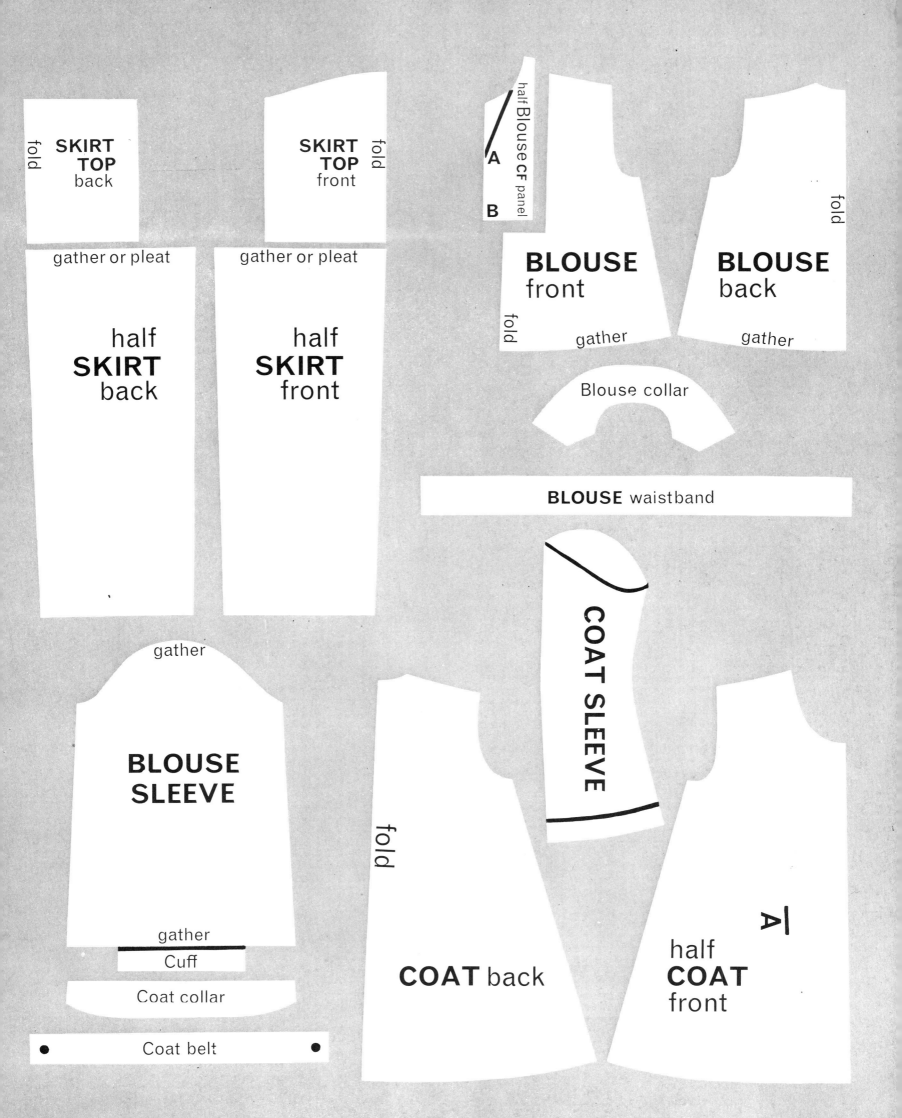

SKIRT TOP back

fold

SKIRT TOP front

fold

half Blouse CF panel

A

B

BLOUSE front

fold

BLOUSE back

fold

gather or pleat

gather or pleat

half SKIRT back

half SKIRT front

gather

gather

Blouse collar

BLOUSE waistband

gather

COAT SLEEVE

BLOUSE SLEEVE

fold

gather

Cuff

Coat collar

Coat belt

COAT back

A

half COAT front

1926 George V

Fabrics: Women — thin silks, ninon, foulard, shantung, georgette, voile, lace (particularly black). Heavy tweeds, rep. Fur trimmings. Knitted wear.

Colours: Women — black, white, red, beige, fawn, brown, orange, cream, bright blue. Colour combinations are usually harmonic or monochromatic.

Decoration: Women — futuristic, geometric, or barbaric designs, embroidered, made up in beads, or printed or appliquèd to total surfaces or restricted to panels, plaques, etc. Striped and spotted fabrics. Skirts often composed of a deep silk or bead fringe or floating panels (Handkerchief skirt).

Padding and restriction, women: Every effort is made to give the body a straight slim boyish look. Lightly-boned straight corsets, with a 30-inch waist and elastic insets, hide the natural waist and flatten the breasts, hips and bottom.

Movement, men: ("bored or bright young things"). Young people are carefree and very casual, almost to sloppiness, in their behaviour.

Movement, women: Young girls are sport- and dance-crazy — they run, fling themselves about and give the impression that they can never stay still. Behaviour is in violent contrast to the quiet dignity of the middle-aged or elderly.

Men

General characteristics: Coats are waisted, shorter, and fit close to the body. Trousers become excessively wide in the leg (sometimes 28 inches or more — Oxford bags).

Under garments — similar to the previous fashion, but made in a variety of styles to suit the various age groups. Ties are broader.

Blazer — usually navy blue, with a regimental, sport or school badge decorating the breast pocket. Single breasted with patch pockets and metal buttons.

Trousers — pleated in the fronts at the waist, and cut loose in the seat and legs. Trousers have turn-ups. Grey flannels very popular for weekend and casual wear.

Socks — patterned and in many colours.

Shoes — in black, brown, and black and white or tan and white for casual wear. Round toes and laced up fronts.

Hats — similar to the previous fashion.

Hair — similar to the previous fashion.

Accessories — cuff-links, cigarette case, wallet, signet ring. Handerkerchief in breast pocket of coat and another, for use, tucked up the coat sleeve.

Women

General characteristics: Essentially youthful in style. All garments are very similar and uniform in cut — very short hip to knee-length straight skirts and long (often sleeveless) straight tops. Boyish short hair and helmet-shaped (cloche) hats. Two-piece costumes, cardigan coats and jumper sets very fashionable. Increased interest in make-up — not natural but mask-like in effect.

Under garments — made up in white, black or light colours, and decorated with flatly applied lace (bands, flowers, birds, butterflies, etc.) Vest, slip, knickers confined at the leg, garters.

Dress — sleeveless (if cut with sleeves — usually long and tightish), with a boat-shaped neck, the dress is belted and slightly pouched at hip level. Two panels of narrow pleats continue the line of the embroidered decoration down the fronts of the skirt.

Coat — cut broadly at the shoulders and tapered to the knees, the coat is fastened with a single large button positioned at hip level. Narrow revers develop into a deep fur collar. The sleeves are long, fur cuffed, and fit close to the arm.

Stockings — transparent flesh coloured. Real or artificial silk.

Shoes — in leather, suede, lizard, alligator or crocodile. Court shoes with high Cuban heels and less pointed toes. Shoes, with one or two narrow straps placed high over the instep. Russian boots.

Hair — shingled, bobbed, straight or waved, with centre or side parting, the hair is dressed flatly and close to the head to curl past the ears onto the sides of the face.

Hats — (colour matches the ensemble), high-domed helmet-like crowns with narrow brims — turned up in front or pulled down well over the eyes. Little or no trimming — feather or stiff bow on the side. Felt hats very popular. Large-brimmed summer hats in lace or transparent material.

Accessories — envelope handbags (containing amongst other things, cigarette case and lighter, etc., make-up — orange lipstick, rouge, compact with puff, eyebrow pencil). Deep fringed shawls. "Apache" scarves, tightly wound around the throat with the ends hanging down the back. Fur necklets. Long bead necklaces and drop earrings, crystal necklaces, slave bracelets (worn at wrist or around upper part of the arm).

Notes on patterns: Women

Corselet — make up in firm fabric (reinforced), with the V-shaped elastic inserts positioned on either side of the lower part of the C.B. panel. A. on back and front indicates positioning of shoulder straps.

Petticoat or slip — adapt dress pattern — cut with a wide low neck, or terminate pattern at chest and support with ribbon shoulder straps.

Dress — open up and extend the front skirt pattern to form the two pleated panels. Face neckline and sleeves, form a placket on left side seam, and attach narrow straps to the side seams at low waist level to control the narrow belt.

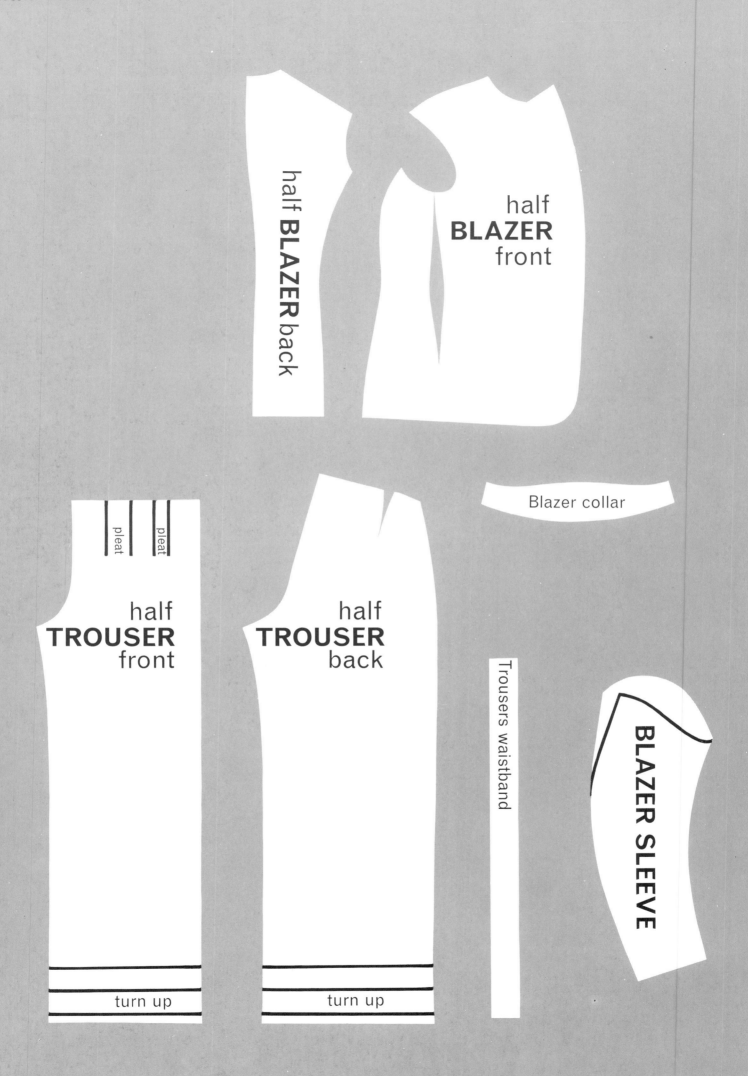

half **BLAZER** back

half **BLAZER** front

half **BLAZER** back

Blazer collar

pleat pleat

half **TROUSER** front

half **TROUSER** back

Trousers waistband

BLAZER SLEEVE

turn up

turn up

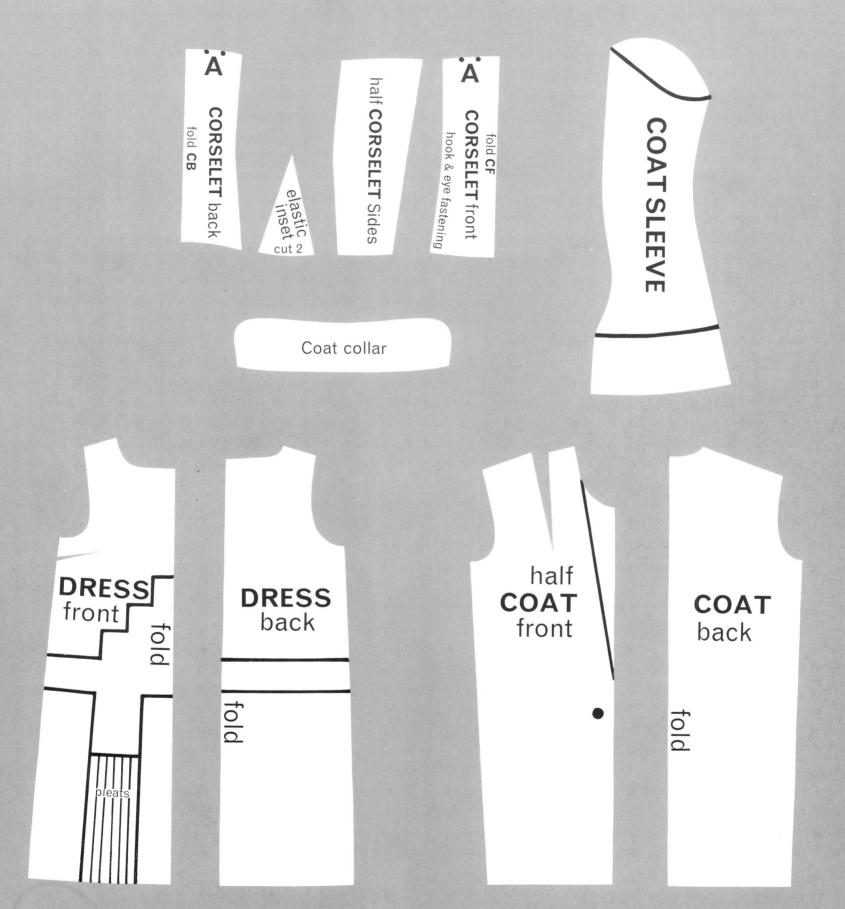

Ä

CORSELET back

fold CB

elastic
inset
cut 2

half **CORSELET** Sides

Ä

fold CF
CORSELET front

hook & eye fastening

COAT SLEEVE

Coat collar

DRESS
front

fold

pleats

DRESS
back

fold

half
COAT
front

COAT
back

fold

1930 George V

Fabrics: Women — clinging materials such as crêpe georgette, satin, rayons, heavy silks, shantung, jersey, supple woollens, etc.

Colours: Women — neutral browns, beige, pinks, etc.

Decoration: Women — floral printed fabrics in soft large designs. Elaborate cutting (particularly on the bias).

Padding and restriction, women: Corsets worn to control excess weight. To be tall and slim, with slender hips, and have a mannish figure with broad shoulders, a small bosom and small bottom, is the craze.

Movement, men: Mature, natural and relaxed.

Movement, women: Mature and elegant.

Men

General characteristics: Similar to the previous fashion. Trousers are no longer so monstrously wide at the hems. Ready-made clothes, of questionable fit, flood the market.

Under garments — similar to the previous fashion.

Sports jacket — mean and narrow in cut, tightly fitted, waisted, with broad lapels.

Pullover — (waistcoat discarded for casual wear), knitted plain or in Fair Isle patterns.

Plus fours — (popular for country wear — in particular golf), cut loose and baggy to terminate below the knee in deep knee-bands. Worn with plaid or plain woollen stockings, and brogue shoes with fringed leather flaps to hide the lacing.

Socks — similar to the previous fashion.

Shoes — similar to the previous fashion.

Hair — similar to the previous fashion. Small clipped moustaches.

Hats — similar to the previous fashion.

Accessories — similar to the previous fashion.

Women

General characteristics: Clothes cling to the body "like a wet cloth". Line is long and sinuous. Dresses are pouched and slackly belted at the waist. Skirts are longer with hemlines flared and dipping at the sides. Picture hats and longer hair. Make-up emphasises angular features. Coats of all lengths.

Under garments — similar to the previous fashion. Slips shaped like the dress, with or without a brassiere top.

Dress — (side and wrist plackets), wherever possible it is cut on the bias to produce the fashionable clinging effect. The very low V neckline, softened by a loosely pleated collar and deep jabot, is partially filled in by an undervest of similar material. The side panels of the skirt (echoed in bodice and sleeves) are set, well below hip level, in soft pleats. The jabot neckline is echoed in the cutting of the lower part of the tight-fitting sleeves. (Flared cape-like short sleeves also popular.)

Stockings — similar to the previous fashion.

Shoes — often in two materials (e.g. kid and lizard), with a Cuban high heel, narrow foot and pointed toe, and narrow straps positioned high across the instep.

Hair — waved, longer and looser with a side parting, the hair lengthens to form a roll at the back of the neck.

Hats — deep, close-fitting crowns with small or large brims. Brims dip down all round, turn up in front, dip over one eye, or dip down at the sides. Trimmings are very modest — flowers, a few loops of ribbon, etc.

Accessories — gauntlet suede gloves. Matching handbag, shoes and belt. Red or grey fox furs slung over one shoulder with the head of the fox forming a clasp to hold the back legs. Batik and fine silk scarves. Heavy finger rings. Gem-set wrist watches. Costume jewellery — ear, neck, and belt clips.

Notes on patterns: Women

Foundation garment — use a ready-made girdle and a simple, slack, unstiffened brassiere.

Slip — make up to semi-fit the figure.

Dress — (wherever possible, cut on the bias), ease bodice waistline to the skirt waistline forming a placket on the left side seam. Set side panels into pleats — three on either side, front and back. Attach narrow straps to the side seams at waist level to control the belt. Form a placket from A. to B. — marked on the sleeve pattern. The back collar and jabot front is set into pleats — extend the pattern if deeper pleating is required. Sew down the back collar to the back bodice and tie-catch the top part of the jabot to the bodice front. A vest, or plastron front pinned inside the bodice and made of the same material as the dress, partially fills the V neckline.

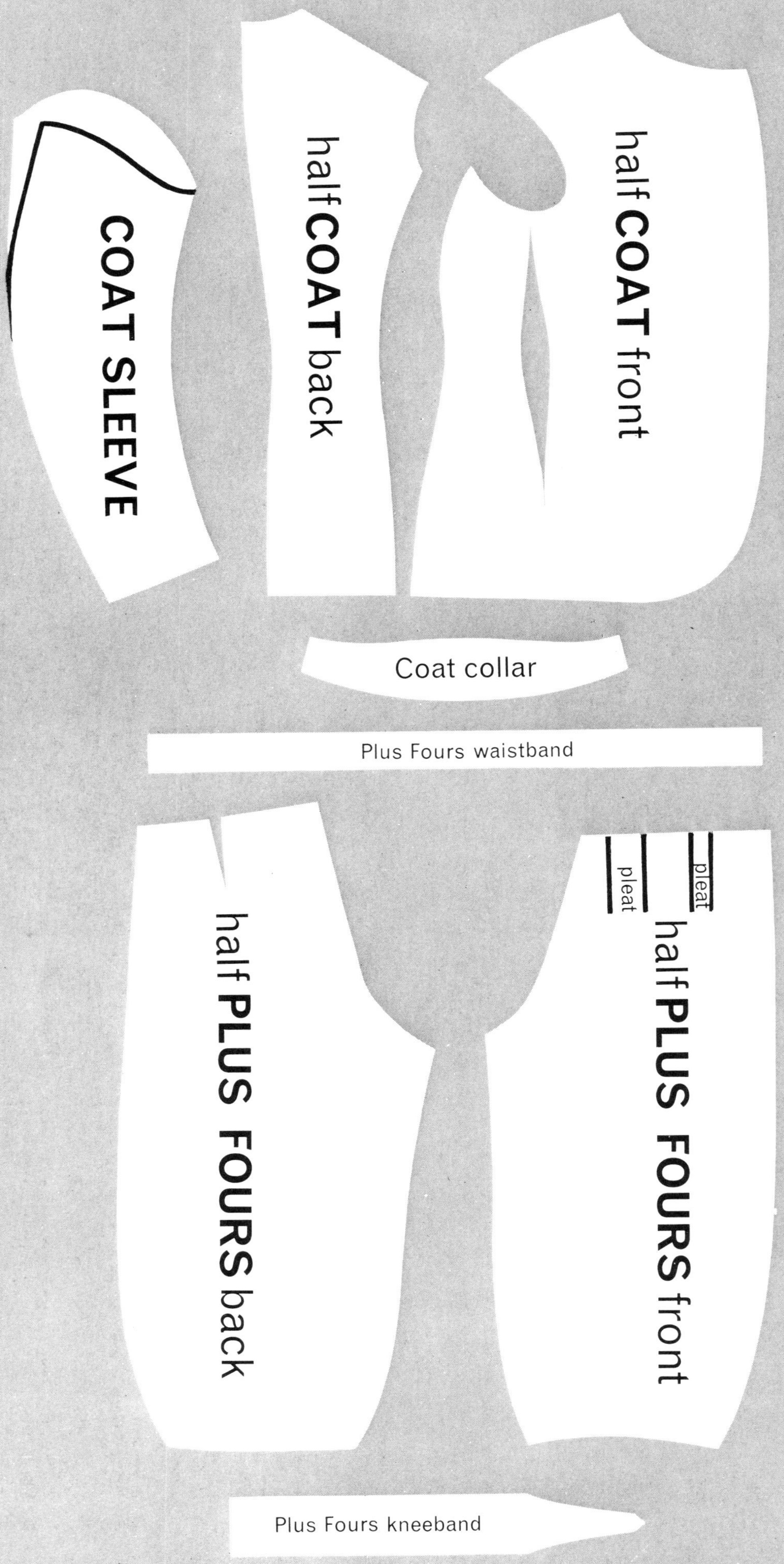

COAT SLEEVE

half **COAT** back

half **COAT** front

Coat collar

Plus Fours waistband

half **PLUS FOURS** back

half **PLUS FOURS** front

pleat

pleat

Plus Fours kneeband

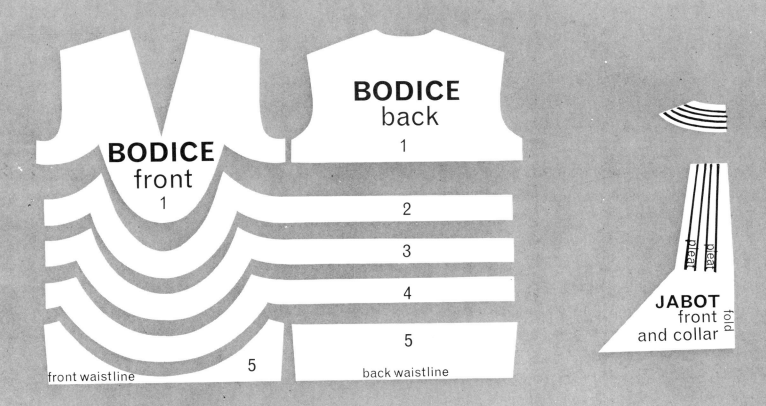

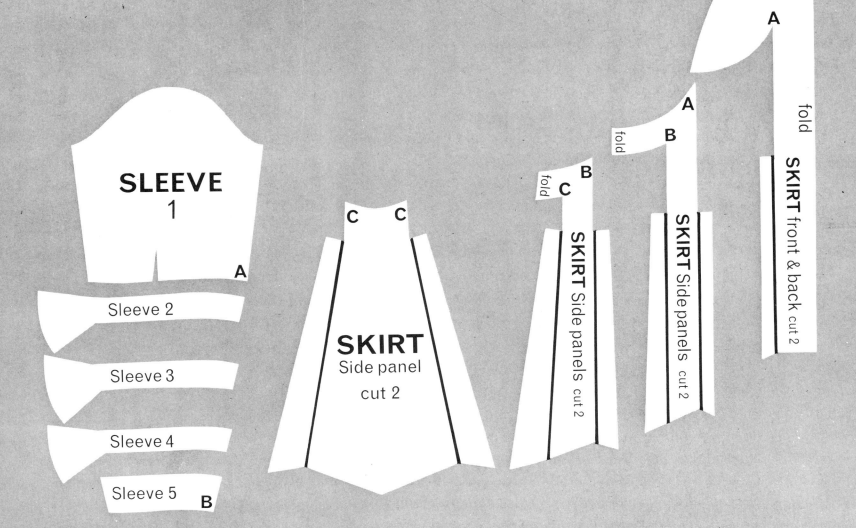